On Brokeback Mountain

Meditations about Masculinity, Fear, and Love in the Story and the Film

Eric Patterson

LEXINGTON BOOKS

A division of
ROWMAN & LITTLEFIELD PUBLISHERS, INC.
Lanham • Boulder • New York • Toronto • Plymouth, UK

LEXINGTON BOOKS

A division of Rowman & Littlefield Publishers, Inc.
A wholly owned subsidary of The Rowman & Littlefield Publishing Group, Inc.
4501 Forbes Boulevard, Suite 200
Lanham, MD 20706

Estover Road
Plymouth PL6 7PY
United Kingdom

British Library Cataloguing in Publication Information Available

Library of Congress Cataloging-in-Publication Data

Patterson, Eric, 1948-
  On Brokeback Mountain : meditations about masculinity, fear, and love in the story and
the film / Eric Patterson.
     p. cm.
  Includes bibliographical references.
  ISBN-13: 978-0-7391-2164-1 (cloth : alk. paper)
  ISBN-10: 0-7391-2164-2 (cloth : alk. paper)
  ISBN-13: 978-0-7391-2165-8 (pbk. : alk. paper)
  ISBN-10: 0-7391-2165-0 (pbk. : alk. paper)
  1. Brokeback Mountain (Motion picture) 2. Proulx, Annie. Brokeback
Mountain. I. Title.
  PN1997.2.B75P38 2008
  813'.54—dc22   2007036042

Printed in the United States of America

⊚™ The paper used in this publication meets the minimum requirements of American
National Standard for Information Sciences—Permanence of Paper for Printed Library
Materials, ANSI/NISO Z39.48-1992.

For Jack Twist and Ennis del Mar

Contents

Introduction: About the Book

Along with many others, I've been strongly moved by Annie Proulx's story, "Brokeback Mountain," and by the film that Larry McMurtry, Diana Ossana, and Ang Lee based on it. My boyfriend, T. R. Forbes, had read *The Shipping News* (1993) and *That Old Ace in the Hole* (2002) and liked them, so when *The Advocate* reported that *Brokeback Mountain* was being made into a movie, we both read it in the collection, *Close Range: Wyoming Stories* (1999), and were floored by it. In Ennis del Mar and Jack Twist we recognized many feelings and experiences similar to those in our own lives and in the lives of friends, and were impressed by Proulx's insight and artistry. We're both interested in fiction about men who love men, but we'd never read anything that got the lives of those who feel pressured to pass for straight—with all the difficulties that can involve—the way Annie Proulx's story does. It's great that today more and more people whose sexuality and gender differ from the majority are out about their identities, and that some, especially in certain urban and academic communities, are able to explore the boundaries of sexuality and identity, but it's important to be aware that others don't, or can't, identify in terms of their sexual difference and that some continue to struggle with sexual orientation and gender in the ways that Proulx depicts, especially in Ennis's experience.

T.R and I hoped the movie version of *Brokeback Mountain* would live up to the story, but like lots of men who looked forward to the film, had our doubts, given the resistance in Hollywood and among American audiences to films that deal in a respectful way with the lives of men who love men. When we saw the movie a few days after it was released, we were impressed by how well the screenplay built on Proulx's story, and by the directing, acting, and cinematography. Within a few minutes of the start of the film, our doubts began to fade, and by the end were replaced by admiration for the filmmakers' achievement. After we saw it, we talked about it for hours, then went to see it again a couple of days later. I re-read the story, then got the screenplay and read it. So many aspects of the story and the movie impressed me that I began writing them down, and within a few days began planning this book.

WHO THE BOOK IS FOR

What I've written here is intended to be useful to a general audience of readers who, like T.R. and me, have been moved by the story and the film. Both versions of the narrative are being widely discussed, as shown by the many sites and references to *Brokeback Mountain* on the Internet and in the press, and academic responses are starting to appear as well. My discussion draws on my background in teaching American cultural studies, American literature, and gay and lesbian studies, and I hope will interest some in those fields, but my goal is to provide a generally accessible discussion of the significance of both the story and the film, examining and comparing the two versions of the narrative closely in order to explore their depictions of the experience of men who have sexual and emotional relationships with men. Over the past three decades a valuable academic discussion has developed, especially among those involved in lesbian and gay studies, gender studies, and queer studies, of theories about the cultural constructions through which a society understands the meanings of sexuality and gender. I've used some important ideas from this discussion, though I've tried to present them in a way that those with a general education, rather than specific knowledge of the language of cultural theory, can appreciate. Engaging in the ongoing debates in lesbian and gay/queer studies isn't my goal; also, I'm not concerned to engage in the current sophisticated academic discussion of narrative representation in fiction and film. Because the analytical insights offered by much contemporary cultural theory often are presented in language that's inaccessible to many general readers, and that sometimes may be alienating to them, these useful ideas unfortunately often are unavailable to a general audience, and remain the privilege of an enclosed, elite academic community. I strongly believe that progressive academics have a responsibility to share analytical perspectives with those outside academia, to make these perspectives available to people who aren't academics so they can develop, change, and apply them in efforts to create a more fair and just society. I've sought to present the theoretical ideas that I've used in language that's accessible to thoughtful general readers and, I hope, not only to encourage these readers to think about the story and the film, but also to introduce them to some significant ideas about sexuality and gender from lesbian and gay/gender/queer studies with which they may not be familiar. Rather than quoting extensively from scholars, I've summarized important ideas from them, indicating sources in endnotes for readers who want to learn more. The endnotes aren't intended to provide comprehensive listings of the scholarship in each area, which often is very extensive, but simply to direct general readers to some of the most relevant, easily accessible scholarly sources. I'm sure that other, more theoretically sophisticated discussions of *Brokeback Mountain* will be forthcoming, but my intention is to reach a wider range of readers.[1]

Certainly the story and the film have many implications for sexually different people other than men who love men, raising issues that lesbians and transgender people also have to confront and that need to be considered by everybody who wants to resist discrimination based on sex and gender. My purpose here, though, is to focus on what *Brokeback Mountain* says about the lives of men who love men, especially those who may not have access to knowledge about men like themselves because of the circumstances of their lives, including poverty, hostile religion, lack of education, and dominant cultural constructions of masculinity and homosexuality. The narrative is set in the American West in the mid to later twentieth century and deals with characters who are white (though it's important to note that Ennis's last name suggests that he may be perceived as being partly Hispanic, which also is true for Joe Aguirre), and so my discussion will be limited in regard to place, time, and race as well, though at points I'll seek to consider how the experiences of white, rural men who desire men may differ from those of other men who desire men. Of course, I hope that anybody interested in the story and the movie, regardless of academic background or race or sex, including straight allies of people who differ from the majority in sexuality and gender, will find my discussion useful. My main purpose is to support other men who love men, including those who may identify as gay, as queer, as bisexual, as questioning their sexual orientation, or in other ways, as they think about the implications of *Brokeback Mountain*. While they won't agree with some of my ideas, I hope that reading what I say will encourage them to think about and discuss the significance of the story and the film. Both are major and welcome additions to the representation of the experiences of men who love men.

In my discussion I make no pretense of a neutral perspective. Though I have criticisms of limitations in both the story and the movie versions of *Brokeback Mountain,* I admire both and am moved by both. My discussion is shaped throughout by my experience of the emotional power of the two narratives and by my perspective as a man who identifies as gay and is in a committed, long-term relationship. Both my partner and I have life experience of the difficulties involved in passing for straight and of homophobic hostility and violence. My discussion also is influenced, I'm sure, by other individual factors, including Irish/English/Swiss/German-American background; middle-class family; access to higher education; commitment to progressive politics, due in part to my family's working-class origin and to personal experience; and aspiration to understand and oppose homophobia, sexism, racism, and other forms of discrimination and inequality. I've sought to consider the narrative in relation to factors of race and class, but of course am limited by my own experience. While I've sought to make a serious analysis of the significance of the story and the movie in terms of dominant American constructions of masculinity and of sexual and emotional relationships between men, I can't do so without also acknowledging the ways they speak to me and to men I care about. As I've said, both T.R and I, as we read and watched *Brokeback Mountain,* felt the shock of recognition, encountering depictions of situations we knew all too well. Undoubtedly the story and the film don't speak in the same ways to many others, those who are sexually different and the straight majority, academics and non-academics, but I hope that what I have to say may stimulate some of them as they consider the story and the film. Many responses to *Brokeback Mountain* are possible, and those who aren't interested in the approach I've outlined here surely will provide others that are very different. Some, I'm sure, will be far more skeptical and critical. To stress the personal nature of my perspective to potential readers, I've followed a good friend's suggestion and have described this book, in its title, as a series of meditations about the significance of *Brokeback Mountain.* What I offer here uses ideas from current academic discussion to make a personal reading and reflection on the meanings of the story and the film.

OVERVIEW OF THE BOOK

Here's a brief overview of the main issues that I discuss in the book. Probably the most important aspect of *Brokeback Mountain* is that it's based on the recognition that many men who love men don't fit the assumptions and stereotypes that the majority holds about them, and seems to need so badly. Men who love men are in every kind of work and in every place in the country. The varieties of sexual and emotional experience between men certainly have been described in literature, but commercial movies and TV, when they represent such men, tend to cater to the straight majority and usually offer the kinds of depictions that the majority is comfortable with, although this certainly is changing. For years the main representations that the media have found acceptable are of sexually different men as a threat or as comic relief, and sometimes as victims, but it's been rare for TV and commercial movies to attempt to show the perspectives that men who love men may have on themselves, each other, and the rest of society. Usually what's been shown in entertainment that reaches straight audiences is what men who are sexually and emotionally intimate with men mean to straight people, not their own points of view. Also, the media tend to focus on stereotypes of men who are part of urban, affluent gay-identified communities. The media tend to have difficulty acknowledging that many men who love men aren't different in their appearance or language or work from the majority of men, and that they live in every region and community in the country. Both versions of *Brokeback Mountain* challenge the majority's assumptions and stereotypes, representing men who love men and who also are conventionally masculine. For some masculine-identified men who desire men, given what the dominant culture teaches about masculinity and homosexuality, their sexual difference is in conflict with their masculinity. Such men often can pass for straight, which can allow them to retain their masculine status in a homophobic society, evading much of the hostility that American society directs at those who are sexually different and who become visible to it. The ability to pass and to remain invisible to the majority because a man doesn't fit its assumptions about gay men may seem like an advantage to some, but, as the story and the film show, it raises many complex possibilities and can incur many costs. In particular, it can lead some men who love men to become involved in heterosexual relationships, often including marriage and having children, which can be difficult for everyone involved. Of course, trying to pass also forces men to hide and deny their most important relationships with other men. Both the story and the film depict the damage that can result for a man who loves men and for the others in his life when the threat of homophobia and the concern to maintain traditional masculine status cause him to try to pass for straight.

Brokeback Mountain also raises the question of how much difference there really is between friendship between men and love between men, though American society tries very hard to define and maintain a boundary separating the two, celebrating male friendships and attacking male love. Friendship is constructed in the most positive terms, including altruism and self-sacrifice, whereas eroticism between men is denigrated as obscene and shameful. Friendship is an important element of the social relationships between men that bind them together and can give them masculine status and power, while male-male eroticism is constructed as negating masculine status and power. One of the many achievements of both the story and the movie is in their recognition that love between men can be continuous with friendship, and can include the exalted values we're taught to associate with friendship and with love between men and women. Both versions of *Brokeback Mountain* are remarkable for their awareness of the profound spiritual dimensions of love between men.

In their depiction of male love, the story and the movie also are remarkable for the direct way in which they present men having sex, though there are significant differences between the two versions. If the subject of sex between men ever is directly discussed among the majority, it's almost always totally from the majority's perspective, and it's treated with ridicule and disgust. The majority's judgments about men having sex together make understanding the experience and feelings of men who have sex with men impossible. This is one of the strongest instances of the inability of many in the majority to begin to consider the experience of being a man who loves men from the standpoint of such men themselves. Indeed, as some critics of contemporary gay culture have pointed out, some gay men today seek to promote "tolerance" by the majority and assimilation into its culture by avoiding the subject of sex between men. Though our society is a long way from even beginning to "tolerate" sexual difference, I believe our ultimate goal must be affirmation, not mere toleration. One of the major strengths of the story and the film, in my view, is their refusal to cater to prejudice against sex between men, and their direct and positive presentation of the sexual passion men can share, particularly anal intercourse. While the story's depiction of men having sex is more unequivocally positive than that in the film, both the story and the film show a commitment to respecting the perspective of men who love men that extends to their depiction of sex between men.

One of the foremost achievements of both versions is their powerful representation of the hatred of same-sex desire, and the ways this hatred affects the feelings, behavior, and relationships of men who love men. Proulx and the filmmakers perceptively convey the way hatred and fear can damage and destroy lives, presenting these forces with an intensity that may be equaled in some works of fiction, but that hasn't been seen before in a major Hollywood movie. Their depictions of homophobia also are highly perceptive concerning the forms it can take and the motivations that cause it. In relation to this, both the story and the film are particularly insightful about the ways homophobia distorts the interactions between parents and children, and the ways the fear and shame men have been taught about homosexuality can damage relationships between them.

A different but related dimension of both versions of the narrative concerns its setting in the Rocky Mountain West, which connects it to representations of nature in established cultural traditions, especially in literature and in film. For many Americans, the traditions of the Western in literature, art, and popular culture, particularly movies, have played a defining role in shaping an understanding of national identity and of masculinity. The Western has been important in defining the relationships between men and each other, men and women, and culture and nature, and *Brokeback Mountain* relates to all of these established ideas in suggestive and challenging ways. Also, the fact that the narrative is an account of the love between two sheepherders in a setting at the boundary between an agricultural landscape and wilderness connects *Brokeback Mountain* directly to one of the most ancient literary forms, and the one that's most profoundly associated with love between men, the pastoral. Greek, Roman, Medieval, and Renaissance literature all enriched a tradition of homoerotic pastoral poetry, that then was added to in brilliant and innovative ways by Walt Whitman, who some see as America's greatest poet, and who can be thought of as the first great literary artist of modern gay culture. Both versions of *Brokeback Mountain* also are significant in that, unlike many representations of sexually different men, they don't concern characters who are urban and affluent, but seek to present the lives of rural, working-class men who love men and who aren't part of the gay culture that has emerged in American cities. It's important to relate both the story and the movie to what can be known about the history of man-loving men in rural America.

Finally, along with all of its other meanings, *Brokeback Mountain* is a great love story, and like other love stories raises profound questions about the nature and power of love that are widely understandable, regardless of sexuality. As in the most moving stories of romantic love between men and women known throughout the global cultural tradition that originated in Europe, *Brokeback Mountain* makes readers and viewers think about the limitations and strengths of love between two people when it's confronted by obstacles in the society around them and within their own minds and hearts, about the connection between love and memory and between love and spirituality, and about the relative power of death and of love. The creators of the two versions of *Brokeback Mountain* have had the courage to locate love between men in two of the traditional genres of expression that are most strongly established and most highly valued in America, especially in popular commercial culture, and that the majority associates exclusively with heterosexuality: the genre of the Western and the genre of the romantic, tragic love story.

The book is organized in the following way to address the issues that I've outlined in the last six paragraphs. After this Introduction comes a Prologue on the significance of what happened at the Academy Awards ceremony on March 5, 2006, in relation to the movie, and the parallels between the reaction of the Motion Picture Academy to the movie and other significant reactions to both the movie and the story. Such reactions have been marked by intense hostility to love between men, and illustrate many of the ugliest aspects of the homophobia that's central to understanding *Brokeback Mountain*. A discussion of the reception of the movie can assist readers of this book by providing examples of some of the most powerful negative stereotypes that are confronted in the story and the film. Following the Prologue come seven chapters. The first chapter, on friendship, examines the development of the relationship between Ennis and Jack, considering the ways that the story and the film challenge the artificial distinction that American society makes between male friendship and male love. The second, on sex, discusses the representations of the sexual relationship between Jack and Ennis, and the degrees to which the story and the film depart from the assumptions the majority makes about sex between men. This chapter also examines ways that the depictions of Ennis and Jack address the experiences of man-loving men who aren't part of the urban gay world that's become visible over the past four decades. The third chapter, on nature in both versions of the narrative, considers the relationship of *Brokeback Mountain* to the homoerotic pastoral literary tradition and to the tradition of the American Western. The fourth, on hatred and fear, examines the presentation of homophobia in both versions, looking closely at their accounts of its impact on men who are sexually and emotionally intimate, as well as what both suggest about the causes of homophobia and the forms it takes, relating the insights presented in the two versions to important current analytical ideas about homophobic prejudice. The fifth and longest chapter, on love, looks in detail at the relationships of Ennis and Alma, Jack and Lureen, and Jack and Ennis, considering the effects and costs of passing for straight on the two men and their families. The sixth chapter deals with the central role played by memory in the love between Ennis and Jack, and the significance of memory, especially in relation to death and spirituality, for Ennis after Jack is gone. In the seventh chapter I discuss ways that *Brokeback Mountain* can be related to the dominant culture's other great myths of love.

Though in what I've written here I've drawn on my teaching and scholarship, those who enjoy literature and film and think about their significance shouldn't need any particular academic background to follow my discussion. In general, my method is to look closely at Proulx's text, which is wonderfully rich, especially in its recognition of the power of Western American vernacular speech, to compare and contrast it with the superb screenplay written by Larry McMurtry and Diana Ossana, and to discuss the sensitive realization of the screenplay by Ang Lee and the fine actors and filmmakers who worked with him. I make a close, comparative examination of the two versions of the narrative, rather than discussing the story in relation to Proulx's other fiction or the film in relation to other work by the director and screenwriters. Throughout this discussion, my goal is to relate the story and the film to the larger cultural issues that I've outlined above. In doing this, where I've employed ideas drawn from literary history and cultural history or from theories about gender and homophobia, I've sought to make them accessible to the general reader who shares my interests and my admiration for the story and the film. For the convenience of readers, in the next section of this Introduction I've explained the analytical words and ideas that I'll use.

BASIC TERMS AND CONCEPTS

It's important to tell both general and academic readers how I use basic terms and concepts in the book. The study of sexuality, especially of same-sex desire and relationships, is continuing to evolve, and there's much debate over the significance and appropriateness of many words and ideas. My intention here isn't to pursue those important debates, but to explain the approach that I've used in my discussion. Given my concern to address a general audience, my use of these words and ideas necessarily will be more simplified than that in current discussions of lesbian and gay/queer studies. I hope that what's lost by not engaging in sophisticated academic debate will be made up for by offering a discussion that a larger audience can read and use.

I accept the perspective that the word sex refers to a person's anatomical sex, that the words sexuality and sexual orientation refer to the forms of sexual attraction and arousal that people feel, which may involve complex and profound emotions, and that the word gender refers to the understanding people have of the significance and meanings of their anatomical sex, their maleness or femaleness. I agree with the view that sexuality and gender are constructed and understood differently in different societies and times.[2] What many contemporary Americans understand as "homosexuality" and "heterosexuality" are relatively recent cultural constructions of sexual feelings and behaviors that can't be assumed to have existed in the past, or to exist in other societies today, or indeed to be accepted by all Americans now. Understandings of the feelings and behaviors now constructed as "homosexual" or "heterosexual" differ greatly with time and place. What many Americans now think of as "masculinity" and "femininity" aren't innate, unchanging characteristics linked to a person's anatomical sex; instead gender involves forms of self-understanding and behavior that are taught to people by the societies they live in. Because experiences of sexuality and gender differ with social context and time period, it really is more accurate to think in terms of sexualities and genders, femininities and masculinities.[3]

The dominant construction of gender in the United States is organized in terms of a strong binary opposition between masculine and feminine, associating masculinity with rationality, control, action, and authority, and femininity with emotion, nurturance, and submission. American economic, social, and political systems stress individual autonomy and competition for men, and so constructions of masculinity in American culture place particular emphasis on individual self-reliance and aggressiveness, even more so than in the European societies that American culture is related to. Although fortunately the feminist movement has caused a degree of change, men continue to occupy privileged positions in relation to women throughout society. The qualities associated with masculinity have been accepted as those required in all aspects of public life, whereas those associated with femininity have been understood to be relevant largely in the restricted environment of the home and in associated "nurturing" professions such as primary education. In terms of sexual behavior, masculinity is equated with sexual penetration and domination, femininity with sexual receptivity and submission. In American society, space is understood by many in terms of gender: the home is the "place" of women, though even there they aren't dominant, and all other spaces, including workplaces, public urban space, and the natural environment itself are understood as being primarily the provinces of men. Many women and some progressive men have challenged this division of space, but for many Americans it continues to be taken for granted. The prevailing system of sex and gender in the United States supports a patriarchal form of heterosexuality, and teaches people to believe that it's innate and natural.[4]

American economic, social, political, and cultural systems historically have privileged people of Northern European, Protestant Christian background, which also affects the social construction of gender. The masculine ideal, as it's been constructed in America, presents a man who's not only rational, capable of controlled action and of exerting authority, and interested in penetrating and dominating women, but who's also depicted as white, Christian, and Protestant, and who is, or aspires to be, successful and affluent. Of course, in actual experience this ideal is an impossible one for most men, and so they often feel inadequate or insecure, and continually struggle to conform, at least as much as they're able, to the ideal. The feminine ideal is similarly linked to factors of race, ethnicity, religion, and class, and causes many women to work hard to conform as well. Indeed, the feminine ideal is even more difficult to attain, since it involves exacting factors of age and appearance. Social institutions, particularly families, schools, religious and political organizations, and the commercial mass media, usually strongly encourage individuals to conform to the established social constructions of masculinity or femininity, whatever their actual sexual desires or their feelings about the kinds of gender behavior that seem natural to them. While constructions of gender may vary with social and cultural factors, and with sexual orientation as well, the ideals of gender just outlined occupy a privileged, hegemonic position in American culture.[5]

Although many Americans resist accepting the fact, there are large numbers of people who experience sexual attraction to those of their own sex, and many of them also experience strong feelings of emotional attachment to people of their own sex. Also, there are many who feel that forms of gender behavior that don't fit rigid models of masculinity or femininity are more natural to them. The human experience of sexuality and gender is vastly more varied, complex, and rich than the simplistic binary system of sex and gender admits, and many people experience a wide range of differences from the system of heterosexuality that American society prescribes as being normative. Certainly many people do experience attraction only to the opposite sex, but many others experience it only to the same sex, and many others to individuals of both sexes in differing degrees and combinations. Some people may feel same-sex attraction while also feeling that traditional constructions of gender are appropriate for them; others who feel same-sex attraction may be uncomfortable within these traditional constructions of gender, and may feel more comfortable with forms of gender expression that diverge from what the society says is right for people of their sex. In relation to this, it's important to note that some of those who feel attraction to the *opposite* sex also may not be comfortable with the boundaries of gender behavior as defined by American society. The varieties of experience of sexuality and gender are affected by many other factors, such as a person's ethnic, racial, or religious background and community, as well as social class and education. There's ongoing debate about how to refer to those who don't conform to the dominant systems of sexuality and gender; in my discussion, I'll refer to them as sexual minority groups.[6]

Because gender is socially constructed rather than innate, for all people it involves the performance of what can be thought of as various cultural scripts, though many can't recognize this, and perceive gender as a natural manifestation of anatomical sex. But at least for some people it's possible to treat gender as a conscious performance, to deliberately adapt, transform, combine, subvert, and reinvent aspects of traditional gender scripts. Some members of sexual minority groups have evolved cultural forms in which they treat gender creatively and often ironically, as in the forms of drag developed by some men and women, and in hypermasculine, hyperfeminine, or androgynous styles of gender expression. Some people also explore varieties of sexual experience that depart in many ways from the norms of procreative, long-term monogamy endorsed—if frequently not practiced—by the dominant culture. The hostile stereotypes of sexual minorities accepted by much of the majority often focus on those sexual minority people who differ strongly in terms of gender and sexual behavior, not recognizing that there are many other members of sexual minorities who experience traditional forms of gender as being appropriate for them or who desire monogamous relationships.[7]

It's also important to note that there are some people who experience their anatomical sex as being in contradiction with their sense of sexual identity;

some may seek to deal with this sense of being transgendered through medical treatment to change their anatomical sex.[8] It should be noted, too, that some people are born intersexed, with anatomical characteristics of both sexes.[9] Hostility to sexual minorities pervades American society, and unfortunately often is especially strong toward transgender and intersex people.

While individual experiences vary a great deal, in general the major institutions in this society seek to force everyone to conform to the dominant binary system of heterosexual gender and sexual behavior, making many people struggle to repress desires, emotions, and behaviors that they may feel are appropriate for them. In relation to this, the word natural deserves comment. The society often presents the forms of gender and sexual behavior that it prescribes as being natural, ignoring their social construction and disparaging those who deviate from them, condemning them as unnatural. In order to challenge these implications of the word, rather than rejecting it altogether I'll use it in reference to the perspective of members of sexual minorities and to what many say feels appropriate *to them*. For good reason the concept of the natural has been analyzed and criticized extensively in academic discussion, but for many outside of academia it continues to be used, by those who accept same-sex desire and those who reject it. Many men who love men attest that forms of gender and sexual behavior that the dominant society repudiates feel natural to them.[10]

Despite the efforts of many people, particularly women, to challenge the American system of organizing sex and gender and so to reduce repression and inequality, traditional understandings of sex and gender remain dominant, strongly affecting the lives of everyone. The system of sex and gender rejects those who don't conform in terms of sexual or gender behavior, placing them in the stigmatized category of homosexuality. As historians have shown, this category and the category of heterosexuality are relatively new constructions, having been established by medical and legal authorities in the later nineteenth century and only gradually affecting the rest of society. As homosexuality has been constructed in medical and legal discourses and in commercial mass culture, it equates same-sex attraction with sexual and gender behavior that differ from prescribed norms. The majority associates same-sex attraction with what it perceives as unusual gender behavior, although there's no necessary link between the two. Men who desire men are assumed to be somehow feminine, women who desire women are assumed to be somehow masculine. The dominant construction of homosexuality also tends to reduce the relationships of members of sexual minorities to sex alone, negating the depth of their emotional relationships and often demonizing their sexual experience. Same-sex intercourse, especially between men, is denigrated as dirty and violent, and often is equated with rape.[11]

Anxiety about being located in the category of homosexuality, which the majority has constructed in terms of negative and hostile stereotypes, is a major factor in causing most members of the society to try to conform to hegemonic constructions of acceptable sexual and gender behavior. The fear of being labeled homosexual operates to enforce conformity throughout society. For straight people, it serves as a constant reminder of the need to conform to prescribed models of gender behavior, and as a constant threat for the vast majority of them who don't feel that they fully measure up to the exaggerated ideals of masculinity and femininity. For people who experience various degrees of same-sex physical and emotional attraction, it often creates intense fear of accepting their own sexual orientations, and so can pose a major obstacle to developing relationships that are physically and emotionally appropriate and satisfying. For people for whom it feels right to act in ways that depart from rigid gender "norms," the fear of being labeled homosexual often imposes an additional struggle of attempting to conform to what the society prescribes as acceptable masculine or feminine behavior. Given the pressures exerted by the dominant system of sex and gender, it takes courage and independence to accept that one needs physical and emotional intimacy with people of one's own sex, or that one doesn't feel right conforming to traditional boundaries of gender behavior. People who act on their sense of sexual or gender difference often must confront the ridicule, harassment, discrimination, and violence that are endemic in American society toward those perceived as different in terms of sexuality or gender behavior. Because of the negative connotations that the words homosexuality and homosexual hold for many who love people of their own sex, where it's possible I've sought to employ more positive alternatives, although in some contexts where it seems appropriate, such as discussion of hostility to men who love men, I've deliberately used these words.[12]

Though the main characters in *Brokeback Mountain,* Jack Twist and Ennis del Mar, both marry and have children, it's stated explicitly in the story and strongly indicated in the movie that their primary sexual and emotional attractions are to men. Both strongly identify as masculine in a culture that constructs desire between men as negating masculinity. Because of the region in which they begin their relationship, the gay social and cultural world that had developed in many American cities, becoming increasingly visible after the Second World War, is quite distant from their lives. While it's possible to think of Ennis and Jack as gay in the sense that they love men, this isn't a word that either of them use, and it's very unlikely, at the start of the narrative, that they'd know this meaning of the word; the one time that they employ a term for men who love men, they use the label queer, which in context has strongly negative implications, but is the only word available. A fundamental part of the struggle Ennis and Jack face is that they've been denied positive language or ideas for understanding themselves. Rather than labeling Ennis and Jack gay, at least as they are when they meet, it's more appropriate to describe them in terms of the experience of rural men who may have sexual and emotional relationships with other men, but who don't consciously share the identity of being gay, particularly as that which has emerged among groups of men who desire men, especially in urban areas. I'll briefly discuss scholarship about rural man-loving men, and then, in light of it, return to the issue of how to refer to Jack and Ennis.

Only fairly recently have those studying sexual minorities begun examination of the lives and history of rural man-loving men. Significant recent studies in social history have been made of men of various backgrounds in rural areas of the Pacific Northwest, of white and African American men in Mississippi, of men in the region of Mormon cultural influence, and of men in farming and ranching areas of the Midwest and the Great Plains.[13] Geographers, sociologists, and social workers also have begun to examine the ways that social space is organized for sexual minorities in rural areas.[14] These studies show that sexual and emotional relationships between men have been and continue to be widespread, and have been constructed and understood in many different ways. Evidence from the mid to late nineteenth century indicates that culturally constructed boundaries separating acceptable social and physical intimacy between people of the same sex from intimacy deemed unacceptable were drawn differently than they came to be in the twentieth century. Today, some of those studying sexuality and gender use the words homosocial and homosociality to refer to the forms of same-sex social, physical, and emotional intimacy accepted in the dominant system of sex and gender, in contrast to what the system labels homosexual and unacceptable.[15] In the nineteenth century, while of course these terms weren't used, divisions between homosocial activity and homosexual activity were unlike those today. Though dominant cultural institutions strongly condemned some forms of sexual interaction between people of the same sex, placing them in the negative, religion-based category of "sodomy," it appears that many forms of physical intimacy, including ones that today we think of as homosexual, may not have been understood to fall into this category and may have been understood as acceptable forms of homosociality. Also, those involved in same-sex sexual relationships usually weren't understood to belong to a distinct human category differentiated by their sexual desires.[16] The development and publicizing of the medical-legal categories of homosexuality and the homosexual during the twentieth century changed this, making people far more aware of same-sex sexual relationships and constructing those who participated in them as a distinct human type. The negative impact of these new constructions began to be evident early in the twentieth century, but didn't reach its height until the Second World War and afterward. Though these constructions reached different social and cultural contexts in the United States at different times, in general they caused many forms of same-sex intimacy that had been relatively tolerated or accepted to come to be perceived negatively, as signifiers of homosexuality and the homosexual.[17]

Studies of rural man-loving men challenge the simplistic assumptions some urban people make that conditions for sexual minorities in rural areas are so hostile that most are isolated or are obliged to migrate to cities. They demonstrate that in rural areas before the development of automobile transportation and electronic communication, when social life centered on the family and on local communities and institutions, particularly church and school, sexual relationships between men often occurred in these contexts. Extended families were typical in agricultural communities, and often also included hired men, and neighbors were brought together in many types of work, church, and school activities. Males might become sexually and emotionally involved with each other in many of these settings.[18] Sexual play between adolescent males seems to have been tolerated or even accepted in some contexts, a pattern that persisted in some areas well into the twentieth century. Among the majority in some regions, until the growing social change of the 1960s there seems to have been an attitude of permitting sexually intimate relationships by pretending ignorance.[19] In the nineteenth century and into the twentieth, men who lived and worked in rural areas but did so outside the contexts of the family and the local community, such as men involved in logging, mining, and tending and moving livestock and men who traveled widely doing migrant labor, as well as men who went to sea, appear to have established and accepted various patterns of same-sex relationships. Work communities that were largely or all male clearly allowed physical and emotional intimacy between men. Those who've studied the cowboys involved in the cattle business cite considerable evidence of intimate male relationships in the later nineteenth century, though the degree to which these may have been sexual and the ways they were understood by the participants are difficult to reconstruct.[20] Men who worked in logging camps in the Pacific Northwest had well-established patterns of intimacy that clearly included sexual intercourse.[21] In the society of hoboes, men who lived on the road and sometimes did itinerant work, into the first third of the twentieth century there was a well-established pattern of a mutually supportive intimate committed relationship including sexual intercourse between an adult man, sometimes called a jocker, and an adolescent, sometimes called a punk.[22] The history of Mormon communities in Utah in the late nineteenth and early twentieth centuries reveals a high degree of acceptance of types of male-male intimacy that would be construed as homosexual today, and records of Mormon and non-Mormon residents reveal many instances of same-sex couples living together as partners for long periods, though they didn't overtly identify themselves as having sexual relations, and whether they did remains conjectural.[23]

In the twentieth century, some factors facilitated same-sex desire, while others opposed it. Although the spread of the medical-legal construction of homosexuality made same-sex attraction less acceptable, the development of transportation and communication added to the possibilities of sexual relationships between rural men. In particular, the automobile made it possible to reach towns and cities, to engage in "car cruising" with pedestrians and other drivers, and provided a relatively safe, private space for encounters.[24] Men who desired men developed social practices that facilitated sexual relationships, learning that it was possible to meet men in certain public spaces, such as particular parks, theaters, bus and train stations, public restrooms, and highway rest stops, though it was necessary to do so in ways that didn't attract hostile attention.[25] Although there hasn't been extensive study of the history of men who desire men in most of the Rocky Mountain West in the twentieth century, scholarly discussion of conditions in some parts of the area and in the Midwest and South indicates that men who interacted in such spaces often sought to maximize social invisibility, and therefore often minimized the exchange of personal information. Social networks certainly developed, but tended to be tightly knit and to keep a very low profile.[26] Certain bars, particularly in or near cities, served as places to meet and socialize for men who sought men, but interactions usually had to be relatively cautious. Sometimes authorities knew about homosexual activity and ignored it, but there also was danger of police entrapment and arrest, particularly as official discussion and condemnation of homosexuality increased.[27] In some areas in the West, sources of support and information such as bookstores and political organizations for sexual minorities only began to appear in the mid to late 1970s.[28] In the mid twentieth century, before the visible emergence of sexual minority political activism, men who desired men increasingly were threatened with exposure and punishment because of the development and spread of the medical-legal categories of homosexuality and the homosexual and efforts by medical and government authorities to suppress homosexuality.[29] There's evidence that religious condemnations of homosexuality increased as medical-legal discourses developed and were publicized, and then as urban gay communities became more visible to American society. Many religious organizations, some of which had been relatively tolerant of same-sex sexual relationships, became aggressively homophobic, particularly from midcentury on.[30]

Scholarship increasingly has recognized the spatial dimension of the social construction of sexual orientation. Geographers, sociologists, and social workers have explored the ways that space, both within cities and towns and in the countryside, has come to be understood by the majority in relation to the dominance of supposedly normative masculinity and heterosexuality. The public space of communities and the outdoors itself generally have been constructed as male space, in which the presence of women is acceptable as long as they remain subordinate, and in which the visible presence of sexual minorities is unacceptable. Sexual difference is constructed as a transgression of the supposedly natural order of heterosexuality, as something unnatural that is out of place and doesn't belong, and so, when it becomes visible, must be excluded or eradicated.[31] Although detailed historical investigation of the frequency of instances of homophobic discrimination, harassment, and violence in rural areas isn't available, it certainly seems probable that as official condemnation grew there was increasing likelihood of individual aggression or even more organized group violence against those perceived as sexually different.

Some scholars argue that lack of access to positive information and support about same-sex desire meant that many in rural areas who experienced such desire faced particular difficulty in understanding or acting on their feelings. For some men, there was no information at all, and so they had no sense that others shared their feelings. For those men who became aware of negative constructions of homosexuality, the stereotypes of effeminacy, deviance, immorality, criminality, and pederasty could pose serious obstacles to recognizing or acting on their attraction to other males, since these stereotypes constructed male-male sexuality in forms that many men could not connect with themselves.[32] Other scholars emphasize the degree of resourcefulness, endurance, and resistance among those in rural areas who did understand themselves as being sexually different in various ways.[33] In general, the evidence presented by those who've studied the history of rural men who loved men suggests that while male-male sexual relationships frequently occurred, they necessarily had to remain relatively clandestine except perhaps in largely male work communities, and that the growing official hostility to homosexuality caused such intimacy to become less acceptable everywhere, including male work communities. In rural areas of the United States in the mid twentieth century, as in much of the society, male-male sexuality was constructed by the majority as a defect or a perversion incompatible with masculinity, and increasingly was the subject of condemnation. It involved the risk of exposure, often with serious consequences, including harassment, ostracism, job loss, and physical violence. Visibility could be very dangerous.[34]

As scholars who've studied same-sex relationships among rural men observe, in many instances their construction of their experience should be described using different terms from those used by and for men who identify as

gay. They point out that in the twentieth century some urban men came to perceive themselves in terms of a distinctive sexual identity, denoted by their use
of the slang term "gay"; but that many men, some in cities and many in rural
areas, engaged in sexual and emotional relationships with other men but
didn't share a sense of this same distinctive sexual identity. The language and
ideas used by such men to describe themselves varied considerably with time
and place, and with ethnic, racial, and religious community.[35] Sometimes the
word that was used for and by such men was "queer," and some scholars suggest using that term to distinguish their experience from that of men who
identified as gay.[36] Clearly it's not accurate to use the word "gay" to describe
the entire variety of sexual and emotional relationships that are possible between men, since to do so applies as a generic term a word that really refers
only to a particular set of ways of constructing male-male intimacy. Still, it's
important for academics discussing this issue to respect the fact that, in the
struggles to resist discrimination, harassment, and violence against sexual minorities over the past forty years, the word "gay" has come to be used by
many people of many backgrounds in many different contexts outside of academia as a significant generic term for sexual minorities.[37]

It's important too, in considering the use of the words "gay" and "queer,"
to recognize the implications of the fact that constructions of gay identity and
community have tended to be shaped by men in urban areas, and particularly
by middle-class, white men. Certainly men of other racial backgrounds and
working-class men have been involved in gay culture in important ways, but
many working-class men and men of color have experienced gay communities as being inhospitable.[38] Some rural men who love men find urban gay
communities unaccepting, especially given the simplistic assumptions made
by some urban people that rural life is backward or that life for sexual minorities is impossible in the country. It's important to note that many sexual
minority people value the positive aspects of rural life, some choosing to remain in rural areas where they grew up, others moving from towns and cities
to the country.[39]

In relation to differences between urban and rural sexual minority experience, it's also important for urban gay men to recognize that the concept of
coming out of the closet may not have the same significance for some rural
men who desire men. Especially since the emergence of sexual minority political movements, for many men who identify as gay, affirming their involvement in an urban community of other men who desire men can be one
of the most important and defining experiences in their lives. Man-loving
men in rural areas also go through the process of understanding their sexuality, of course, but may not come out in the same sense of widely acknowledging their sexual orientation to others or participating in a large community

of men like themselves.[40] Indeed, as some who've studied sexual minority men have observed, in some contexts, often including rural areas, remaining closeted is necessary in order to remain in the community, and in fact can be used creatively and resourcefully to permit the pursuit of same-sex relationships, though it necessarily also may limit how fully these relationships can develop. From the perspective of urban men who identify as gay, the closet may seem only to signify oppression, but it must be recognized that in many contexts it also can be a crucial means of survival and even of facilitating some kinds of same-sex relationships.[41] Even with these important limitations, though, the concept of the closet can be a powerful instrument for conceptualizing various effects of hostility to sexual minorities. As some scholars have noted, it's not merely a metaphor for the necessity of hiding sexual difference, but a recognition of the actual spatial dimensions that patriarchal heterosexuality has taken: public space has been constructed as the realm of heterosexual men, limiting participation by women and often excluding sexual minorities from visibility altogether. Exclusion has occurred through prejudice and policy at the national and state levels, in religious and educational institutions, in science and medicine, in representation in the media, and in local communities and the activities of daily life. For many sexual minority people today, it still is true that only limited safe spaces are available for the expression of desire: bars, bookstores, the private spaces of their apartments or houses. Some have even more limited space, such as those who only can act on same-sex desire in the clandestine meeting places of certain parks, restrooms, or theaters. Some have almost no space at all, monitoring their own behavior and bodies to exclude signs of sexual difference, perhaps not even being able to articulate or acknowledge their desires to themselves. The closet can be thought of as taking a vast range of forms, as simultaneously global in scale and as existing within the individual body and mind.[42]

Concerning the use of the word "queer," it should be noted that throughout American society it's also widely been used as a term of abuse; it's been, and continues to be, used to attack men who are attracted to men, and, in varying degrees in different times and places, has been part of the effort to marginalize or exclude them from their families, schools, religious organizations, work, and other aspects of community life controlled by the majority. The adoption of the slang term "gay," particularly as communities of politically active men who loved men emerged in the 1960s and 1970s, was in part an attempt to reject the negative connotations of the word queer.[43] Over the past twenty years, especially in academic and urban contexts, some sexual minority people and their allies have sought to appropriate and redefine the word "queer" in positive ways, using it to refer to those who experience their sexuality and gender as setting them apart in various degrees not only from the majority but also from the gay communities that have emerged, and also using it to refer to various forms of current theory about the social construction of sex and gender, as in the term "queer studies."[44] As mentioned before, many who identify as queer in this sense of the word do so in part because they reject what they see as the assimilationism of some gay and lesbian people, particularly as embodied in gay and lesbian acceptance of the models of monogamy and marriage endorsed—if not necessarily practiced—by the majority.[45]

To relate these various points about language to the issue of what words to use to discuss the two major characters in *Brokeback Mountain,* it's my view that when Jack and Ennis begin their relationship, neither man yet has a degree of experience or knowledge that allows him to describe his sexuality. During their summer together, they address the question of whether they're queer, in the older sense of the word, meaning men who are conventional in terms of gender but desire men, and who don't share a connection with the type of identity and community connoted by the word gay. Ennis rejects labeling himself queer, and Jack complies. Ennis never gets involved with any man other than Jack, but Jack does become involved in the type of connections with other rural men that can be described as queer (in the older sense of the word) rather than gay, and then eventually moves toward a degree of open self-identification as a man who loves men that seems to me to be better described as gay rather than queer. Over the course of the narrative, many of the tensions between the two men result because Jack develops an understanding of himself that's like that of many gay men, while Ennis doesn't.

In the ongoing discussion of *Brokeback Mountain* some have said that Ennis and Jack should be thought of as bisexual. I strongly support the right of people to decide for themselves about their own sexual orientations and to name them in the ways they feel appropriate. I know there are many people who, in various degrees, desire physical and emotional intimacy with people of both sexes, and for whom the word bisexual accurately describes their experience of their sexual orientation. In my view, given the evidence of the text and the movie, if men with the feelings Ennis and Jack are represented as having were allowed to accept and express them, it seems apparent to me that their primary attraction would be to other men. The two versions of the narrative present considerable evidence that, for Ennis and Jack, their relationships with women are the result of societal pressure, and aren't freely chosen. Because of this, I don't think the term bisexual is appropriate for them, though there certainly are people for whom it is. In a society that wasn't hostile to homosexuality, or even, to imagine what I hope one day will be the case, a society that affirmed sexual and gender difference and variety, people would be able to explore and embrace forms of gender expression and consensual sexual behavior that were appropriate for them. People who now feel unable to accept same-sex attraction, and often deny it or hide it, even becoming involved in opposite-sex relations that aren't right for them or for their partners, as I think is the case for Ennis and Jack, would feel able to accept their love for people of their own sex. Rather than being suppressed, such same-sex relationships would be affirmed and encouraged by the larger society. The world today has an enormous range of problems, but an overabundance of love sure isn't one of them. I can't see any harm coming from accepting and encouraging love between people of the same sex, whatever degree of it they feel, and I can see a great deal of good, for them and for others.[46]

As I've mentioned, for many readers and viewers perhaps the most striking aspect of the two main characters in *Brokeback Mountain* is that they want sexual and emotional intimacy with each other and also fit traditional constructions of masculinity. The story and the film thus challenge homophobic stereotypes and assumptions about men who love men. But in doing so they don't uncritically endorse traditional masculinity, and neither do I. Both versions of *Brokeback Mountain* suggest the substantial costs of traditional masculinity for men who accept it and for those involved with them, and suggest alternative ways of understanding being a man. For myself, like many men who love men, I've found the society's assumptions and stereotypes concerning man-loving men damaging, oppressive, and offensive. Certainly among many men who identify as gay, especially over the past several decades, one way of challenging these negative constructions has been to assert their masculinity, indeed to construct a form of hypermasculinity. I can't deny the erotic appeal of many signifiers of masculinity, or the fact that demanding access to them is satisfying for men who've been told they're inferior because they're sexually different. But aspiring to be like traditionally masculine men is filled with problems, since it involves aspiring to be treated like them, having their privileges and power, and implicitly excludes others, particularly women and more feminine men, from these advantages. Butch guys can be sexy, but challenging the culture's treatment of men who desire men needs to be different from trying to be like them. It needs to be part of a larger change that will allow freedom and respect for varieties of sexuality and gender, not just for masculine men, and this involves confronting traditional masculinity.[47]

While I seek to locate the story and the film in relation to important cultural attitudes, including religious ideas, my own perspective is a secular one that perceives the assumptions and beliefs of people as being influenced by economic, social, political, and cultural conditions, and not as the product of any ideal power beyond the human. Although I certainly recognize that religion can express important ethical concepts as well as a yearning, borne from life's struggles, for spiritual assurance, my perspective is that of a historical materialist and an agnostic. Various religions raise profoundly important questions, but I don't subscribe to any as providing final answers. I realize, however, that religion is an important aspect of the lives of many sexual minority people and their allies, and that many are involved in the ongoing effort to build religious organizations that affirm sexual minorities, challenging doctrines and policies that promote hostility and discrimination. Christianity is significant to many who've read or seen *Brokeback Mountain,* especially outside the limits of the world of academia, and because of this I believe it's important to address the relation of the story and the movie to Christian religious ideas and images. I don't share a belief in such ideas and images, but I wish to respect those who do, and to appreciate the significance for them of the many connections between *Brokeback Mountain* and religious discourse and iconography.

Concerning the pervasive hostility to same-sex attraction and to gender difference that damages and destroys the lives of so many people, I'll refer to it here with the term homophobia, in the broad sense that it's come to be used to describe the disapproval, disgust, contempt, hatred, and fear that many Americans unfortunately feel for sexual minorities. Homophobia takes many forms, from silent disapproval and willful ignorance to the most horrible acts of violence. Homophobia is inseparable from larger patterns of thought and behavior that privilege heterosexuality and value men above women; homophobia is part of patriarchal heterosexism. It ranges along a spectrum, from its most subtle but fundamental element, the pervasive assumption that everybody who matters is straight, to the casual but endemic disapproval that warns sexual minority people that they're unwelcome, to uncritical acceptance of stereotypes of sexual minorities, to condescension and ridicule, to favoritism toward straight people and discrimination against members of sexual minorities, to overt homophobic insults and harassment and ultimately to the intimidating threat, and sometimes the terrible reality, of violence. It can vary depending on the person who's targeted. For gender-conforming men, if it becomes known that they're sexually different, many perceive them as being "discredited," denigrating them as "failed men" because they supposedly somehow are like women. Woman-loving women face the combined prejudices of misogyny and homophobia, and often are denigrated for supposedly "wanting to be men." People whose gender expression differs substantially from the "norm" may be targets of particular hostility and violence. In recent years, courageous transgender people have repeatedly been the victims of horrific murders.

Homophobia injures everyone in American society. By targeting those the society perceives as being different in terms of gender and sexuality, it not only hurts them, but intimidates and silences those whose differences aren't readily apparent, and indeed forces all men and women into the confining restrictions of traditional constructions of accepted sexuality and gender. Homophobia works to silence or discredit those who might challenge the established order of gender and power, in particular functioning as an impediment to feminism.[48]

Those who are eager to minimize the problem of homophobic prejudice often try to define it only in terms of the most obvious hate words or hostile acts. This ignores—and thus perpetuates—the subtle ways many in the majority marginalize and silence discussion of sexual minorities by assuming that people are heterosexual, by acting uncomfortable when sexual minority issues are raised, by using language and images that affirm heterosexuality as the society's norm, by employing code words that indicate negative assumptions about sexual minorities but that make it possible to evade accusations of homophobia, and by including and promoting the interests of people who are perceived as heterosexual, especially those in coupled relationships who reproduce, while ignoring and excluding those perceived as sexually different. As with other forms of prejudice, it's a mistake to make assumptions about where homophobia can be expected; like racism, sexism, and other prejudices, it pervades American society, and often occurs, especially in its more subtle and easily deniable forms, in contexts and institutions, such as academia, that publicly present themselves with a rhetoric claiming diversity and inclusion.

The general climate of hostility toward homosexuality in American culture can push members of sexual minorities to try to pass; for men who desire men, passing is required in many contexts in order to retain the status and privileges conferred by masculinity. But passing necessarily damages the self of the person who attempts to do it and prevents the development of sexual minority communities and so prevents progress. To try to pass can be a form of suicide, or perhaps, more accurately, murder, since it's one of the most pervasive ways the majority in society destroys the lives of sexual minority people.

The characters in *Brokeback Mountain* grow up and establish their relationship in the period when many historians find that homophobia was becoming especially widespread and intense in the United States. The story and the film indicate that in their sense of themselves as men, Ennis and Jack don't depart in any substantial way from the boundaries that define socially constructed norms of gender, and indeed that they exemplify many of the characteristics Americans associate with the dominant ideal of masculinity, but both must confront and struggle with a society in which homosexuality is equated with unacceptable gender behavior. In America, homophobia constructs attraction to other men as negating masculinity. For Ennis especially, the central problem of his life is that he can't square his attraction to Jack with his identity as a man.

My understanding of homophobia is based not only on academic study, but also, as unfortunately must be the case for most members of sexual minority groups, on direct personal experience. I've had plenty of lessons about homophobia in my family, in my education, in my work, and in daily life, although of course these also have been shaped by factors of race, gender, and class. Though I certainly didn't want to get the direct knowledge of homophobia that I've been given, my experience of it has increased my appreciation of *Brokeback Mountain*. The many people I've encountered in my life and work who promote the interests of straight people against those of sexual minorities, and who engage in various forms of harassment and even violence to maintain heterosexual privilege, make me feel it's necessary to speak up about the value of the story and the movie in challenging these problems.[49]

Of course, prejudice operates not only among the majority, and it's important to recognize and challenge it among sexual minorities. Unfortunately, feeling desire for those of one's own sex doesn't exclude homophobia. Some gender-conforming sexual minority people are hostile to those who don't conform in terms of gender. Members of sexual minorities can be divided by sexist assumptions on the part of men toward women, and by racial, ethnic, religious, and other cultural prejudices. Differences in class, education, age, and physical ability also can divide members of sexual minorities and prevent them from working together, as does prejudice toward transgender and intersex people. The gay culture that has become increasingly visible in America is, in many of its aspects, the creation of men who are white and middle class, and unfortunately often perpetuates the racial and class discrimination of the larger society. And as some queer activists and theorists have pointed out, the assimilationist perspective of some gay and lesbian advocates of certain issues, such as same-sex marriage, sometimes functions to marginalize those who advocate greater sexual freedom, including freedom from what some perceive as the confines of established relationship models, such as the model of the monogamous couple. Because such models follow the "norms" of gender and sexuality endorsed by the heterosexual majority, those who criticize them sometimes describe them as "heteronormative."[50]

Certainly some who support same-sex marriage do have an assimilationist agenda that queer critics are right to challenge, but it's also possible to advocate marriage equality without assuming that other sexual minority people should accept heteronormative models, and to affirm their right to diverse sexual and gender experience and expression. While I'm deeply committed to my partner and support efforts to gain marriage equality, I also want to support and respect those for whom monogamy and marriage aren't appropriate goals. Sexual minority people face enough misunderstanding, discrimination, and hostility from members of the majority; they don't need to experience more of it from other sexually different people. I hope that it can be possible for those who are sexually different to understand and accept their various experiences and perspectives and yet to work together to challenge all the ways the dominant society and culture limit their lives. I believe that people of all identities have the right to receive respect and equal and fair treatment.

ACKNOWLEDGMENTS

Like many other people who've read and seen *Brokeback Mountain,* I'm grateful to Annie Proulx for her creation, and to everyone involved in making the movie. Thanks to her, and to them, Ennis and Jack are the kinds of fictional characters sometimes created by great literature and cinema, who many readers and viewers come to think of almost as real people, whose thoughts and feelings have so much truth that they seem like people we've known. She herself has come to acknowledge the vitality of the characters she created, though certainly not in a way that's self-regarding. When she was asked, in an interview with the *Missouri Review* in 1999, whether she ever had fallen in love with one of her characters, she rejected the question, saying that she thought the "notion . . . repugnant."[51] On reconsideration, she's corrected herself, saying of that response, "There is one lie in this interview where I said I had never fallen in love with any of my characters. I think I did fall in love with both Jack and Ennis, or some other strong feeling of connection which has persisted for the eight years since the story was written."[52] She's not alone. I've written this as an expression of my appreciation for the author and the filmmakers, and of course to honor the two men they've made seem so real. The book is for Jack and Ennis, and for all those people, especially men who love men, who see themselves in them. I'm also grateful to the millions of other people, particularly men who identify as gay, bisexual, questioning, or queer, but also many women and those straight men who actually have made the effort to be allies of sexual minorities, for their enthusiasm for the story and the film. I hope they find this book a useful contribution to their interest in *Brokeback Mountain.*

My good friend, Prof. Carol Mason of the Department of English, Oklahoma State University, Stillwater, generously read this book and made many helpful suggestions, especially for improving chapters 2 and 3. Her advice and support have been invaluable. I'm grateful to Robert Ballantyne and the readers at the Arsenal Pulp Press and Charlie Perdue of McFarland Publishing for their advice for improving my discussion and to Joseph Parry and Ryan Quick of Lexington Books for the guidance and Dr. James Berg of Lake Superior College for his critical comments. Any errors here aren't their responsibility, but mine.

The friendship of many people provided encouragement for me in writing; they include Chris Ryan, Christopher Westfall, David Hirsch and John Campione, Joe Laquatra and Greg Potter, Michael Busch, Michael Lanieu, Peter Johnson and Ron Keeney, Karl Niklas and Ed Cobb, Gaurav Kampani and LeBron Rankins, Craig McClain and Wayne Lightsey, Keith Nightenhelser, Blake Thurman, Juan Liebana, James-Henry Holland, Susan Henking, Sigrid Carle, Regi Teasley, Bert Adams, Richard Salter, Stefan Baer, and Marilyn Kallet. I'm also grateful for the friendship of T.R.'s sisters Susie and Sandy; Sandy's husband, Tom Beyerle; and T.R.'s brother Tim, and for the affection and kindness of my cousin, Nancy Peregrine. Bo Decker and Mitch Guthrie always have given particular inspiration. The many good students, including members of sexual minorities and straight allies, who've taken the courses I've taught on sexual minority history, culture, film, and literature also have encouraged me. They give me hope that, while many academic administrators and faculty may think talking about "tolerance" for sexual minorities is enough, students will demand equality, fairness, and affirmation. I've found encouragement, too, in the beautiful, brilliant writing of J.G. Hayes. As always, my thanks and love go most of all to my friend Terry, for nearly twenty years "a companion where none had been expected," and to our "little darlin," Mina; I never would have been able to write this without the two of them.

NOTES

1. My education at Amherst College (B.A.) and at Yale University (M.A., M. Phil., Ph.D.) was in American (that is, United States) cultural studies and literature, and I teach in these areas and in Lesbian, Gay, Bisexual, Transgender, Queer Studies at Hobart and William Smith Colleges, Geneva, New York. In working with students, I take an approach similar to what I offer in this book, emphasizing close attention to texts and other artifacts, presenting and applying a variety of analytical ideas in ways intended to be accessible, and also acknowledging the importance of personal responses. Popular discussion of *Brokeback Mountain* already has resulted in a book, *Beyond Brokeback: The Impact of a Film* (Livermore: WingSpan, 2007), by members of the Ultimate Brokeback Forum, one of a number of Internet sites for discussion of the film and the story. The book presents scores of accounts of personal responses to the film and story. Many of the men who contributed identify themselves as sexually different, and a number are from rural areas, some in the West; some of their testimony eloquently and movingly describes substantial parallels between their experience and that of Annie Proulx's characters. There also is testimony from women who identify as sexually different and from women and men who identify as straight. Early in 2007 *GLQ: A Journal of Lesbian and Gay Studies*, published at Duke University, presented a "*Brokeback Mountain* Dossier," edited by Scott Herring, including essays by Dwight A. McBride, Martin F. Manalansan IV, John Howard, Michael Cobb,

Corey K. Creekmur, and Dana Luciano, which suggests some of the perspectives that academic discussion of the film and story may take (see *GLQ*, volume 13, number 1, 93–109.) (There already is a good critical discussion of Annie Proulx's career, including a brief section on *Brokeback Mountain*: Karen L. Rood, *Understanding Annie Proulx* [Columbia: University of South Carolina Press, 2001)]. While I value the insights of such academic discussion, I can't pretend to a neutral or negative position on the story and the film, and share some of the strongly positive subjective responses many nonacademics have had.

2. As anyone who becomes interested in the discussion of sexuality and gender will find, there's a vast and continually growing literature on these issues with contributions from many fields. It's not my intention to survey this literature or to discuss the evolution of theory within it, but merely to locate my general perspective in relation to it. My approach to male-male desire, masculinity, and homophobia in *Brokeback Mountain* is based on discussions of the social construction of sexuality and gender in the areas of lesbian, gay, bisexual, queer studies and men's/masculinities studies by such scholars as Michael S. Kimmel, Martin Levine, Jonathan Ned Katz, Gregory Herek, Brian Pronger, Peter Nardi, Michael Messner, David Plummer, and Robert W. Connell. Sources that I've found particularly relevant are Michael S. Kimmel, "Masculinity as Homophobia: Fear, Shame, and Silence in the Construction of Gender Identity," in *Theorizing Masculinities,* Harry Brod and Michael Kaufman, eds. (Thousand Oaks: Sage, 1994), also published in Kimmel, *The Gender of Desire: Essays on Male Sexuality* (Albany: S.U.N.Y. Press, 2005); Kimmel, *Manhood in America: A Cultural History* (New York: Free Press, 1996); Martin Levine, *Gay Macho: The Life and Death of the Homosexual Clone* (New York: New York University Press, 1998); Jonathan Ned Katz, *Love Stories: Sex between Men before Heterosexuality* (Chicago: University of Chicago Press, 2001); Katz, *The Invention of Heterosexuality* (Chicago: University of Chicago Press, 1995); Gregory Herek, ed., *Stigma and Sexual Orientation: Understanding Prejudice against Lesbians, Gay Men, and Bisexuals* (Thousand Oaks: Sage, 1997); Brian Pronger, *The Arena of Masculinity: Sports, Homosexuality, and the Meaning of Sex* (New York: St. Martin's, 1990); Peter Nardi, ed., *Gay Masculinities* (Thousand Oaks: Sage, 2000); Michael Messner, *Politics of Masculinities: Men in Movements* (Thousand Oaks: Sage, 1997); David Plummer, *One of the Boys: Masculinity, Homophobia, and Modern Manhood* (Binghamton: Harrington Park, 1999); Robert W. Connell, *Gender and Power: Society, the Person, and Sexual Politics* (Stanford: Stanford University Press, 1987); and Connell, *Masculinities* (Berkeley: University of California Press, 1995.) To some degree I've also drawn on E. Anthony Rotundo, *American Manhood: Transformations in Masculinity from the Revolution to the Modern Era* (New York: Basic Books, 1993.)

3. On the development of constructions of heterosexuality and homosexuality, see Katz, *Invention of Heterosexuality* and *Love Stories*; David F. Greenberg, *The Construction of Homosexuality* (Chicago: University of Chicago, 1988); Kimmel, *Manhood in America*; and Rotundo, *American Manhood*. Useful introductory explanations of the social construction of gender are provided in Kimmel's "Masculinity as Homophobia" and the Introduction to Kimmel and Amy Aronson's *Men and Masculinities: A Social, Cultural, and Historical Encyclopedia* (Santa Barbara: ABC-Clio,

2004.) On the general history of people in the United States who differ from the majority in sexuality and gender, see Neil Miller, *Out of the Past: Gay and Lesbian History from 1869 to the Present* (New York: Alyson, 2006) and Barry Adam, *The Rise of a Gay and Lesbian Movement* (New York: Twayne, 1995).

4. On general characteristics of masculine and feminine gender constructions, see Kimmel, "Masculinity as Homophobia" and *Manhood in America*; Plummer, *One of the Boys*; and Connell, *Gender and Power* and *Masculinities*.

5. Plummer, *One of the Boys*, provides a detailed discussion of processes and institutions, including family, school, peer groups, religion, and media, involved in masculine gender socialization.

6. Estimates of the numbers of people who experience same-sex attraction are difficult to make given widespread hostility, which silences many people. The Human Rights Campaign gives estimates, based on voter exit polls, of approximately 5 percent of the population for men and women who identify themselves as experiencing same-sex attraction; the British National Survey of Sexual Attitudes and Lifestyles for 1999–2001 gives estimates of about 8–9 percent. I recognize that the ways in which those who differ from the majority in terms of sex, sexuality, and gender are referred to are very important. Not all people who differ from the majority in these various ways describe themselves as being part of a minority, or wish to participate in organizations and activities based on a consciousness of being a minority, and certainly the many groups who differ from the majority don't form a single minority. Nonetheless, men who desire men, women who desire women, people who experience desire for people of both sexes, transgender people, and intersex people are treated by the majority as being different, often as "Other," and so, in this discussion, I'll refer to them with the general term sexual minorities. My intention isn't to suggest that they share a consciousness of difference or that they have related social and political goals, but rather that, regardless of their perceptions and feelings, many in the majority perceive and often stigmatize people with their various needs and desires as different. On the words gay and queer and the acronym LGBTQ, see notes for this Introduction numbered 33–37 below.

7. Discussion of gender as performance follows the insights of Judith Butler in *Gender Trouble: Feminism and the Subversion of Identity* (New York: Routledge, 1990). On sexual minority men and hypermasculine gender performance, see Levine, *Gay Macho*, and Steven Zeeland, *The Masculine Marine: Homoeroticism in the U.S. Marine Corps* (Binghamton: Haworth, 1996).

8. On transgender people, see Susan Stryker and Stephen Whittle, eds., *The Transgender Studies Reader* (New York: Routledge, 2006); Joanne Meyerowitz, *How Sex Changed: A History of Transsexuality in the United States* (Cambridge: Harvard University Press, 2004); as well as Dallas Denny, ed., *Current Concepts in Transgender Identity* (New York: Garland, 1998).

9. On intersex people, see Anne Fausto-Sterling, *Sexing the Body: Gender Politics and the Construction of Sexuality* (New York: Basic Books, 2000).

10. Over the last several decades, the development of intellectual discussion of the social construction of reality in sociology, cultural studies, and many other fields has involved the recognition that many concepts and behaviors that society assumes to be

natural and hence inevitable in fact are social constructs and can be changed. Significant examples are racist concepts and practices and sexist concepts and practices, which long were defended (and still are, by some, unfortunately) as being the inevitable result of natural conditions. Virtually any aspect of society and culture can be analyzed as a social construct; of course, the ways of understanding same-sex desire in our society, including the attitudes of sexual minorities as well as homophobic constructions of them and their relationships, are important examples. Among those discussing social construction there's an ongoing debate about whether any aspects of human experience can be thought of as natural, and if all aren't affected by social construction. That debate is far beyond the range of my discussion, but what's important to note here is that as a result of the insights of social constructionism the argument that any idea or behavior is natural, in the sense that it's the inevitable, unchangeable result of natural conditions, should be met with skepticism. Of course, nevertheless, many outside of academia continue to use the word to justify or explain what they think is right or inevitable. And many members of sexual minority groups use it to describe what feels appropriate *to them*, in terms of sexual and gender behavior, and to refute those who say that what they feel or do is unnatural. My deliberate use of the word is in the sense that such sexual minority people use it and is intended to affirm their perspective.

11. For the history of the construction of homosexuality and heterosexuality, see Katz, *Invention of Heterosexuality* and *Love Stories*; Greenberg, *Construction*; Kimmel, *Manhood in America*; and Rotundo, *American Manhood*. On negative stereotypes of sexual and emotional relationships between men, see Kimmel, "Masculinity as Homophobia;" Levine, *Gay Macho*; Plummer, *One of the Boys*; Herek, *Stigma and Sexual Orientation*; Warren J. Blumenfeld, ed., *Homophobia: How We All Pay the Price* (Boston: Beacon, 1992); R. S. Byrne Fone, *Homophobia: A History* (New York: Picador, 2000); Roger E. Biery, *Understanding Homosexuality: The Pride and the Prejudice* (Austin: Edward-William, 1990); Eric Marcus, *Is It a Choice? Answers to the Most Frequently Asked Questions about Gay and Lesbian People* (New York: Harper, 2005); and James T. Sears and Walter L. Williams, eds., *Overcoming Heterosexism and Homophobia: Strategies That Work* (New York: Columbia University Press, 1997). Also see historical overviews of these issues in Miller, *Out of the Past*, and Adam, *Rise*.

12. See Kimmel, "Masculinity as Homophobia," and Plummer, *One of the Boys*, on the policing effects of the negative category of homosexuality on men.

13. I've drawn on the following recent works of social history that examine the lives of sexual minority men: on the Northwest, Peter Boag, *Same-Sex Affairs: Constructing and Controlling Homosexuality in the Pacific Northwest* (Berkeley: University of California Press, 2003); on Mississippi, John Howard, *Men Like That: A Southern Queer History* (Chicago: University of Chicago Press); on the Mormon cultural area, D. Michael Quinn, *Same-Sex Dynamics among Nineteenth Century Americans: A Mormon Example* (Urbana/Chicago: University of Illinois Press, 1996); on the Midwest, Will Fellows, ed., *Farm Boys: Lives of Gay Men from the Rural Midwest* (Madison: University of Wisconsin Press, 1996), Karen Lee Osborne and William J. Spurlin, eds., *Reclaiming the Heartland: Lesbian and Gay Voices from the Midwest*

(Minneapolis, University of Minnesota Press, 1996), and Frank Tobias Higbie, *Indispensable Outcasts: Hobo Workers and Community in the American Midwest, 1880–1930* (Urbana/Chicago: University of Illinois Press, 2003); on North Dakota, Jerry Lee Kramer, "Batchelor Farmers and Spinsters: Gay and Lesbian Identities and Communities in North Dakota," in David Bell and Gill Valentine, eds., *Mapping Desire: Geographies of Sexualities* (New York: Routledge, 1995); on West Texas, Laurence Tate, "How They Do It in West Texas," *Harvard Gay and Lesbian Review*, Vol. 13, No. 4, Jl./ Ag., 2006; and on same-sex relationships in the pre-industrial period, William Beneman, *Male-Male Intimacy in Early America: Beyond Romantic Friendships* (Binghamton: Harrington Park, 2006). The general historical overviews in Miller, *Out of the Past*, and Adam, *Rise*, provide a useful context for understanding these studies.

14. Recent studies in these fields on which I've drawn include: Rini Sumartojo, "Contesting Place: Antigay and Lesbian Hate Crime in Columbus, Ohio," and Todd Heibel, "Blame It on the Casa Nova? 'Good Scenery and Sodomy' in Rural Southwestern Pennsylvania," both in Colin Flint, ed., *Spaces of Hate: Geographies of Discrimination and Intolerance in the U.S.A.* (New York: Routledge, 2003); Michael Brown, *Closet Space: Geographies of Metaphor from the Body to the Globe* (New York: Routledge, 2000); Jo Little, *Gender and Rural Geography: Identity, Sexuality, and Power in the Countryside* (New York: Prentice Hall, 2001); Taryn Lindhorst, "Lesbians and Gay Men in the Country: Practice Implications for Rural Social Workers," in James Donald Smith and Ronald J. Mancoske, eds., *Rural Gays and Lesbians: Building on the Strengths of Communities* (Binghamton: Haworth, 1997); B. Van Hoven, ed., *Spaces of Masculinities* (New York: Routledge, 2004); and Paul Cloke, *Country Visions: Knowing the Rural World* (Upper Saddle River, N.J.: Prentice Hall, 2003).

15. There are useful discussions of homosociality in Kimmel's "Masculinity as Homophobia" and *Manhood in America*; Levine, *Gay Macho*; and Plummer, *One of the Boys*.

16. The relative acceptance of many forms of same-sex intimacy before stigmatization by the development of the negative category of homosexuality is discussed in Beneman, *Male-Male Intimacy*; Katz, *Invention of Heterosexuality* and *Love Stories*; Quinn, *Same-Sex Dynamics*; Boag *Same-Sex Affairs*; and Howard, *Men Like That*.

17. The growing influence of negative constructions of homosexuality in the twentieth century is discussed in Quinn, *Same-Sex Dynamics*; Boag, *Same-Sex Affairs*; Howard, *Men Like That*; Katz, *Invention of Heterosexuality* and *Love Stories*; Greenberg, *Construction*; and Jennifer Terry, *An American Obsession: Science, Medicine, and Homosexuality in Modern Society* (Chicago: University of Chicago, 1999). The overviews provided by Miller, *Out of the Past*, and Adam, *Rise*, also are useful.

18. The contexts of same-sex attraction for rural men in the extended family, agricultural and other rural work, and social and religious community activities is discussed by Fellows, *Farm Boys*; Quinn, *Same-Sex Dynamics*; Howard, *Men Like That*; and Boag, *Same-Sex Affairs*.

19. On the toleration of sexual play between males in the past and in rural communities, see Howard, *Men Like That*; Quinn, *Same-Sex Dynamics*; Beneman, *Male-Male Intimacy*; Katz, *Love Stories*; and Martin Duberman, "'Writhing Bedfellows' in

Antebellum North Carolina: Historical Interpretation and the Politics of Evidence," in Duberman, Martha Vicinus, and George Chauncey Jr., eds., *Hidden from History: Reclaiming the Gay and Lesbian Past* (New York: Penguin, 1989). Quinn, *Same-Sex Dynamics*, indicates that accommodation of sexual minority men continued until the 1950s among Mormons, and Howard, *Men Like That*, indicates that it continued into the 1960s in Mississippi.

20. See Chris Packard, *Queer Cowboys and Other Erotic Male Friendships in Nineteenth Century American Literature* (New York: Palgrave Macmillan, 2005).

21. See Boag, *Same-Sex Affairs*, on same-sex relationships among loggers.

22. See Boag, *Same-Sex Affairs*, and Higbie, *Indispensable Outcasts*, on same-sex relationships among hoboes.

23. See Quinn, *Same-Sex Dynamics*, on past Mormon toleration of same-sex couples living together.

24. See Howard, *Men Like That*, and Kramer, "Batchelor Farmers," on the effects of the automobile in facilitating same-sex relationships.

25. On the widespread clandestine demarcation of certain public spaces for male-male sexual relationships, see Howard, *Men Like That*; Kramer, "Batchelor Farmers"; and Tate, "How They Do It."

26. On the necessity of minimizing visibility for sexual minority men, see Howard, *Men Like That*; Kramer, "Batchelor Farmers"; and Tate, "How They Do It." Of course, as Tate indicates, today many men continue to be involved in clandestine sexual activity in the area he discusses, and this continues to be the case throughout the country.

27. See Howard, *Men Like That*, on instances of toleration of gay bars by authorities in Mississippi.

28. On the gradual appearance of resource and support organizations for sexual minorities in rural Western areas, see Kramer, "Batchelor Farmers."

29. On the growing threat of exposure for sexual minority men due to the expansion of the influence of negative medical-legal categories of homosexuality, see Quinn, *Same-Sex Dynamics*; Howard, *Men Like That*; and Boag, *Same-Sex Affairs*.

30. On increasing religious intolerance toward sexual minorities, see Howard, *Men Like That*, and Quinn, *Same-Sex Dynamics*.

31. On the construction of public space as heterosexual, see Sumartojo, "Contesting Place"; Heibel, "Casa Nova"; Brown, *Closet Space*; Little, *Rural Geography*; Lindhorst, "Practical Implications"; Van Hoven, *Spaces*; and Cloke, *Country Visions*.

32. The deterrent effect of homophobic stereotypes on identification for some sexual minority men is discussed in Kramer, "Batchelor Farmers."

33. Howard, *Men Like That*, and Tate, "How They Do It," particularly emphasize the endurance and resistance of sexual minority men in rural areas.

34. In general, scholars who discuss sexual minority men in rural areas emphasize that visibility became more dangerous in the twentieth century as a result of the expansion of the influence of negative medical-legal categories of homosexuality.

35. On the limitations of the word gay for describing the variety of sexual minority men, see Howard, *Men Like That*, and Tate, "How They Do It"; also relevant are the discussion of class prejudice in the gay community in "Afterword: Passing Notes

in Class," by Wendell Ricketts, in his edited volume, *Everything I Have Is Blue: Short Fiction by Working-Class Men about More-Or-Less Gay Life* (San Francisco: Suspect Thoughts Press, 2005), and the discussions of race prejudice in the gay community in Keith Boykin, *One More River to Cross: Black and Gay in America* (New York: Anchor, 1996), and Dwight A. McBride, *Why I Hate Abercrombie and Fitch: Essays on Race and Sexuality* (New York: New York University Press, 2005).

36. On reasons for using the word queer rather than gay for many rural sexual minority men, see Howard, *Men Like That*.

37. There's continuing debate over use of the word gay as a generic term. It isn't appropriate for many reasons: it refers to a particular way of constructing same-sex orientation today, not all present constructions, and not earlier ones; although some women refer to themselves as gay, many find that the term excludes women; and many men are critical of it because gay communities often are more welcoming and supportive to middle class and affluent white men. Some, especially younger, urban, political activists, use the word queer as a generic term, but some who've experienced it as a term of abuse understandably aren't comfortable with it. The acronym LGBTQ (for Lesbian, Gay, Bisexual, Transgender, Queer, and Questioning) is widely used, but is awkward, and is objected to by some who find that the various groups don't share common perspectives and concerns. Still, as also noted, for many people, including many who are not middle class, affluent, or white, the word gay has come to function as a generic term, both in the United States and around the world. I believe that all who want to be supportive of those who differ from the majority in sexuality and gender need to engage in dialogue, listening to and respecting their various concerns about language, and trying to develop language that's acceptable to all of those it describes. Finding language that adequately describes their experiences is an important aspect of their efforts toward freedom and equality, and necessarily is an ongoing and open-ended process.

38. For a critique of gay culture and class, see Ricketts, "Afterword"; on gay culture and race, see Boykin, *One More River*, and McBride, *Abercrombie*.

39. See Fellows, *Farm Boys*; Howard, *Men Like That*; and Osborne and Spurlin, *Reclaiming the Heartland*, for insightful discussions of the negative assumptions and stereotypes that many urban people make about rural life and sexual minority people in rural contexts. Substantial numbers of sexual minority men and women have chosen to live in rural areas, especially in certain parts of the nation, as is the case for some involved in the Radical Faerie movement and some involved in lesbian separatist communes.

40. Howard, *Men Like That*, provides insightful criticism of negative assumptions about rural life implicit in personal and social narratives that stress the value of coming out and identifying as gay.

41. As discussed in Howard, *Men Like That*, it's important to recognize the potential positive aspects of remaining "closeted" for men in many different social contexts, and the ways in which it actually can facilitate certain forms of relationships between men.

42. Brown, *Closet Space*, provides useful discussion of many aspects of the concept of the closet. For a contrasting perspective, providing a critique of limitations of

the concept of the closet, see Howard, *Men Like That*, as well as Steven Seidman, *Beyond the Closet: The Transformation of Gay and Lesbian Life* (New York: Routledge, 2003).

43. The circumstances of the adoption of the word gay as a generic term have been discussed by historians of sexual minority political movements; see Miller, *Out of the Past*; Adam, *Rise*; and John D'Emilio, *Sexual Politics, Sexual Communities: The Making of a Homosexual Minority in the United States, 1940–1970* (Chicago: University of Chicago Press, 1983).

44. On the effort to recuperate the word "queer" as a positive, assertive, generic term, see Michael Warner, *The Trouble with Normal* (New York: Free Press, 1999) and the edited collection, *Fear of a Queer Planet* (Minneapolis: University of Minnesota Press, 1993); also see Annemarie Jagose, *Queer Theory: An Introduction* (New York: New York University Press, 1996).

45. Warner presents insightful queer critiques of gay culture in *Fear of a Queer Planet* and *The Trouble with Normal*.

46. For introductory discussion of bisexual experience and perspectives, see Beth Firestein, ed., *Bisexuality: The Psychology and Politics of an Invisible Minority* (Thousand Oaks: Sage, 1996), and William E. Burleson, *BiAmerica: Myths, Truths, and Struggles of an Invisible Community* (Binghamton: Haworth, 2005).

47. For important critical perspectives on the masculinization of gay culture and masculine privilege, see Levine, *Gay Macho*; Seymour Kleinberg, *Alienated Affections* (New York: St. Martin's, 1980); and Leo Bersani, "Is the Rectum a Grave?" in Douglas Crimp, ed., *AIDS: Cultural Analysis, Cultural Activism* (Cambridge: M.I.T. Press, 1989). The work of many currently involved in the study of masculinities, particularly those listed in endnote number 2 above, along with the extensive and significant work of lesbian and feminist scholars on sexuality, gender, and many other topics, is providing analytical and critical perspectives that can assist in changing constructions and relations of sexuality and gender and making them less unequal and discriminatory. The critique of these issues available within academia is vast and valuable, but the most important challenge, I believe, remains making this critique accessible, sharing it with those outside academia, involving them in participation in discussing and developing it, and particularly working with women and sexual minorities throughout the society in using it to take action for change.

48. The word "homophobia" only was created in the late 1960s, and indeed its meanings continue to be discussed and contested. It's become widely understood not to mean only a phobia in the literal sense of an irrational fear, but the entire complex system of negative ideas, attitudes, and practices directed at homosexuality and those identified as homosexual. Dr. George Weinberg, a progressive clinical psychologist active in efforts to challenge homophobic prejudice and its effects, was the first to popularize it, in his *Society and the Healthy Homosexual* (New York: St. Martin's, 1972). Some constructive critics of the word who oppose hostility to sexual minorities have proposed words such as "homoerotophobia" or "homonegativity." Others point out that the use of the prefix "homo" implicitly locates the problem that the word describes in those who are its targets and victims, which is unjust, and that a better word would emphasize that the real responsibility for the problem lies with those

who think straight people are better than sexual minority people; these critics propose words such as "heterosexism," whose structure parallels that of "racism" and "sexism," and which refers to the general privileging of the present dominant system of patriarchal heterosexual relations of which hostility to sexual minorities is an integral part. Though there are good arguments for these proposed replacements, they haven't displaced "homophobia." Those who are hostile to sexual minorities often reject the word "homophobia" for various reasons as part of their efforts to minimize the problems caused by hostility to sexual minorities. Some argue that it only should be used to refer to a phobia in the strict sense of the word as it is used in psychology; this is one of the criticisms made by the small minority of psychologists and psychiatrists who continue to argue that sexual orientation can and should be "changed." Others dismissively say that as it's constructed the word must mean an irrational fear of sameness, and so that it really has no meaning. Religious homophobes sometimes indignantly claim that the use of the suffix "phobia" makes their hostility sound irrational, when of course they believe it's a divinely ordained and revealed truth.

49. On various forms of homophobia, see Plummer, *One of the Boys*; Sears, *Overcoming Heterosexism*; Blumenfeld, *Homophobia*; Fone, *A History*; Herek, *Stigma and Sexual Orientation*; Biery, *Understanding Homosexuality*; and Terry, *American Obsession*. I've discussed the concept of the spectrum of homophobia in detail in "Toward Inclusion and Equality for Sexual Minorities" (2005), a handbook on heterosexism and homophobia which I wrote and have distributed on my own initiative at Hobart and William Smith Colleges, where I teach, with the intention of informing students, faculty, and administrators and reducing homophobic discrimination, harassment, and violence on the campus. I intend eventually to publish a version of this handbook for use at other colleges and universities. In my experience as a teacher, it's evident that harassment of students perceived as members of sexual minorities still is far more prevalent—and far less opposed by many administrators and faculty—than other forms of prejudice. "Gay" is widely used among students as a term of abuse without official opposition, whereas a serious effort would be made to stop the negative use of other identity terms. And while liberal academic institutions may pretend—in every sense of that word—to diversity, inclusiveness, and fairness, straight people in academia enjoy substantially more professional and social advantages, continually being empowered by heterosexism to pursue their interests, as in heterosexual couple hiring, an advantage historically denied to same-sex couples and entirely unavailable to single people. Traditional gender socialization still shapes behavior in conducting the processes of daily life even at supposedly progressive educational institutions, and so straight white men continue to be disproportionately enabled to make their voices heard over others and to throw their considerable weight around. Some continue to resort to homophobic abuse or more easily excused code words in efforts to marginalize and silence criticism of heterosexist privilege. Even in the supposedly progressive world of academia, there's a long way to go before some men relinquish what Annie Proulx perceptively refers to as the "hard need to be the stud duck in the pond" and such institutions truly become diverse, inclusive, and fair.

50. On heteronormativity, see Warner, *The Trouble with Normal* and *Fear of a Queer Planet*.

51. "Interview with Annie Proulx," *The Missouri Review*, Vol. 22, No. 2, 1999.

52. Annie Proulx corrected herself about loving Ennis and Jack in her comments on her interviews on her website; "Note on Interviews" (http://www.annieproulx .com/).

Prologue: Reactions To
Brokeback Mountain

When he accepted his award for Best Director at the 78th Academy Awards ceremony, Ang Lee expressed his gratitude to those who worked with him and to his friends and his family, as recipients of awards usually do. But he began in a way that's seldom if ever been heard in an acceptance speech before, thanking "two people who don't even exist."[1] He went on to explain,

> or I should say, they do exist, because of the imagination of Annie Proulx and the artistry of Larry McMurtry and Diana Ossana. Their names are Ennis and Jack. And they taught all of us who made *Brokeback Mountain* so much about not just all the gay men and women whose love is denied by society, but just as important, the greatness of love itself.[2]

Many, among general readers and viewers at least, agreed, feeling that in both its forms, *Brokeback Mountain* is extraordinary because it goes inside the lives of two men who love each other, showing many dimensions of the longing, fear, pain, and joy that often are experienced by that minority of people who are drawn to others of their own sex and who consequently are rejected by much of the majority. For most members of the majority, the lives of members of sexual minorities go unconsidered and remain invisible, and if they're noticed at all, it's often with contempt, ridicule, and hatred. Many in the majority see sexual minorities only in terms of their own assumptions and beliefs, and particularly their own anxieties and fears, and never are capable of understanding what it's like to be one of the people whose love they react to with so much disgust and disdain. Few straight men, in particular, have the security in their own sexual identity to make the effort to imagine what it's like, given the attitudes of the majority, for a young man growing up and discovering that his sexual and emotional needs are for other men. Sexual difference is so threatening to many straight men that they only can think of it in relation to themselves, as a possibility that disturbs and repels them, and so can't begin to imagine at all what it's actually like to be a man who's attracted to men. For many straight men, feeling secure in being straight depends on perceiving and treating sexually different men as Other, perpetuating the hostility and destructiveness of homophobia.

Fortunately, there are straight people who are able to make the effort to set aside the assumptions taught by the dominant culture, and to try to imagine what the world is like for sexual minorities. Such straight people are real allies in resisting prejudice against gay, lesbian, bisexual, transgender, queer, and questioning people because they've begun the process of understanding and challenging the fear and hatred so many in the majority feel toward sexual minorities. In both its versions, *Brokeback Mountain* demonstrates the capacity of straight people to become allies in the struggle to overcome homophobia, since the story is the creation of an author who is heterosexual, and the movie was based on her story by two screenwriters, a director, actors, and many others who are heterosexual. The *Production Notes* for the film show that during the process of making it, the straight people involved made a serious effort to think about the lives of men who love men and to learn from sexual minority people who were involved in the production. In being able to imagine what it's like to be a man who's attracted to men, the story's author, Annie Proulx, and Ang Lee, Larry McMurtry, Diana Ossana, Heath Ledger, Jake Gyllenhaal, and the many other straight people involved in making the film version all demonstrate that it's possible for members of the majority to understand homophobia and to work to end it, and many sexual minority people feel respect for them as a result. Annie Proulx deserves particular praise for the depth with which she thought about the lives of men like Ennis and Jack, and the brilliance with which she depicted them.

As is the case with all other forms of prejudice, the fundamental requirement for overcoming homophobia is the ability to imagine being another person, to imagine what that person's experience may be, to imagine what that person may feel, to respond with compassion, and to begin to act in ways that respect that person's identity. One of the basic reasons people write books and make movies, and that people read and go to movies, is to try to understand what it's like to be someone else. In his grandest poem, "Song of Myself," Walt Whitman, one of the most original American writers and the first to assert directly the value of love between men, celebrates the power of imagination to take us into the lives of others and to begin to learn the sympathy that can make society a community. He proclaims, "I am he attesting sympathy,"[3] and offers hundreds of brief depictions, almost like snapshots, of poignant, funny, terrifying, beautiful moments in the lives of men and women, seeking to imagine their circumstances and what they might feel. To live without this capacity of imagination and compassion, as he says, not only allows us to injure others, but also injures ourselves: "whoever walks a furlong without sympathy walks to his own funeral drest in his shroud . . ."[4] The achievement of both the story and the film of *Brokeback Mountain* is a sign that the power of imagination to show people the lives of others as they themselves may experience them, so admired by Whitman, can be a real force for positive change in the world.

Both Annie Proulx's story and Ang Lee's film have been widely honored. After it first was published in the *New Yorker* in October 1997, the story received the O. Henry Award; the author also has received the Pulitzer Prize and the P.E.N. Faulkner award for other works. The movie has received so many awards that it's difficult to make a complete list, and I won't attempt it here. Some of the most important are: Independent Spirit Awards: Best Feature, Best Director; Golden Globe Awards: Best Motion Picture-Drama, Best Director, Best Screenplay, Best Original Song; Producers' Guild of America: Producer of the Year Award; Directors' Guild of America: Director of the Year Award; Critics' Choice Awards: Best Picture, Best Director, Best Supporting Actress (Michelle Williams); British Academy of Film and Television Arts Awards: Best Film, Award for Achievement in Direction, Best Supporting Actor (Jake Gyllenhaal), Best Adapted Screenplay; Gay and Lesbian Alliance Against Defamation: Best Wide Release Film; Venice International Film Festival: Golden Lion Award for Best Film; best picture awards by London Film Critics Circle, Los Angeles Film Critics Association, New York Film Critics Circle, Boston Society of Film Critics, Dallas-Fort Worth Film Critics Association, Florida Film Critics Circle, Las Vegas Film Critics Society, San Francisco Film Critics Circle, Southeastern Film Critics Association, Utah Film Critics Society, among others. The Motion Picture Academy of Arts and Sciences awarded it Best Musical Score, Best Adapted Screenplay, and, as already noted, Best Director. At the MTV Awards, what's perhaps the award to the film that's been most appreciated by many gay men was given to Heath Ledger and Jake Gyllenhaal for Best Kiss. According to Universal Studios, *Brokeback Mountain* was the most honored film of 2005. If money is to be the measurer of success, it was quite successful, having been made for about 14 million dollars, and earning more than 83 million dollars in the United States and 95 million dollars abroad during its 133 day run; of course, with its DVD and cable TV releases, the movie is earning large additional sums. The story and the film continue to be widely discussed, as shown by the many sites and references to *Brokeback Mountain* on the Internet and in the press.[5]

Yet the Academy Awards, at which Ang Lee made his moving acceptance speech, also gave a powerful reminder of the limits of imagination and compassion. Some straight people, like Proulx, the screenwriters, and the filmmakers, are able to try to imagine and understand the lives of others whose sexual orientation is different from their own, but to many, those others remain entirely Other, separate, alien, unimaginable. Despite the remarkable quality of *Brokeback Mountain,* it didn't receive awards in five of the eight categories for which it was nominated, Best Actor (Heath Ledger), Best Supporting Actor (Jake Gyllenhaal), Best Supporting Actress (Michelle Williams), Best Cinematography (Rodrigo Prieto), or Best Picture. Of course, many films that receive nominations in a large number of categories never receive all the awards that some believe they deserve, but the case of *Brokeback Mountain* is remarkable because of the widespread reports that many members of the Academy refused to watch the film because of its content, or rather, because of their preconceptions and prejudices about its content. This information comes from a number of sources, including two elderly white male actors, Tony Curtis and Ernest Borgnine, both members of the Academy. Curtis told an interviewer on Fox News that he had no intention of seeing the film, and that most of his friends in the Academy didn't either. He went on to pass judgment on the movie, even though he hadn't seen it, saying that it wasn't as important as people had said, that the only reason it was widely discussed was that it concerned "gay cowboys," and then invoked two straight male figures from Hollywood's past as supposedly representing his standards where male homosexuality is concerned: "Howard Hughes and John Wayne wouldn't like it."[6] Borgnine had a similar view, saying, "I didn't see it and I don't care to see it. If John Wayne were alive, he'd be rolling over in his grave."[7] While it's bizarre, Borgnine's statement, like Curtis's, points to the centrality of traditional homophobic constructions of masculinity in the reactions of many straight men to the film.

Particularly because the Academy has no means of assuring that its members actually see the films that have been nominated for the various categories on which they vote, the statements of Curtis and Borgnine give reason to think that the judgment of the Academy wasn't really a judgment at all, since it was based in part on willful ignorance, not on a fair evaluation of the qualities of the film compared with those of others that were nominated.[8] Los Angeles journalists who cover the Academy confirmed this problem. Nikki Finke of *Los Angeles Weekly* commented, "I found horrifying each whispered admission to me from Academy members who usually act like social liberals that they were disgusted by even the possibility of glimpsing simulated gay sex. . . . Turns out Hollywood is as homophobic as Red State country."[9] Of the Academy members who participated in making the awards decisions without seeing *Brokeback Mountain,* she said, "There are those for whom the cowboy is an iconic figure in Hollywood, old guys who boast about their friendships with John Wayne. This is something that really offends them."[10] Kenneth Turan of the *Los Angeles Times* commented about the atmosphere preceding the awards, "[Y]ou could not take the pulse of the industry without realizing that [*Brokeback Mountain*] made a number of people distinctly uncomfortable," and argued that the homophobic attitudes of Academy members prevented the film from winning Best Picture.[11] It's notable, too, that straight members of the Academy who claim to be allies of sexual minorities didn't raise the strong objection to the refusals of some Academy members to see the film that they deserve.

The failure to watch and to fairly evaluate *Brokeback Mountain* is a direct manifestation of the central subject of *Brokeback Mountain,* the destructive impact of the fear, hatred, and ignorance concerning sexual minorities that comprise homophobia. Not surprisingly, of course, many of the more than six thousand members of the Academy belong to exactly the group that's most likely to be fearful and hostile toward men who are sexually different and to cling to homophobic prejudice—older heterosexual men. Though many who admired the film were disappointed by the failure of the Academy to recognize its quality with the award of Best Picture, that failure hardly can come as a surprise, given the nature of the Academy as a social and economic institution that manifests the attitudes of the dominant group, in terms of sex, race, and sexual orientation, that shapes much of American society.[12]

The refusal of some in the Motion Picture Academy to consider *Brokeback Mountain* for the Best Picture award is paralleled by the response to the movie of a substantial sector of the American public. On TV, on radio, on the Internet, in the press, in popular music, in politics and religion, and in everyday interactions between people, many, particularly straight men, have subjected the film to an extraordinary degree of hostility, contempt, and ridicule, often without seeing it. (Few of those who've made public negative comments have discussed the short story, apparently not having read it.) To anyone who thinks about the stereotypes that the majority imposes on sexual minorities, and the destructive impact of these stereotypes, their comments speak for themselves.

Here are a few of the most notable examples of the ways the movie has been attacked in the media: John Gibson of Fox News expressed his opinion of *Brokeback Mountain* with a "question," asking which would be harder to watch, the scenes depicting Ennis and Jack making love or the scenes in the movie *Syriana* in which a character is tortured by having his fingernails pulled out.[13] Also on Fox News and on his radio program, Bill O'Reilly repeatedly complained about the film, stating, "this movie [is] being pushed and pushed and pushed by every media [sic] you can imagine. Why? Because they want to mainstream homosexual conduct."[14] Interestingly, Gibson,

O'Reilly, and others who attacked the film stressed that they refused to see it, apparently making it a point of pride that their opinions were based on ignorance.[15] Joe Scarborough, a Republican former Congressman who now has a program on MSNBC, presented a view similar to O'Reilly's, again, like Gibson, posing it as a "question": "Is Hollywood pushing a subversive agenda? Is Hollywood trying to push a radical agenda?"[16] Scarborough's rhetoric is especially disturbing, since it constructs *Brokeback Mountain* as an element of an "agenda" of "radical subversion," much as the hysterical McCarthyite rhetoric of the early 1950s often equated homosexuality with Communist subversion, as part of the concerted effort by McCarthyites at the time to drive sexual minority people as well as those who had supported the New Deal out of government, the media, education, unions, and many other areas of American life.[17]

Various right wing groups have made accusations about *Brokeback Mountain* similar to those of O'Reilly and Scarborough, constructing the movie as part of an "agenda" by "Hollywood liberals" who are "out of touch with America" and who are trying to "homosexualize" the country. According to Robert Knight, who—rather amusingly—belongs to Concerned Women for America, the movie is "the product of two decades of a pro-homosexual agenda by Hollywood and the media."[18] He lamented the success of what he and other opponents of the film present as an organized effort to change attitudes about homosexuality, saying "the constant promotion of homosexuality in the media has lowered resistance to the idea that homosexuality is normal and healthy."[19] In his view, the film

> combines high production values with a lowdown attack on morality. It's a mockery of the Western genre embodied in every movie cowboy from John Wayne to Gene Autry to Kevin Costner. I can't think of a more effective way to annoy and alienate most movie-going Americans than to show two cowboys lusting after each other and even smooching.[20]

(Apparently not having seen the movie, Mr. Knight was spared the distress of learning that it shows Ennis and Jack doing considerably more than "smooching.")

The perception that the movie is part of a general conspiracy to promote homosexuality was the basis of a widely quoted column, entitled "The Rape of the Marlboro Man," by David Kupelian of World Net Daily, an ultra-rightwing Internet site. Kupelian argued that *Brokeback Mountain* was equivalent to a film supporting heroin addiction or one supporting child molestation.[21] His views on the movie were given prominence by Fox News, on which he stated,

. . . all of the talents of the acting and the directing and the music, everything
that goes into it, is geared towards making homosexuality seem like, you know,
a wonderful lifestyle and it makes the adulterous relationship of these two men
which destroyed both their marriages and left their children bereft of a father
into something like a wonderful, magnificent love story, which is what the critics are calling it.[22]

Ted Baehr, operator of the ultra-right-wing movie review site, MovieGuide
.org ("A ministry dedicated to redeeming the values of the mass media according to Biblical principles . . ."[23]), denounced the film as subversive and
abhorrent, calling it anti-family, anti-American and "laughable, frustrating,
and boring Neo-Marxist homosexual propaganda."[24] Unlike Concerned
Women for America's Knight, Baehr actually seems to have watched the
movie, and to have seen the depiction of Ennis and Jack enjoying anal intercourse, which to him was a "San Quentin–type rape scene."[25] Others, such as
Andrea Sheldon Lafferty of Louis Sheldon's Traditional Values Coalition,
based their attacks on long-discredited homophobic psychological theories:

Hollywood screenwriters and producers think that it's their duty to teach Middle America that homosexual conduct and cross-dressing are normal behaviors
that should be affirmed in American culture. They're wrong, and we will never
accept the belief that same-sex relationships or transvestism are simply normal
variations of human sexuality. These behaviors reveal deep-seated psychological problems that should be treated, not affirmed.[26]

More than three decades ago, the American Psychiatric Association repudiated this mental illness model of homosexuality, and it and other responsible
mental health care professional organizations condemn those who continue to
promote such hostile views as well as the related belief that it's possible, and
preferable, to change a homosexual orientation.[27]

Many other homophobic groups, of course, construct same-sex love not so
much as sickness but as sin, and base their attacks on their interpretations of
religion. When the film was released, the United States Conference of
Catholic Bishops initially issued a review praising the acting and filmmaking
and labeling the movie with an "L," indicating that the church found it acceptable for a limited adult audience because it had "problematic content
many adults would find troubling."[28] A few days later, after vocal protest by
many within and outside the church who were hostile to the film, the review
was changed. While still praising the film's quality of presentation, it now labeled the film with an "O," for "morally offensive,"[29] citing the contorted arguments employed in Catholic doctrine to attack same-sex love, that "homosexual inclinations" are "objectively disordered," that "homosexual acts" are

"intrinsically disordered," and that the relationship in the movie thus was "objectively immoral."[30] The review justified this judgment because of the film's "tacit approval of same-sex relationships"[31] as well as a long list of other elements of the movie that alarmed church leaders, ranging from adultery to such shockers as " . . . profanity, rough and crude expressions, irreligious remarks, [and] alcohol and brief drug use;"[32] perhaps the most laughable to make the list of horrors was what church officials intriguingly described as "shadowy rear nudity."[33] Typically, as in other attacks on the film, church leaders showed no ability to recognize the connection between the destructive repression and hideous violence toward men who love men depicted in the film and the hostility to homosexuality that they propagate in their own official church teachings. As members of sexual minorities know all too well, the harassment, discrimination, and violence that they face in American society are continually reinforced and encouraged by the homophobia of many religious organizations and leaders, which makes the understanding and support of sexual minorities by some progressive religious denominations, and indeed by some progressive people within denominations that are officially hostile, including the Catholic Church, all the more admirable.[34]

Pat Robertson, the Southern Baptist head of the Christian Coalition and of the Christian Broadcasting Network, didn't indulge in any jesuitical logic chopping, simply dismissing the movie as "moral pollution"[35] in line with his earlier statements that acceptance of homosexuality could cause terrorist attacks, earthquakes, hurricanes, tornadoes, and "possibly a meteor."[36] CBN strongly promoted the belief that *Brokeback Mountain* is the result of a homosexual conspiracy, attacking the film as part of "a well-planned propaganda campaign . . . laid out all the way back in the 1980's,"[37] that employs "tactics . . . remarkably similar to the brainwashing methods of Mao Tse-Tung's Communist Chinese—mixed with Madison Avenue's most persuasive selling techniques."[38] As is the case for many other American right-wingers, Robertson's religious/media/political empire is haunted by twin specters, the specters of Communism and homosexuality.

Certainly the most hysterical and venomous denunciations of the film that received substantial TV coverage were those of "Michael Savage," a radio talk show "personality." "Savage," whose actual name is Michael Weiner, formerly had a call-in program on MSNBC, but was fired after he abused a caller who had identified himself as gay, referring to the caller as a "sodomite" and telling him to "get AIDS and die."[39] On his syndicated radio program, "Savage" labeled *Brokeback Mountain* "disgusting," "vile filth," "refuse in a sewer pipe," and a result of "the dementia of Hollywood."[40] He "renamed" the film "Bareback Mounting," in a typical homophobic effort to reduce its content to sex acts and to demonize those sex acts, and repeated this parody of the title over and over.[41] He also subscribed to the model of Hollywood as part of a conspiracy to "homosexualize" America, stating, "[I]t is true the pink hand of Hollywood is in total control and all stops were removed in order to push homosexually-themed films."[42] The derogatory use of the word pink in this attack perfectly epitomizes the conflation of homosexuality with left-wing politics in a grand fantasy of "subversion" that's typical of so much current Neo-McCarthyite rhetoric. This might be dismissed as just another vicious homophobic rant, but "Savage" received a remarkable degree of endorsement from two highly visible individuals on MSNBC, Chris Matthews, who has a regular evening program, and Don Imus, who at the time had one in the morning (in 2007 he was fired for gross insults directed at the Rutgers University Women's Basketball Team.) When Matthews appeared on Imus's program, they both ridiculed *Brokeback Mountain,* sharing parody titles that reduce the film's meaning to a hostile representation of anal sex between men. Matthews's behavior was particularly irresponsible and destructive, since some people take him seriously as a news commentator. In his conversation with Imus, Matthews praised "the wonderful Michael Savage"[43] and cited with approval "Savage's" shrill denunciations of the movie as "Bareback Mounting."[44] Imus responded with another parody title which he found amusing, which similarly reduces the film to sex, and similarly reduces that sex to the level of disgust: "Fudgepack Mountain."[45] The loathsome statements of all three men typify the depth of hatred and contempt toward men who love men that permeate the media and American culture generally.

Brokeback Mountain was the subject of endless "jokes" by late night TV "personalities," as well as parodies in the press and on the Internet, which of course then shaped conversation about the movie around the country. David Letterman, Conan O'Brien, and Jay Leno repeatedly referred to it on their TV shows, sometimes in ways that were relatively supportive of sexual minorities, but also in ways that were offensive.[46] Leno made fun of it so frequently that he was publicly criticized in an open letter by Jeff Whitty, a successful gay playwright and actor. Whitty's perceptive and eloquent letter summed up the feelings of many gay men. He said, in part:

Dear Mr. Leno,
    . . . . When you think of gay people, it's funny. They're funny folks. They wear leather. They like Judy Garland. They like disco music. They're sort of like Stepin Fetchit as channeled by Richard Simmons. Gay people, to you, are great material. Mr. Leno, let me share with you my view of gay people. . . . When I think of gay people, I think of suicide. I think of a countless list of people who took their own lives because the world was so toxically hostile to them. Because of the deathly climate of the closet, we will never be able to count them. You think gay people are great material. I think of a silent holocaust that continues

to this day. I think of a silent holocaust that is perpetuated by people like you, who seek to minimize us and make fun of us and who I suspect, really, fundamentally, wish we would just go away . . . [47]

Many simply dismiss the comments of Leno and others as merely being "humor," and criticize those like Whitty who object, accusing them of "not being able to take a joke" and of being excessively "sensitive," thus attempting to dismiss them by feminizing them. It's useful, however, for anyone who's concerned about homophobia to consider what the reaction would be to "humor" of this kind about movies dealing with other sorts of prejudice and violence. How long is it since there's been an analogous case in which a serious film dealing in a respectful way with the lives of members of another minority group has been subjected to the sort of prolonged, pervasive ridicule that's been directed at *Brokeback Mountain*? It's difficult to imagine how a similar reaction could occur today to a film dealing with any other minority group. Would most Americans tolerate such a response to *Schindler's List* or to *Do the Right Thing*? Would the same degree of contempt be acceptable toward a film dealing with women, who aren't a minority, but often are treated like one? Would it be acceptable toward one that dealt with Arab Americans, who certainly have been unfairly represented, though seldom with the kind of crude disparagement directed at sexual minorities? There have been many films in recent years that have addressed the experience of other groups that have struggled against irrational hatred and fear, and those films usually have been met with respect, admiration, and praise, as they should be. But this isn't the case for a movie that deals with the lives and perspectives of men who love men. While "humor" of the type directed at *Brokeback Mountain* may be discounted as trivial by some people, it has serious destructive effects. In general, the ridicule directed at the movie tends to operate in two important ways.

First, such ridicule concentrates on the sexual relationship between the two main characters in the film, and especially on the sex act that many in the majority assume all sexual minority men, and virtually no heterosexuals, desire: anal intercourse. Ridicule thus serves a very serious purpose, reducing the complexity of the characters' relationships to sex, and constructing that sex as being disgusting and repulsive. This successfully eliminates any consideration of the emotional depth of the characters' connection with each other or of the difficult problems caused for them and their families by the pervasive homophobic hostility that forces many men who desire men into trying to pass for straight. Especially for straight people who haven't seen the movie, its meaning thus is contained at a minimal level that confirms their contempt for it and for men like those it depicts: it's just "that gay cowboy movie" showing "gross" gay sex. In this regard, ridicule achieves much the same dehumanizing effect as the attacks by Gibson and the other "news" commentators and by the various right-wing groups.

The second important aspect of the "humor" directed at the film involves the mobilization of the well-established stereotypes of men who are attracted to men as effeminate, weak, and contemptible. Such "jokes" operate by imposing on the film the stereotypes of the gay man as a silly, hysterical queen or a stylish urban sophisticate, often playing on the contrast between these stereotypes and the cultural ideal of the supremely masculine cowboy in order to get a "comic" effect. In these "jokes" the concept of "gay cowboys" is constructed as preposterous: they juxtapose the idealized image of the cowboy, the epitome of the "real man," with the supposed interests and activities of stereotypic gay men. The resulting constructs are deliberately absurd, imagining cowboys who are interested in interior decorating, fashion, grooming, trendy consumer goods, Broadway shows, and transvestism, all the stereotypical trivial or bizarre concerns of the "faggot" as constructed by homophobes. Such "jokes" maintain the dominant culture's unremitting attack on those men who do fit parts of traditional homophobic stereotypes, an attack that of course it takes great strength to withstand (directly contradicting the assumption that sexually different men are weak, though this certainly isn't recognized by the majority). The construction of these "jokes" also has the powerful effect of denying the fact that there are men who love men throughout American society who don't fit homophobic stereotypes and so are invisible to the majority, that gender behavior and sexuality aren't necessarily linked. This pattern of construction functions to reimpose and perpetuate the stereotypes that *Brokeback Mountain* challenges, reassuring the majority that sexually different men really are merely the weaklings and clowns that they want to think they are. Also, this sort of "humor" demonstrates the inability of many straight men to tolerate the fact that there are men who love men who are as masculine as they are, and who, given assumptions about masculine superiority, they might thus have to acknowledge as their equals. Their "jokes" are a verbal attempt at castration. And as Jeff Whitty so powerfully pointed out to Leno, such "humor" renders invisible all of the problems of homophobia and all of the lives that are damaged and destroyed by it, and at the same time reinforces homophobia.

Such "comic" responses to the film are more insidious than the overt attacks by those who denounce same-sex attraction and relationships, since they allow the "comedians" who make them to excuse themselves by saying that they only are "joking" and that they actually know gay people and "like" them. They adopt the pose that they're "kidding," acting playful and lighthearted, but meanwhile reinforcing the beliefs that men who love men somehow are separate and inferior, and supporting and encouraging people who refuse to see the film. At least people like those mentioned above who have denounced the movie aren't evasive or duplicitous about the reality of their dislike of sexual minorities. "Michael Savage" hates sexually different men and doesn't hide the implications of his hatred behind some claim about actually having gay friends or the pose of being "funny" and "cute." He's a homophobic bigot, but at least he's honest, unlike those who mention that someone's gay and then add, "not that there's anything wrong with that," slyly indicating that to them there *is* something wrong with sexual difference.

Since country music always has celebrated the cowboy as an icon of traditional masculinity, it hardly was surprising when a major country singer, Alan Jackson, who performs in cowboy attire, with a white cowboy hat, boots, and well-fitting Wranglers, attacked the movie. In a concert in Houston he altered the Hank Williams Jr., song, "Texas Women," adding the lines "I'm a cowboy fan/Not a Brokeback man," drawing cheers from homophobes in his audience.[48] For Jackson, as for so many others, being a cowboy or a cowboy fan excludes the possibility of being a man who loves men. It's important to note, though, that this hostile stance isn't that of some other country music performers, such as Dolly Parton, Emmylou Harris, Mary McBride, and Willie Nelson, who've done songs about same-sex love or provided musical accompaniment for movies dealing with sexual minorities. Harris, McBride, and Nelson all performed in the soundtrack for *Brokeback Mountain,* Harris singing the beautiful ballad, "A Love That Will Never Grow Old," McBride the twangy love song, "No One's Gonna Love You Like Me," and Nelson the poignant elegy that concludes the movie, "He Was a Friend of Mine."[49]

An offensive TV commercial for the Kraft/Nabisco product Fig Newtons has been perceived by some viewers as alluding to *Brokeback Mountain*. It depicts two stereotypically masculine men, one in a plaid shirt, the other in a tan canvas jacket like that worn by Heath Ledger in the film, leaning against a fence in a wheat field, watching a "comic" advertising character, the "Snack Fairy." The "Fairy," presented as a bumbling man in a pink tutu, appeared in Kraft/Nabisco ads beginning in 2005, first in a commercial during the Academy Awards of that year. In the new ad, as the "Fairy" runs away from a tractor, one of the men says to the other, to whom the "Fairy" has given some Fig Newtons, "So you're saying he's a fairy?" to which the other replies, "A Snack Fairy." They then watch in amusement as the "Fairy," who's now on the tractor, falls off it backwards; one of the men shouts contemptuously, "Walk it off, Snack Fairy." Neither man wears a cowboy hat, and one has a cap, which seems to portray them less as ranch hands than as farmers, but still, the "humor" works like that in many of the "jokes" about the movie, presenting the incongruous association of stereotypically masculine men with their supposed antithesis, the exaggeratedly effeminate homophobic stereotype of the sexually different man as a "fairy." The ad operates like many of the "jokes" about the film, inscribing on masculine imagery similar to that of *Brokeback Mountain* the concept that men who love men really aren't men at all.[50]

Perhaps the most grotesque and ludicrous attack on the film that many Americans were exposed to was by the NBC TV film reviewer, Gene Shalit. Although Shalit has a gay son and has spoken supportively about him, his interpretation of the movie was built on the one standard negative stereotype of sexually different men that grants them any degree of power, in contrast to the stereotypes of clownish queens and ineffectual dandies. He said, "Jack, who strikes me as a sexual predator, tracks Ennis down and coaxes him into sporadic trysts. But sporadic isn't enough for Jack. He wants Ennis full-time! He whines, he pleads, he shouts that when they're apart, he's desolated."[51] This construction manages to have it both ways, not only presenting Jack according to the model of the "sexual predator," the specter of the dangerously aggressive gay man that homophobes often invoke in order to justify excluding sexually different men from the armed forces and other homosocial organizations, but also as overly emotional, "whining," "pleading," "shouting," and "desolate," as in the model of the effeminate hysteric. In its response to this offensive distortion of the characters and the plot of the film, the Gay and Lesbian Alliance Against Defamation pointed out that Shalit's interpretation of *Brokeback Mountain* made about as much sense as describing the Leonardo DiCaprio character in *Titanic* as a "sexual predator" who pursues and "coaxes" the Kate Winslett character into "trysts."[52] For many straight men, unfortunately, it's impossible to perceive relationships between men as being based on mutual sexual and emotional attraction and thus as being equal to the ideal of heterosexual love.

Given the accelerating efforts over the past several decades of right-wing politicians to cater to homophobic prejudice, it was inevitable that hostile references to *Brokeback Mountain* would be exploited as part of the rhetoric used by some of those seeking enough votes to win elections. In September 2006, with the midterm elections approaching, the Republican Party struggling to maintain control of both houses of Congress due to growing discontent with the catastrophic invasion and occupation of Iraq, and various Republicans trying to position themselves as the political heirs of the second George Bush, the reactionary Family Research Council held a "Values Voter Summit" in Washington. In one of his last major political appearances, Jerry Falwell gave the opening prayer, and in attendance was his influential ally, James Dobson of Focus on the Family, as well as the homophobic commentators Ted Baehr and Ann Coulter (who subsequently distinguished herself by publicly insulting Democratic presidential candidate Senator John Edwards, calling him a "faggot"). Among the many presidential aspirants were then Governor Mitt Romney of Massachusetts, Senator Sam Brownback of Kansas, then Senator Rick Santorum of Pennsylvania, and then Senator George Allen of Virginia (who recently had gained considerable notice for directing a particularly crude racial insult at an American citizen of Indian background, calling him "Mr. Macaca"). A common factor among those hoping to become the Republican candidate for the presidency was their effort to draw votes by competing with one another in attacks on the attempt of same-sex couples to gain status and benefits equal to what opposite-sex married couples can take for granted. Not to be outdone by the others, Governor Mike Huckabee of Arkansas, attending a session on what the religious right calls "covenant marriage," proclaimed that the country should keep marriage like it is "until Moses comes down from Brokeback Mountain with two stone tablets saying we've changed the rules."[53]

Predictably, some are eager do what they can to try to render invisible the aspects of male love that the film and story make visible. In June 2007 the American Film Institute, a nonprofit organization based in Los Angeles and composed of approximately 1,500 people involved in filmmaking and media commentary on film, released its list of the one hundred best films, updating and revising a list released ten years earlier. *Citizen Kane* led the list, which ranged from other great films such as *Sunset Boulevard* and *Vertigo* to such works as *Forrest Gump* and *Toy Story*. *Brokeback Mountain* was omitted. Kevin McDonough, a columnist for United Features Syndicate, which supplies opinion columns and comic strips to newspapers around the nation, summarized the stated criteria on which the list was based as "contemporary critical reaction, prizes, nominations, historical significance, cultural impact, and enduring popularity,"[54] and asked whether films such as *Brokeback Mountain* belonged on the list. He answered, "Given these criteria, I'm not sure some of these films should make the cut. *Brokeback Mountain* is the perfect example of a movie that gets talked about in the period leading up to the Oscars and is forgotten soon after."[55] At least by Mr. McDonough.

The ugliness of the hostile reactions to *Brokeback Mountain* is self-evident to many sexual minority people and to those straight people who are able to make the effort to imagine what it's like to live in a world in which comments of this sort are made on a routine basis about you and those you love. Gay, lesbian, bisexual, transgender, queer, and questioning people hear this sort of hostility and contempt directed at them and the people they care about every day, not only in the media, but from family members, at school, at work, and while trying to go about the business of daily life. The level of discussion in the media about *Brokeback Mountain* shows how acceptable homophobic prejudice continues to be for many Americans today. Many religious organizations are unrelenting in their promotion of hostility toward sexual minorities. Instead of speaking out against this prejudice, most of the nation's political leaders timidly avoid it or actively exploit it. Many of these leaders not only enforce a policy of excluding from the armed services anyone who acknowledges belonging to a sexual minority group, but also support a constitutional amendment that would exclude people in committed same-sex relationships from the status, rights, and benefits of marriage, categorizing them as an implicitly inferior class of citizens. In schools, the word gay is used routinely by students to mean stupid or worthless, and now the word "brokeback" is being used as a term of homophobic abuse. Harassment, discrimination, and attacks on people who are perceived as sexually different happen throughout the country, but national legislation protecting sexual minorities from discrimination in obtaining education, employment, housing, and various important benefits and services or addressing hate crimes against them has repeatedly been blocked, particularly by members of the Republican Party. With far too few exceptions, their Democratic opponents have been too fearful and self-interested to challenge the political exploitation of homophobia.[56] At a time when many other nations around the world are making significant progress toward achieving full equality for sexual minority people, in the United States well-organized and well-funded homophobic religious and political groups continue to prevent legislative change that would lead to greater inclusion and equity for sexual minorities.[57]

With all the attention that's been given to the subject matter of the two versions of *Brokeback Mountain,* sometimes not enough is paid to the high degree of artistry each shows in the methods through which it presents the lives of the characters. Of course, because of the differences between the media of writing and moviemaking, the methods of presentation of the lives of Jack and Ennis and the people connected with them are different in the story and the film. But as works of art, both reach high levels of accomplishment. Perhaps the most significant difference between them is the fact that the story is told by a narrative voice that often employs a rich variety of vernacular language like that used by the characters it describes. The movie doesn't use a voice-over narrative drawing on the narrative voice that Proulx has created, but presents the actions and words of the characters without comment, in a clear, deliberate, chronological sequence, with one significant flashback scene when Ennis describes to Jack the murdered man he saw as a child, one when Jack and Ennis argue and Jack recalls Ennis's gentle, extended embrace during their summer on the mountain, and one scene representing Ennis's thoughts about Jack's murder as he listens to Lureen on the phone. Because the movie is based on a story rather than a novel, it wasn't necessary for the screenwriters to condense, and instead it was possible to expand the narrative, and McMurtry and Ossana ably and sensitively add numerous scenes and de-velop some characters, particularly Lureen and her family, Cassie, and Alma Jr. Like the film, the story presents the experiences of Ennis and Jack largely in linear, chronological order, with one important exception: Proulx frames the story by beginning with a brief section describing Ennis's thoughts and actions one morning as he gets up, perhaps a few months after he's learned about Jack's murder, and then returns to the same point in Ennis's life at the end of the story. As I'll discuss in detail in chapter 6, the movie drops this frame and begins with Ennis's arrival in Signal on the morning that he and Jack meet for the first time.

The narrative voice that Proulx creates to tell *Brokeback Mountain* is vivid and powerful. To capture the grandeur of the landscape and the complexity of the characters' feelings, thoughts, and actions, it seamlessly combines the ca-sual conversational sentence structure and the colorful language of Western vernacular speech with a sophisticated vocabulary that allows minutely de-tailed depiction of external appearance and internal meaning. The narrative moves smoothly from objective description of the settings and characters to descriptions that clearly indicate the perspectives of the characters about what's going on, paraphrasing their thoughts and feelings. In defining the nat-ural, economic, and social conditions of the characters' lives, as well as their inner experience, the narrative employs vernacular expressions that convey a sense of their poverty and lack of formal education but also emphasize their knowledge of the hard realities of their world as well as the strength with which they confront them. As so often is the case with vernacular American speech, the Wyoming idiom is homely, concrete, funny, and sometimes ex-travagantly obscene and yet simultaneously intensely poetic, perceptive, sen-sitive, and moving. Some passages in the story directly paraphrase conversa-tions between Jack and Ennis, and are full of their pungent, powerful vernacular; the shift in the narrative from such passages to quoted dialogue between Ennis and Jack is so smooth that the voices of the characters and the narrator seem almost to merge.

The popular response to the story and the movie show how much readers and viewers appreciate Proulx's use of vernacular speech as well as the per-ceptive additions made by McMurtry and Ossana. In discussions of *Broke-back Mountain,* lines like "I wish I knew how to quit you,"[58] "There's no reins on this one,"[59] and "If you can't fix it you gotta stand it"[60] get quoted repeat-edly and now are showing up on t-shirts worn by fans. The power of the con-versations between Ennis and Jack isn't just in the vivid metaphors they use but in the tone they take with each other, showing the intimacy, playfulness, and emotion of a male friendship that's also intense romantic love. When they talk to each other, both men frequently use irony, at once deprecating themselves, deflating any egotistic pretensions and so indicating respect and consideration for each other, and yet also sometimes gently and playfully teasing and flirting. As so often is the case for men, affection can be easier to express under the mask of joshing each other.

Proulx's narrator doesn't consistently speak in the vernacular, but the narrative voice she creates so effectively incorporates the sentence structure and vocabulary of Western speech, and so frequently paraphrases the conversations and thoughts of the characters, that it almost seems as if it's told by one of them. Proulx has an ear for how people talk that bears comparison to one of the greatest students of American speech, and one of America's greatest writers, Mark Twain. At times *Brokeback Mountain* recalls *The Adventures of Huckleberry Finn* (1885) not only in its often comic, sometimes touching rendition of the eloquence of ordinary Americans, but also in its juxtaposition of characters who are sensitive and vulnerable with a society in which brutality and violence are everywhere. While Huck Finn confronts a society that's poisoned by greed, fraud, and racism, rather than hatred of sexuality, the communities he explores along the Mississippi always are on the verge of violence, much like the society that surrounds Jack and Ennis. The little river towns Huck ventures into repeatedly spawn lynch mobs that threaten him and his friend Jim. Of course, Ennis's life is shaped by his fear of being the victim of a homophobic lynching, like the rancher Earl, whose tortured body Ennis's father exhibited to him when Ennis was a child, and Jack finally becomes the victim of a homophobic lynching. Both *Brokeback Mountain* and *Huckleberry Finn* describe characters who really have no place in their societies, and only can find a refuge in nature. As many critics and readers have noted about *Huckleberry Finn*, though the connection between Huck and Jim isn't sexual, and is more like a familial relationship, it is strongly homosocial, demonstrating the intense bond two males can form.[61] In this, of course, it challenges the racism that would keep black and white Americans separate. Part of the achievement of Proulx's great story is to challenge another of the vicious prejudices that damages the lives of many Americans, and to show that there really is no clear distinction between friendship and love between men, that for some men it's possible for a close friendship to evolve naturally into a passionate physical and emotional connection that should be allowed to form the basis of their lives.

In its presentation of the lives of Jack and Ennis, the film uses a style as distinctive as Proulx's. Without any reliance on spoken narrative explanation, it slowly and clearly shows what happens between the characters. This method succeeds because of the uniformly fine quality of the screenwriting, the direction, the acting, and the filming and music. The main actors in the movie are extraordinarily convincing as their characters; they clearly thought with care about how the characters would speak, move, and look, and undoubtedly worked closely with the director and others in considering how to present the meanings of the screenplay and the story. Michelle Williams and Anne Hathaway strongly convey the confusion, suffering, and anger of Alma and Lureen. The achievement of Heath Ledger and Jake Gyllenhaal is especially impressive, since to succeed they had explore a territory of male emotion and experience that many straight men are incapable of treating with any respect. It's evident that they must have put serious effort into understanding the situations of men who are attracted to other men in a hostile society. As the film unfolds they persuasively and powerfully present the struggles of Ennis and Jack with feelings and needs that are essential to the characters but that they've been taught to fear and hate and to try to reject. Though the film doesn't use a narrator to delineate the thoughts and feelings of the characters, the actors are so skilled, and have put so much effort into understanding their characters and their relationship, that their gestures, postures, and facial expressions subtly and effectively indicate what they think and feel. To do this must have been particularly challenging for the actors because the very nature of the problem that damages the lives of the characters, the hatred of their sexuality felt by everyone around them and that's been instilled in them as well, necessarily makes it almost impossible for the characters to put their feelings into words. A central part of the problem Jack and Ennis confront is that they've been denied any words to say what they feel and who they are. Yet the acting is so fine that in every scene it's easy to understand the emotions each man struggles with. For many men who love men, the actors are able to present feelings and situations that are painfully familiar.

The film version of *Brokeback Mountain* is remarkable for the respect it shows toward the conditions of the social world that Proulx describes, particularly since it's a product of the American commercial movie business. The filmmakers largely resisted the impulse to moderate the depiction of the hard lives of the characters or to sentimentalize Proulx's account of what happens to them. Few American films, at least from major studios, make any effort to recognize the economic limitations faced by the majority of the people in this country, but McMurtry, Ossana, Lee, and those working with them are willing to present the working and living conditions of the characters, especially the poverty of Ennis and Alma, much as it's presented in the story. Certainly Ledger and Gyllenhaal are more physically attractive than Ennis and Jack as Proulx describes them, but that's hardly a surprise in a film intended for a large audience. The filmmakers could have cast unknown actors who were more physically like the characters in the story, but probably at the expense of reaching as large an audience as the movie actually did. Part of what makes the film remarkable is that the filmmakers crafted a strategy of presentation that honored Proulx's vision but could bring it to a general audience and make her devastating depiction of the destruction of love between men part of a national discourse. It's difficult for me to knock an approach that forced more Americans to think for once about how homophobia can ruin lives. In this, as in other aspects of the project, the filmmakers seem to have been motivated by recognition of the potential significance of the film in challenging prejudice against sexual minorities, and to have been guided by the principle, as Ang Lee put it when he received the award for the film from the Gay and Lesbian Alliance Against Defamation, that "when the world is made better for one gay or lesbian person, it's made better for everyone."[62]

The film is very beautiful to watch. Rodrigo Prieto and Ang Lee create a visual style that perfectly presents the story's contrast between society and the wilderness where Ennis and Jack fall in love and to which they periodically are able to return together. The settings in the towns and buildings are as rough and poor as what Proulx describes, and the cramped, dingy interiors are filmed to suggest how confining they are; the cinematography used to present the magnificent landscape of the mountain is a striking contrast. The manner in which the mountain scenes are filmed, stressing light and space and clarity, suggests the freedom the men feel there. The effect of the cinematography is reinforced by Gustavo Santaollala's beautiful, lyrical score. In its filming, *Brokeback Mountain* clearly recalls the sweeping, epic visual style of major Hollywood Westerns of the past, inviting the audience to recognize the commentary that it provides on American constructions of masculinity and sexuality that have been so fundamental to the national tradition of the Western. The film's slow pace and visual beauty also reinforce its relationship to the rich traditions of homoerotic poetry, and particularly to the tradition of the pastoral elegy, in which a man laments the death of a beloved male friend.

Both the story and the movie versions of *Brokeback Mountain* offer powerful insights into the lives of a substantial number of American men, at least for those who are open to them and are able to feel empathy. To those who only can perceive love between men in terms of their own fears about themselves, these two works of art necessarily must remain meaningless. But both versions can be deeply moving to people, whatever their sex or sexuality, whose hearts are open and capable of feeling.

NOTES

1. Gay and Lesbian Alliance Against Defamation: *"Brokeback Mountain* Resource Guide": Ang Lee, acceptance speech, Academy Awards Ceremony, March 5, 2006 (http://www.glaad.org/eye/brokeback_mountain.php., July 29, 2007).

2. Lee, acceptance speech.

3. Walt Whitman, "Song of Myself," line 461, *Leaves of Grass* (Ninth edition/1892.) A word about my approach to Whitman is in order. Over the last several decades, as sexual minority people have been able to shape the discussion of same-sex love, rather than having it continue to be dominated by those who condemn or misunderstand it as once was the case, there has been substantial recognition of Whitman's love for men. It's become increasingly difficult for critics and teachers to minimize it or ignore it—or to fabricate heterosexual relationships for the poet—the way they did for nearly a century, and there's been extensive discussion of his work and life by sexual minority scholars and readers. Still, there continue to be many who are eager to focus on equivocal statements Whitman made about his sexuality, especially late in life when he had become famous, or to stress the limitations of evidence about actual sexual activity with other men, and to construct his male relationships as emotional rather than physical. (Interestingly, it seems to me far less common for those discussing apparently heterosexual writers to be as concerned to find direct evidence of *their* sexual activity, or to construct *their* desire as emotional rather than physical in the absence of such evidence.) The critical and biographical literature on Whitman is vast, and I don't intend to review it or the contentions over his sexuality here. In general, I accept the position of the important critic, Robert K. Martin, that Whitman was a man who loved men both emotionally and physically, that "no other poet, until the present time, has so clearly defined himself in terms of his sexuality and so clearly defined his poetic mission as a consequence of his homosexuality" (Robert K. Martin, *The Homosexual Tradition in American Poetry* [Austin: University of Texas Press, 1979], xvi.) A valuable corrective to biographical and critical approaches to Whitman that ignore or fail to understand the significance of same-sex desire and relationships in his life and work is available: Gary Schmidgall, *Walt Whitman: A Gay Life* (New York: Plume, 1998.) Of course, I recognize the significance of social constructionist approaches that emphasize the differences between constructions of gender and sexuality in various contexts and times; certainly ways of understanding love between men in Whitman's time, and in different social contexts in that time, were unlike those today in many ways. While he can't be understood as gay in the contemporary sense of the word, I don't believe that that means that his poetry and other writings don't continue to speak directly to readers now about many dimensions of love between men, as they have ever since they were published. Whitman, and other man-loving men, many of whom were inspired by him, had important influence in articulating constructions of man-loving men, which formed a significant alternative to negative constructions, particularly those articulated by the medical and legal systems, and helped lead to the current construction of gay identity. As I've noted in the Introduction, the approach that I take in this book is informed by my interests in literary and cultural criticism, but it's based on a personal response to literature and film as a man who loves men. Throughout my discussion of *Brokeback Mountain* I'll note parallels with poems by Whitman, responding to them not primarily as a literary and cultural critic, but as a reader to whom they speak about situations and feelings that I, and many other men who love men, recognize from experience.

4. Whitman, "Song of Myself," 1. 1272, *Leaves of Grass* (Ninth edition/1892).

5. Detailed listings of the various awards given to the film version of *Brokeback Mountain* and of the film's earnings are provided by Internet Movie Database and by GLAAD in its "*Brokeback Mountain* Resource Guide." (http://www.imdb.com/title/tt0388795, July 29, 2007; http://www.glaad.org/eye/brokeback_mountain.php, July29, 2007).

6. Internet Movie Database biographical listing for Tony Curtis (http://www.imdb.com/name/nm0000348, July 29, 2007); "Curtis Berates *Brokeback Mountain*," Feb. 5, 2006 (http://www.contactmusic.com/new/xmlfeed.ns/mndwebpages/curtis%20berates%20brokeback%20mountain_05_02_2006, July 29, 2007).

7. Internet Movie Database biographical listing for Ernest Borgnine (http://www.imdb.com/name/nm0000308, July 29, 2007).

8. On the possibility that many members of the Academy who participated in the choice of Best Picture in 2006 actually may have failed to watch *Brokeback Mountain* see Erik Lundegaard, "Oscar Misfire: *Crash* and Burn: The Academy Takes Yet Another Step toward Irrelevance with Its Latest Pick," March 6, 2006 (http://www.msnbc.msn.com/id/11700333, July 29, 2007).

9. Nikki Finke, "What Did I Tell You?," *Los Angeles Weekly*, March 5, 2006 (http://www.deadlinehollywooddaily.com/what-did-I-tell-you, July 29, 2007).

10. As quoted by Eric Boehlert, "Cowboy Controversy," *Rolling Stone*, Feb. 10, 2006 (http://www.rollingstone.com/news/story/9257407/cowboy_controversy, July 29, 2007).

11. Kenneth Turan, "Breaking No Ground; Why *Crash* Won, Why *Brokeback* Lost and How the Academy Chose to Play it Safe," *Los Angeles Times*, March 5, 2006 (http://theenvelope.latimes.com/awards/oscars/env-turan5mar05,0,5359042.story, July 29, 2007).

12. Erik Lundegaard, "Playing It Safe, Academy Awards Style," Jan. 26, 2005 (http://www.msnbc.msn.com/id/6725814, July 29, 2007).

13. "Conservatives Quick to Opine on *Brokeback*, Slow to Actually See Film," Jan. 20, 2006 (http://www.mediamatters.org/items/200601200005, July 29, 2007).

14. "Conservatives Opine."

15. "Conservatives Opine."

16. "Scarborough Country," transcript, Jan. 17, 2006 (http://www.msnbc.msn.com/id/10907413, July 29, 2007).

17. The ways in which the McCarthyite purges of progressives equated liberal-left activism and homosexuality have been widely discussed; see Miller, *Out of the Past*; Adam, *Rise*; and D'Emilio, *Sexual Politics*.

18. Ben Frichtl, Robert Knight, "*Narnia* Gets Lion's Share of Box Office While Critics Hail 'Gay Cowboy' Flick," Concerned Women For America, Culture and Family Issues, Dec. 13, 2005 (http://www.cfa.org/articles/9689/CFI/misc/index.htm July 29, 2007).

19. "*Narnia* Gets."

20. "*Narnia* Gets."

21. David Kupelian, "The Rape of the Marlboro Man," Dec. 27, 2005 (http://www.WorldNetDaily.com/news/article.asp?ARTICLE_ID=48076, July 29, 2007).

22. Kupelian expressed his views on *Brokeback Mountain* on Fox's *Dayside* on Dec. 30, 2005 and on *Your World* on Jan. 13, 2006.

23. http://www.MovieGuide.org, July 29, 2007.

24. Internet Movie Database quotes MovieGuide.org in "*Brokeback* Crossing Sexual Preference Divide," Dec. 29, 2005 (http://www.imdb.com/news/sb/2005-12-29, July 29, 2007).

25. "'Profam' Critic: *Brokeback*" (http://www.goodasyou.org/good_as_you/2005/12/profam_critic_b.html, July 29, 2007).

26. "Homosexual-Themed Films Assault Christmas Moviegoers," Dec. 14, 2005 (http://www.traditionalvalues.org/modules.php?sid=2535, July 29, 2007).

27. The American Psychiatric Association ceased classifying homosexuality as a mental illness in 1973 and repudiated so-called "reparative therapy" for homosexuality in 1998; the American Psychological Association declassified homosexuality as a mental illness in 1975 and repudiated "reparative therapy" in 1997. For introductory historical discussion of these changes, see Miller, *Out of the Past*; Adam, *Rise*; and Ronald Bayer, *Homosexuality and American Psychiatry* (Princeton: Princeton University Press, 1987).

28. "U.S.C.C.B. Reclassifies Gay Western *Brokeback Mountain* after Complaints," Dec. 16, 2005 (http://www.catholicnewsagency.com/new.php?n=5643, July 29, 2007).

29. United States Conference of Catholic Bishops, Office for Film and Broadcasting, *Brokeback Mountain* Full Review, Dec. 30, 2005 (http://www.usccb.org/movies/b/brokebackmountain.shtml, July 29, 2007).

30. USCCB review.

31. USCCB review.

32. USCCB review.

33. USCCB review.

34. In contrast to the vocal condemnation of sexual minorities by Catholic, Southern Baptist, Mormon, and many Evangelical and Pentecostal leaders, many denominations, including the Unitarian Universalist Association, the United Church of Christ, the Episcopal Church, the Evangelical Lutheran Church, the Society of Friends, Reform Judaism, and the Presbyterian Church, have made it clear that they welcome and affirm sexual minorities. The Metropolitan Community Church primarily was created by and for sexual minority people.

35. Pat Robertson, as quoted by Eric Boehlert, "Cowboy Controversy," *Rolling Stone*, Feb. 10, 2006 (http://www.rollingstone.com/news/story/9257407/cowboy_controversy, July 29, 2007).

36. Statement made by Pat Robertson on the "700 Club" TV program, June 8, 1998, as part of his condemnation of "Gay Days" at Disney World; "Pat Robertson's Contradictory Theology," May 2, 2005 (http://www.mediamatters.org/items/200505020002 July 29, 2007.).

37. Paul Strand, "Homosexual Agenda Pushed in Movies Like *Brokeback Mountain*" no date (ca. Jan 13, 2006) (http://www.cbn.com/cbnnews/news/060113d.asp, July 29, 2007).

38. "Homosexual Agenda."

39. "MSNBC Airs Juvenile Homophobia on 'Imus in the Morning,'" Jan. 20, 2006 (GLAAD Action Alert: http://www.glaad.org/action/alerts_detail.php?id=3854, July 29, 2007).

40. "Juvenile Homophobia."

41. "Juvenile Homophobia."

42. "Juvenile Homophobia."

43. "Juvenile Homophobia."

44. "Juvenile Homophobia."

45. "Juvenile Homophobia."

46. GLAAD, "*Brokeback Mountain* Resource Guide" (http://www.glaad.org/eye/brokeback_mountain.php, July 29, 2007).

47. Jeff Whitty, "Open Letter to Jay Leno," April 24, 2006 (http://queerty.com/queer/entertainment/an-open-letter-to-jay-leno-20060424.php, June 17, 2006).

48. "Alan Jackson Sets the Mood," *Houston Chronicle*, March 16, 2006 (http://www.chron.com/disp/story.mpl/chronicle/3726986.html, July 29, 2007).

49. For the songs by Emmylou Harris, Mary McBride, and Willie Nelson, see *Brokeback Mountain,* Original Motion Picture Soundtrack, Verve/Forecast B0005604-02. Though unlike the others mentioned, Dolly Parton doesn't sing in *Brokeback Mountain*, she provided the song, "Travellin' Thru" for the 2005 film, *Transamerica,* and has made many positive comments about sexual minorities and embraced her many gay fans.

50. "Snack Fairy: Cowboys" (http://www.commercialcloset.org/cgi-bin/iowa/portrayals.html?record=2660, July 27, 2006).

51. "Gene Shalit Offers Defamatory *Brokeback* Review on NBC's 'Today,'" Jan. 5. 2006; "'Today' Show Reviewer Regrets *Brokeback* Comment," Jan. 10, 2006 (GLAAD Action Alert: http://www.glaad.org/action/alerts_detail.php?id=3849, July 29, 2007).

52. "Shalit Defamatory."

53. Sean Cahill and Cynthia Burack, National Gay and Lesbian Task Force Policy Institute, "Internal Enemy: Gays as the Domestic Al-Qaeda; A Report from the Family Research Council's Values Voters Summit, Sept. 22-24, 2006" (http://www.thetaskforce.org/reports_and_research/internal_enemy, July 29, 2007).

54. Kevin McDonough, "Tune in Tonight: Do Movies of the Past Decade Make the Cut?" United Features Syndicate, June 20, 2007 (http://www.2.ljworld.com/news/living/columns/tunein/?page=2, July 29, 2007).

55. McDonough, "Tune in Tonight."

56. Homophobia pervades American life. For introductory discussion of the problem of homophobia in families, see Sears, *Overcoming Heterosexism*; Blumenfeld, *Homophobia*; and Biery, *Understanding Homosexuality*. In education, see Sears, *Overcoming Heterosexism*, and Human Rights Watch, *Hatred in the Hallways: Violence and Discrimination against Lesbian, Gay, Bisexual, and Transgender Students in United States Schools* (New York: Human Rights Watch, 2001). In religion, see Sears, *Overcoming Heterosexism*, and Biery, *Understanding Homosexuality*. In government policy, see Sears, *Overcoming Heterosexism*; Eric Marcus, *Making Gay History: The Half-Century Fight for Lesbian and Gay Equal Rights* (New York: Harper,

2002); and John D'Emilio, William B. Turner, and Urvashi Vaid, *Creating Change: Sexuality, Public Policy, and Civil Rights* (New York: St. Martin's, 2000). In the media, see Larry Gross, *Up from Invisibility: Lesbians, Gay Men, and the Media in America* (New York: Columbia University Press, 2002); Suzanna Danuta Walters, *All the Rage: The Story of Gay Visibility in America* (Chicago: University of Chicago Press, 2001); and Harry M. Benshoff and Sean Griffin, *Queer Images: A History of Gay and Lesbian Film in America* (Lanham: Rowman and Littlefield, 2005). On homophobic violence, see Gregory M. Herek and Kevin T. Berrill, eds., *Hate Crimes: Confronting Violence against Lesbians and Gay Men* (Thousand Oaks: Sage, 1992), and Lacey M. Sloan and Nora Gustavsson, *Violence and Social Injustice against Lesbian, Gay, and Bisexual People* (Binghamton: Harrington Park, 2000.)

57. Unlike most European nations and a number of others around the world, the United States has no national legislation protecting sexual minority people from discrimination in employment, housing, or human services. Only two other nations in N.A.T.O., Portugal and Turkey, ban military service by sexual minority people. Many other nations around the world permit sexual minorities to serve, including some with particularly formidable armed forces, such as Israel. More than thirty nations have national legislation permitting same-sex civil unions, and the Netherlands, Belgium, Canada, Spain, and South Africa have full marriage equality.

58. Annie Proulx, *Brokeback Mountain* (New York: Scribner, 2005), 26.

59. Proulx, *Brokeback Mountain*, 27.

60. Proulx, *Brokeback Mountain*, 30.

61. The famous discussion of *The Adventures of Huckleberry Finn* that initiated this perspective on the novel (and raised the issue of same-sex attraction and relationships in other works of American literature) is Leslie Fiedler's essay, "Come Back to the Raft Ag'in, Huck Honey," *Partisan Review*, June 1948; see also his *Love and Death in the American Novel* (New York: Stein and Day, 1960).

62. Ang Lee, 17th Annual GLAAD Media Awards, New York, March 27, 2006 (http://www.glaad.org/events/mediaawards/index.php, July 29, 2007).

Chapter One

A Companion Where None Had Been Expected: Friendship

The fundamental achievement of both the story and the film of *Brokeback Mountain* is to go inside the shared emotional and sexual experience of two ordinary American men and explore their feelings as they discover their love for each other, and as they discover what this means for them as individuals and in relation to each other in a society that hates love between men. Many gay writers have depicted the experience of men discovering attraction, sex, and love with other men and the ways this affects a man's relationship with his society, and some women have done so in their writing as well, though few writers, regardless of sex or sexual orientation, have done it with the insight of Annie Proulx. Many gay filmmakers have depicted this experience too, usually in small-budget, limited-release films, some of which are powerful and beautiful and deserve to be much more widely seen. But, with a few significant exceptions, such as the sensitive adaptation of E. M. Forster's *Maurice* (1914; 1971) released in 1988, this is almost uncharted territory for commercial movie production companies, and especially so for straight screenwriters, directors, and actors, and for general audiences in the United States. The landscape of male-male desire, the passions and conflicts of male couples, and the larger landscape of homophobic contempt and hatred in which men who love each other must define themselves and their relationships and try to establish a place for both, all have been largely ignored by commercial Hollywood movies and by straight audiences.[1]

The story and the film depict that landscape, at least one part of it, as it's been for some white, rural, working-class men in the later part of the twentieth century, mapping its beauty and ugliness in great detail. They take us inside the lives of two young men, not even out of their teens at the start, whose experiences and perspectives have been limited by economic necessity, interrupted education, demanding work, and the lack of any knowledge about men who love other men except hostile stereotypes. The ways Ennis and Jack understand themselves have been shaped by others who despise love between men, particularly by their fathers. Both young men are strong and stoical, and, despite the hard economic limitations of their lives in rural Wyoming, like many men aspire to the American Dream of success through individual effort. Neither is able to name the passion they feel for each other, or to challenge the hostile beliefs and behaviors toward male love that pervade the society around them as well as their own thoughts and feelings. Yet their passion for each other is so strong that it leads them into a profound union that, while continually thwarted, can't be destroyed.

When we first encounter them, in the spring of 1963, Jack and Ennis both are nineteen, "high school dropout country boys with no prospects, brought up to hard work and privation, both rough-mannered, rough-spoken, inured to the stoic life."[2] Both are broke and need work, but both clearly prefer the outdoor work with stock they've grown up doing. Jack apparently has quit school to work on his father's ranch, but for good reason wants to get away, and already has worked one summer on his own, employed to herd sheep on Brokeback Mountain. Ennis has grown up even poorer than Jack, being reared by his older brother and sister after their parents' deaths in a driving accident, forced to quit high school before becoming a sophomore because the pickup he drove to school broke down, "pitching him"[3] into work as a ranch hand. The movie emphasizes Ennis's poverty even more than does the story; it's clear from the text that when they meet both he and Jack have trucks, but in the movie, Ennis hitchhikes into Signal to get to the Farm and Ranch Employment Agency trailer, one change of clothes in a paper grocery sack. Jack's pickup is a junker that keeps breaking down, but Ennis is on foot.

Like millions of other American men who've grown up in poverty, Ennis and Jack have been taught to believe in the possibility that some day, through hard work, saving, and maybe some good luck, each of them will be able to get a little property of his own and to work independently, rather than for somebody else who owns property and calls the shots for the propertyless men he hires. Throughout American history, many young men without property have striven for the goal of owning a small farm or a small business, so that they can make decisions for themselves about their lives rather than having them made for them by others. Their hope has been to rise from the ranks of those who only own their own bodies and must survive by selling their ability to labor, and to obtain a small amount of property, joining the lower level of the middle class. For Jack and Ennis, success means having a little ranch of your own and being able to be your own boss. But though each claims to be saving money for a small place, it's not realistic, given their circumstances; for Ennis all it means is two five-dollar bills in a tobacco can.

For every poor boy who makes it, whose ship eventually really does come in, allowing him to claim to belong to the middle class, there are many others in America who never do, though the dream of success continues to dangle in front of them, keeping them working hard for other men in the hope that someday they'll make it after all.[4] A man who has a place, like Joe Aguirre, the foreman who hires them, easily dismisses them: "pair of deuces going nowhere."[5]

To young men like Ennis and Jack, a real man should be able to make it on his own, and shouldn't need anyone else; to admit that you do is to admit that you aren't really a man. Women and weaklings show their feelings and are dependent on other people, but a real man can stand alone. American masculinity is virtually synonymous with individualism. For many men, to acknowledge needing support from another man is to acknowledge inferiority, and puts you in the position of a dependent, like a woman or a child. Though individual friendships between men are valued, strict controls are placed on them, limiting their intensity. To express any emotional dependence on another man is especially threatening; American culture has defined women in terms of emotion, so a man who feels an emotional need for another man is seen as being feminized. A man who acknowledges that he loves and needs another man is perceived to be like a woman, and is despised. To many American men, such a man can't really be a man at all.[6]

Americans are taught always to conceive of individualism as an unqualified good, in terms of thinking and acting for oneself and being self-reliant and independent, but it has negative consequences that often go unrecognized in the dominant culture. The American ideal of individualism can make it difficult to share an awareness of common problems and to work together to find solutions for them. To effect change, a united effort often is required, but individualism functions to separate people, teaching them to expect that they can achieve a better life entirely through their own efforts. Individualism divides man from man, making men see one another as competitors and fear any admission of dependence, reducing their ability to challenge things as they are. The American ideal of masculine individualism functions to discourage the possibility of any collective effort to change the distribution of property and power in American society. The racism and ethnic prejudice that pervade American culture only divide men further. Unfortunately, some American men of European background have been taught that one thing that supposedly gives them status is their race; some men with little or no property have been told that, along with their maleness, the "possession" that sets them above other people is their whiteness.[7]

Not only have Ennis and Jack been taught the traditional model of American masculinity, but they aspire to meet the standards of what's probably its most intense expression, the ideal of manhood exemplified by the cowboy. All Americans are aware that cowboy heroes in Western fiction and films define a particular extreme of American culture's construction of masculinity. Even though John Wayne died in 1979, for many he's still the personification of what an American man ought to be. People who live outside the American West often are unaware of the particular strength with which the cowboy ideal applies for many men in that part of the country. Of course, some Westerners treat it with skepticism, but for many this model of masculinity is taken very seriously, strongly affecting male behavior and self-presentation. Both Jack and Ennis clearly are deeply enamored of it, and both aspire to a Western version of the American Dream, hoping that they can become independent ranchers. As Proulx has noted in her comments on the story, "both wanted to be cowboys, be part of the Great Western Myth, but it didn't work out that way . . ."[8]

Into the hard, difficult, and all too common circumstances of the lives of Ennis and Jack, the story and the film introduce a force that transforms them, that provides a different way of thinking of being a man and of thinking of success, interfering with the ideals that they've been taught, although perhaps if they could fully embrace this force it actually could help them, uniting them in their efforts to achieve their dreams. Friendship gradually develops between Jack and Ennis. Though as they begin to work together it takes the form of convivial comradeship, from the start there's an element of unspoken mutual physical interest and attraction, which eventually is fulfilled in intense mutual sexual passion and then deepens into a continuing commitment, both emotional and sexual, that persists despite all the difficult and painful obstacles that their lives impose.

Straight people, especially straight men, who perceive love between men in terms of homophobic stereotypes may reject defining the relationship between Ennis and Jack as friendship, instead trying to define it—and dismiss it—as only being sexual desire. For most straight men, the homophobia enforced by American culture sets a boundary between male friendship, which supposedly is a pure form of comradeship in which physical attraction plays no part, being unthought and unthinkable, and male-male sexuality, which is constructed as mere lust without any emotional connection, as aggressive, promiscuous sex marked by domination and submission. When many members of the majority do acknowledge the emotional dimension of relationships between men who have sex with men, they construct it in terms of negative feminine stereotypes, as excessive and hysterical. Friendship and sex, of course, aren't so easy to separate as many in the majority want to believe. As most men grow up, whatever way they ultimately identify their sexual orientation, they experience a spectrum of intense physical and emotional intimacy with other males, including playing and roughhousing with each other as well as competing in sports, in which it's difficult to draw any clear line between homosocial and homosexual activity. Engaging in competitive games together often leads to teasing and horsing around, and can involve wrestling, which frequently can be sexually arousing for some of the men who participate or who watch. In order to be able to continue to engage in sports and other physical activities that they value because they enact masculinity and bond them with other males, in a homophobic culture like that of the United States most men have to draw a strict—though artificial—line between the homosocial, which is permitted and often valued, and the homosexual, which is banned and reviled. Among organized male groups in America today some kinds of contact, like the sort of erotic wrestling just mentioned, though clearly sexual, usually are excused and tolerated as mere "fooling around," and so can just barely be included on the "safe" side of the boundary, at least if they don't happen frequently. Repeated, overtly sexual attraction and interaction with other males are repudiated and are constructed in accordance with intensely negative homophobic stereotypes.[9]

As those studying gender have pointed out, homosocial interaction among men is fundamental to establishing masculine status in American society. Relationships with women are a significant way in which masculinity is defined, of course, but relationships with other men ultimately are more important. In working, playing, and socializing together, men define hierarchies of status and power in relationship to one another in which each man's place depends on his ability to enact various accepted manifestations of masculinity. One manifestation is a man's ability to succeed in social and sexual relationships with women, particularly women that men find attractive and value, but others involve his ability to compete with and assert himself in relation to other men. For young men, games and sports are especially important, but competition in manifesting masculinity shapes most social interactions between young men, and continues to be a major factor in work and socializing among men as they get older. Work, school, sports, social and public life define a wide arena in which men continually seek to display adequately masculine characteristics to other men.[10]

Masculinity is constructed almost as a possession that some men have more of than others; those perceived as having a great deal of it are admired and emulated, and those who supposedly have little are disparaged and ignored. Men who are ranked higher because of age, position, size, or aggression often engage in bullying in an attempt to discredit and marginalize those they perceive as inferior. Men who are suspected or known to be sexually different are particular targets. Young men suspected of sexual difference sometimes avoid situations, such as school athletics, in which they may be bullied, but increasingly today there are those who realize that the best response is resistance. Some hide their difference and seek to pass; others don't and confront and reject the supposed superiority of heterosexual men. Generally for men, as they compete with each other for rank, they experience constant anxiety about being masculine enough, and fear of being shamed before other men for failing to be adequately masculine. Unless a man continues to perform in sufficiently masculine ways before other men, he may be condemned by them as not really being a man. Masculinity, at least as it's understood in contexts dominated by the straight male majority, easily can be damaged or lost entirely. The way it's constructed creates a parallel with the anxiety men may experience about the possibility of impotence or castration. Men perceived as having little masculinity are told they don't "measure up" or aren't "real men," and of course one of the ultimate ways of judging a man is in terms of whether or not he's "got balls." Another word for a bully, indicating the phallic significance of aggression between men, is a "prick." Though in traditional constructions of masculinity women are valued as possessions, for a man to be perceived as being *like* a woman impairs his masculine identity. Homosexuality, as it's been constructed by the dominant society, supposedly feminizes a man, erasing his masculinity. For most men, in the competition with other men for masculine status the greatest possible source of shame and failure is to be labeled homosexual.[11]

Though they often entail competition and anxiety about masculine status, homosocial relationships are important to most men because they establish the alliances necessary to work together, to advance individual careers, and to maintain male power in society. By organizing male relationships and establishing and maintaining hierarchy among men, homosociality allows cooperation among men. It permits men to form strong bonds of friendship, both among groups and between individuals. Such male relationships can occur in many occupational and social contexts, but some kinds of activity allow more intimate and intense physical contact between men than others, in particular forms of work and recreation that cause men to dress and shower together, and in some cases, to travel and live together for periods of time. Strong homosocial relationships are especially necessary in all-male organized groups under stressful conditions, as on athletic teams or in military forces. Of course, the intensity of contact between men in such settings stimulates physical desire and emotional involvement for some men, and so, in a culture like that in the United States today, men learn to set boundaries that discourage or deny same-sex attraction. In social environments such as schools, fraternities, athletic teams, and military forces that bring large numbers of young men together, authorities maintain surveillance and discipline to prevent homosexual behavior and relationships, but peer pressure also constantly acts against any who feel or express same-sex desire. Men who are identified with it risk forfeiting their masculine credentials among their peers. Other cultures, unlike that in the United States, instead of banning male-male sexual relationships, have encouraged them, recognizing the intense commitment they can create among men, and using them as part of the system of male status and power. In some societies, such as ancient Greece, same-sex desire often functioned to build intense loyalty between soldiers, whereas the American armed forces value homosociality but seek to exclude any actual sexual involvement between those of the same sex.[12]

Contrary to homophobic stereotypes, some men who desire men may be drawn to the homosocial climate of sports, fraternities, police or military forces, or certain largely male work environments because of the bonding that occurs there between men. It's understandable that such homosocial settings would have particular appeal to men who desire men but who also identify as masculine, and who, as a result, may not identify as gay or queer. Stereotypes associated with gay or queer men, especially those that construct male-male attraction as being incompatible with masculinity, may deter some masculine, man-loving men from involvement with those perceived as gay or queer, and may incline them toward activities perceived as strongly masculine and heterosexual, but providing intense male intimacy. However, there's always the danger, for such a man, that visible expression of male-male desire may lead to its labeling and condemnation as homosexuality.[13]

Of course, intense homosocial bonding occurs in the sport in which Jack Twist seeks to make his career, professional rodeo. Stock handlers, rodeo clowns or bullfighters, and riders all work and compete under very dangerous conditions with huge, powerful animals that can kill a man in an instant, and the men all have to be able to trust and rely onone another completely. There's great emphasis on competition between individual riders, but there's also intense camaraderie, and riders often learn from each other and are supportive of each other. Also, working the rodeo circuit necessarily puts men together traveling, sharing meals and hotel rooms, and cooperating in doing all the daily work that makes rodeo competitions possible. Proulx doesn't say so explicitly, but for Jack, this powerful connection with other men, as well as his desire to prove himself to men like his father and also to himself, may be part of what attracts him to rodeo.[14] In relation to this, she chooses a striking and suggestive word to describe his enthusiasm, not just for bull riding but for living on the rodeo circuit, in her first substantial description of him as he talks to Ennis on the day they meet; as she puts it, Jack's "infatuated"[15] with life in rodeo.

In the system of homophobic stereotypes that American culture has created to deter homosocial relationships from becoming homosexual, men who are attracted to men are constructed in extremely negative terms. They supposedly are driven by sexual desire so strong that it makes them unable to establish real commitments, and are seen as engaging in continual sexual pursuit and an endless series of one-night stands. In such constructions, men who desire men are either sinister predators, who eye every man as a potential sex partner, or silly queens who posture and gossip with each other like stereotypic women, dithering over their episodic affairs. The anxieties of straight men are articulated in the form of the hypermasculine gay rapist, an object of fear, and the effeminate "girlieman," an object of contempt. When they encounter gay couples, many straight people project onto them their own constructions of relationships between men and women, assuming that one partner must be more masculine and one more feminine, one "playing" the man and one "playing" the woman. The possibility that two men who have a sexual relationship may form lasting bonds with each other as friends, or that two male lovers often may interact with each other in their daily life together like any other close male friends, is unimaginable.[16]

Central to the urge to relegate male-male sexuality to the far side of the boundary separating it from "real" friendship between "real" men is the intense and persistent anxiety of many straight men, which surfaces as both ridicule and rage, about the sex act that they equate with male-male sexuality, anal intercourse. Simultaneously, faggots are constructed as wanting to fuck any man, threatening even "real" men with rape, and as wanting to submit to other men "like women," thus supposedly negating their maleness. This demonization of men who have sex with men leaves little space for emotions other than the hysteria and despair supposedly involved in a life of promiscuous couplings, of endless domination and submission, and none at all for real friendship.[17]

As many men who love men attest, and as they've recorded in fiction, memoirs, and film, in fact there aren't necessarily any strong boundaries between friendship, attraction, sex, or love between men. Men who love men aren't some alien, distinct, separate species, but experience many relationships with other men that are like those of straight men. While many explain that they felt a sense of difference early in life, others only recognize their sexual orientation in adolescence or even later. Some identify as gay, but many others never embrace this identity, and others define their identities in other ways. Because American culture assumes to begin with that all young people are heterosexual, making heterosexuality compulsory, men who realize they're attracted to men grow up along with straight men amid the same male relationships and activities. Men who desire men come to an understanding of their sexuality in many different ways, and at different times in their lives, but many explain that their friendships with other boys and other young men often played a crucial part in this process in their youth. In childhood and adolescence most boys have strong friendships and enmities; they play, explore, and engage in games and sports together, enjoying physical competition and contact. As they grow up some gradually realize that the intensity of their feelings for their friends is part of a physical and emotional desire for other men analogous to what all the voices of the culture tell them they should be beginning to feel for women. For some, the intensity of commitment to a friend, the anxiety about his distance or indifference, the sense of competition with others, particularly women, for his attention, along with sexual arousal because of him, all may precipitate an awareness of being sexually oriented partly or entirely toward men. If American culture weren't pervaded by hostility to love between men, it's likely that many more men would be able to recognize a degree of physical and emotional desire for other men. For many of the men who do come to think of themselves as gay, their sexual attraction to men goes along with a desire for male companionship, for a group of close gay male friends and particularly for a friend who also is a lover. Walt Whitman recognized this, repeatedly coupling the words "friend" and "lover" in his poems about male love, although homophobic teachers and scholars still suppress these poems or seek to explain them away as being "merely" about friendship in the usual limited heterosexual sense.

> . . .When I wander'd alone over the beach, and undressing
>   bathed, laughing with the cool waters, and saw the sun rise,
> And when I thought how my dear friend my lover was on his
>   way coming, O then I was happy,
> O then each breath tasted sweeter, and all that day my food
>   nourish'd me more, and the beautiful day pass'd well,
> And the next came with equal joy, and with the next at evening
>   came my friend,
> And that night while all was still I heard the waters roll slowly
>   continually up the shores,
> I heard the hissing rustle of the liquid and sands as directed to me
>   whispering to congratulate me,
> For the one I love most lay sleeping by me under the same cover in
>   the cool night,
> In the stillness in the autumn moonbeams his face was inclined
>   toward me,
> And his arm lay lightly around my breast—and that night I
>   was happy.[18]

Today gay men often use the words "partner," "lover," or "boyfriend" for the men they love; with the struggle for marriage equality for same-sex couples, some use the word "husband," but some simply use the word "friend" to refer to the man they share a life with. Some heterosexuals may dismiss the use of the word in this way as a mere euphemism, as an attempt to mask the "real" nature of the relationship, which they reduce to being only a sexual one, and a sexual one that they construct in the crudest terms at that, but many men who love men recognize that its use isn't euphemistic, but indicates the completion and fulfillment of what they felt as boys or young men for their best friends, the physical and emotional need to be with another man. For many men who love men, the kind of friendships all men experience in fact are continuous with, rather than distinct from, their social and intimate relationships with other men who love men.[19]

The story and the movie of *Brokeback Mountain* depict with insight and sensitivity the gradual, tentative discovery of friendship, in all its gradations from boyish comradeship to intense physical passion, between Jack and Ennis. Annie Proulx's description of the unfolding of their feelings for each other, though brief, is subtle and rich in nuance and detail, and Larry McMurtry and Diana Ossana perceptively expand her account in their screenplay. Those who convey their vision in the film, particularly Ang Lee and Heath Ledger and Jake Gyllenhaal, provide an impressive example of the ability of straight filmmakers to understand and respect the depth of emotional and sexual intimacy possible between two men, especially given the lack of precedent in the work of most Hollywood directors and actors. Both the written and the visual representations show the continuity that's possible, in some men's lives, between friendship and intense emotional and sexual love.

The film augments the story's description of the evolution of the friendship between Jack and Ennis in many ways, starting with the episode in Signal when the two men meet and begin to get to know each other. The scenes outside the Farm and Ranch Employment Agency trailer before Aguirre arrives and orders Ennis and Jack inside indicate their poverty, their dignity, and their awareness of each other. Ennis gets there first, dressed in old boots and Levis and an old tan canvas jacket buttoned up, his hat tilted low; he leans against the trailer, and smokes and strips a cigarette. His isolation as he waits in the empty lot, surrounded by shabby commercial buildings, a little church steeple behind them, the railroad tracks and the empty plain in front of him in the bright sun, suggests the dimensions of the hard, isolated life he's had so far. Then Jack pulls up in his old, rough-running truck, kicks it in frustration, and turns and looks at Ennis, who keeps his head lowered so his hat brim hides his face. Where Jack is animated, Ennis is withdrawn; Jack walks forward as if he's about to say something to Ennis, who remains leaning against the trailer, huddled up, hands thrust in his pockets, and keeps his head down. When Jack hesitates and turns back toward his truck, Ennis briefly looks up, watching as Jack walks back, his blue cowboy shirt and jeans showing his young, strong body. Jack then leans back against his truck, taking a self-consciously relaxed pose, perhaps trying to hide his nervousness, and also continuing to display himself, and looks toward Ennis, but Ennis looks down, avoiding Jack's gaze. Whereas Ennis wears his jacket closely buttoned, Jack's shirt is open at the neck, already suggesting the differences between their personalities. Jack cleans up, looking in the outside rearview mirror of his truck, making himself presentable to apply for a job, but perhaps also for meeting Ennis, who he watches closely in the mirror as he shaves. Both actors subtly and effectively suggest the awareness the two characters have of each other, and the efforts of each not to allow the other to see it. Neither man speaks, but both size each other up—as workers, potential competitors for jobs, possible partners in shared employment, and perhaps in other ways neither would want to articulate fully, certainly not to the other and probably not even to himself. While neither character has the boldness and assurance of an out gay man, each looks at the other with a degree of interest that almost suggests cruising—and which, with interesting and suggestive irony, echoes many scenes in earlier Westerns in which two men stare intently at each other, taking each other's estimate, often as a prelude to a fistfight or a gunfight. With this, the film begins its process of challenging fundamental assumptions about the solitary, aggressive, competitive nature of masculinity inherent in representations of men in the traditional Western.

In the trailer in the next scene, Aguirre gruffly explains their work with an edge of contempt for the Forest Service regulations and for the two men he's telling to ignore them when they herd sheep together on the mountain. Except as employees, Ennis and Jack are invisible to him; he makes no greeting to them when he arrives, even though he knows Jack from the previous summer, and he orders them inside with an insult. His patronizing treatment of them as subordinates contrasts with their deference to each other: neither asserts himself or takes the lead, but instead each remains silent, giving the other a degree of respect. When Aguirre is interrupted by a phone call, again Ennis briefly glances at Jack, who's looking away, and then, when Ennis drops his gaze, Jack in turn looks at him; their cautious interest in each other contrasts with Aguirre's hostility toward the man on the phone. Ennis and Jack are quiet and deferential, but Aguirre's the kind of man who posts a sign on the door where he works reading, "Trespassers will be shot, survivors will be shot again."

As Jack and Ennis leave the trailer, the film suggests their different personalities, and just the beginning of a friendly mood of acceptance between them. Jack smiles, reaches out and shakes Ennis's hand, and introduces himself, eliciting Ennis's taciturn offer of his first name only. Jack's response is to tease, asking Ennis, "Your folks just stop at Ennis?" which gets him a muttered

"Del Mar," to which Jack smiles and replies, "Nice to know you, Ennis del Mar." The exchange indicates the basic difference between them, Jack's warmth and openness and willingness to take a risk, and Ennis's insularity and caution. Also, by playfully raising the question of whether Ennis's parents gave him their last name, it subtly points to the issue, crucial in the lives of both men, of their difficult relationships to their families, and of the factor of sexual difference in those relationships. They walk to a bar, Jack in the lead, and there, over beers, gradually warm to each other a bit, sharing a little about their backgrounds, though characteristically Jack does more of the talking.

In the story, this episode is conveyed briefly by the narrative voice, which paraphrases Jack's account of his previous summer's experience on the mountain and of his attraction to rodeo and describes the contrasting appearances of the two men; the movie expands the scene, showing Jack's lively, friendly manner with Ennis, Ennis's taciturn account of his parents' deaths and the impact on him and his brother and sister, and Jack's startled sympathy. What Jack says in their conversation in the film hints at the hostility of his father, which Ennis eventually will see firsthand. After telling Ennis about the hard work they'll do on the mountain, Jack comments that it beats working for his old man, adding that there's no way to please him. His conflict with his father also is evident when he asks Ennis if his folks ran him off; clearly this is something Jack realizes is well within the range of possibility. Ennis's stoicism comes across in the way he tells Jack about his parents' deaths: he responds to Jack's question with the ironic comment that his folks ran themselves off, and explains that they missed the one curve in the road and were killed in an accident, leaving him to be raised by his older brother and sister after the bank repossessed the ranch. As Ledger presents him, Ennis clearly is the epitome of a type of man every American knows, that's found everywhere in the country, but that's especially characteristic of the West. However intense his feelings, he holds them in, keeps them to himself, and says very little about himself or about anything else. Jack, in contrast, though similarly masculine, is more able to show what he feels and wants, in words, in facial expressions, in gestures. Gyllenhaal repeatedly looks at Ledger as they talk in the bar scene, while Ledger delivers his lines staring straight ahead at his beer bottle. As the screenwriters note, Jack comes across as less stoic and more of a dreamer.[20] But where the film convincingly presents the characters from the outside, the story can take us into their thoughts, and in the text this scene is particularly important because it confirms the reader's sense of the awareness and interest the men show in each other, including, in this passage, Ennis's awareness of Jack's body. As will be discussed in more detail below, in Proulx's description of Jack in the episode it's clear that she's presenting him as he appears to Ennis, and the physical qualities about him that strike Ennis.

The friendship between the two men intensifies as they go from society and the limitations it imposes to the greater freedom of the mountain. Signal is presented in the film as a dusty little town; Aguirre's trailer is dirty, cramped, and stuffy, but the mountain is dazzling: its forests, cliffs, meadows, and peaks are clear and detailed under a brilliant, windy blue and white sky. In both the story and the film, the sense of open space and clarity is emphasized by the dramatic movement of the men, horses, mules, dogs, and hundreds of sheep up the mountain, away from roads and towns and buildings and machines, "out above the tree line into the great flowery meadows and the coursing, endless wind."[21] In the film, Rodrigo Prieto's camerawork in these scenes creates a wonderful sense of liberation amid the light and shadow and color of the mountain, which is emphasized by the gentle sound of pump organ and acoustic guitar in Gustavo Santaolalla's lyrical musical score. In contrast to the preceding close shots of the men as they meet with Aguirre in the trailer and then talk in the bar, now they're shown from a distance as they take their animals up the mountain, and in shots that show the immense scale of the landscape and the sea of sheep moving up the slope.

When Ennis and Jack arrive on Brokeback Mountain, they enter the kind of space that historians of sexual minorities have documented and discussed in which men live and work together apart from society and particularly from the company of women, making physical and emotional intimacy between men more likely. Among men involved in work such as logging and mining, and possibly also in the cattle business, sexual relationships seem to have been more frequent, and at times more accepted, than in other parts of American society.[22] Proulx herself, in her discussion of the process of writing the story, has commented on learning about the patterns of male-male sexual relationships in all-male work environments. She explains that she developed her ideas for the story partly as the result of a trip in the Big Horn Mountains on which she "noticed distant flocks of sheep on great empty slopes,"[23] which caused her to realize that "in such isolated high country, away from opprobrious comment and watchful eyes . . . it would be plausible for the characters to get into a sexual situation."[24] Her hunch was confirmed by talking with an "old sheep rancher, dead now, [who] used to say he always sent up two men to tend sheep 'so's if they get lonesome they can poke each other.'"[25]

At the beginning of her description of the time Ennis and Jack spend on the mountain, Proulx builds on the sense of contrast between life in the towns below and the feeling of liberation in nature, suggesting the developing bond between the two men. She starts by describing their first morning on the mountain, after both sleep in the main camp the first night, the "glassy orange"[26] light of dawn making the "sooty bulk"[27] of the mountain gradually pale until it's the color of the smoke from the breakfast fire Ennis has made, causing the smallest pebbles and bits of soil to cast long shadows and revealing the "somber malachite"[28] of the massed lodgepole pines. Then she describes the dawning awareness of each other the two men experience as Ennis works at the main camp and Jack tends the sheep far up the slope of the mountain: "During the day Ennis looked across a great gulf and sometimes saw Jack, a small dot moving across a high meadow as an insect moves across a tablecloth; Jack, in his dark camp, saw Ennis as night fire, a red spark on the huge black mass of the mountain."[29]

The film also shows the two men watching each other across the clear, far distances of the mountain, suggesting the emerging connection between them. Once the men have set up their base camp on the first day on the mountain, Jack rides up to the alpine meadow above to spend the night with the sheep. After a sunset that turns the soft gray clouds to pink and orange and gold, we see him sitting in the light of the full moon, looking out over the sheep in the meadow, and down the slopes of the mountain, clear in the moonlight, to the valley below where Ennis's campfire glows and sends up a plume of smoke. Shown in close-up, Gyllenhaal's face suggests Jack's loneliness, his curiosity about Ennis, and his desire for his company. The soft, plaintive music reinforces his mood. In a scene a day or so later, when the sun has come out after a sudden shower, Ennis is shown washing dishes in a stream; he hears thunder, and looks up at the heights of the mountain above him, seeing Jack riding amid the herd of sheep on a steep meadow near a sharp ridge, with the clouds of the storm beyond. Again, as with the parallel shot of Gyllenhaal, a close shot of Ledger's face conveys a sense of the concern he's begun to feel for his friend, and again the movie's score suggests his feeling.

The film provides a much more extensive and detailed depiction of the development of friendly intimacy between Jack and Ennis, through a series of episodes not present in the story. For a man who loves men, or for anyone else actually able to respect the development of a passionate friendship between two men, the slow, subtle, gradually intensifying pace with which the director and actors convey the growth of the silent physical and emotional attraction between the two men is moving to see. As many men can attest, the development of such a relationship often is tentative and often occurs with little actually being said about what's being felt, since neither man's sure what the other feels, and both have been conditioned to fear emotion and sexuality between men. Many men who love men spend part, or perhaps all, of one of the most important portions of their lives, their adolescence, when they first understand and perhaps act on their attraction to other men, hiding what they feel. The climate of contempt and hatred for male-male desire expressed in

insults, ridicule, "jokes," harassment, and violence, which young men encounter often at home, and always at school, teaches many of those who feel
attraction for other young men to remain silent and to hide what they feel
from others, even from themselves, and to try to pass for straight. For straight
people, it isn't possible to know from experience what it's like, when you're
in your teens, beginning to feel the power and intensity of sexual desire, to be
able to tell no one, in fact, to fear that the very friend you find yourself attracted to may respond with disgust and condemnation, quite likely with
anger and violence. For straight people, even if they're drawn to individuals
who reject them or who are unattainable, the entire culture still validates, supports, and encourages their desire. For a young man to be physically and emotionally drawn to another young man, and to admit it to himself, much less to
express it to his friend, can be loaded with risk, shame, and fear. This would
have been especially so in the rural West forty years ago. Though there's substantial evidence of intense sexual and emotional relationships between men
in both rural and urban areas throughout this period, and indeed before, a man
who felt attracted to another man knew that, until he was certain of the feelings of the man he desired, there was danger. Given endemic homophobia, the
possibility of intimacy with another man had to be negotiated with care. At
the least, the expression of desire might result in ridicule and humiliation; at
worst it might result in violence and injury, even in death.[30] In the movie, both
Gyllenhaal and Ledger skillfully suggest how two men, each with feelings he
can't speak or perhaps even think, and neither of whom is sure of the other or
really of himself, may gradually edge toward intimacy. Gyllenhaal conveys
the tentative yet consistent way that the attraction a man feels may lead him
to dare to risk testing the possibility of physical intimacy with his friend. It's
much to the credit of both actors, and of the director and screenwriters, that
they could understand and respect this fundamental aspect of life for men
who are unsure about expressing same-sex attraction, which is obvious to gay
or queer men, and virtually invisible to most of the straight majority.

McMurtry and Ossana wrote several original episodes that Lee, Gyllenhaal, and Ledger present suggesting the deepening of feeling between Jack
and Ennis. The most significant begins by depicting Ennis, probably a week
into their summer on the mountain, toward the end of May, picking up supplies at the bridge down below, then packing them back up on mules. By a
stream a bear spooks his horse, Ennis is thrown, and the mules take off, tear-
ing the packs and scattering the supplies. After dark, Ennis finally makes it
into camp; the screenwriters indicate that Jack's worried but, when Ennis
rides in, hides his concern with a show of indignation, shy of saying directly
that he's been worried about Ennis and cares what happens to him.[31] Seeing
the blood on Ennis's head, Jack quickly takes off his bandana, dips it in hot

water, and hesitantly begins to wipe Ennis's wound, wincing slightly as he does so; Ennis then grabs the bandana and cleans the cut. The scene captures an experience many men attracted to men have known, especially when young, of being concerned for the well-being of another man but of fearing to express it, since men generally aren't supposed to express emotion or to minister to the physical needs of others, and certainly not to do so for other men.

This original episode is linked to the one that follows; it raises the question of what Ennis and Jack will do to get more—and better—food, since about all they've got left is beans, which they're already sick of. With typical impulsiveness, Jack suggests shooting one of the sheep, but Ennis stoically refuses, saying he'll stick with beans; Jack's reply that he won't reflects his general sense that he ought to get more from life than the little that other men will allow him. Apparently Ennis's concern for his friend keeps him from insisting that Jack put up with just eating beans; the men hunt together, Ennis shoots an elk, and Jack congratulates him with a yell and a shove, to which Ennis gruffly jokes, "Was gettin tired of your dumb ass missin." As often happens in male friendships, including those between men who have sex with each other, affection is expressed playfully, through teasing and horseplay. After Ennis's successful shot, Jack excitedly tells him they need to get a move on so they won't get caught with the elk by the Game and Fish Department. Again, as often is the case for young men, their sense of intimacy is intensified by the excitement of doing something together that's deemed illicit by authority.

The growing affection between the two men is presented in other scenes shared by both the film and the story. When Jack complains about Aguirre's demand that he violate Forest Service rules and sleep with the sheep, which requires commuting four hours a day in order to get breakfast and dinner cooked by Ennis in the main camp, Ennis generously and easily offers to switch. Jack's pleased, but jokes about his own cooking, warning Ennis that he can't cook, though he's pretty good with a can opener. Ennis reassures him, and so they switch jobs. As happens when two men like and trust each other, Jack and Ennis work smoothly together, each readily accommodating his friend. Also, the discussion of the issue of violating rules subtly reminds the reader or viewer of the fact that the two men are in the process of approaching a degree of intimacy that will violate the artificial boundary between the homosocial and the homosexual imposed by their culture, although this parallel only is implied and never is articulated explicitly in either version.

Over their meals together in the main camp, the two men share more about their backgrounds, families, lives, and hopes. The film and the story develop their conversations in different ways. Some of what we learn about the characters through the narrative voice in the story is presented in the film through their conversations by their campfire. In one scene in the movie, as he comes over to join Ennis by the fire, Jack proudly flicks his brass belt buckle won for bull riding, showing off for his friend, which leads to a discussion of rodeoing. Jack sits down, pours Ennis some whiskey, and opens up, telling Ennis about his ambitions as a bull rider and then making the spare but painful comment that despite a successful career in rodeoing his father never shared his knowledge with Jack and never came to see him ride. The sadness implied in his comment about his father's failure to encourage him leads Jack, with characteristic sensitivity toward Ennis, to ask whether Ennis's brother and sister did right by him. Ennis replies with a more complete account of his family after his parents' deaths, explaining that he got a year of high school but had to quit when the pickup broke down, that his sister married an oil worker and moved away, and that he and his brother then got work on a ranch, but when his brother got married Ennis had to move out, and so ended up getting the job on Brokeback Mountain. For the first time in the film, Ledger presents Ennis as being relaxed and a little animated as he speaks, though he indicates Ennis's continuing cautiousness by looking straight ahead toward the campfire, only occasionally venturing a glance at Jack. What Ennis says, and the way he says it, elicits a smiling look from Jack, which causes puzzlement for Ennis; Jack explains that it's more than Ennis has said in the past two weeks, which makes Ennis smile for the first time and joke about his own silence, saying it's more than he's said in a year. This marks a crucial shift in their relationship: from the start, Jack's been more open and friendly than many men, but now in response to him Ennis begins to break away from the strictures of traditional masculinity that have bound him, and to share emotion with his friend. He trusts Jack enough to take the risk of compromising his commitment to complete independence and self-reliance. The warmth of their growing friendship is in marked contrast to the burden of sadness each carries about failed family relationships, especially with fathers and a brother who, as we gradually learn, all were similar in their hostility. Unlike the angry, violent men each has grown up with, Jack and Ennis, in just a couple of weeks together, have treated each other first with respect and consideration, then with trust and compassion, and now with acceptance and gentle humor. In the film this quickly becomes mutual playfulness; the talk about rodeoing leads Ennis to say that his father was a fine roper, and then to tease Jack, glancing at him and adding that his father thought rodeo cowboys "was all fuck-ups." Jack objects, "The hell they are!" and launches into a "pretend bull ride around the campfire, bucking and twisting."[32] He acts up a storm, shouting that he's spurring the bull's guts out, waving to the girls in the stands, and staying on no matter how high the bull kicks—and then trips and collapses in a heap over the saddles, proving Ennis's father's point about rodeo cowboys. Ennis smiles and says he thinks his dad was right, and they both have a good laugh. Their shared humor consistently has an element of playful self-mockery, of self-directed irony that reduces any sense of egotistic competition, further reinforcing the quality of mutual respect and deference that marks their intimacy.

In the story, Proulx emphasizes different details, but with a similar effect of indicating the deepening respect, trust, and affection between the two men. On the evening that Ennis agrees to switch camps, her narrative notes that he doesn't ride out to the sheep right after supper, but rather that together he and Jack "fend off"[33] the night—and the necessity of parting company—for an hour with the light of the kerosene lamp. Their next evening together, they have a "high-time supper,"[34] sharing beans and fried potatoes, keeping warm by the fire as the day ends and it gets cold, drinking whiskey, smoking, getting up to piss, and throwing more wood on the fire to prolong their time together. One descriptive detail in this passage stands out especially on rereading the story, and subtly hints at the element of male sexual attraction still unexpressed at this point in the emerging friendship between Ennis and Jack: the description of the evening sky above them as "lavender,"[35] one of the colors that are conventionally emblems, for gay people and homophobes alike, of same-sex desire. The conversation the men enjoy so much is about things that often are part of the experience and interest of young men in the rural West, including horses and rodeo as well as "dogs each had owned and known."[36] They share a love of the country and of working with and knowing animals in a context that few city people ever get to experience or understand. They also talk about topics of particular concern to young men in 1963, including the draft, which necessarily was an ever-present factor in the plans of every young man, even before the escalation of the Vietnam War two years later. For young, fit, unmarried men who didn't have the money or education to attend college, it was a likelihood that they'd be drafted and would serve two years in the army.

In Proulx's account, talking about the draft leads Ennis and Jack to talk about the dangers of military service, particularly a recent disaster with considerable significance for men like them, sensitive to the possibilities of the profound bonds between male companions. They discuss the wreck of the submarine *Thresher* two months before and what it must have been like for the ship's men "in the last doomed minutes."[37] A highly advanced nuclear attack submarine, the *Thresher* was on a deep diving exercise about two hundred miles off Boston on April 10, 1963; from a depth of more than a mile she sent garbled distress messages, and then shortly afterward was lost with all hands. The investigation indicated that a sudden pipe failure probably had flooded the engine room, leading to the shutdown of all electric power, which made it impossible to control the ship; she slowly went down to a depth so great that the tremendous pressure finally caused her to implode. On board were sixteen officers, ninety-six enlisted men, and seventeen civilian technicians who were monitoring the ship's dive tests. The circumstances of the wreck are particularly horrific, and particularly moving, because the men of the *Thresher* knew what was happening, probably for many minutes, but could do nothing to stop it.[38] Thinking of the men in the darkened ship, gradually drifting down to her destruction, forces one to imagine the fear, courage, stoicism—and also the compassion for one another—among the doomed sailors. The wreck of the *Thresher* was compelling for everyone who heard about it, but especially so for those, like Ennis and Jack, awake to the potential of strong emotional connections between men.

Like the screenplay, the story's narrator describes the differing views that Jack and Ennis express about rodeoing during their talk by the campfire. To Jack's enthusiasm for bull riding, Ennis says he's more interested in the kind of riding that goes on for more than eight seconds and has a point, to which Jack counters that the money you can make in rodeo is a good point, and Ennis has to agree. Proulx notes that they treat each other's opinions with respect, underlining the fact that each man is "glad to have a companion where none had been expected."[39] So strong is Ennis's happiness in his new friendship with Jack that, at the end of the evening when they have their "high-time supper,"[40] as he rides back to the sheep he thinks to himself that he'd "never had such a good time, felt he could paw the white out of the moon."[41] It's unfortunate that this important moment in the development of Ennis's feeling for Jack is omitted from the screenplay, since in Proulx's narrative it stresses Ennis's sheer animal joy, especially after his rough relationship with his brother and father and his hard struggles on his own, at having found a buddy in Jack.

In both the story and the film, the ordinary processes of daily life close together in the main camp accelerate the pace with which physical and emotional intimacy grow between the two men. When they eat and drink together, they show no self-conscious, fastidious squeamishness about having to urinate, but stand up from the fire, take a piss, and sit back down to talk and drink again. Before they have their "high-time supper,"[42] as Jack's preparing their meal, Ennis heats water and shaves and washes, telling Jack that early that morning he shot a coyote, "'balls on him size a apples,'"[43] then easily offers to share the hot water with Jack. Ennis goes ahead and pulls off his boots and jeans and, as he says in the story, proceeds to "'warsh'"[44] everything he can reach, right in front of Jack. In the movie, whereas when he first met Jack,

Ennis wore his coat like armor, buttoned up to the neck, now he's relaxed with his friend, unself-conscious about being naked. As Ennis bathes, both the story and the film clearly show Jack's awareness of Ennis's slim but muscular body. In the film, Gyllenhaal effectively conveys a sense of Jack's intense awareness of Ennis—who squats down, washing himself, naked except for his hat—without ever looking directly at him and allowing himself to be seen to watch. The story comments that, when Ennis strips, Jack notices that he wears no socks or drawers. When Ennis offers to share the hot water, the film adds a subtle visual pun: whereas in the story at this moment Jack's peeling potatoes, here he's lying back next to the fire, opening a can of beans, and nearly spills it when he declines Ennis's offer. The implication is that Jack refuses because to strip and join Ennis in bathing might be sexually arousing, and so could "spill the beans" about the attraction he feels to his friend.

It's clear in the text that Jack's interest in Ennis's body is reciprocated, indeed, that Ennis already has looked closely at Jack. As has been mentioned before, in the episode in the bar on the morning the two men meet, when Proulx describes the appearance of each, she indicates, in describing Jack, that she's describing him as he appears to Ennis. As they talk in the bar, Jack proudly tells Ennis about the eagle he shot on his first summer on Brokeback, turning his head to show the feather in his hat; Proulx explains that Jack "seemed fair enough,"[45] but that though small he "carried some weight in the haunch"[46] and that his smile "disclosed buckteeth."[47] Ennis appreciates Jack's looks but also considers him somewhat critically, noting his bucktoothed smile and the heaviness of his haunches; while this seems to qualify his sense that Jack is "fair," it also indicates, interestingly, that one of the things Ennis notices first about his new friend is his thighs and butt. With this detail Proulx suggests a degree of potential erotic interest indicative of the current of sexual attraction toward men present in Ennis, and soon to develop in his sexual relationship with Jack. She reinforces this with Jack's name; his first name has obvious sexual connotations, being a vernacular synonym for ejaculation, and his last name of course can be taken to suggest sexual difference. But as Gyllenhaal explained in an interview, Proulx also told him, in her inscription in the copy of the story that she gave to him expressing her gratitude for his fine performance in the movie, that the last name of his character refers to the muscles needed by a bull rider to move with, and keep on, a huge, powerful bull as it tries to throw him off. Gyllenhaal said:

> Annie Proulx wrote me a note very recently . . . with a limited edition of *Close Range*, which is the book that "Brokeback Mountain" . . . is in. And in it she said that Jack Twist refers to, "twist" refers to the strength of the thighs and butt muscles that a bull rider has to have in order to stay on the bull. I had never thought

of it that way. It's so funny. It's so clearly in your face the whole time and you never really know what that is.[48]

Jack Twist's name is charged with suggestions of the erotic attraction his body holds for Ennis.

Proulx's indication of Ennis's awareness of Jack's body doesn't seem to have been missed by the filmmakers. In the episode when the men drive the sheep off the trailers and ready their horses and gear for the climb up the mountain, Jack has a moment of trouble with his horse, which, as Ennis warns him, has a low startle point. Jack's reply is to brag about his riding ability, to which Ennis just responds with a long, slightly amused look as Jack leans back in the saddle, pulling in the reins on the jumpy horse. The significance of what Ennis sees as he looks at Jack can't be indicated in the film the way it can in a written narrative, and certainly many viewers would assume he's merely observing how Jack rides, but it's notable that the scene displays just those features of Jack's body, the muscles of his thighs and butt as they strain against the tight denim of his Wranglers, that Proulx says Ennis notices.

In both versions, each man watches the other in ways that suggest his interest and appreciation, although each does so guardedly. Each looks, though neither wants to get caught looking, since he's unsure of the other. Looking at other people in an obvious way, especially looking at women in a way that indicates sexual interest, historically has been one of the many privileges of heterosexual men. In the traditions of European and American high art, in advertising images, in the movies, and of course, in the individual interactions of daily life, men look at women. Women, at least until the efforts of feminists began to challenge the inequalities of traditional patriarchal sexist culture, were expected to submit to being looked at, to welcome being evaluated, to compete with each other for male evaluation, and to hope to be evaluated and found deserving. A woman who looked back, or who wasn't bashful and dared to do her own looking at men, was deemed "available" or "loose," and often was labeled in many worse and uglier ways than these. In the European and American cultural traditions, "men act and women appear. Men look at women. Women watch themselves being looked at."[49] The gaze is charged with meaning in terms of double standards and relative power.

Men who look at other men, of course, are even more reviled in this cultural system than women who dare to look at men. Women who look at men challenge the male prerogative, daring to assume the same degree of agency, of sexual autonomy, as men; they raise the possibility, deeply disturbing to many men, that *men* should "appear" for women who "look," that *men* should be objects for women to evaluate and even to use sexually. But a *man* who looks at another man raises an even more disturbing possibility, at least for men who hate and fear love between men: that he himself may be the object of the desire of another man. Given that a patriarchal, sexist culture equates being male with having a penis, and having a penis with penetration, and penetration with domination, this causes many heterosexual men to be unable to tolerate being looked at in any but the most casual, incidental ways by other men. To be the object of the male gaze, for homophobic men, signifies vulnerability to what for many is their worst fear, anal penetration, which they equate with submission and the loss of the status of masculine independence. As a result, in most everyday interactions with men they don't know, and especially in all-male spaces such as men's rest rooms, locker rooms at a gym, or a military barracks, straight men follow well-defined unspoken rules that regulate and limit looking at others. Particularly in potentially intimate situations, they learn to be aware of who's around them, and to interact with them, if necessary, without looking too much or too long. When men are naked together in a locker room and have a conversation, they'll often do so while carefully avoiding looking directly at each other's bodies. Many straight men may want to look at other men's bodies in these situations in order to compare themselves to others, but they learn to do so without looking too closely, and especially without being *seen* to look, which they strongly avoid because they realize it may be taken to indicate sexual interest.[50]

For men who are attracted to other men, the gaze is of particular importance. Men who desire intimacy with other men know, as part of the general system of meaning concerning looking and being looked at as it's been defined by heterosexual male power, that looking can indicate sexual attraction. From an early age, of course, most men who are attracted to men are acutely aware of the rules about looking, and learn how to avoid looking in the "wrong" ways and provoking hostile reactions. Men who desire men can be and often are present in any intimate all-male space, such as a rest room, a locker room, or a barracks, but they become adept at negotiating these situations in ways that allow them to look, and even to identify and respond to other men who share their desire, without arousing the suspicion of straight men. One of the many pleasures of male-male desire is the enjoyment of the beauty of other men, but to enjoy it entails mastering the skill of looking at men while seeming to be looking at something else, or not to be looking at all.[51] How one looks at other men is one of the most fundamental aspects of cruising among men; to look at another man, and to look him directly in the eyes, is one of the clearest indications of male-male desire and potential sexual interest.[52] Whitman describes it eloquently in the *Calamus* poems, which he added to *Leaves of Grass* in 1860. He recounts the excitement of seeing and being seen by other men on the streets of New York, in passages such as this:

> . . .as I pass O Manhattan, your frequent and swift flash of
>   eyes offering me love,
> Offering response to my own—these repay me,
> Lovers, continual lovers, only repay me.[53]

Or this:

> Among the men and women the multitude,
> I perceive one picking me out by secret and divine signs,
> Acknowledging none else, not parent, wife, husband,
>   brother, child, any nearer than I am,
> Some are baffled, but that one is not—that one knows me.
> Ah lover and perfect equal,
> I meant that you should discover me so by faint indirections,
>   and I when I meet you mean to discover you by the like in
> you.[54]

Though Whitman sometimes includes references to women in these episodes, an understanding of individual poems in the context of the entire *Calamus* group, which is filled with homoerotic poems, and especially recognition of the ways in which he altered his work in different editions, indicates that because of condemnations of his poetry by homophobic critics he often sought to make the sexually charged situations involving men less alarming to the majority by referring to women as well or, in the case of some of his revisions, even to "heterosexualize" poems by changing pronouns from masculine to feminine. Some straight readers continue to use these textual evasions to try to claim that Whitman did not depict sexual attraction between men, which is laughable and insulting to him and to man-loving men who know and love his work.[55]

Gay men often joke about having "gaydar," an intuitive ability to tell whether another man is gay; some heterosexuals mistakenly think that this simply means noting the obvious signifiers of unusual, possibly effeminate gender behavior that constitute the stereotypes of the homosexual man as many heterosexuals understand and perceive them, but that hardly describes this perceptive sense, particularly because most men who desire men don't fit the simplistic stereotypes. Gaydar is far more subtle, and one important element of it is noticing where, at what, and for how long other men—particularly the majority of man-loving men who don't meet the criteria of the stereotypes recognized by the heterosexual majority—look.[56] Looking not only is a signifier of being a man who desires men, a way of recognizing men who share a minority sexual orientation who don't otherwise stand out from the heterosexual majority, and of indicating potential openness to knowing

another individual man, but it also is charged with the pleasure of appreciating male beauty, and also with risk, since if straight men do notice such looking, the result sometimes is confrontational. Especially for young men like
Ennis and Jack still in the process of understanding their sexuality, and passing as straight in a strongly macho and homophobic male culture to boot, the
gaze is fraught with significance.

Both Ledger and Gyllenhaal convey with skill and subtlety the tentative
nature of the growing intimacy and attraction between Ennis and Jack, and
the gradual pace at which it develops through the incremental steps of their
simple daily interactions. Both are adept at suggesting the mutual respect and
consideration of the two men, the pleasure they take in each other's conversation and humor, and, in particular, the cautious intensity of each in his
awareness of the other. It's a tribute to them as actors, to Ang Lee's direction,
to the screenwriters, and to all others involved with this aspect of the film that
their presentation of the two characters is so convincing. Interestingly, it's
been reported that one way that the actors sensitized themselves to the situations of men in rural America who are attracted to men was by reading *Farm
Boys: Lives of Gay Men from the Rural Midwest* (1996), collected and edited
by Will Fellows, in which he presents statements from scores of men who
now identify as gay and who grew up in agricultural areas from Ohio to Nebraska.[57] The men who contributed to the book provide detailed, moving, eloquent testimony about the isolation, lack of information or support, and frequent hostility that they encountered as they gradually questioned and
understood their sexuality, and many give accounts of clandestine, passionate
friendships with other young men with clear parallels to the relationship between Jack and Ennis. One, in fact, describes his intense, secret emotional
and sexual involvement over many years with a friend who married and
raised a family. The filmmakers also had advice directly from sexual minority men who had grown up in contexts like those of Ennis and Jack: among
the technical advisors to the film during production in Canada were two Alberta rodeo riders, Tim Cyr and Shane Madden, both of whom identify as gay
and who spoke from direct experience about their experience of homophobia
in the rural West. In the film's *Production Notes*, Cyr comments, "When I
read the short story, I could identify with the traits and feelings that the characters had, especially coming from a background of ranching—where everything out there is looked upon as being different if it's not traditional."[58] Madden adds, "Being raised on a farm, yeah, you had to hide it. It hurt to try and
hide it. There were times when I used to bang my head against a wall. [I read
the story, and] I was losing it after the first six pages. It hit me deep inside."[59]
(Both men are active in ARGRA, the Alberta Rockies Gay Rodeo Association, based in Calgary, whose members appear in several sequences in the

movie.)[60] The experiences of Cyr and Madden and those offered in *Farm Boys* must have been useful to the performers in developing their understanding of the characters they were portraying. As many gay men who've seen *Brokeback Mountain* have said, it's impressive to see the success with which the two straight actors are able to go inside the experience of men who've been compelled to hide their attraction to other men, an experience that many straight men know nothing, and care less, about, and that the dominant culture rarely acknowledges, much less treats with respect. In contrast, of course, some straight viewers, particularly men, and some straight male film critics, complain that they find the film, especially the part set on the mountain, "too slow," which simply confirms their inability or refusal to recognize the complex psychological and sexual situation the film depicts between Jack and Ennis. Their obtuse reactions confirm the fact that many in the majority are so oblivious, indifferent, and often hostile to the experience of men who love men that they can't begin to understand what they're seeing, much less to respect it, and their feeble and predictable limitations only make the achievement of those involved in the movie, especially the two actors, the more impressive.

In addition to being gifted actors who are capable of imagining and representing the experience of men who love men, Ledger and Gyllenhaal are physically well cast for their roles. Ledger is somewhat taller than Gyllenhaal, and has the kind of slim but strong, muscular, and supple body—"made for the horse and for fighting"[61]—that Proulx describes Ennis as having, and a narrow face and eyes with the farsighted squint that Proulx says makes Ennis a poor reader but a good marksman. Gyllenhaal, in contrast, is slightly sturdier, dark haired where Ledger is light, with striking blue eyes that contrast with his hair. Like Ledger, he's fit and athletic, but his looks are softer; Ledger is handsome in a rather hard, austere way, but Gyllenhaal has real masculine beauty. And yet, at the same time, because of his gifts as an actor, he also can make his character come across as slightly geeky in a manner that's endearing, as somewhat more physically awkward and vulnerable than Ledger. Gyllenhaal presents Jack as being a bit of a braggart, and clearly as not being up to everything he claims, but instead of allowing this aspect of the character to be irritating, he makes it touching, since Jack so obviously cares about his friend's opinion and wants to impress him. In turn, as Ledger embodies Ennis, his greater physical competence and confidence contrast strikingly with the sense of fear he conveys of accepting sexual attraction to another man. As in the text, Jack, though the smaller of the two, is the braver about trying to be who he is, and Ennis, though able to fight anyone physically, is the more afraid.

The two actors, however, are more obviously physically attractive than the two very ordinary young men Proulx describes. In her presentation of them, neither one's a looker. But in general the film is notable, for a relatively large-scale Hollywood project, for its refusal to moderate Proulx's story, and its recognition of the harshness of the world of rural Wyoming as she depicts it. The settings, especially the little line cabins, ranches, and trailers that Ennis lives in, are cramped, worn, and dusty, as is the Twists' sad little four-room ranch house, "two down, two up;"[62] unlike many filmmakers who can't resist upscaling and prettifying the conditions in which millions of ordinary working people live, the makers of *Brokeback Mountain* treat Proulx's realism with respect. But the casting of Jack and Ennis does avoid the physical deficiencies attributed to them in the story, which probably was impossible not to do in casting a film intended for a broad audience. In the story, while Ennis is described as muscular and strong, Proulx also notes that he's slightly cave-chested, which certainly doesn't describe Ledger. While Proulx describes Jack as lively, warm, and humorous, she doesn't give him the masculine beauty of Gyllenhaal. Also, incidentally, it's notable that in the film Jack is presented in ways that soften him slightly more than in the story. In both, he isn't quite the bull rider he'd like to be, but the film also suggests that he's not quite as good with a gun as Ennis. As has been mentioned, when the two men hunt and shoot the elk on the mountain, Ennis kids Jack about being a bad shot, and an earlier scene in the film shows Jack taking aim at a coyote and missing; the story doesn't indicate that he's not a good marksman, and indeed it notes that he proudly wears in his hatband the tail feather of the eagle he tells Ennis he shot his first summer on the mountain. But still, as they're presented in the film the two characters are convincingly like the young men Proulx created in the story. They look scruffy and wear simple, cheap work clothes—Ennis's particularly look like they've had a lot of use. Neither is made to seem special, and neither is presented in a way that's out of keeping with the kinds of hard lives Proulx attributes to them.

The story and the film don't qualify the masculinity of Ennis or Jack. Both men exemplify many aspects of the traditional American ideal of masculinity, particularly as it's expressed in its most intensely libertarian, individualistic Western form: they're strong, independent, self-reliant men, competent at any kind of physical work or activity, indeed excelling in many activities that are challenging and dangerous. They're able horsemen, hunters, bull and bronc riders, and can work and live and travel easily in harsh, demanding wilderness conditions. Both know and understand animals well, the domestic ones they work with and the wild ones they hunt. They can do the hard and dirty work of caring for domestic animals and of butchering game. Both are outdoorsmen, and indoor life holds little appeal for them; Ennis isn't a reader, and Jack, as Ennis tells Alma, isn't the restaurant type, preferring cooking over a campfire. Both have grown up in impoverished and difficult circumstances, learning early on how to fend for themselves. Both speak in the rough, pungent vernacular of ranch life; though neither is grammatical, each is adept in the use of vivid, homely, sometimes obscene metaphor that can capture exactly what he means. While Jack is loquacious, particularly with Ennis, Ennis usually is a man of few words with anyone except Jack. Jack's greater demonstrativeness is related to a subtle but important difference between him and Ennis; Ennis is more emotionally closed, and not only speaks less to others about what he feels than Jack does, but is less able to acknowledge his feelings to himself. As the story and the movie progress, both develop the implications of this difference, using it to provide an important critique of the limitations of traditional constructions of masculinity.

Although in the world of the American West men who work with sheep often are looked down upon by men who work with cattle, to a general American audience of readers or filmgoers Ennis and Jack fit closely the ideal icon of American manhood which has been repeated over and over for nearly two centuries, first in popular fiction and performance, then in film, TV, music, and advertising, the heroic image of the cowboy. Dime novels; Buffalo Bill's Wild West Show; more than a century of Western movies (starting with the first American film, *The Great Train Robbery*, in 1903); innumerable TV "horse operas", generations of country music stars in boots, jeans, Western shirts, and cowboy hats; the enormously successful ad campaign for Marlboro cigarettes; and wealthy and well-connected politicians who seek to garner votes by trying to present themselves as hardworking ranchers all continually reinforce the iconic status of the cowboy as the epitome of American masculinity. For a lot of Americans, their heroes have always been cowboys. What makes both versions of *Brokeback Mountain* so powerful in their critique of traditional assumptions about masculinity and sexuality is that the two "cowboys" they present desire men. As Willie Nelson sings in his recent song, recorded years ago but released on Valentine's Day, 2006, "Cowboys Are Frequently, Secretly (Fond of Each Other)."[63]

In both the story and the film, the friendship between the two men, with the intense but silent mutual attraction that's developed over their first several weeks of living and working on the mountain, finally builds to a passionate fulfillment. After their "high-time supper"[64] they move to a new camp farther from the sheep. Ennis has to ride an even longer distance for meals at the main camp, and, because of his enjoyment of Jack's company, he spends more and more time away from the sheep. As the screenplay indicates, they've become friendlier with each other.[65] Gyllenhaal continues to portray Jack as lively and humorous, and Ledger becomes more animated, his face lighting up with a smile when he talks and jokes. In the evening at their new camp, as Ennis finishes setting up the tent, Jack plays his harmonica, flattened from a fall off his skittish mare. (Incidentally, a subtle detail is worth noting: the tune Gyllenhaal plays is "He Was a Friend of Mine," the elegaic song about male friendship that closes the film.) The movie uses Jack's music-making to develop the playful, affectionate teasing between them. Listening to Jack on the harmonica, Ennis observes that the harmonica doesn't sound quite right, eliciting Jack's explanation about being thrown by the mare, to which Ennis replies by joshing Jack about the way he bragged about his ability as a rider. To this, Jack excuses himself by saying that the mare got lucky, bringing Ennis back to the harmonica with the wry crack that if *he* got lucky, the harmonica "woulda broke in two," which makes Jack laugh. The kidding about the harmonica continues through the film during the part set on Broke-back Mountain and on the later trips Ennis and Jack make together, a signifier of the playful affection between the two men. One of the many subtle insights into the continuity between friendship and love between men that's offered by both the movie and the story is the recognition that teasing between men often can be a form of flirtation.

In the story, during their evenings by the fire after supper in the new camp, Ennis joins Jack in singing, and though their singing's rough, it's enthusiastic. The songs Proulx says they sing are suggestive of the forces that draw them together. "The Strawberry Roan" is a cowboy song about a rider who takes on, and comically is defeated by, a famous, unrideable bucking horse:

> With a big forward jump he goes up on high
> Leaves me sittin on nothin way up in the sky
>
> I turns over twice, and I comes back to earth
> I lights in a-cussin the day of his birth
> I know there is ponies I'm unable to ride
> Some are still livin, they haven't all died.
>
> Well, it's oh, that strawberry roan,
> Oh, that strawberry roan!
> I'll bet all my money the man ain't alive
> That can stay with old strawberry when he makes his high dive!
> Oh, that strawberry roan![66]

The "salty" version of it, which Proulx says Ennis sings, is salty for sure, and in a way that attests the rough realities of work with animals on a farm or a ranch, and also celebrates the indomitable sexual energy of the stallion. After commencing with a scene in a whorehouse and providing a long, comically obscene account of the struggles of the rider and his boss to ride the roan, the song tells how the rider's boss, in a frustrated rage, declares that they should castrate the roan, which turns out to be bad for all involved, but worst of all for the boss. The two men succeed in holding the horse down and removing one testicle, but the horse breaks loose, and castrates the boss!

> Just then I heard one of them blood-curdlin squalls
> And I looked and the roan had the boss by the balls
>
> I tromped on his head, but it wasn't no use,
> He was just like a bulldog, he wouldn't turn loose
> So I untied his legs, and he got to his feet,
> But the boss's voice changed, and I knew we was beat.
>
> Oh, the strawberry roan, I advise you to leave him alone
> He's a knot-headed cayuse with only one ball,
> And the boss he's a eunuch with no balls at all,
> Lay off of the strawberry roan![67]

Ennis's choice of the salty version of "The Strawberry Roan," of course, suggests his consideration of Jack's love of the challenge and skill involved in bronc and bull riding, but it also indicates his complex awareness of masculine sexuality and relationships. The song celebrates the male sexual energy of the roan, his refusal to submit, and his success in keeping his maleness at least partly intact, yet it also warns of the danger of an assault by other males, the terrifying and sickening threat of violence whose specific aim is castration. In these aspects, the song hints at the mixture of joy and fear that will mark Ennis's relationship with Jack, his struggle as a man who loves another man in a homophobic society that denies the masculinity of man-loving men and that may try to destroy both of them because of their love.

In the story, Jack first sings a Carl Perkins song, though it's hard to be sure which one, since all we get is the wild rockabilly wail "'what I say-ay-ay'"[68]; still, Jack's version of this one line evokes the manic, reckless sexiness of the songs that made Perkins famous in the 1950s, like "Honey Don't," "Glad All Over," and "Don't Step on My Blue Suede Shoes." But in contrast to this, Proulx tells us that Jack's favorite is a slow, sad hymn, "Water-Walking Jesus,"[69] that Jack learned from his mother "who believed in the Pentecost."[70] A world of meaning about Jack's character, and the developing relationship between him and Ennis, lies in this detail. It suggests the sadness, loneliness, and fear that marked Jack's childhood, which Ennis only will understand when he visits the Twist ranch after Jack's death and meets his embittered, brutal, threatening father and his beaten, weakly compassionate mother. Jack's had little love from anyone except his mother, who's entirely dominated by his father; John C. Twist, rather than love, feels only contempt for his son, as we eventually learn in sickening detail. Neither Ennis or Jack has had much of the unconditional love and support that supposedly are the fundamental contribution parents make to their children; as for so many men attracted to men, the story and the film suggest that their families' responses to them were conditioned, even in childhood, by their fathers' unarticulated but strong and hostile awareness of sexual difference. Part of the power and poignancy of the love between Jack and Ennis is that, if it too weren't conditioned and limited by the hatred of men who are sexually different that both have witnessed in childhood, it could provide both of them with the kind of family neither ever has had.

Though in the story Proulx only gives the title of the hymn that she imagines Jack singing, her involvement in the film, and the sensitivity of those who made it, allowed her to assist the musicians in writing the two lines that Gyllenhaal hoarsely belts out. The movie doesn't depict Ennis as singing on his evenings with Jack, but in this scene he accompanies the hymn by beating time with a stick, and Ledger continues to present Ennis as being far more animated than earlier. Gyllenhaal's husky singing voice is complemented by the country/bluegrass sound of Santaolalla's beautiful, gentle score. Santaolalla's music accompanies the scenes depicting the men arriving on the mountain, setting up camp, and establishing their routine, and then falls silent, but returns at the close of their "high time supper,"[71] becoming more expansive with the exuberant sound of a pedal steel guitar during the scenes in which they shift to the new camp and joke about the harmonica. The music suggests the growing feeling the two men have for each other, subtly emphasizing the development of their mutual attraction and anticipating the ensuing episodes depicting them making love.

The hymn and the reference to the Pentecost are significant for the consummation of the love between the two men in profound ways. In the story and the film, on an evening of drinking and singing, they stay up so late and drink so much that Ennis can't get it together to ride back to the sheep, and eventually sleeps in the tent with Jack, leading to their overwhelmingly intense first sexual experience together. Each man has been drawn to the other, but neither has planned that their attraction will be consummated when and how it is; the moment comes upon them by chance. In both versions, the scene preceding that in which Ennis joins Jack in the tent and they make love is the one by the campfire where Jack sings the Pentecostal hymn; of course, one effect of this juxtaposition of Pentecostal Protestant belief and male intercourse is ironic, reminding us, even just when Jack and Ennis are about to consummate their attraction, of the legions of pious, self-righteous Americans who condemn same-sex love, of the profound distrust of sexuality in general in much of American religion and of the strident hatred of homosexuality in particular. Indeed, while Pentecostalism generally places more emphasis on the shared ecstatic experience of the Holy Spirit than most other brands of

Protestantism, and usually somewhat less on the enthusiastic condemnation of others to hellfire that's characteristic of many Evangelicals, nonetheless many Pentecostals are relentless in their denunciation of what they label "sodomy," which they perceive as being caused by demonic possession requiring exorcism.[72] But there's a further, much more powerful and subversive irony in what Proulx has done—she suggests that Jack and Ennis are about to enjoy their *own* miracle of Pentecost together. To each young man, after a life of ignorance about his own sexuality, and isolation and loneliness enforced by living in a homophobic society that permits little discussion of homosexuality other than official condemnation, there's come a revelatory moment when the power of love frees him from his limitations, allowing him to commune with the other in a way that's as full and complete as possible. Each speaks freely in his native tongue, and each is completely understood by the other. Each expresses what he needs, and miraculously the other is able to comprehend his need and give it to him. On a late spring night—indeed, right at the time of Pentecost, which came on the second of June in 1963—they share a communion that simultaneously is physical and emotional, and which initiates a spiritual connection that lasts until death, and indeed, beyond it. Proulx doesn't say so directly, but as she presents it the episode implies that, much as for Walt Whitman in "Song of Myself" and indeed for many others who have conceived of sex in terms of divine power (and perhaps of the divine in terms of sexual power), the Holy Spirit of divine love pours out as a sexual ecstasy, a gift that creates a union between Jack and Ennis that proves to be indissoluble.[73]

What happens between the two men is miraculous for both, but perhaps especially so for Ennis. As Proulx presents him and as he's depicted in the film, he's the more repressed of the two, the more committed to the ideal of American masculinity that allows no emotion to show. And Ennis is a particularly striking example of this model of American manhood, since he has so much emotion to hide, and those emotions are ones that he and most other men believe have to be hidden, because they're focused on another man. For Ennis, the love he discovers with Jack offers the opportunity of release from the constraints of masculinity that he's been taught by his father and brother and the other men he's known, the possibility of a form of salvation, not only in companionship with another person, but in the acknowledgement of himself to himself.

The screenplay expands the episode when Jack sings the hymn in important ways, showing that McMurtry and Ossana recognize the significance of what Proulx has done in her reference to the Pentecost. After Jack sings, he comments to Ennis, by way of explanation, that his mama believes in the Pentecost, to which Ennis replies with friendly curiosity that his folks were

Methodist, and asks what exactly the Pentecost is. Jack starts to explain, but doesn't get very far, realizing he doesn't have a clue. This slightly drunken, comical moment adds to the serious point, which becomes clear as the night continues and Ennis and Jack discover their mutual passion, that they at last *do* find an explanation of it, and of themselves as individuals and as selves in communion with each other, in the sexual and emotional revelation that transforms their lives. Also, in the film, after Jack realizes he has no idea what the Pentecost is, he comments ironically, indicating his awareness of the self-righteous intolerance and sexphobia of so much American religion, "I guess it's when the world ends and fellas like you and me march off to hell." Ennis's jesting reply is "Unh uh, speak for yourself. You may be a sinner, but I ain't yet had the opportunity," indicating an important fact about Ennis's own experience: apparently he's a virgin. He has no experience with women, though he's already become engaged, and now is just about to discover that what really is right for him, given his sexuality, is sex and love with a man. This detail thus forecasts the dilemma in which Ennis is forced to place himself, and Jack, and Alma, and even eventually Lureen, when he goes ahead with his marriage to Alma because the fear of fully accepting his sexuality forces him to try to conform to the homophobic, heterosexist expectations of his society.

The discovery that Jack and Ennis make on Brokeback Mountain, of course, is one that lots of ordinary young men have made, and continue to make. In a culture that teaches that love between men negates masculinity, for such young men the process of realizing and acting on a desire for men can evoke intense shame and fear. Some realize from it that they need to have their physical and emotional lives with men, and come to think of themselves as gay; others may engage in sexual relations with men and sometimes establish emotional connections with them, but never make such an identification. As noted earlier, particularly in rural contexts men who may have sexual and emotional relations with men, but don't identify as gay, sometimes have referred to themselves, and are described by some who study their experience, as queer. For some men who are queer in this sense of the word, it's possible, and sometimes preferable, to maintain intimate relationships with men that remain partly or entirely hidden from others, but this also can shape and limit the possibilities of their relationships in significant ways. For most, it's necessarily not possible to live with another man with whom they have a strong sexual and emotional relationship. Some queer men establish heterosexual relationships, marriages, and families, but still continue to feel and often act upon their feelings for other men; sometimes they're able to balance these parts of their lives and to meet the needs of those with whom they're involved, but sometimes this situation becomes one that neither they, or their wives or their male partners, are able to live with.[74]

Although Ennis and Jack aren't able to talk about their sexuality, and refuse to label themselves as "queers," after their initial night together they don't withdraw from what they've experienced or from each other, but continue their lovemaking, which becomes even more exuberant over the course of their summer together on the mountain. And not only is their communion profoundly physical, but it also is profoundly emotional. They delight in each other, playing, teasing, chasing, wrestling, fucking, and sleeping in the warmth of each other's arms. The film, perhaps reflecting assumptions about the heterosexual audience's resistance to the representation of love between men, depicts Ennis as feeling a degree of hesitation and doubt when he first sleeps with Jack, though he overcomes these feelings; there's none of this in the story, which tells us, after describing Jack sleeping "butted against"[75] Ennis after intercourse on their first night together, that though they say nothing about what's happened, both of them "knew how it would go for the rest of the summer, sheep be damned. As it did go."[76]

The depth of the attraction between the two men, as mentioned before, is manifested in the repeated use of the word "friend." Jack, who's more emotionally open than Ennis, uses it repeatedly in their conversation, during the summer on the mountain and then later in his message to Ennis reinitiating contact after four years, and in their conversations together over the next sixteen years. Ennis, indicating his greater reserve, particularly his fear of fully embracing his sexuality and his relationship with Jack, never uses it as a way of directly addressing Jack, though he does use the word to refer to him to Alma and to Lureen. With the sensitivity and insight concerning men who love men that marks the entire film, the filmmakers recognize the significance of the word, and, as the film closes, leaving Ennis alone with only the memory of Jack, use the Willie Nelson performance of the touching traditional song, "He Was a Friend of Mine," which takes an ordinary phrase employing the word and exalts it to the level of a tragic vernacular elegy, expressing the pain and grief of a man over the death of his friend.

In insisting on the depth and power of emotion between Ennis and Jack—as well as the depth and power of their sexual attraction and fulfillment—both the story and the film offer a strong and healthy challenge to the endlessly repeated homophobic stereotype of men who love men as being motivated only by sex, and so as being sexually promiscuous, shallow, and incapable of sustained commitment or stable relationships. For many straight people, when they think of man-loving men, they immediately think only in terms of sex acts between them, and immediately express their disgust at what they think such sex is like. Being such a man, as they construct it, is reduced to indulging in sex acts that they imagine as violent, filthy, and obscene. When they see a man and a woman kissing or holding hands, or when they see images of a heterosexual couple in a romantic situation, or of a bride and a groom, they don't immediately think in terms of the sex acts that the two people probably are soon to perform, but they often do when they see two gay or queer men together. To heterosexuals, other heterosexuals are complete human beings, for whom sexuality is only one aspect of their existence with other people, along with a complete spectrum of possible shared emotion and human companionship; gay or queer men often are reduced to mere signifiers of the sex acts they supposedly perform. The story and the movie challenge this appropriation of the complete range of human feeling by heterosexuals alone, and powerfully insist on the full humanity of man-loving men as both lovers and as friends. In both versions of the narrative, the intensity of emotion between the two men is palpable every time they're together, but whereas in traditional American culture emotion is associated with femininity, the emotion Jack and Ennis display, including gentle affection, humor and playfulness, intense frustration and anger, profound longing, and passionate, ecstatic desire, isn't presented in ways that feminize them. The story and the film show the deep, complex feelings between the two men over a twenty-year period, but while both men exhibit a great range of intense emotion toward each other, both consistently are presented in terms of the iconic masculinity of the American West. For a society struggling to move beyond the confining limits of traditional gender ideology, as well as homophobia, *Brokeback Mountain* demonstrates to Americans that it's possible to be a man and to express emotion, and to do so to another man.

One last point about Proulx's representation of the profound spiritual significance of the friendship between Jack and Ennis, and the subtlety with which she challenges the pervasive hatred of love between men by many who like to claim to be "Christians." As has been mentioned, in her description of their first full day and night of work on the mountain, when Ennis tends camp and Jack first stays overnight on the meadow above with the sheep, Proulx notes how each of them looks at the other across the distance: "During the day Ennis looked across a great gulf and sometimes saw Jack, a small dot moving across a high meadow as an insect moves across a tablecloth; Jack, in his dark camp, saw Ennis as night fire, a red spark on the huge black mass of the mountain."[77] In this description, Proulx's use of the famous phrase "a great gulf," which comes from the parable of Dives and Lazarus in the Gospel According to Saint Luke, has richly suggestive, ironic significance in terms of her presentation of the transcendent, redemptive power of love between men. In recounting the teachings of Jesus to the Disciples, Luke retells the parable, which is one of the saddest depictions of human estrangement in the Gospels. Dives, a rich man, is incapable of feeling any compassion for the sufferings of Lazarus, a poor beggar dying at his gate; after Lazarus dies, he is "carried by the angels into Abraham's bosom,"[78] while Dives dies too, and "in hell . . .

lift up his eyes, being in torments, and seeth Abraham afar off, and Lazarus in his bosom."[79] Dives begs Father Abraham to send Lazarus to bring him water "and cool my tongue, for I am tormented in this flame,"[80] but Abraham refuses, observing Dives's failure to have ministered to Lazarus in life, adding, "And beside all this, between us and you there is a great gulf fixed: so that they which would pass from hence to you cannot; neither can they pass to us, that would come from thence."[81] The great gulf is that between Heaven and Hell, but also between people who are incapable of compassion for one another. The unbridgeable distance between them condemns them to the Hell of individual isolation, denying them the Heaven of companionship with another human being. In her depiction of the intense awareness Jack and Ennis have of each other across the great gulf between the high meadow and the camp, which grows into a love that binds them together for life and even after Jack's death, Proulx indicates the potential of love to bridge the separation of selves which is perhaps the fundamental source of pain in the human condition. Whitman, and some writers influenced by him who affirmed love between men, such as Edward Carpenter, E. M. Forster, and Allen Ginsberg, could see the potential of same-sex love to assist in reducing human isolation and indifference, and in particular see how male love could bind together men who were separated by the competitive, individualistic, materialistic values and even, potentially, the differences of class, race, religion, and ethnicity that divide modern society.[82] Like them, Proulx does not limit her understanding of love to that between man and woman, or to love in the general, nonsexual sense of empathy, but recognizes and affirms the power of love between people of the same sex to be as much a source of unity, bridging the estrangement and differences between selves, as any other form. She sees that love between two men can be equal to any other love.

NOTES

1. For a general overview of the representation in literature of men who love men, probably the best basic resource is Claude J. Summers, ed., *The Gay and Lesbian Literary Heritage: A Reader's Companion to the Writers and Their Works, from Antiquity to the Present* (Revised edition; New York: Routledge, 2002). Gregory Woods provides a useful survey in *A History of Gay Literature: The Male Tradition* (New Haven: Yale University Press, 1998). On representations of man-loving men in film, see the pioneering study by Vito Russo, *The Celluloid Closet* (New York: Harper and Row, 1987), as well as Benshoff and Griffin, *Queer Images*.
2. Proulx, "Brokeback Mountain," 4.
3. Proulx, "Brokeback Mountain," 5.

4. On the American Dream, constructions of masculinity, and their effects, see Kimmel, *Manhood in America*.

5. Proulx, "Brokeback Mountain," 7.

6. See Kimmel, *Manhood in America* and "Masculinity as Homophobia."

7. There is thoughtful discussion of the divisive effects of individualism in *Habits of the Heart: Individualism and Commitment in American Life*, by Robert N. Bellah, Richard Madsen, William M. Sullivan, Ann Swidler, and Steven M. Tipton (Berkeley: University of California Press, 1985.) The development of whiteness as a privileged category is discussed in David R. Roediger, *The Wages of Whiteness: Race and the Making of the American Working Class* (New York: Verso, 1991).

8. Annie Proulx, "Getting Movied," in Annie Proulx, Larry McMurtry, Diana Ossana, *Brokeback Mountain: Story to Screenplay* (New York: Scribner, 2005), 130.

9. On male homosocial and homosexual relationships and the maintenance of boundaries between the two, see Kimmel, "Masculinity as Homophobia"; Plummer, *One of the Boys*; and Levine, *Gay Macho*.

10. On the homosocial arena in which men compete with each other for masculine status, see Kimmel, "Masculinity as Homophobia"; Plummer, *One of the Boys*; and Levine, *Gay Macho*.

11. On fear of losing the possession of masculinity, see Kimmel, "Masculinity as Homophobia."

12. On the importance of homosocial bonding in all-male groups, see Kimmel, "Masculinity as Homophobia," and Plummer, *One of the Boys*.

13. The attraction many man-loving men feel for homosocial groups such as fraternities, sports teams, and military forces has been widely discussed, especially in personal narratives; see Shane Windmeyer, Pamela Freeman, eds., *Out on Fraternity Row: Personal Accounts of Being Gay in a College Fraternity* (Los Angeles: Alyson, 1998); Shane Windmeyer, ed., *Brotherhood: Gay Life in College Fraternities* (New York: Alyson, 2005); David Kopay (with Perry Deane Young), *The David Kopay Story* (New York: Arbor House, 1977); Billy Bean (with Chris Bull), *Going the Other Way: Lessons from a Life In and Out of Major-League Baseball* (New York: Marlowe, 2003); Esera Tuaolo (with John Rosengren), *Alone in the Trenches: My Life as a Gay Man in the NFL* (Napierville: Sourcebooks, 2006); Jon Barrett, *Hero of Flight 93: Mark Bingham* (New York: Alyson, 2002); Steven Zeeland, *Masculine Marine*; Jeffrey McGowan (Major, U.S. Army, Ret.), *Major Conflict: One Gay Man's Life in the Don't -Ask-Don't-Tell Military* (New York: Broadway Books, 2005).

14. Useful discussions of rodeo are provided in Wayne S. Wooden and Gavin Ehringer, *Rodeo in America: Wranglers, Roughstock, and Paydirt* (Lawrence: University of Kansas, 1999); Dirk Johnson, *Biting the Dust: The Wild Ride and Dark Romance of the Rodeo Cowboy and the American West* (New York: Simon and Schuster, 1994); and W. K. Stratton, *Chasing the Rodeo: On Wild Rides and Big Dreams, Broken Hearts and Broken Bones, and One Man's Search for the West* (New York: Harvest, 2005.)

15. Proulx, "Brokeback Mountain," 7.

16. On the various homophobic stereotypes of men who love men, see Herek, *Stigma and Sexual Orientation*; Sears, *Overcoming Heterosexism*; Blumenfeld, *Homophobia*; and Biery, *Understanding Homosexuality*.

17. On attitudes toward anal eroticism and sexual minority men, see sections on "Anal sex" in Wayne Dynes, ed., *The Encyclopedia of Homosexuality* (New York: Garland, 1990).

18. "When I Heard at the Close of the Day," ll. 5–13, Whitman, *Leaves of Grass* (Ninth edition/1892).

19. See Peter Nardi, *Gay Men's Friendships: Invincible Communities* (Chicago: University of Chicago, 1999), and his edited volume, *Men's Friendships* (Thousand Oaks: Sage, 2004.) Many personal narratives by men who love men discuss the importance of adolescent friendships in the process of their recognition of same-sex desire.

20. Larry McMurtry, Diana Ossana, "Brokeback Mountain: A Screenplay," in Annie Proulx, Larry McMurtry, Diana Ossana, *Brokeback Mountain: Story to Screenplay* (New York: Scribner, 2005), 2 of screenplay.

21. Proulx, "Brokeback Mountain," 8.

22. See Boag, *Same-Sex Affairs*, and Packard, *Queer Cowboys*.

23. Proulx, "Getting Movied," 131.

24. Proulx, "Getting Movied," 131.

25. Proulx, "Getting Movied," 131–32.

26. Proulx, "Brokeback Mountain," 9.

27. Proulx, "Brokeback Mountain," 9.

28. Proulx, "Brokeback Mountain," 9.

29. Proulx, "Brokeback Mountain," 9.

30. Quinn, *Same-Sex Dynamics*; Fellows, *Farm Boys*; John Gerassi, *The Boys of Boise: Furor, Vice, and Folly in an American City* (Seattle: University of Washington Press, 2001/1966); and Miller, *Sex-Crime Panic: A Journey to the Paranoid Heart of the 1950's* (Los Angeles, Alyson, 2002) all provide evidence of the danger of homophobic condemnation for men who desired men in the time period when Proulx imagines Ennis and Jack growing up.

31. Proulx, "Brokeback Mountain," 10.

32. McMurtry and Ossana, "Screenplay," 15.

33. Proulx, "Brokeback Mountain," 10.

34. Proulx, "Brokeback Mountain," 11.

35. Proulx, "Brokeback Mountain," 11.

36. Proulx, "Brokeback Mountain," 12.

37. Proulx, "Brokeback Mountain," 12.

38. Norman Polmar, *The Death of the U.S.S. Thresher: The Story behind History's Deadliest Submarine Disaster* (Stonington: Lyons Press 2004/1964).

39. Proulx, "Brokeback Mountain," 12.

40. Proulx, "Brokeback Mountain," 11.

41. Proulx, "Brokeback Mountain," 12.

42. Proulx, "Brokeback Mountain," 11.

43. Proulx, "Brokeback Mountain," 11.

44. Proulx, "Brokeback Mountain," 11.

45. Proulx, "Brokeback Mountain," 7.

46. Proulx, "Brokeback Mountain," 7.

47. Proulx, "Brokeback Mountain," 7.

48. "Jake Gyllenhaal Talks about *Brokeback Mountain*: Jake Gyllenhaal on *Brokeback Mountain* and His Love Scenes with Heath Ledger." Rebecca Murray, Your Guide to Hollywood Movies, About.com, *New York Times*, no date, 2006 (http://www.moviesabout.com/od/brokebackmountain/a/brokeback112905.htm, July 29, 2007).

49. The extensive scholarly literature on the significance of the gaze began with John Berger, *Ways of Seeing* (London: BBC/Penguin, 1972), and Laura Mulvey, "Visual Pleasure and Narrative Cinema" (originally published 1975) in John Caughie *et. al.*, eds., *The Sexual Subject: A Screen Reader in Sexuality* (London: Routledge, 1992). Suzanna Danuta Walters provides a useful discussion of women and the gaze in *Material Girls: Making Sense of Feminist Cultural Theory* (Berkeley: University of California Press, 1995). Levine, *Gay Macho*, and Plummer, *One of the Boys*, discuss men and social codes of looking. The quotation is from Berger, 47.

50. On homophobic codes limiting men looking at men, see Levine, *Gay Macho*, and Plummer, *One of the Boys*.

51. On looking and cruising, see Plummer, *One of the Boys*; Dynes, "Cruising," in *Encyclopedia*; and Levine, *Gay Macho*.

52. On cruising, see Dynes, "Cruising," in *Encyclopedia*, and Levine, *Gay Macho*.

53. "City of Orgies," ll. 7–9, in Whitman, *Leaves of Grass* (Ninth edition/1892).

54. "Among the Multitude," in Whitman, *Leaves of Grass* (Ninth edition/1892).

55. On efforts to suppress recognition of Whitman's concern with male-male desire, see Robert K. Martin, *The Homosexual Tradition in American Poetry*, and Byrne R.S. Fone, *Masculine Landscapes: Walt Whitman and the Homoerotic Text* (Carbondale: Southern Illinois University Press, 1992).

56. Though the phenomenon of "gaydar" is widely recognized, scholarly literature tends to treat it as gay folklore; the closest any scholar I've read comes to really analyzing it is Levine, in his discussion of "cruising, searching, stalking, and signaling," Levine, *Gay Macho*.

57. University of Wisconsin, Madison: Campus News: "A Local Author's Work Inspires *Brokeback Mountain* Production," Jan. 10, 2006 (http://news.wisc.edu/11998, July 29, 2007).

58. Tim Cyr, as quoted in *Brokeback Mountain: An Ang Lee Film: Production Notes*, 4.

59. Shane Madden, as quoted in *Production Notes*, 4.

60. *Production Notes*, 17.

61. Proulx, "Brokeback Mountain," 8.

62. Proulx, "Brokeback Mountain," 47.

63. The song, "Cowboys Are Frequently Secretly (Fond of Each Other)," was written by Ned Sublette in 1981, with Willie Nelson in mind as a performer. Nelson recorded it in the mid 1980's, but only released his version in 2006, coinciding with the attention being paid to *Brokeback Mountain*. His performance of the song was debuted on Valentine's Day on the Howard Stern show; there are other versions, including one by Pansy Division. "Willie Nelson's Gay Cowboy," Feb. 14, 2006 (http://www.365gay.com/newscon06/02/021406nelson.htm, July 29, 2007).

64. Proulx, "Brokeback Mountain," 11.

65. McMurtry and Ossana, "Screenplay," 16.

66. The widely popular folk song, "The Strawberry Roan," exists in many versions, and apparently was based on a poem, "The Outlaw Bronco," probably published in an Arizona newspaper in 1915. Some versions are relatively tame, others quite "salty."

67. The "salty" version of "The Strawberry Roan" cited here is referred to as "The Castration of the Strawberry Roan" (http://www.sniff.numachi.com/pages/tiCAS TROAN;ttSTRWROAN.html, July 29, 2007.)

68. Proulx, "Brokeback Mountain," 13.

69. Proulx, "Brokeback Mountain," 13.

70. Proulx, "Brokeback Mountain," 13.

71. Proulx, "Brokeback Mountain," 11.

72. On homophobia among Pentecostals, see the Encyclopedia of Gay, Lesbian, Bisexual, Transgendered, and Queer Culture (glbtq.com): entry by Jeffrey Dennis under "Social Sciences/Evangelical Christians," 2004; also see J. Gordon Melton, *The Churches Speak on Homosexuality: Official Statements from Religious Bodies and Ecumenical Organizations* (New York: Gale, 1991). For a general overview of the homophobia of the Christian Right, see Didi Herman, *The Antigay Agenda: Orthodox Vision and the Christian Right* (Chicago: University of Chicago Press, 1997).

73. *The Holy Bible*, King James Version: The Book of Acts, Chapter 2.

74. Howard, *Men Like That*, and Tate, "How They Do It," provide important perspectives on the experience of rural queer men.

75. Proulx, "Brokeback Mountain," 14.

76. Proulx, "Brokeback Mountain," 15.

77. Proulx, "Brokeback Mountain," 9.

78. *The Holy Bible*, King James Version: The Gospel According to Saint Luke, Chapter 16, Verse 22.

79. St. Luke, 16:23.

80. St. Luke, 16:24.

81. St. Luke, 16:26.

82. In his important essay, "Democratic Vistas," (1870) Whitman expresses his hope that "adhesiveness," the "manly love" he so often celebrated, can overcome differences between men. The possibility that attraction and love between men can become a counterforce correcting the divisiveness and competitiveness of a society in which men are separated by class, race, and possessive individualism was explored by man-loving men influenced by Whitman, such as the English social reformer and poet Edward Carpenter, the great novelist E. M. Forster, and the American Beat poet, Allen Ginsberg.

Chapter Two

"Gun's Goin *Off"*: Sex

Until movements to end discrimination against sexual minorities began to develop about four decades ago, the homophobia of the heterosexual majority kept sexual minorities mostly silent about their own perspectives on themselves and their sexualities. Before this change began, although men and women who loved those of their own sex sometimes described their relationships in positive terms in literature, members of the majority usually weren't interested in what they wrote and condemned it if they became aware of it. Same-sex love was dismissed as the "love that dare not speak its name,"[1] and the commercial mass media usually either ignored its existence or presented it according to the negative representations required by homophobic religious, medical, and political authorities. Hollywood had a well-established policy, until almost the time when the action of *Brokeback Mountain* begins, of refusing to represent sexual minorities; from the establishment of the Motion Picture Production Code in the early 1930s until the code began to break down in the early 1960s, films only could hint at the existence of sexual minorities, employing stereotypes of effeminate men and masculine women. This changed in the 1960s and 1970s, and especially in the past twenty-five years sexual minority people have become widely visible in the mass media, but they still often are presented in terms of the stereotypes the majority wants, and their sexual relationships often are ignored or are presented in terms of the majority's assumptions and prejudices. Most in the majority never consider the fact that members of sexual minorities must live in a culture that constantly represents and honors heterosexual sex, while lovemaking between people of the same sex usually is kept invisible or is presented with ridicule or with disgust.[2]

Central to the pervasive policy of rendering homosexuality invisible and silencing discussion of it was the majority's construction of same-sex intercourse as a "crime against nature" that was "unspeakable." Though gay, lesbian, bisexual, transgender, questioning, and queer people have forced American culture to break the silence about them, when it addresses their sexual relationships, especially sex between men, it's still consistently in negative ways. For homophobic straight men, anal intercourse between men is a particular source of both fear and fascination. As they construct it, it's obscene, repulsive, and brutal. Because in the dominant culture's patriarchal sexist ideology concerning intercourse between men and women the penis is associated with power and domination and the vagina with passivity and submission, anal intercourse is similarly constructed in terms of domination and submission. The man who enters is constructed as aggressive, and the man who is entered is constructed as passive. The "aggressor" is perceived in terms of male power, often as the potential gay rapist that some straight men fear will threaten to "come on to them" in the shower at the gym, the barracks, or the dorm; the "submissive" man, because his supposed submission associates him with women and femininity as they're constructed in the patriarchal sexist system, isn't perceived as a real man at all, but as an effeminate weakling who actually "lets" another man "stick it up his ass." For the majority of straight men, intercourse between men necessarily implies forcible entry of one man's body by another. Anal intercourse is constructed as anal rape, as in the rantings of the homophobes who denounced the sex scene in *Brokeback Mountain* as a "San Quentin–type rape."[3] The possibility of mutually gratifying erotic play between two men, of sexuality involving two penises, of male-male sexuality not requiring some pattern of domination and submission, aggression and passivity, is unimaginable, as is the possibility that anal intercourse could be mutually desirable and mutually pleasurable. Perhaps it may be remotely conceivable to homophobic straight men that a man of some sort might want to fuck another man, but the idea that a man might want to be fucked and still could be a man, and that two men might engage in fucking in ways in which each recognizes and seeks to satisfy the desires of the other, is inconceivable to most men in the majority. So too is the possibility that two men might alternate in giving and receiving this form of sexual pleasure. Perhaps least possible to imagine is that sharing this form of physical intimacy could be connected to sharing the deep emotional intimacy that's fundamental to a lasting relationship characterized by mutual respect and love.

But while the dominant culture has constructed anal intercourse as so repulsive and frightening as to be unimaginable, many straight men *do* seem to spend a lot of time imagining it, almost whenever the growing visibility of men who love men obliges them to think about them. Many straight men

seem to think of anal intercourse almost automatically, like some sort of homophobic Pavlovian conditioned reflex, whenever gay or queer men intrude
on their consciousness. In their awareness of these men, it's almost the only
thing they *can* think about. Certainly this was the case with many of the hostile reactions to *Brokeback Mountain,* such as those of Imus, Matthews, and
"Savage." Often straight men assume that anal sex is what all gay or queer
men do, ignoring the facts that many prefer other, different forms of sexual
interaction and that some straight couples have anal sex, and indeed the even
more inadmissible fact that some straight men themselves, in their sexual relations with women, desire anal stimulation. All men are born with prostates,
after all. It's difficult not to recognize that this may be an instance in which
fascination with a forbidden practice—and perhaps, for some, with a forbidden desire—causes the hysterical projection of both the practice and the desire onto an Other, a despised stereotype that represents all those things that
real men supposedly are not and never could be—and indeed supposedly
never would *want* to be. This process reassuringly locates the fascinating, forbidden issue of anal sex far away from the construction of the normal, heterosexual masculine self, as a practice unique to faggots, queers, fairies,
fruits, girliemen—men who are "butt pirates" and "fudgepackers." The projection of anal eroticism onto gay and queer men, and the reduction of their
existence to signifying anal intercourse, probably is one of the chief sources
of the ridicule, disgust, insult, hostility, and violence continually aimed by
straight men at gay and queer men.[4]

It also is likely the chief source of their discomfort with *Brokeback Mountain.* After all, the story and the film not only directly present scenes of anal
intercourse, but present it as the consummation of a passionate attraction between two men who correspond entirely to the culture's construction of masculinity. As has been discussed, the story and the film insist on the masculine
credentials of Jack and Ennis. The fact that the film repeatedly has been referred to with contempt in the media and in conversations around the country
as "that gay cowboy movie" demonstrates the anxiety that this causes for homophobic straight men—*Brokeback Mountain* is especially disturbing and
threatening because it locates male-male desire, and what it "really" means to
them, anal sex, in *their* territory, in the iconic world of the American West, the
ultimate national symbol of masculine independence and power. Thus it challenges all of their assumptions about sexual minority men, anal intercourse,
and American masculinity.

The degrees of candor and respect with which both versions of *Brokeback
Mountain* present sex between men are impressive given the particular inten-
sity of homophobic hostility toward anal intercourse in the dominant culture.
Until recently, homophobia made it virtually impossible to mention this form

of sexual activity at all, at least without the culturally requisite formulas of disgust and condemnation, and certainly to attempt to present it in a neutral way, much less to recognize or affirm the perspective of those who desire and enjoy it, was impossible. In its depiction of the love that the two men share during their summer on the mountain, the story entirely rejects the burden of negative meaning that the dominant culture has imposed on anal sex between men, and the film does so for the most part, though it includes elements not in the story that indicate anxiety on Ennis's part when he and Jack first make love. Of course, one of the fundamental points throughout both versions of the narrative is that the fear and shame that have been instilled in Ennis since childhood by a homophobic society prevent his acceptance of the desire he feels for Jack, with tragic consequences, but in the story his anxiety about Jack only starts as they leave the mountain. The screenwriters, though, suggest it before this, although this isn't in keeping with Proulx's depiction of the experience of the two men. As she describes them, in their union on the mountain they feel entirely free; when Ennis thinks back, after Jack's murder, on their experience there together, he remembers it as "that old, cold time on the mountain when they owned the world and nothing seemed wrong."[5] The mountain, especially for Ennis in the story, is a world elsewhere, free from the anxieties caused by homophobia.

For many men who love men, one of the most impressive aspects of Annie Proulx's imagination in creating "Brokeback Mountain" is her ability to affirm the reality of sexual passion between men without evasion or euphemism. She gives candid and substantial descriptions of the way that Ennis and Jack make love, with no explicit or implicit judgment from a perspective that's heterosexist or homophobic, and in fact with real recognition of what their sexual experience is like for them and what it means to them. All their lives men who love men witness the disgust, ridicule, contempt, condemnation, and hatred with which most in the heterosexual majority judge and represent sex between men, and many must struggle with their own internalization of the dominant culture's continuous hostile propaganda about male-male desire. Because of the anxiety about all forms of sexuality that pervades American culture, heterosexual intercourse certainly often is presented in negative ways, as dirty, obscene, degrading, scandalous, pruriently interesting, and titillating, but it also continually is presented as beautiful, romantic, and even, through religious ideology, as pure, exalted, and even sacred. The representation, or even the mention, of male-male intercourse never is accorded positive status by the dominant culture, but either is the subject of discomfort and so is avoided altogether as something repellent, or is overtly repudiated. It's a positive contrast, then, for many readers who are gay or queer to find that a major heterosexual writer represents intercourse between men on a level of acceptance equal to that often automatically given by the dominant culture to intercourse between men and women.

The movie's presentation of the sexual relationship between Ennis and Jack not only adds elements that suggest a degree of hesitation on Ennis's part when he and Jack first have sex, but later on, during their first reunion, omits some of the elements of the story that indicate how much both men desire and enjoy sexual intercourse with each other. Fortunately, however, the movie also adds an important episode when Jack and Ennis sleep together the second night that strongly and convincingly affirms the value of their sexual relationship. When the film was in production, many who were anticipating it doubted that the filmmakers would be capable of respecting the story's frank and sympathetic presentation of the way Ennis and Jack make love, and would eliminate any depiction of sexual intercourse or would entirely reject the positive way Proulx presents it. The changes made by the filmmakers aren't so major that they negate Proulx's approach, but they do alter the meaning of the narrative in significant ways, especially for viewers who haven't read the story. Despite these differences, the filmmakers had the conviction not to avoid depicting sex between men, and do depict some aspects of it much as Proulx does in the story. Overall, the film's presentation of the sexual relationship between the two men remains a positive one, showing that it's pleasurable and satisfying to both of them, but it's not as boldly affirming of their lovemaking as Proulx's story is. This difference is one of the most substantial that many viewers have objected to in the film, and though it doesn't by any means undercut the importance of the film as a remarkable effort to present intimate male-male experience from the perspective of men who love men, it does avoid challenging homophobic prejudices as strongly as Proulx's story and at least to a degree it even may allow some viewers to impose their negative views of male intercourse on what they see. In order to understand the significance of the changes made by the film, first it's important to appreciate what Proulx achieves in her presentation of the physical passion between Ennis and Jack.

As Proulx depicts it, the consummation of the attraction between Ennis and Jack comes easily, without any self-consciousness or hesitation. It's passionate and energetic, but clearly, like lots of men who love men, that's what both of them want. She explains that late one cold night after an evening of drinking and talking, joking and singing, Ennis, so drunk he's dizzy, decides it's too late to ride back to the sheep. At first he says he'll sleep by the fire, but Jack tells him he'll freeze his ass off, and so Ennis goes into the tent with his friend. He lies on the ground cloth, leaving Jack the single bedroll, but the sound of his teeth clacking from the cold wakes Jack, who irritably tells him to get under the covers with him, since the bedroll's big enough. Neither man is described as being consciously aware of the possibility of any physical involvement; it just happens as a natural result of their friendship and their intimacy in the situation. As Proulx presents the episode, the cold night, the warmth and limited size of the bedding they share, and the feeling of friendliness that's developed between them simply cause them to lie next to each other because it's warm and comfortable, and so this contact leads to sexual arousal. She comments that the bedroll *was* big enough, and warm enough, and so they soon "deepened their intimacy considerably."[6] It's the kind of contact many young men can wind up having together, if working or traveling or recreation puts them in a situation where they're sleeping next to each other. Close contact of this sort can cause one or both men to get sexually aroused; some stop at that point, aware of what's happened but afraid to act on it, but sometimes one man will take the risk of going farther. Sometimes his friend will want to go along, other times he'll retreat, and either way, in a homophobic society like ours, there's the question of what they'll do or say about it afterward.

In her description of what happens between Jack and Ennis as they lie together in the bedroll, Proulx deliberately makes the reader think for a moment that she may be about to describe anxiety or even anger on Ennis's part when Jack makes the first move, but she balks that expectation, instead emphasizing how completely Ennis embraces his passion for Jack. In her description of how it is that they come to have anal intercourse, she uses a complicated metaphor about Ennis's approach to life whose meaning isn't fully evident at first. She begins by saying Ennis "ran full throttle on all roads whether fence mending or money spending, and . . . wanted none of it when Jack seized his left hand and brought it to his erect cock."[7] This almost sounds as if she's about to tell us that Ennis rejects Jack, but then in the course of the next sentence she startles the reader by making the meaning of the "full throttle"[8] figure of speech clear, saying that Ennis "jerked his hand away as though he'd touched fire, got to his knees, unbuckled his belt, shoved his pants down, hauled Jack onto all fours and, with the help of the clear slick and some spit, entered him . . ."[9] Ennis is anything but resistant—as soon as Jack makes his own sexual desire known, Ennis takes charge and acts on what he wants to do. He doesn't reject sex with Jack, but rejects merely playing with his cock, and wants to fuck him—and Jack wants to be fucked. Jack makes the first move, but it's Ennis who goes the whole way.

In contrast to most of those who aren't gay or queer men, Proulx has the imagination and empathy and, above all, the freedom from homophobic assumptions to be able to conceive that both Ennis and Jack like what they're doing. When most straight people and even some lesbians actually try to discuss male anal intercourse, they frequently construct it as being coercive and violent; some who seek to be understanding of male-male sexual experience may perceive it as perhaps being desirable and necessary for the man who wants to enter the other man, but still as unpleasant and painful for the man who's entered. They seem to think of male intercourse as an inferior substitute that gay or queer men resort to because vaginal intercourse isn't possible. What's so impressive about Proulx is that there are none of these patronizing assumptions in her writing about Jack and Ennis. For them, as for lots of men who desire men, fucking isn't something that they "put up with" because it's the only way they can have a kind of intercourse approximating the "real thing," and that even the participants themselves find troubling and perhaps even disgusting, though somehow necessary.[10] Proulx repudiates this homophobic construction of male intercourse, and recognizes that the two men like it and want it, that it feels good to them, not just for Ennis to fuck Jack but for Jack to get fucked by Ennis. For those who aren't gay or queer men but who aspire to be accepting of them, this last point probably is the most difficult of all to deal with: there are men, many of them who identify as being masculine, who want to get fucked by other men. For many of them, it's not only an issue of sexual pleasure, but also of attaining an intense degree of physical closeness to a man they care about, affirming their mutual emotional connection. Perhaps the most remarkable thing about Annie Proulx's remarkable story, in this episode and subsequent ones, is that she gets this. There's no hesitation on Jack's part when Ennis enters him, and in fact, Proulx's language implicitly shows that she recognizes that their mutual desire for intercourse causes them to collaborate in doing it: she doesn't say that Ennis goes at it but rather that *they* go at it, they interact together to make intercourse satisfying for both of them. And instead of protesting, Jack actually makes a joke, a comic exclamation—filled with extraordinary implications—when Ennis comes inside him. The experience then ends easily and satisfyingly for both men; Ennis pulls out and they lie down and go to sleep. Jack's appreciation is evident in the way he sleeps for the rest of the night, "butted against"[11] Ennis. There's no worry, no concern, no anxiety, the next morning or until they leave the mountain; without saying anything about what they've done, they both "knew how it would go for the rest of the summer, sheep be damned. As it did go."[12]

The joke that Jack makes when Ennis comes not only demonstrates the pleasure and satisfaction he takes in getting fucked by Ennis, but also resonates with extraordinary significance in relation to Proulx's challenges to traditional constructions of homosexuality and masculinity, particularly her daring in locating male love within the iconic system of the American Western landscape and the figures of masculine Westerners. Proulx tells us that as they go at it together, they're silent except for their breathing and Jack's "choked 'gun's goin *off* . . ."[13] Her challenge to the dominant construction of heterosexual masculinity dares to go so far as to appropriate the foremost signifier of phallic power in the American national fantasy of the Western, the gun itself, making it the metaphor for the ecstatic consummation of male anal intercourse! Later on in the story, in her description of the argument Jack and Ennis have on the last day they ever spend together, Proulx, with her gift for the vernacular, employs a telling Western expression that perfectly describes what she's done in this sex scene by having Jack say what he does at the moment of sexual climax: with the metaphor of the gun going off that she has Jack use in his ejaculation when Ennis ejaculates, she's "cutting fence . . . trespassing in the shoot-'em zone!"[14]

Even though neither Jack or Ennis can identify as gay or queer, and the feelings of sexual attraction to men that they have remain silenced, perhaps even to themselves, Proulx makes it clear that there's an easiness for both of them about sex. Both are country boys who've grown up on ranches, constantly around horses, dogs, cattle and many other animals, and always aware of the continual processes of sex, birth, life, death, and new life among stock and wild animals. Both also are hunters. Both obviously like and understand the animals they work with. As they go up the mountain for the first time with their horses, mules, ewes, lambs, and dogs, Proulx tells us that the men bring along three puppies of one of the blue heelers in a pack basket, and that Jack takes the runt inside his coat, "for he loved a little dog."[15] Later in the story she indicates the love Ennis feels for his horses, who he speaks to more affectionately than to his wife. No matter what their families' attitudes were toward sex, for young men who like being outdoors and who like working with animals, sexual intercourse can't be an invisible, forbidden mystery—it's everywhere in their world. In corrals, barns, and farmyards, and on the plains and in the mountains, they've seen all types of it, over and over, throughout their lives, in contrast to young people in towns and cities for whom knowledge about it often is suppressed, distorted, and mystified, at least as much as possible, by adults. As Proulx observes in her essay on writing the story, "livestock workers have a blunt and full understanding of the sexual behaviors of man and beast."[16] The language the two men use reflects their easy awareness of the sexual lives of living things—Ennis describes the coyote, "balls on him size a apples,"[17] and notes the muscularity of Jack's butt—his "haunch"[18]—using a word taken from his work with stock. So the first time they make love, there's no doubt about what to do; as Proulx says, it isn't something Ennis ever has done but there's "no instruction manual needed."[19] Ennis and Jack have intercourse in a time-honored way, with a time-honored lubricant, available whenever the right circumstances arise.

The screenwriters and filmmakers present Ennis as being more hesitant about his sexual involvement with Jack, though they eventually confirm the

fundamental feeling of joy and satisfaction that he finds with Jack and that
Jack finds with him. The changes in the movie version begin before the men
get ready for sleep on the first night that they have sex in the tent. Ennis is depicted as being more physically distant from Jack than in the story; he
chooses to sleep outside by the fire, until the "hammerin" of his jaw from the
cold wakes Jack, who tells him to come inside. In the story, sharing the tent
with Jack isn't such a big deal for Ennis; in fact, Proulx indicates that he's already done it on the night of their first day on Brokeback, before Jack went
out to set up the illegal camp by the sheep, a detail that the film changes, having Jack go up to the sheep as soon as they've set up the main camp. The film
makes a number of other changes and additions that subtly suggest that Ennis is somewhat anxious at the start. It completely omits representation of
Proulx's observation that once they begin sharing the bedroll they take mutual pleasure in lying intimately together, which then leads to Jack moving
Ennis's hand to his cock. Instead, in the movie at the moment that Jack takes
hold of Ennis's hand, we see Ennis lying next to him, but no more closely
than he was when he first lay down. And more significantly, when Jack moves
Ennis's hand to his cock, instead of instantly taking charge as he does in the
story, Ennis at first responds with confusion. He sits up and pulls back sharply
as Jack sits up in front of him; Jack grabs Ennis by the shoulder and the lapel,
pulling him closer and then getting out of his coat, which causes Ennis to ask
what he's doing. But this immediately is resolved: they grapple, and each man
holds the back of the other's head, roughly caressing his hair, as they lean
their foreheads together for a moment almost as if they're about to kiss. Then
Jack unbuckles his belt, Ennis turns him around, unbuttoning his own fly, and
Jack raises his butt and Ennis pulls down Jack's Wranglers, exposing the pale
skin of his ass, and mounts him.

As the actors present the scene, the sexual experience the men have is passionate, energetic, and powerful, as it is for many gay or queer men. Ledger
presents Ennis, once he's overcome his confusion, as knowing just what he
wants, much as in the story, and Gyllenhaal indicates no hesitation or resistance on Jack's part when they start going at it. Just as Proulx says, it's evident that Ennis uses spit as a lubricant, and there are plenty of sudden intakes
of breath indicating Ennis is entering Jack. The camera initially concentrates
on Ennis's intent expression as he enters Jack, but then cuts to a shot of Jack's
reaction; as Gyllenhaal presents him, Jack rocks up and down under his
friend, grunting and gasping at the sensation of having him inside him, tightly
shutting his eyes at the intensity of it but for just a moment almost smiling,
indicating the pleasure he feels. As Ennis comes, Jack slams his hand down
and then puts his hand over his friend's, grasping hand-over-hand, as Ennis
finishes. Unfortunately, Proulx's brilliant touch in having Jack exclaim,
"'gun's goin *off*'"[20] apparently proved to be too much for the screenwriters.

Not only does this omission erase her ironic juxtaposition of male intercourse with the ultimate American symbol of traditional masculine phallic power, but more importantly it eliminates the clearest indication she makes in the episode of Jack's positive feelings about what Ennis is doing. Still, anyone who follows the scene closely can see that the actors present the intercourse between the two men as something that they're both eager for and that they both enjoy, but it does lack the positive, humorous detail Proulx uses to show just how much pleasure Jack takes in having Ennis inside him.

Without Jack's exclamation, and given the less intimate way that Ennis and Jack are presented before they have sex and the shortness of the sex scene itself, the depiction of the first time the men fuck thus is susceptible to misinterpretation by homophobic viewers. There's little to offend male viewers who are gay or queer, but there's also little to challenge the assumptions that so many viewers who aren't often impose on male-male sex. What happens between Jack and Ennis is abrupt and aggressive and passionate, and instead of recognizing that that's sometimes the way sex between men is, and that some men like it, viewers who are inclined to do so may be enabled to mobilize their assumptions about anal sex between men as a form of violence. Hence we get the reactions by those like Kupelian, Baehr, and other homophobes, who want to construct the sex scene as rape. What happens in the film between the men on the second night, of course, makes this hostile distortion of their intercourse impossible to accept, but that hasn't stopped the homophobic commentators who hate the movie.

The possibility of making a negative interpretation of the scene of the men on the first night in the tent is reinforced by some aspects of the episodes that the filmmakers add depicting what happens between Ennis and Jack on the following day, some of which show more doubt and hesitation on Ennis's part. The film presents Ennis waking up, looking at Jack peacefully asleep beside him in the tent, seeming confused at first and then realizing what's happened. Ennis then gets ready to ride off to the sheep without having breakfast, silent as Jack comes up to him and says in a friendly, expectant way that he'll see him for supper. Up on the mountain, Ennis rides fast to investigate why one of the dogs is barking and finds that a sheep is down, gutted by coyotes, with the blue heeler guarding the carcass, trying to do the job Ennis should've done. In the scene, Ledger presents Ennis as responding with a sense of guilt to what the character perceives as the consequences of sleeping with Jack. The image of the slaughtered sheep resonates with Christian iconography, and so can be interpreted as implying the negative judgment made by some Christians on male-male sexual relationships, a judgment that a man in Ennis's time and place undoubtedly would be well aware of. Throughout the episode, Santoalalla's beautiful score turns brooding and ominous, and there's also the whistling of the wind and the low sound of distant thunder, all reinforcing the sense that Ennis feels shame at what's happened. Ennis's feelings are contrasted with Jack's developing commitment to him: the film cuts from the scene with Ennis finding the dead sheep to one showing Jack, naked except for his boots, squatting down by a sunlit stream washing clothes, and taking particular care with Ennis's shirt—the one that he'll eventually take as a token of his feeling for Ennis. This, of course, is one of the many indicators in the film ignored by homophobic viewers that shows that Jack's desired and enjoyed the sexual experience that he and Ennis have shared.

In a particularly significant change that emphasizes a sense of anxiety on Ennis's part, the film locates the one discussion the men have that summer about their sexual relationship late on the afternoon of the day after they first have sex. In the story, Proulx doesn't place this conversation at this point, simply telling us that during the course of the summer, as they continue to have sex together, they say nothing about it, except that once Ennis says, "'I'm not no queer,'"[21] and Jack replies with "'Me neither. A one-shot thing. Nobody's business but ours.'"[22] By placing the conversation on the day after the men first have sex, the film presents their physical relationship as a more problematic issue between them, one that Ennis apparently feels he has to address immediately. The film also changes the dialogue slightly; as the screenwriters word it, Ennis denies his sexuality by saying, "You know I ain't queer," which unfortunately eliminates the double negative that he uses in the story. Proulx, in having him use a double negative, the vernacular way of being emphatic, indicates with brilliant irony the truth that Ennis can't actually speak about his sexuality: for him to say he's "'not no'"[23] queer in fact is for him to say, without his realizing it, that he *is* a queer. Still, the way the screenwriters word it, Ennis's statement has its own irony, though of course it's also unconscious on Ennis's part. He doesn't just say "I ain't queer," but starts by locating his denial in reference to what Jack "knows"—and of course what Jack actually *knows* includes the fact that Ennis wanted to fuck him, which thus negates Ennis's denial! Where Proulx has Jack say the rest of the dialogue, in the movie Ennis approaches Jack and starts the conversation by defining and limiting their relationship as a "one shot thing," anticipating his termination of the relationship at the end of the summer. The dark mood created by Ennis's concern and Jack's inability to counter it or to encourage Ennis to affirm their relationship and perhaps even their sexual orientation is reinforced by the weather in the scene, which is overcast and dark, and by the continuation of the ominous music. Then that night, in the film, when Jack already has entered the tent and bedded down, Ennis is shown alone by the fire; he hasn't left to go back to sleep in the camp by the sheep, but nevertheless he sits with his head lowered and pensive, apparently worrying about his intimacy with Jack.

When Ennis finally joins his friend in the tent, Jack has his shirt off, and gently embraces and kisses him, just barely whispering that it's all right, re-assuring him, as Ennis begins to respond. Only then are Ennis's worries sus-pended, and he and Jack gently embrace and lie back on the bedroll, holding and kissing each other. The scene is beautifully acted and filmed, and effec-tively represents the way in which Ennis gradually adjusts to Jack, and to himself, that the screenwriters appear to have wanted to convey. Also, this added scene is significant because it strongly refutes the homophobic as-sumption that men who desire men only care about sex, and that the sex they have necessarily is violent and brutal—nothing could be more gentle and lov-ing, affirming the depth of emotion two men can share, than the way Ledger and Gyllenhaal portray Ennis and Jack on their second night together in the tent. Their lovemaking is as affectionate as any scene depicting a man and a woman. Gyllenhaal embraces Ledger tenderly, and the way Ledger responds, laying his head on Gyllenhaal's chest, eyes closed, as Gyllenhaal holds him against him, clearly indicates the isolation, loneliness, and intense need for in-timacy with another man that are central to Ennis's character. The music in this episode confirms the change in mood, gradually becoming sweet, peace-ful, and reassuring. Thus, while some aspects of the additions made by the film do present the relationship with Jack as being problematic for Ennis, and may be objectionable to gay or queer viewers, especially those who've read the story, the addition depicting the men on the second night actually is quite affirming of the emotional depth of their relationship. Some viewers may per-ceive the depiction of the first night as conforming to their negative assump-tions about male-male intercourse, but certainly the manner in which the sec-ond night is shown challenges this misperception. After seeing the affection the men share on the second night, it's difficult to believe anyone could char-acterize the way they make love as "rape" or label either of them a "sexual predator." That some men have said so is a testament to the intensity with which their own fears drive them to cling to their disgust at men who love men, not to a shortcoming of the film. The significance of this episode in the film's representation of the development of the love between Jack and Ennis, and the gradual decrease in Ennis's anxiety, is confirmed by the scene that follows immediately, in which they tease and laugh and chase and wrestle and then embrace and kiss, half stripped, in the sun.

The film's changes and additions thus significantly alter the presentation of Ennis at the start of the summer on the mountain. Perhaps the filmmakers were seeking to develop the viewer's sense of the homophobia Ennis has in-ternalized and the intense fear he feels, which Proulx only fully reveals in the reunion episode set four years later when Ennis tells Jack about Earl's mur-der, but the way they depict Ennis also can be seen as an adjustment of the narrative in preparation for homophobic reactions of potential audiences, an effort to anticipate the hostility of some viewers to the film's direct depiction of male love. It's as if the filmmakers wanted to reassure homophobic viewers, validating their reactions to some degree by including them in Ennis's behavior. By introducing episodes in which Ennis has qualms about his involvement with Jack, the movie avoids provoking the shock that straight audiences might have felt if Ennis's attitude during the summer were presented as being as positive as it is in the story. The difference isn't a major one, but it certainly is noticeable to many gay or queer men, who are all too used to the media's willingness to cater to the homophobic assumptions of the dominant culture. Also, certainly unintentionally, the changes the film makes have tended to play into the hands of those hostile or merely stupid reviewers who present laughably distorted misinterpretations of the film, in complete contradiction to the overall presentation of the characters in the film, and of course the story. For whatever reason, the film makes Ennis more worried than he is in the story at the start of his relationship with Jack. Part of the story's brilliance and power is in its contrast of the complete, unqualified freedom to love as he wants to love that Ennis feels just once in his life, on Brokeback Mountain, with the fear that controls his life before and afterward.

Once the film gets past its depiction of Ennis's anxiety the first time he and Jack have sex, it adopts a position similar to Proulx's in presenting their relationship over the course of the summer. As mentioned, she makes it clear that Jack and Ennis share intense sexual passion, not only on the first night they make love, but during their entire time together on Brokeback Mountain, and after that whenever they can be together. Their passion is so powerful that it quickly extends from the night into the day as well, and from the private space of the tent out onto the landscape of the mountain. They make love in the sunshine and by the fire, "quick, rough, laughing and snorting, no lack of noises . . ."[24] For them as men, given the society's system of gender, the landscape is a space which they've been taught they have a right to, and now, rather than hiding their passion for each other, they can embrace the landscape as men who love men. The movie adds to what Proulx says, showing that their coupling runs the gamut—sometimes aggressive, as on the first night, sometimes gentle, as on the second, sometimes playful, as when they chase and wrestle and kiss in the sunshine. Both the story and the film recognize the intense physical energy that men in love can share, the way it can erupt in teasing, horseplay, and wrestling, and then quickly become fucking. They acknowledge the particular nature and possibilities of love between strong, healthy, active men, what Whitman called "manly," "robust," and "athletic" love.[25] For Ennis and Jack, their lovemaking smoothly goes back and forth between shared work and chores, to friendly play, to physical

competition, to shared sexual ecstasy. Friendship and sexual desire are integrated and continuous with each other. The film not only frankly presents
their intercourse in the tent at night, but also their ribald horseplay with each
other, half naked, in the camp during the day. In a long shot we see both of
them, wearing just boots, jeans, and hats, in the sunny green meadow by their
tent and fire circle: Ennis comes up behind Jack, suddenly knocks his hat off
his head, Jack whirls around, chases Ennis, grabs him, then embraces him
from behind, Ennis twists free, pushes Jack down on the grass, comes down
on top of him, and they embrace and kiss. In their interactions with their
friends, all young men experience the first part of the spectrum of physical intimacy, working and playing and competing in sports together, and many
more than ever will say so reach the point of wrestling with a friend and becoming sexually excited, even so far as orgasm; Ennis and Jack go the length
of the spectrum, and extend their friendship into erotic play and mutual sexual fulfillment.

Despite the differences between them, the story and the movie affirm sex
between men with a directness that's new to mainstream culture. Both present anal intercourse as what these two masculine men want; it brings them
mutual physical joy, and they delight in it. Neither one is the "aggressor" or
the "submitter," neither one is a rapist or a victim. When Ennis and Jack couple, it's intense and energetic, but it's what they both like and want. Again,
it's much to the credit of those who made the film that the culture's homophobia didn't prevent them from conveying a sense of the shared energy,
closeness, and ecstasy that two men can experience in a sexual relationship.
In their discussions with the media, both actors generally have made very
positive comments about the film and its popularity, although on a few occa-
sions they've conformed somewhat to the expectations of the majority, expressing discomfort with the intimate physical contact that their roles required, but to their credit professionally, this doesn't come across in their
performances. Certainly it's been noted that at showings of the film sometimes during the scenes of intimacy between Jack and Ennis there are gasps,
murmurs, and nervous giggles, particularly from straight men in the audiences, but this says considerably more about their fears and insecurities than
it does about any on the part of those who made the film. As many cultural
analysts have noted, the fact that historically cultural production has been
dominated by straight white men has meant that all those who consume cultural products, regardless of their sex, sexual orientation, or race, often must
entertain and tolerate the point of view from which straight white male writers, artists, and filmmakers present experience, which frequently is shaped
and limited by straight, white, male experience, and by degrees of sexism,
racism, and homophobia as well. To some men who love men, it's satisfying

to see the tables turned by *Brokeback Mountain.* For once, general American audiences have been provided with a depiction of sex between men not in the form of the hostile, distorted constructions that so many straight people find necessary to impose, but as it actually can be for many men, a source of intense sexual pleasure and frequently part of the basis of a profound emotional bond that can unite two men, often for life.[26]

The story and the movie don't just present the sexual relationship between the men one time and then avoid the subject with relief. In both versions, the two men clearly have sex frequently on the mountain, and when they finally see each other again four years later, it's almost all they can do to hold off until they can get to a motel. The motel scene is much more substantial in the story than in the film; unfortunately, the elimination of some of the dialogue between Ennis and Jack concerning the intensity of their sexual attraction to each other and the pleasure they take in the type of sex they have may interfere with the understanding some viewers have of their relationship. Proulx begins her description as the men just have finished having intercourse. Ennis is stretched out on the bed, sweating and breathing heavily, and still half-hard, as Jack, lying next to him smoking, praises his partner's ability, and speculates about its source: "'Christ, it got to be all that time a yours ahoresback makes it so goddamn good.'"[27] As noted before, many straight people, if they allow themselves to think about male-male anal sex at all, tend to consider it only from the perspective of the partner who they perceive as the "real" man, since he's the one who inserts his penis, though they often project their own anxieties and conceive of his actions almost as rape. Proulx, however, is open to imagining the perspective of the man who receives the other's penis, and is free of any assumptions that project onto him the usual homophobic horror at being anally penetrated, instead recognizing and affirming the pleasure he feels, and his appreciation of his partner. Her depiction also is free of any of the usual homophobic cultural assumptions that the man who's entered by his partner must somehow be the more "passive" or "feminine" of the two; there's nothing effeminate in Jack's exclamation praising Ennis's ability in intercourse, with its blunt profanity and its horseman's insight into how Ennis's experience as a rider accounts for how good he is at riding Jack.

While the candid way Jack praises Ennis's ability in bed seems to have been more than the filmmakers could handle, fortunately they do retain what he says next; he tells Ennis he didn't think they'd get into sex with each other again, and then laughingly corrects himself, saying yes, he did, and that's why he "redlined"[28] it to get there! As Gyllenhaal delivers the lines, with Ledger lying back against his chest, he shows that he gets the point, presenting Jack as smiling at the intensity of his own desire for his friend. This moment has to make the pleasure Jack takes in being fucked by Ennis clear to any but the most complete homophobe.

This mutually satisfying kind of sex remains a fundamental aspect of Jack and Ennis's physical and emotional connection; on their last trip together, in May 1983, twenty years after having met, Proulx says that at the end of a day of riding through the mountains, Jack opens a bottle of whiskey, drinks, tosses it to Ennis, and remarks, "'That's one a the two things I need right now.'"[29] Later on this trip, when he and Ennis argue, Jack exclaims in frustration to his friend, "'I'm not you. I can't make it on a couple a high-altitude fucks once or twice a year.'"[30] One particularly sad aspect of the decline of the marriage in which Ennis's fear traps him and Alma is that his nostalgia for the kind of sex he prefers, anal intercourse with Jack, causes him to try to insist on it with Alma, which isn't right for her. The significance of Jack Twist's last name, as Proulx explained it to Gyllenhaal, already has been discussed, but it's also important to note her daring and startling reference to anal intercourse even in Ennis's name, which can be perceived as a homophone for "anus." Comical, suggestive references appear in both versions; especially in the film, the men repeatedly complain and joke about beans, a food whose flatulent properties long have been celebrated in scatological American folk poetry. The visual pun about Jack "spilling the beans" already has been noted. The screenplay also adds a scene in which, when the men meet in the mountains for one of their many riding trips, Ennis makes a joking, nostalgic gesture about beans; unfortunately, in the film it's shot from a distance and its significance can't be clear to audiences. As he walks into camp, Ennis tells Jack to look at what he's brought, giving him a paper sack containing cans of beans, a memory of their summer on the mountain, and perhaps also a playful reference to the physical intimacy they share.[31] The connection between the references to beans and intercourse may seem far-fetched, but it's borne out by a detail of Ennis's erotic dreams about Jack, which Proulx mentions in the descriptions of Ennis alone in his trailer, some time after Jack's murder, which frame the story. In the part of the narrative frame that closes the story, she describes Ennis's dream vision of being with Jack on Brokeback Mountain: Jack comes to Ennis as he was at nineteen, with his curly hair and bucktoothed smile, and in the dream the open can of beans with the spoon sticking out is there too, "in a cartoon shape and lurid colors that gave the dreams a flavor of comic obscenity."[32] Though the dreams also are significant in other ways that will be discussed later, this sentence seems to suggest that Jack and Ennis have shared the sort of mood of earthy, robust, Rabelaisian intimacy that can develop between a couple who love each other and know and completely accept and enjoy each other's bodies, in both their sublime and their preposterous aspects.

As Proulx and the filmmakers have constructed the relationship between Ennis and Jack, one of the many negative stereotypes about male-male sexual relationships that it challenges is perhaps the most deeply entrenched, the construction of them as casual, shallow, and brief. In both versions, it's evident that the relationship between the two men not only is intensely sexual but also deeply emotional, and that they love being together not simply because of sexual attraction but also because of the pleasure they take in each other's company. Ennis's fears eventually force Jack to look elsewhere for sex and for love with a man, but neither he or Ennis fits the standard hostile construction of the promiscuous homosexual male who's driven only by lust. Resistance to their relationship originates in their society, and without this their attraction likely would keep them together. This construction resonates strongly with the experiences of many men who love men, and is especially relevant in a period when concerns about HIV/AIDS have reinforced awareness of the problems that can be involved in promiscuity and when many gay men are active in the legal struggle for marriage equality.

In their frank depiction of the love of the two men for each other, the story and the film not only challenge the homophobic misrepresentation and suppression of intercourse between men, but also assist in the process of increasing the visibility of the variety of men who love men. By portraying the mutual sexual attraction of two masculine working-class Westerners dressed in what the majority sees as the garb of working "cowboys" (though in fact they're employed as sheepherders), both narratives show that man-loving men can be anywhere, that there's no necessary connection between appearance and sexuality. Gender presentation and sexual orientation aren't linked, homophobic stereotypes of gay men to the contrary. The homophobic ideology that pervades American culture consistently constructs men who love men in terms of characteristics related to sexist constructions of women, repeatedly rendering them in some way as "feminine." Men who desire men are constructed as exotics, as stylish, sophisticated, affluent urban types, sometimes elegant dandies, sometimes effeminate queens, sometimes comical "fairies," sometimes devious, sinister sexual predators, but not as ordinary American working men. Certainly there are men who desire men and who fit elements of the dominant stereotypes, though there's no necessary connection between these elements and the burden of negative meaning that the heterosexual majority imposes on men whose self-presentation is stylish or feminine. But there are many others who don't fit them at all. The traditional indicators of masculine gender—the signifiers of masculinity in clothing, speech, gestures, occupation, interests, and all the other factors that are used in American society to identify and judge the degree of gender conformity of men—have no necessary or inherent connection to heterosexuality. Everywhere in American society there are men who desire men and who, because they don't conform to the majority's expectations of what a man who desires men supposedly looks and acts like, are virtually invisible, at least to the majority. Some may identify as gay, some as queer in either of the two major senses of this word discussed in the Introduction, and others may identify in other ways. Indeed, it's important to recognize that for some men who have sex with men, their sexual feelings and activities may not be a source of any particular identification. Men who have intense sexual and often emotional connections with other men live in rural and urban areas, they belong to all racial, ethnic, cultural, and religious groups, they have every level of education, they play sports and engage in other activities that don't fit the dominant stereotypes, they work at every sort of job, on farms, in factories, in offices, in the police, in the military services, in every form of labor and every occupation. And some are high school dropout ranch boys, reared in families that go to Methodist and Pentecostal churches, who like dogs and horses and working outdoors and hunting in the mountains.

The straight majority's stereotypes of sexual minorities have been developed as a result of its perceptions of those it regards, in terms of gender behavior and self-presentation, as "deviating" from its definitions of appropriateness. As historians of sexual minorities in America have shown, by the late nineteenth century and probably considerably before that, in major urban areas the possibilities of economic and social freedom for individual men had allowed the development of social networks and meeting places that permitted connections between men who wanted sexual and emotional involvement with other men.[33] Much of the developing urban social world of men who loved men was invisible to the majority, since many of the men involved seemed similar to all other men. It allowed the development of groups of man-loving men whose clothing, speech, gestures, occupations, and interests were more feminine than those acceptable to the majority, and who thus did stand out to some observers and critics of urban life. To the majority, with its acceptance of a rigid traditional gender ideology concerning men and women, which it believed to be based on "natural" differences between the sexes, men whose clothing, speech, gestures, occupations, and interests it perceived as being associated with women and therefore effeminate increasingly were relegated to the developing negative category that came to be labeled "homosexual." As this construction became established, it was assumed to represent all men who felt sexual attraction to other men: the more feminine men whom the majority derided, dismissed, and often attacked as "fairies" and "pansies" were perceived as typifying all man-loving men.[34] Historians suggest that the sensational trials in 1895 of Oscar Wilde, who was internationally famous as a dandy, aesthete, and wit, helped to set the pattern, both in medical-legal discourses and in the public mind, of constructing male homosexuality in terms of effeminacy.[35] Stereotypes of the flamboyant fairy were clearly evident in Hollywood films before the full enforcement of the Production Code, and though homosexuality couldn't be addressed directly in films after 1934, it continued to be referred to obliquely in minor "sissy" characters embodying elements of the fairy stereotype.[36] The persistent construction of male-male desire in terms of effeminacy obscured the fact, as many urban and rural man-loving men knew, that all sorts of men had sexual relationships with other men.

While the challenges made to traditional gender ideology by heterosexual women and sexual minorities since the Second World War have resulted in a degree of progress toward a less repressive system of gender, traditional gender ideology still pervades American culture and shapes the lives of men and women whatever their sexual orientations, causing many of them to conform to established models of masculinity and femininity. "Effeminate" men and "masculine" women continue to be particular targets of abuse, which all people concerned with diversity and equality must work together to stop. As it affects men, gender ideology causes many who are heterosexual but who depart in some ways from rigid gender models to be perceived as possibly being sexually different. And for large numbers of men whose clothing, speech, gestures, occupations, and interests are conventionally masculine, and who are attracted physically and emotionally to other men, it makes their sexual difference invisible to the majority.

The pioneering research on sexual behavior by Dr. Alfred Kinsey and his associates, which began to be published in the late 1940s, made the general public aware that many apparently "gender normative" men actually were having sexual experiences with other men.[37] Critics of Kinsey's work argue that the methodology that he and the others working with him used exaggerated the numbers of men involved in sexual contact with one another, but even acknowledging other, lower estimates, it became evident that men who desired men were more numerous, and less stereotypic, than had been widely thought. Many today continue to assume that men who desire men fit homophobic stereotypes, and that men who seem masculine to them are straight. As a result, in both urban and rural areas, many men who desire men and who are "straight-acting" and "straight-appearing," to use the language sometimes seen in gay personals ads, still usually are assumed to be heterosexual. Some may identify as being gay and may decide to come out as gay in various social contexts, though depending on location and community this can entail substantial risks. Many others may participate in sexual and emotional relationships with men, perhaps identifying their sexual difference in other ways or not identifying as sexually different at all. Because of the great costs often imposed on sexual minority people in homophobic contexts if their sexual orientation becomes known, many man-loving men whose appearance and behavior are conventionally masculine, whatever construction of sexual orientation they may identify with, pass for straight. One of the most important requirements for continuing to pass, in many urban and rural social contexts, is to avoid the visible degree of intimacy with another man that would cause suspicions or accusations of homosexuality. Thus, for many man-loving men, whatever their identification, seeking to pass may eliminate the possibility of living with a man with whom they're intimate. Some all-male work environments that require men to live together, such as military or religious organizations, may create conditions that permit a high degree of intimacy between two men without making them visible as homosexual. Urban society can allow a high degree of anonymity for a male couple, but in general, in many contexts in the United States, for two adult men who are unrelated to live together, even if they're perceived as conventionally masculine, makes it very likely that they'll be identified as homosexual.[38] For Ennis and Jack in *Brokeback Mountain,* the question of being willing to take the risk of living together becomes the central issue of their relationship.

In their presentation of Ennis and Jack, Proulx and those who created the movie make visible the existence of the millions of sexually different men who the majority still simply is incapable of seeing. The story and the film not only contradict simplistic assumptions concerning the supposed link between gender behavior and sexual orientation, but they also resonate strongly with constructions of masculinity that have been developed by men who love men and who identify as gay. The story and the movie come at a time when gay men have constructed models of masculinity for themselves that defy the stereotypes that much of the majority continues to accept. While many heterosexuals still don't want to see gay men at all, or only want to see them as what they perceive as the reassuring stereotypes purveyed by *Will and Grace,* *Queer Eye for the Straight Guy*, or *The Birdcage*, many gay men have created masculine styles that are far more congruent with the masculinity of Jack and Ennis in *Brokeback Mountain*. This isn't to say that gay culture has rejected its long-established creative traditions of drag, camp, and other forms of ironic, subversive gender behavior and performance; it hasn't, and many gay men who value and delight in the richness of gay culture understandably don't want it to. Their pleasure in such exaggerated enactments of gender demonstrates a degree of awareness that, for them and for all members of American society, whether they realize it or not, gender is socially constructed and so *is* a performance. Because of the situation imposed upon them by the majority as they grow up, as outsiders with a different, "unspeakable," and often unspoken sexual orientation, and because of their long experience in dissimulating and passing as straight, many gay men are acutely, intuitively aware that gender is not innate but is constructed. And so, as gay communities have emerged, many gay men have constructed styles of masculine, and often hypermasculine, self-presentation and performance that put many straight men to shame.[39]

Because of the eruption of Gay Liberation in 1969 and the affirmation of gay pride and calls to sexual minorities to come out and to resist discrimination and harassment, gay male culture was transformed. Not only did gay men repudiate the homophobic ideology of medical and scientific "experts" along with the hostile policies of government and the hatred preached by many religions, but also, in their celebration of their sexuality, they sought to define for themselves their own ideals of gender behavior and presentation.[40] Earlier in the twentieth century, particularly prior to the Second World War, many men who identified themselves as sexually different seem to have accepted and internalized the dominant culture's stereotypes of them, perceiving themselves as feminine and emphasizing more feminine styles of gender behavior and presentation. Some constructed their models of gay male identity in relation to the European model of the stylish, elegant, aristocratic dandy as exemplified by Wilde. Historians of sexual minorities have found that in major urban communities, many men who loved men followed the larger society in differentiating between men less on the basis of sexual activity and more on the basis of gender performance. Men whose self-presentation was effeminate were perceived and labeled as being different from other men, whereas those who were more masculine in their self-presentation, even though they had sex with other men, were still understood as being much like the majority of men. Relatively masculine men who had sex with other men were thought of as queer, but not as fundamentally different from other men, and strongly masculine men who had sex with men still were understood as "normal" straight men.[41] Gradually a shift occurred, and many began to identify themselves less in terms of gender behavior and more in terms of sexual orientation, using the term "gay" to refer to all men who desired men, regardless of the degree of effeminacy or masculinity in their gender behavior. Following the Second World War, and perhaps partly because of their experiences in it, some in the communities of sexual minority men that grew in major cities began to develop a stronger emphasis on masculine forms of gender presentation, sometimes involving uniforms and leather, sometimes simply involving a generally more masculine style of dress and behavior. Many masculine-looking and-acting men, who formerly might have been thought of as queer or straight but whose sexual orientation was toward other men, now identified as gay. Rather than desiring men that they idealized as being more "straight" than they were, many gay men masculinized themselves, becoming objects of sexual desire for one another. With the vast expansion of gay communities in major cities in the 1970s, gay men generally developed strongly masculine styles, based in part on the modes of self-presentation among working class American men—including rural Westerners—with boots, jeans, flannel shirts, and facial hair, celebrating the masculine appearance that the dominant culture naively assumed excluded the possibility of same-sex attraction. In some places, like San Francisco's Castro District in the late 1970s, this form of hypermasculinity became a kind of gay uniform in and of itself. And of course, one of the "macho man" archetypes presented in this period by the popular gay disco band, the Village People—which the majority took an amusingly long time to realize was a gay group—was the Cowboy.[42]

The development of more masculine constructions of being gay has had both positive and negative effects. With considerable reason, some have pointed out that in embracing and even exaggerating aspects of traditional masculinity, gay men uncritically adopted and endorsed ways of being men that were markers of the status and privilege of straight men. Also, as urban gay communities moved away from the radical aspirations of early gay liberation groups, masculine gender performance became deeply commercialized and commodified, both in the sense that there developed an extensive market in consumer goods connoting masculinity, and that relationships between many gay men became like a sexual marketplace, increasingly stressing the "marketability" of masculinity. Many women saw this as a manifestation of the lack of understanding and solidarity of gay men with feminism and the concerns of lesbians. The masculinization of gay culture distanced it from the struggles of women against sexism and against homophobia toward lesbians. Others have argued that the "sexual scripts" associated with hypermasculinity caused many urban gay men to become involved in sexual behaviors that unintentionally facilitated the spread of HIV.[43] Also, it's important to recognize that the urban gay culture that produced this hypermasculine style was limited in terms of race and class, and while available to many white, middle-class men, was not as open to men of working-class background or men of color. The hypermasculine style may have been based on the appearance of some working-class men, but, like a great deal of gay pornography, appropriated and fetishized that appearance as part of a fantasy about the supposed sexual prowess of working-class men that had particular appeal to many middle-class men. Despite the idealization of a working-class "look," urban gay society continued to be marked by prejudice against men from rural and working-class backgrounds and men who did manual and service jobs. Gay culture was not part of the lives of many man-loving men, both rural and urban.[44] For many men who could identify as gay, however, the more masculine style was empowering, allowing the integration of traditional aspects of masculinity in their lives as a way of repudiating the dominant culture's construction of them in terms of homophobic stereotypes, and of overcoming the sense of inferiority they had been taught to internalize.[45] Interestingly, some have argued that in this period, for many lesbians as well, elements of traditional masculine gender appealed because they connote strength, independence, and assertiveness.[46]

While the particular gay masculine style of the 1970s changed in the 1980s and 1990s, the emphasis on masculine forms of self-presentation didn't, and more and more gay men became seriously involved in bodybuilding. The emphasis on male strength and health may have been partly a reaction to the fear and grief of the growing HIV-AIDS pandemic, and for some men, especially those who became HIV positive, regular, intensive exercise was a very practical and valuable component of their regimen in resisting the disease and remaining as healthy as possible. It's important to note, though, that here too class is an important factor: working out at a gym takes time and money that many men don't have. Some gay men, unfortunately, have taken the concern with creating a masculine image too far, seeking to attain the appearance of a perfect body not through exercise but through drugs, using steroids. Still, for many more men the stress on exercise and fitness has been very positive, improving their health, making them even more attractive to one another, and countering the disempowering damage of homophobic abuse in childhood and adolescence. And as gay men have created cultural styles celebrating their masculinity, and as sexual minority communities have evolved and have organized to fight homophobia, increasing numbers of men who desire men and whose gender presentation is masculine have identified as gay.[47]

The past twenty-five years have seen a burgeoning of interest among gay men not only in regular exercise at gyms but also in competitive sports. In earlier generations, many sexually different men avoided sports because of the endemic hostility toward anyone perceived as not conforming to cultural constructions of masculine aggressiveness, and today for many sexual minority men, especially during childhood and adolescence, sports continue to be fraught with homophobic abuse. But increasingly many men who identify as gay revel in the competition, comradeship, bonding, and erotic attraction provided by gay teams that compete in sports including football, basketball, baseball, soccer, rugby, and lacrosse, and also in clubs that engage in biking, hiking, wrestling, swimming, gymnastics, weightlifting, mountain-climbing, and every other sport. In organizing these activities, gay men have had the supportive parallel example of many straight women, and especially of lesbians, who also have embraced the pleasure of competition and bonding through sports, once supposedly a privilege of straight men only.[48] The enthusiasm for sports among sexual minorities not only has produced local teams and activities, but competitive regional and national sports groups and organizations, as well as organized international competition in the Gay Games.[49] And in the rural United States and Canada, especially in the West, for those who identify with the gay community, the gay sports movement has produced the many regional gay rodeo groups that form the International Gay Rodeo Association, providing an affirming social environment for those from ranches and farms who love outdoor life—and people of their own sex.[50]

In considering the development of masculine gender styles among men who identify as gay, it's important to recognize that for some, more feminine forms of self-presentation feel natural. Man-loving men whose gender presentation is masculine need to respect this, and to work as allies of those whose gender presentation differs from theirs; all of them face homophobia, and to confront it effectively it's necessary for them to accept each other and work together and to accept and work with women as well. Feminine men who love men are those most visible to the dominant culture, and face the most intense homophobia, and they shouldn't have to face discrimination from other sexual minority men as well. There ought to be room among sexual minorities, and in the entire society, for varieties of masculinity; indeed, masculinity shouldn't be available only to men as a mode of gender expression, but to women as well. Some criticize more masculine forms of self-presentation as an imitation of the dominant, patriarchal culture and an effort to retain the status and privileges of straight men, but it's important for them to recognize that a masculine style does feel natural and appropriate for some men who love men. The adoption of masculine forms of self-presentation among men who identify as gay can function as a way of resisting the destructive effects of growing up in a strongly homophobic society. Also, the masculinization of gay culture has helped to make space for the involvement of masculine-identified man-loving men.

Although many straight people who read or see *Brokeback Mountain* are shocked at the notion that there could be "gay cowboys," many men who desire men aren't surprised at all, since they themselves look as masculine as the majority's ideals of masculinity, or more so, and indeed many who identify with gay culture set styles of masculine dress and physique and looks that many men in the majority imitate without any awareness of their source.[51] Also, many men who desire men know that there are men with such desires everywhere, in the city and in the country, and that some, in appearance, occupations, and interests, aren't any different from the two men in *Brokeback Mountain*. They realize that a man can desire men and look like—and be—a weightlifter, a police officer, an electrician, a rugby player, a building contractor—or a man who works outdoors with stock on a ranch. Rather than constructing themselves in terms of some alien Other, as many in the majority expect, many men who love men present themselves in ways that are part of the traditional patterns of American masculinity. Some consciously identify as being gay, and some don't; some present themselves with a degree of self-consciousness, deliberately defining and exaggerating a masculine ideal, and others present themselves in masculine ways simply because it's part of who they've grown up being.

Whitman has proven to be an accurate prophet of the development of masculine forms of self-understanding among some men who love men. In his poetry he envisioned ways of being man-loving men that rejected the assumptions that men who loved men necessarily were feminine, that sexuality and gender behavior were connected. He explicitly repudiated the established European paradigm of the fastidious dandy, which increasingly came to be associated with male sexual difference through the nineteenth century and into the twentieth; in the first edition of *Leaves of Grass* in 1855, he deliberately presents himself as a man-loving man who is "one of the roughs,"[52] celebrating and eroticizing the ordinary working-class appearance of other men, and emphasizing it as part of his own performance of gender.[53] In the famous photograph that Whitman used at the start of the 1855 volume, he represents himself in the garb of a carpenter, shirt open at the neck, sleeves pushed up, and hat aslant, and in the text he announces the delight he takes in the bodies of other men and in his own naked body, including his body hair and beard: "Washes and razors for foo-foos . . . for me freckles and a bristling beard."[54] As Whitman constructs it, emotional and physical love between men does not preclude masculinity, and indeed, he characterizes it as particularly masculine, democratic, and American:

> Behold this swarthy face, these gray eyes,
> This beard, the white wool unclipt upon my neck,
> My brown hands and the silent manner of me without charm;
> Yet comes one a Manhattanese and ever at parting kisses
>   me lightly on the lips with robust love,
> And I on the crossing of the street or on the ship's deck
>   give a kiss in return,
> We observe that salute of American comrades land and sea,
> We are those two natural and nonchalant persons.[55]

In what's probably his most famous poem about the exuberance of male love, made the subject of an early explicitly homoerotic painting (1961) by the important gay artist David Hockney, Whitman conveys the feeling of the joyful,

ecstatic energy two young men who love each other can find in every aspect
of being with each other:

> We two boys together clinging,
> One the other never leaving,
> Up and down the roads going, North and South excursions
>   making,
> Power enjoying, elbows stretching, fingers clutching,
> Arm'd and fearless, eating, drinking, sleeping, loving,
> No law less than ourselves owning . . .
> Fulfilling our foray.[56]

The delight in shared masculine sexual energy expressed in the poem is much
like that Proulx describes between Jack and Ennis during their summer on the
mountain, having sex first at night in the tent, then in full daylight, "quick,
rough, laughing and snorting, no lack of noises . . . there were only the two
of them on the mountain . . ."[57] Both Whitman and Proulx envision the possibility, for men who love men, of not having to disavow their love or to con-
fine it to a limited number of private, safe spaces, but of being free to express
it together spontaneously, in their bodies, their gestures, their speech, and
their movement through every dimension of public space.

Although in the decades following the Second World War gay culture developed in ways that were increasingly empowering for many gay men, the
men in *Brokeback Mountain,* whose relationship begins in 1963, well before
the emergence of Gay Liberation in urban areas, are isolated from gay communities and from gay culture. More masculine constructions of gay identity
were evolving in this period, but due to lack of information and resources, as
well as increased propagation of homophobic stereotypes, were unlikely to be
known to men like Ennis and Jack. While throughout America, including rural areas, men engaged in sexual and emotional relationships together, as historians have shown, they also have shown that the 1950s and early 1960s saw
increasing hostility toward men who loved men. The growth of sexual minority communities in urban port cities such as San Francisco and New York
after the war caused more aggressive condemnation by scientific, political,
and religious organizations, which was widely reported and supported by the
commercial mass media. The McCarthyite Red Scare of the early to mid
fifties demonized and attacked homosexuals, and there were sensational "sex-
crime panics" in which men were arrested and imprisoned or institutionalized
for having sex with men, the two most widely known both occurring in 1955,
in Boise, Idaho, and in Sioux City, Iowa; in 1958, police in Salt Lake City began extensive entrapment and arrests of men for seeking sexual contacts with
men.[58] Proulx clearly recognizes the intimidating conditions created by this
atmosphere of homophobia in her depiction of Jack and Ennis when they

meet. She presents them as country boys who are aware that there are men who have sex with men and are labeled queer, and who are fearful of being labeled in this way themselves. They know that some men who are perceived as sexually different are rejected as deficiently masculine; as Ennis says to Jack in the story when they talk about their options during their reunion in 1967, "'I don't want a be like them guys you see around sometimes.'" [59] Beyond this, they have little other information or language for describing themselves, their feelings, and their experience together.

But even so, despite the fact that their culture's hostility to love between men has made them unable to acknowledge or say who they are and how they feel, the physical and emotional force that draws them together is so strong that Ennis and Jack, like many men before and since, do have their revelation—their Pentecost.

NOTES

1. Lord Alfred Douglas, "Two Loves," *The Complete Poems of Lord Alfred Douglas* (London: Martin Secker, 1928).

2. See Russo, *Celluloid*, and Benshoff and Griffin, *Queer Images*, on changing representations of sexual minorities in film. In general, in the period before the enforcement of the Production Code in 1934, there were relatively frequent depictions of stereotypes of effeminate men and masculine women, and some positive representations of the perspectives and experience of men who loved men and women who loved women. After 1934, homosexuality only could be suggested indirectly, usually through comic stereotypes such as the sissy, though sometimes in more sinister characters. With the breakdown of the Code in the late 1950s and early 1960s, more representations were permitted, though these usually were negative. In addition to comic sissy and fairy stereotypes, gay men and lesbians often were constructed in terms of mental illness and violence, often as predators and murderers. Over the last forty years independent filmmakers have sought to present the lives and experience of sexual minorities from their own perspectives, though this has continued to be rare in major commercial filmmaking. The past two decades have seen many more independent films as well as some cable TV shows presenting the lives of sexual minority people more as they perceive themselves, although the stereotypes the majority wants still continue in many commercial studio films.

3. Baehr, cited in goodasyou.org, "'Profam' Critic: *Brokeback*" http://www .goodasyou.org/good_as_you/2005/12/profam_critic_b.html, July 29, 2007).

4. The hostile obsession many straight men have with anal intercourse and sexual minority men may be understood as an instance of the hysterical projection of forbidden desires onto an Other. For more discussion of such patterns of hysterical projection and homophobia, see the discussion of the analysis of homophobia by Elisabeth Young-Bruehl in chapter 4.

5. Proulx, "Brokeback Mountain," 4.
6. Proulx, "Brokeback Mountain," 14.
7. Proulx, "Brokeback Mountain," 14.
8. Proulx, "Brokeback Mountain," 14.
9. Proulx, "Brokeback Mountain," 14.
10. The cultural construction of anal intercourse between men according to negative stereotypes is a fundamental example of the way in which discussion of homosexuality in our society has been controlled by the majority, particularly heterosexual men. In general, many in the majority consider homosexuality only as it seems to them, without recognizing the perspectives of people who are attracted to others of their own sex. As a result, of course, the difficult experience of becoming aware of same-sex desire in a homophobic society becomes largely invisible to the majority, and sexual attraction and activity between people of the same sex rarely are considered as they may be to them. Since straight men dominate much of the cultural production in our society, sex between women sometimes is constructed as being intriguing and titillating, but sex between men usually is erased entirely or is presented in terms of violence. The general prejudice against sex in our society and against anal sex in particular have functioned to silence men who enjoy sexual relations with each other and to prevent them from expressing their perspectives.
11. Proulx, "Brokeback Mountain," 14.
12. Proulx, "Brokeback Mountain," 15.
13. Proulx, "Brokeback Mountain," 14.
14. Proulx, "Brokeback Mountain," 41.
15. Proulx, "Brokeback Mountain," 8.
16. Proulx, "Getting Movied," 131.
17. Proulx, "Brokeback Mountain," 11.
18. Proulx, "Brokeback Mountain," 7.
19. Proulx, "Brokeback Mountain," 14.
20. Proulx, "Brokeback Mountain," 14.
21. Proulx, "Brokeback Mountain," 15.
22. Proulx, "Brokeback Mountain," 15.
23. Proulx, "Brokeback Mountain," 15.
24. Proulx, "Brokeback Mountain," 15.
25. Whitman uses the adjectives "manly," "robust," and "athletic" repeatedly in the *Calamus* poems to describe love between men.
26. On statements by the actors about being uncomfortable with their roles, see *Entertainment Weekly*: Movie News: "Western Union: Heath Ledger and Jake Gyllenhaal Put Their Careers on the Line—The Young Actors Play Cowboys in Love in *Brokeback Mountain*," Christine Spines, Dec. 2, 2005 (http://www.ew.com/ew/article/0,,1136232,00.html, July 29, 2007.); *Entertainment Weekly*: Movie News: "Are You Enjoying 'Jokeback Mountain'?" Michael Slezak, Feb. 3, 2006 (http://www.popwatch.ewcom/popwatch/2006/02/are_you-enjoyin.html, July 29, 2007); and MSNBC: Entertainment: Jeanette Walls: Gossip: "Interview with Heath Ledger and Matt Damon," Aug. 25, 2005 (as quoted by the wonderful Andy Towle, in his "TowleRoad: A Blog with Homosexual Tendencies;" http://www.towleroad

.com/2005/08/heath_on_brokeb.html July 29, 2007). Interestingly, Gyllenhaal seems to have been somewhat more equivocal about his role than Ledger—which is disappointing but hardly surprising, given dominant cultural attitudes to the sexual position he takes in the film. On homophobic audience reactions to *Brokeback Mountain,* see "Love Makes *Brokeback* Oscar Favorite: Tale of Star-crossed Lovers Attracts Audience, Academy Votes," Erik Lundegaard, Feb. 1, 2006 (http://www.msnbc.msn .com/id/11102003, July 29, 2007.) For introductory discussions of various analytical approaches to the problem of the prevalence of a straight, white male perspective in literature and other forms of cultural production, see Ellen Rooney, ed., *The Cambridge Companion to Feminist Literary Theory* (Cambridge: Cambridge University, 2006.)

27. Proulx, "Brokeback Mountain," 24.
28. Proulx, "Brokeback Mountain," 24.
29. Proulx, "Brokeback Mountain," 37.
30. Proulx, "Brokeback Mountain," 42.
31. McMurtry and Ossana, "Screenplay," 59.
32. Proulx, "Brokeback Mountain," 54.

33. See George Chauncey's valuable comprehensive study, *Gay New York: Gender, Urban Culture, and the Making of the Gay Male World, 1890–1940* (New York: Basic Books, 1994), for discussion of the development of urban communities of men who desired men, of the various forms of gender performance in these communities, and of the ways in which the visibility of more effeminate men affected the general public understanding of men who desired men. Also see Miller, *Out of the Past,* and Adam, *Rise,* for general historical overviews.

34. See Chauncey, *Gay New York.*

35. On the impact of Wilde and his trials on constructions of men who desired men, see Neil Bartlett, *Who Was That Man?: A Present For Mr. Oscar Wilde* (London: Serpent's Tail, 1988); Ed Cohen, *Talk on the Wilde Side: Towards a Genealogy of Discourse on Male Sexualities* (New York: Routledge, 1993); Michael Foldy, *The Trials of Oscar Wilde: Deviance, Morality, and Late-Victorian Society* (New Haven: Yale University Press, 1997); and Alan Sinfield, *The Wilde Century: Effeminacy, Oscar Wilde, and the Queer Moment* (New York: Columbia University Press, 1994). Also see Miller, *Out of the Past,* and Adam, *Rise.*

36. See Russo, *Celluloid,* and Benshoff and Griffin, *Queer Images.*

37. Alfred Kinsey, *et. al., Sexual Behavior in the Human Male* (Philadelphia: Saunders, 1948). On the impact of the Kinsey study, see Miller, *Out of the Past,* and Adam, *Rise.*

38. On the increased visibility and consequent exposure to homophobia of same-sex couples, see Alfred W. Lees and Ronald Nelson, *Longtime Companions: Autobiographies of Gay Male Fidelity* (Binghamton: Haworth, 1999), and Richard A. Mackey, Bernard O'Brien, and Eileen F. Mackey, *Gay and Lesbian Couples: Voices from Lasting Relationships* (Binghamton: Haworth, 1997).

39. On the awareness among sexual minority men that gender is performance, and on forms of feminine and masculine gender performance among them, see Levine, *Gay Macho,* and Zeeland, *Masculine Marine.*

40. See Levine, *Gay Macho*, on changes in gender expression among gay men relating to Gay Liberation; see Miller, *Out of the Past*; Adam, *Rise*; and Bayer, *American Psychiatry*, on challenges to homophobic theory and practice in psychology.

41. See Chauncey, *Gay New York*, on the construction of difference between "fairies" or "pansies," "queers," and supposedly "normal" straight men who had sex with men.

42. On the masculinization of gay culture, see Levine, *Gay Macho*; Kleinberg *Alienated Affections*; Bersani, "Is the Rectum a Grave?"

43. On the various effects of the masculinization of gay culture, see Levine, *Gay Macho*; Kleinberg, *Alienated Affections*; Bersani, "Is the Rectum a Grave?"

44. See the critiques of gay culture in relation to issues of class by Ricketts ("Afterword") and of race by Boykin (*One More River*) and McBride (*Abercrombie*).

45. See Levine, *Gay Macho*.

46. The positive aspects of a more masculine form of gender expression for some women are discussed in Adam, *Rise*; also see Judith Halberstam, *Female Masculinity* (Durham: Duke University Press, 1998).

47. On changing ideals of gay male beauty and on gay men and bodybuilding, see Edisol Dotson, *Behold the Man: The Hype and Selling of Male Beauty in Media and Culture* (Binghamton: Haworth, 1999); Shaun Cole, *Don We Now Our Gay Apparel: Gay Men's Dress in the Twentieth Century* (Oxford: Berg, 2000); Michael Bronski, *The Pleasure Principle: Sex, Backlash, and the Struggle for Gay Freedom* (New York: St. Martin's, 1998); and Dennis Altman, *The Homosexualization of America* (Boston: Beacon, 1982).

48. On the involvement of sexual minority men in organized sports and the development of organized sports groups for sexual minority men, see Eric Anderson, *In the Game: Gay Athletes and the Cult of Masculinity* (Albany: S.U.N.Y. Press, 2005), as well as the sites of the Gay and Lesbian Athletic Foundation (http://www.glaf.org), OutSports (http://www.OutSports.com), and GaySports (http://www.GaySports.com), July 29, 2007.

49. The International Gay Games were organized by Dr. Thomas Waddell, a gay former Olympian, and began in 1982; see http://www.GayGames.com. July 29, 2007.

50. On the International Gay Rodeo Association, see http://www.igra.com, July 29, 2007.

51. On the influence of gay men in setting masculine fashions, see Dotson, *Behold*, and Cole, *Gay Apparel*.

52. In the first three editions of *Leaves of Grass*, Whitman used this phrase in the first line of what came to be Section 24 of the poem he came to call "Song of Myself."

53. On Whitman's masculine self-construction, see William Pannapacker, *Revised Lives: Whitman, Religion, and Constructions of Identity in Nineteenth Century Anglo-American Culture* (New York: Routledge, 2003).

54. Original version of the poem later entitled "Song of Myself," l. 468, Whitman, *Leaves of Grass*, 1855 edition.

55. "Behold This Swarthy Face," Whitman, *Leaves of Grass* (Ninth edition/1892).

56. "We Two Boys Together Clinging," Whitman, *Leaves of Grass* (Ninth edition/ 1892).

57. Proulx, "Brokeback Mountain," 15.

58. On McCarthyism and homophobia, see Miller, *Out of the Past*; Adam, *Rise*; and D'Emilio, *Sexual Politics*. On the sex-crime panics of the 1950s, see Gerassi, *Boise*, and Miller, *Sex-Crime Panic*. On the arrests in Salt Lake, see Quinn, *Same-Sex Dynamics*.

59. Proulx, *Brokeback Mountain*, 29.

Chapter Three

The Rushing Cold
of the Mountain: Nature

For three months in the summer of 1963, from May to late August, Ennis and Jack are able to develop and share their love because they're living almost entirely apart from society on Brokeback Mountain. When they agree to herd sheep for the summer, they enter the sort of work environment that makes sexual intimacy between men possible. Each man brings with him the fear and shame that's been instilled in him by society, particularly by the hostility of men like Jack's father and Ennis's father and brother, but at least temporarily the separate world of the mountain frees them from these constraints, and allows them to feel and express the physical and emotional attraction, "the need and love of comrades,"[1] as Whitman named it, that's a part of both of them and that society forces men like them to suppress. Being in nature permits them to experience and share a desire that's a basic element of their natures.

In the story, Proulx's descriptions of the mountain, several of which already have been quoted, are brief but powerful, presenting its wild beauty not as something static, a sort of landscape picture seen from a distance, but as a living place where you're exposed to the enormous energy of natural processes, constant wind, changing light, sudden storms, warmth by day and cold at night, the inexorable movement of the seasons. The men work every day with the animals that they've brought to the mountain, but along with the sheep, dogs, horses, and mules there are wild animals as well, particularly the coyotes that continually watch and wait for the opportunity to pick off sheep and that the men hunt and hear howling in the distance at evening. The mountain is so high above the plain below that Ennis and Jack look down on the hawks, even though they soar. The changes in the weather are extreme, sometimes bringing turbulent thunderstorms with lightning and hail that strike the mountain or, in late summer, early snowstorms that leave it covered in snow for a few hours. The warmth of the short summer repeatedly lapses, the cold nights and cold winds warning of the fall and long winter soon to come. The descriptions not only stress the intensity of the natural forces at work on the mountain, but also the constancy of change, the speed with which time passes. While the mountain is a space that allows Jack and Ennis sexual and emotional freedom for the first time in their lives, Proulx's representation of the processes of nature repeatedly emphasizes the temporary aspect of their freedom there.

Ang Lee and those who collaborated with him in making the film expand on Proulx's descriptions of the mountain, presenting it in stunning images that capture and extend the sense that the text gives of the separateness, energy, and intensity of life there. Rodrigo Prieto's wonderful cinematography captures the bright, shifting sunlight by day; the sharpness of detail and the purity of color of the trees, meadows, and sky; the strong contrast of light and shadow on cliffs; the great spaces between one level of the mountain and another; the views toward other ridges and peaks; and the enormous distances out across the plains in the clear air. It particularly shows the size and depth and intense blueness of the Western sky and the feeling, high up on the mountain, of space all around and of being close to the constantly changing clouds. In full sun, the huge size of the cloud shadows moving over the forested slopes gives a sense of the immense scale of the landscape. Sometimes the clouds are backlit by blazing sun and seem incandescent, at others the sky is softly overcast, and the mist rising from the mountainsides makes land and sky seem almost to touch. The brilliant whiteness of the remaining snow against the strong green of grass and pines shows the continuing coldness of summer on the mountain, as do the clear, fast mountain streams and the constant movement of the wind through the grass and trees. The sense of space and light by day contrasts with the intense darkness of night, which in turn is offset by the rich, intimate light of the campfire. Because there are no towns nearby, no artificial lights compete with the moon and stars, and their light can illuminate the landscape at night. Some of the episodes added by the filmmakers increase the sense of the wildness of the place, as when Ennis comes on a bear by a stream, when Jack shoots at a coyote, or when Ennis shoots an elk. Although most of the parts of the film set on the mountain in fact were filmed in Alberta, rather than in the Big Horn Range of Wyoming, where Proulx says she imagined the mountain in her story, she's expressed her satisfaction with the approximation of its appearance by the filmmakers.[2] Some readers who loved the story, in part for the accuracy with which it conveys the language and culture of Wyoming, have said they wish the film had been made there, but still it gives a sense of the drama of the actual Wyoming landscape, the abruptness with which mountain ranges rise from the wide expanse of the high plains, and the pure beauty of its wilderness.

The filmmakers emphasize the contrast between the mountain and the small towns and ranches below, choosing for their settings stores, houses, and trailers of the kind that would have been seen in the early 1960s, none elaborate or prosperous looking, most of them simple, cheaply built, and run down. The range of colors is limited in the scenes involving the buildings that define the social world of Wyoming in the film, stressing shades that look dusty, shabby, and dark, in contrast to the brilliant light and color of the mountain. Many interior scenes, especially in the beat-up ranch houses, apartments, and trailers where Ennis lives, are dingy and poorly lit. This serves to sustain the viewer's sense of the liberating effect for Ennis and Jack of being apart from society in a natural place where they can act on sexual desires that their society expects men to deny. Also, the clothes that Gyllenhaal and Ledger wear, with their brown, blue, and green colors, tend to reinforce the association between Jack and Ennis and the natural landscape of the mountain.

In emphasizing the difference between the social world and the mountain, both Proulx and the filmmakers demonstrate an impressive sensitivity, especially for straight people, to the ways in which sexual minorities experience space in a homophobic society. People who are attracted to others of their own sex learn from an early age that though their society encourages public affection between people of the opposite sex, displays of affection between people of the same sex are severely limited. In most of American society, women are permitted to express physical affection for each other far more than men are; for most American men, a handshake and perhaps a brief hug are all that's acceptable. Affection between men often is expressed by feigning violence, as in the playful punches exchanged by men who are friends. In public, at least, any more sustained or affectionate touching between men is intolerable, as any man who's gone to a public place like an airport or a train station to greet or see off a man he loves can explain. When two men who love each other are together in most public spaces in this society, their lifelong experience of homophobia usually restrains their affection in every possible way, not only keeping them from embracing and kissing, as heterosexuals are able to do whenever they meet or part, but for many even from touching each other or looking at each other with too much intensity of affection. Their physical relationship, and thus their freedom to express emotion, constantly are mediated and restricted by the threat of homophobia. For such men to go ahead and express what they feel for each other with the ease and unself-consciousness, the naturalness, that heterosexuals simply take for granted is to risk a spectrum of hostile reactions, from dirty looks, to insults, to physical attacks. Particularly in small or tight-knit communities, of course, this also means the risk of hostile gossip, of social exclusion, of job loss, and of reprisals. While same sex couples can express affection openly in some areas of major cities where there are large sexual minority communities, there's always the threat, even in West Hollywood or Chelsea, that holding hands or kissing will provoke insults or gay-bashing. In rural Wyoming in 1963 men who felt physical and emotional attraction for other men would have been extremely careful not to show it—as still is the case more than forty years later.[3]

Before the emergence of urban sexual minority communities that could challenge official harassment and provide at least a relative amount of safety, safe spaces for the expression of same-sex desire were limited. In many cities there were bars that catered to men who desired men, but there always was the possibility of police raids and exposure. In more rural areas, men could develop sexual relationships with each other in the context of the extended family and local community organizations such as church and school, but usually they had to be secretive, especially as hostility to homosexuality became more intense in the mid-twentieth century. Men who desired men met furtively in many public places, including parks, theaters, bus and train stations, public restrooms, and highway rest stops, but for many the only really safe spaces for the expression of passion and affection were indoors in a private house or apartment or perhaps a hotel or a motel, or outdoors, in a rural or wilderness area where it could be known for sure that no other people would be. Some in urban gay communities think of rural areas as unremittingly hostile to sexual minorities, and certainly small towns can be so, but for some men, especially those whose work took them away from the local community, the isolation and seclusion of the country allowed the expression of male-male desire. As Ennis tells Jack, the only place they really can be together for days at a time and move naturally from shared work and play to shared affection and sex, is "'way the hell out in the back a nowhere.'"[4] For them, the mountain provides a safe space in which they can begin to express their sexuality. There they can feel as if they own the world and nothing is wrong, as Ennis thinks years later, remembering their summer on the mountain.

Proulx stresses this sense of being physically and emotionally liberated in a natural space where natural desire finally can be expressed, in contrast to the homophobic repression of the social world, in her description of the exuberant passion Jack and Ennis share during their summer on the mountain. After the passage describing their repeated passionate lovemaking, first at night in the tent and then outside in the sunshine during the day, she says that to them being alone together on the mountain feels like they're "flying in the euphoric, bitter air."[5] They look "down on the hawk's back"[6] during the day and on the lights of vehicles driving on the plain at night and feel "suspended above ordinary affairs. . . . They believed themselves invisible . . ."[7] As always is the case in her writing, the passage is rich with implications. It directly compares their shared sexual ecstasy to flying, resonating with the sense of complete freedom that many people experience in sexually charged dreams of being able to fly, and it emphasizes how remote they feel from the society below them, whose daily life, potentially hostile to theirs, they still can hear and see from a far distance. Of course, the pun on "affairs" is particularly striking; the members of the majority, driving their vehicles and living on their ranches below, are free to have their "affairs" without the constant threat of harassment and violence, but they wouldn't react to the love between Ennis and Jack as any "ordinary affair."

As Annie Proulx has explained in interviews, her interest in history, particularly in the methods of the French Annales school "which pioneered minute examination of the lives of ordinary people through account books, wills, marriage and death records, farming and crafts techniques, the development of technologies"[8] has helped to inspire her approach to writing fiction, with its sensitive attention to the implications of the material conditions in which people live and work. She's especially aware of the determining role that the landscape can play in the economic and social environment. In her stories about Wyoming, she demonstrates a sense of irony concerning the landscape, which, while grand and inspiring, also is harsh and difficult and provides few ways of easily making a living. But in the case of "Brokeback Mountain," the beautiful, demanding environment not only impoverishes, it also frees. As she's said, it's a "freedom-granting yet hostile landscape."[9] For man-loving men, the landscape can offer the utopian space that's denied them just about everywhere else by society, in which they can become themselves sexually and emotionally, as straight people are enabled to do in virtually every space in the society they control. The mountain is presented as an active force, almost as a living being, a character in itself, as is recognized implicitly by both Ennis and Jack as the story proceeds. As Jack says later on to Ennis, referring to their summer on the mountain and the intensity of their bond and the ways it influences their lives, "'Old Brokeback got us good . . .'"[10] For Ennis, at the end of the narrative, it becomes a kind of talisman of Jack in the simple shrine he makes of the shirts and the postcard.

Proulx's presentation of the mountain as a liberating space that allows the men to develop their love recalls Whitman's presentation of nature in the *Calamus* poems. Whitman was the first American writer to acknowledge that the secluded edges of the cultivated landscape were a zone apart from society where men could have the freedom to fully express their physical and emotional attraction to each other. He opens the *Calamus* section of *Leaves of Grass* by announcing that by retreating "in paths untrodden . . . away from the clank of the world"[11] he has

> Escaped from the life that exhibits itself,
> From all the standards hitherto publish'd, from pleasures,
>   profits, conformities,
> Which too long I was offering to feed my soul . . .[12]

In the wild landscape, "in the growth by the margin of pond-waters,"[13] he is "no longer abash'd"[14] and finally is free to sing the songs "of manly attachment . . . To tell the secret of my nights and days, / To celebrate the need of comrades."[15] Whitman not only presents the isolation and privacy of nature as liberating him to sing his songs of male love, but also depicts himself as being able to share affection openly with other men in natural places. While in some of the *Calamus* poems he describes the excitement of the mutual attraction he experiences with men on the streets of Manhattan, he also says that we should think of him as a man

> Whose happiest days were far off through fields, in woods,
>   on hills, he and another wandering hand in hand, they
>   twain apart from other men . . .[16]

The parallel between Whitman and Proulx in their recognition that the wild places at the edges of society allow some men the freedom to love each other points toward the connection of their work to an important tradition in the representation of nature and male love. Both the *Calamus* poems and "Brokeback Mountain" can be related to the long and rich literary and artistic history of the representation of men loving men in ideal natural landscapes. For centuries, pastoral places far from cities and near the wilderness have been depicted, especially in poetry, as the site of male love. The tradition begins with the Greeks and continues through Roman, Medieval, and Renaissance writing. Whitman's *Calamus* poems can be understood in relation to it, as creating for the first time a celebration of male love in the American landscape, at the point where agricultural land turns to wilderness. Also, as all Americans are aware, American culture has a long tradition of heroic narratives of Western adventure, depicting the process of extending an agricultural society into the wilderness. Such narratives have been central not only to justifying American national expansion, but also to articulating standards of American masculinity as well as homophobic restrictions on male friendship. "Brokeback Mountain" can be related to both the tradition of homoerotic pastoral art and to the heroic Western tradition, but before doing this it's necessary to briefly summarize the development of the pastoral ideal in art and literature. The remainder of this chapter will discuss the story and the film in connection with the pastoral tradition and then in connection with the tradition of the Western.

~

Since the time of ancient Greece and Rome, European cultural expression has idealized rustic landscapes between the city and the wilderness as places where nature's benevolence can make human happiness possible. Such idealizations of pastoral life were written by and for members of sophisticated urban elites, and masked the exploitative relationship between city and country, ignoring the fact that Greek and Roman cities drained the countryside of its resources and taxed it heavily. Major Classical writers often set their poems and stories in the imagined landscape of Arcadia, an idyllic mountain valley with a mild climate; lush woods and meadows; cool, pure springs and streams; and surrounding mountains and forests that separated it from the cares and troubles of urban society. Arcadia was pictured as being inhabited by a simple community of shepherds whose easy labor in a land of abundance made it possible for them to spend much of their time relaxing in the shade, cultivating simple, enjoyable forms of artistic expression, particularly playing the flute and singing. The playful singing contests in which they were imagined to engage were presented as part of an endless, delightful cycle of flirtation and courtship, erotic flight and pursuit. Ancient culture didn't subject same-sex desire, or sexuality in general, to the kind of hostile moral judgments later imposed by Christianity, and in the pleasant meadows and groves of Arcadia Classical writers not only imagined shepherds courting shepherdesses, but also courting other shepherds. The tradition of pastoral poetry was one of the most important areas of cultural expression in which the Greeks and Romans celebrated love between men.[17]

In Classical literature, the Arcadian landscape was strongly associated with sexual energy. The meadows and woods and mountain forests were imagined as being the home of male and female spirits that represented the sexual power of nature, satyrs, nymphs, and dryads, and of course their great god, Pan, whose physical appearance, half man and half goat, directly manifested his phallic animal sexuality. The actual region called Arcadia on which the myth was based, a secluded area of mountains and valleys in the central Peloponnesus in Greece, was believed to have been the birthplace of Pan. The simple reed flute, the instrument of the idealized Arcadian shepherd, was believed to have been the creation of Pan, who often was depicted as carrying and playing it in his wanderings and sexual adventures in Arcadia. For sophisticated Greek and Roman audiences, this idealized pastoral landscape on the edge of the more primitive mountain wilderness offered the fantasy of an escape from the constraints and responsibilities of society, providing an imaginary world where sexual desire and all the emotions related to it could be fully expressed.[18]

The tradition of lyric, homoerotic poetry set in an idealized pastoral landscape was defined by Theocritus, a Greek probably from the colony at Syracuse on Sicily in the third century B.C., when Hellenistic Greek culture was flourishing around the Mediterranean. Theocritus seems to have lived for a time in Alexandria, and to have written for a powerful aristocratic patron and a privileged circle. His *Idylls*, a series of thirty lyric poems, include many on pastoral themes that established the forms and conventions of pastoral writing that were followed and developed by many other Greek and Roman poets in succeeding centuries, and that have continued to influence many European and American writers until today. Theocritus set them not in Arcadia, but in the sunny rural landscape of his own Sicily, which he idealized in terms much like those associated with Arcadia, and which he depicted with a loving eye for the details of the cycle of the seasons. His poems repeatedly compare the processes of nature, the blooming of flowers in spring, then the flourishing of leaves and fruit, then their decline in autumn and winter, to the changing emotions of lover and beloved. The characters who speak in his pastoral poems are presented as ordinary shepherds, whose idealized, easy way of life allows them time and freedom to engage in romance and to explore their emotions. Although Theocritus describes many situations in which shepherds are attracted to women, including both mortals and minor nature deities, many of the *Idylls* are concerned with love between men, which is presented as being as valid as love between men and women. In some of the homoerotic poems, following a widespread pattern in ancient Greek culture, the speaker is somewhat older than a beautiful young man with whom he's in love, but there are others in which no age distinction is made.[19]

While male sexual intercourse is referred to directly in a few of the homoerotic poems, particularly in a ribald one that presents a comic argument between two former lovers, in most of them Theocritus concentrates on the intense emotions of one man for another, constructing attraction between men in terms of romantic love. He presents a number of specific homoerotic situations: a shepherd yearning for a lover who's absent; a lover's warning, to a young man who's rejected him, about the transience of youth and beauty; the feelings of a man, just getting over a love affair with another, and finding himself falling in love yet again with a young man; a lover who's driven to suicide by a cruel young man who rejects him; one shepherd's lament over the death of another. Other poems deal with more joyful aspects of male intimacy, such as one that depicts a singing contest between two beautiful young shepherds, suggesting the mixture of rivalry and affection between them. In one poem in which the speaker praises the young man he loves, he expresses the hope that their love will never grow old and will be remembered the way the Athenians remember two famous male lovers in whose honor young men held annual kissing contests. In many of the poems, a persistent theme is the lover's desire for a closer, more permanent connection with the man he loves, and his repeated invitations to his lover to come to him or to stay and live with him.[20]

Other Greek writers of the Hellenistic Period continued the tradition of the homoerotic pastoral poem begun by Theocritus. In contrast to the individualistic, innovative approach to literary and artistic expression that's valued in American and European culture now, in the Classical period great importance was placed on working within and maintaining the established conventions of the various arts, and so pastoral writing tended to emphasize certain conventionalized literary forms, settings, characters, and situations. The idealized rustic setting; the shepherds, nymphs, and other figures; even the identities and names of characters that had been created by Theocritus were employed again and again in poetry and in romantic fiction until the eventual decline of Classical culture. Among the stock characters who appear repeatedly are the shepherds Daphnis, Damoetas, Corydon, Alexis, Lycidas, and Thyrsis, to name a few of the most well known. One particular strand of the tradition, the homoerotic elegy, was developed in two famous poems by Hellenistic writers following Theocritus, the "Lament for Adonis" by Bion, in which the author grieves for the youthful, beautiful nature god Adonis, who was believed to die and then be reborn each year, and, in honor of Bion after his death, the "Lament for Bion," attributed to Moschus. Both the invitation to the lover to live together and the lament over the death of a beautiful, beloved man became established as two of the most important themes of homoerotic pastoral.[21] The two themes are evident in some of the most significant English and American pastoral poetry—and of course, they're central to *Brokeback Mountain.*

The homoerotic pastoral tradition was given its fullest form at the end of the first century B.C., by the great Roman poet Virgil in a series of ten poems in Latin often called the *Eclogues* or the *Bucolics.* Like Theocritus and other Greek writers of pastoral, Virgil wrote for a sophisticated urban audience; his patron was the first emperor, Augustus. Strongly concerned to show his respect for the precedents set by Greek culture, Virgil located his *Eclogues* in the lovely imaginary landscape of Arcadia, the "*locus amoenus*" or "pleasant place" where except for the light work of caring for their flocks, people could be free to play, sing, and flirt together. He presents life in Arcadia as an ideal earlier Golden Age, from which his contemporary world, for all its power and grandeur, represents a decline. In his depiction of Arcadia, Virgil created an image of a perfect pastoral landscape, analogous in many ways to the Judeo-Christian myth of the Garden of Eden, which has exerted a continuing influence. For centuries Arcadia has been celebrated not only by poets but also by painters, sculptors, musicians, and other artists. The word "pastoral," used for the kinds of landscapes idealized in the image of Arcadia, and applied to works of art depicting such landscapes, comes from the Latin "pastor," for shepherd.[22]

Several of the *Eclogues* present erotic situations between men, particularly through depictions of shepherds singing together. The Third Eclogue includes a comic singing contest in which two shepherds tease and insult each other, referring to affairs they've had with both women and men, and in the Fifth two shepherds respectfully compete to see who can offer the most moving elegy on the death of Daphnis, a shepherd they've loved for his beauty and sweet singing. The Second Eclogue is by far the most important Classical pastoral poem depicting love between men, and continued to inspire poets who wished to honor male friendship and love through the Middle Ages, the Renaissance, the Romantic Period, and to the present.[23] The poem is largely in the voice of the shepherd Corydon, who, Virgil announces in the famous opening line, "burned for fair Alexis."[24] Much of the poem is a song sung by Corydon, in which he expresses his frustration and sorrow at being rejected by Alexis, and repeats his invitation to him, telling Alexis about the quality of his flocks and pastures, of the gifts he can give, of his fine singing, of his good looks. Before he abandons his effort to persuade Alexis, Corydon makes one last attempt, describing the happy life they could enjoy living together in a shepherd's cottage in the country, hunting, herding, and entertaining each other with music and flute playing:

> Ah that thou wouldst but care to be with me in the rough country,
>   To dwell in low cots, to shoot the deer, or drive a flock of kids to the green mallow bed.
>   With me in the woods together thou shalt copy Pan in singing; Pan first taught to join with wax the row of reeds: Pan is guardian of the sheep and of the shepherds . . .[25]

The poem has been so influential on writers and other artists interested in depicting intimate relationships between men that even the names Corydon and Alexis became signifiers of male love; when Andre Gide published his bold, courageous defense of homosexuality shortly after the First World War, he entitled it *Corydon* (1924).

During the Middle Ages, the pastoral tradition, even with its strong element of homoeroticism, continued to be valued as part of Christian Europe's inheritance from Classical culture, and with the start of the Renaissance, as part of the general enthusiasm for the rediscovery and further development of Classical art, many poets, playwrights, painters, sculptors, composers, and other artists were drawn to the representation of episodes, characters, and settings taken from the ancient traditions concerning Arcadia and its happy inhabitants.[26] Dante, Petrarch, and other Medieval writers turned to Virgil in particular, and wrote Eclogues inspired by his, treating the form as a way to present an ideal of strong but nonsexual friendship.[27] Renaissance writers in Italy, France, Spain, and England were drawn to the pastoral; among the English poets who wrote important pastoral poems and other pastoral works are Edmund Spenser, Christopher Marlowe, Richard Barnfield, and Sir Phillip Sidney. Shakespeare used it as well, in the comedy *As You Like It*, set in the Forest of Arden, an embodiment of the landscape of pastoral fantasy; Andrew Marvell celebrated pastoral landscapes in some of his most famous poems, and Alexander Pope wrote a series of pastoral poems closely based on those of Virgil.[28] In part, the great attraction of the myth of Arcadia and its Golden Age was as a kind of natural utopia that allowed the depiction of human relationships under ideal conditions. For Renaissance writers concerned with male intimacy, and especially with the possibility of love between males, such as Marlowe and Barnfield, it exerted a special appeal, and became the basis of a revived tradition of pastoral male love poetry, often depicting the love of an adult man for a beautiful adolescent.[29] Many other later writers, including John Milton, Percy Bysshe Shelley, and Matthew Arnold used the conventions of the pastoral in important elegies honoring male friendship, though not physical love between men.[30] Whitman's homoerotic poetry uses none of the conventions of Classical pastoral, but often presents an idyllic American landscape whose peace and security welcome male love, much like Arcadia.[31] The modern writer most clearly influenced by the homoerotic pastoral tradition is E. M. Forster. In novels with heterosexual characters, such as *Where Angels Fear to Tread* (1905), *The Longest Journey* (1907), and *A Room with a View* (1908), Forster contrasts English sexual repression with the natural sexual energy of those who live in the countryside, and his great novel about a young man coming to accept his love for other men, *Maurice* (1914; published 1971), ultimately presents Maurice rejecting the homophobic repression of his society for life in the country with his lover Alec, a gamekeeper. Of course, Alec's name directly echoes that of Corydon's beloved Alexis.[32] As contemporary theorists have pointed out, readers shouldn't assume the existence of a transhistorical "gay" identity in all these works; what writers of different periods and different cultures understood desire between males to signify differed substantially. Still, it needs to be noted that this is a recent insight, and that many readers and writers have read—and continue to read—earlier representations of desire between men as speaking directly to them about their own experience as they understand it. The construction and significance of sexuality and gender in Classical culture, including physical and emotional intimacy between men, necessarily were different in many ways from those in succeeding periods, but many later readers and writers understood the constructions of male intimacy that were part of the Classical pastoral tradition as affirming and validating their own concerns with physical and emotional relations between men.

Although *Brokeback Mountain* depicts characters and settings that are entirely modern and American, many connections can be drawn between the homoerotic pastoral tradition and both the story and the movie. Proulx certainly presents Ennis and Jack without idealizing them or their circumstances, in contrast to the idealized presentation of rustic working-class characters in the work of earlier writers of pastoral, and the film generally respects her recognition of the harshness of the lives of the characters, but there still are many obvious parallels with the pastoral tradition. First of all, as Proulx has pointed out to those who keep calling *Brokeback Mountain* a love story about "gay cowboys," Ennis and Jack actually are sheepherders, and many men who work with cattle in the American West look down on those who work with sheep. The fact that the two men are shepherds connects them directly to the shepherd-lovers of poetry. Also, like the poems about shepherds by so many earlier writers, although without their degree of idealization, Proulx's story depicts a rural world apart from the cares of society, close to the primitive wilderness, where working with animals brings men close to nature, and yet also leaves them plenty of time for the shared joys of companionable conversation, play, music, and love. The landscape of Brokeback Mountain is harsher and wilder than the peaceful summer landscapes of Arcadia depicted by many of the poets, being the farthest edge of the continuum from the pastoral to the primitive, where the outer edge of an agricultural society meets the wilderness, but it still allows a life that combines the relatively easy work of tending sheep with the adventure of hunting. Like Virgil's Corydon, the two American sheepherders easily shift from caring for their sheep to hunting on the forested slopes around the meadows where the sheep graze. Their lives on the mountain share many other similarities with those of their counterparts in poetry. Ennis and Jack are surrounded by a natural landscape of incomparable beauty and purity, whose meadows, forests, and streams equal anything imagined by a pastoral poet. While in modern American culture a belief in nature spirits like Pan and his satyrs and nymphs is a largely forgotten mythology, the very mountain itself seems alive with the turbulent energy of the changing weather and the constant Wyoming wind. The men both enjoy living and working outdoors, and understand and work easily and well with their horses, dogs, mules, and sheep, though their romance sometimes causes them to forget their responsibility to their flock. The work that Ennis and Jack have to do usually is easy enough that they're able to enjoy long conversations, and to move gradually toward deeper friendship through erotically charged sessions of eating and drinking on the summer evenings, joking, teasing, playing, and making music together. Like the shepherds of poetry, they sing for each other, offering favorite comic and serious songs. Where the shepherd of the poetic tradition amused himself and his companion by playing on a flute, Jack plays his harmonica. Eventually, their mutual attraction reaches its first passionate consummation, and their alternating passion and play continue for the rest of their summer together. Though the later parts of the story and the film stress the destructive impact of social hostility on their love, the parts of both that are set on the mountain have some of the same mood of innocent, joyful, natural romance between men often found in the pastoral tradition. What occurs on Brokeback Mountain can be seen as a modern version of a homoerotic pastoral idyll.

In locating male love in nature, the story and the film share a fundamental similarity with the tradition of homoerotic pastoral poetry that was redeveloped in the Renaissance, based on the Classical tradition: *Brokeback Mountain,* like much of the poetry of the past five hundred years that celebrates love between men, counters hostility to male love by presenting that love as being fundamentally a *part* of nature. Christianity, unlike the culture of the Classical period, whose pagan religions affirmed and celebrated sexuality, including love between people of the same sex, restricted its approval of sexuality to sex within heterosexual marriage with the goal of procreation, and generally was hostile to same-sex love. The degree of Christian hostility varied, of course, and in some places and times in the Middle Ages and the Renaissance love between men seems to have been tolerated by members of the majority, but still men who loved other men often were subject to ridicule, scorn, religious condemnation, and punishment. The Judeo-Christian tradition, unlike the pagan religions, often condemned same-sex love as an "abomination," using an elaborate and intensely hostile homophobic rhetoric in which same-sex love was denounced as a "crime against nature." These attacks, of course, reduced male love to sex, ignoring emotion, and focused on supposedly "unnatural acts" between people of the same sex, especially anal intercourse. Though the exact meaning of the "crime" of "sodomy" varied in different religious and legal systems, anal intercourse between men was denounced insistently as its worst form; well into the nineteenth century, religious and legal officials found it so "unspeakable" that they used Latin to designate it as *"peccatum illud horribile, inter Christianos non nominandum"*—"that horrible sin not to be named among Christians."[33] In contrast to the dominant culture's construction of male love as "unnatural," the pastoral homoerotic tradition, by locating love between men *in* nature, provided an effective way for its advocates to refute homophobic hostility, and to present their love in terms of naturalness and innocence, stressing emotional as well as sexual connections between men. The revival of the ancient pastoral tradition in the context of a society officially hostile to same-sex love allowed men who loved men not only to invoke the precedent and prestige of ancient culture but also to construct their love as they themselves often experienced it, as innocent, delightful, and natural. From the perspective of men who loved men, their attraction wasn't simply physical, but often also was profoundly emotional. In its advertising, the film does something very similar to homoerotic pastoral poetry with regard to nature; the main poster for *Brokeback Mountain* shows images of Ledger and Gyllenhaal against a beautiful view of the Grand Teton Range, with the slogan, "Love is a force of nature."[34]

One of the most persistent themes of the homoerotic pastoral tradition, the effort of one shepherd to convince another to come and share his life with him in the country, is of particular relevance to *Brokeback Mountain*. This kind of invitation is the subject of Virgil's Second Eclogue, and also of works by the two most important English Renaissance writers of homoerotic pastoral, Marlowe and Barnfield. Marlowe's most famous short lyric poem, given the title "The Passionate Shepherd to His Love" by an editor when it first was published in 1599, shortly after the poet's death, presents a shepherd inviting a lover to come with him to enjoy all the delights of love in a beautiful natural setting. The speaker offers not only the prospect of life and love in nature, but also material gifts to try to get his beloved to agree to live with him:

Come live with me, and be my love,
And we will all the pleasures prove
That valleys, groves, hills and fields,
Woods, or steepy mountain yields

And we will sit upon the rocks,
Seeing the shepherds feed their flocks
By shallow rivers, to whose falls
Melodious birds sing madrigals.

I will make thee beds of roses,
And a thousand fragrant posies,
A cap of flowers, and a kirtle
Embroidered all with leaves of myrtle.

A gown made of the finest wool
Which from our pretty lambs we pull,

Fair lined slippers for the cold
With buckles of the purest gold.

A belt of straw and ivy-buds,
With coral clasps and amber studs,
And if these pleasures thee may move,
Come live with me, and be my love.

The shepherd swains shall dance and sing
For thy delight each May morning,
If these delights thy mind may move,
Then live with me, and be my love.[35]

For centuries readers from the sexual majority, ignoring the considerable evidence of Marlowe's love of young men, have assumed that the speaker in the poem offers his invitation to a woman, thus, from their perspective, "naturalizing" it as a text about love as it's experienced by those in the majority. However, there isn't clear internal evidence in the poem itself for this assumption; no pronouns are used, and the gifts that the speaker describes, in the fashions of the time, could be appropriate for either a woman or a man. In fact, the poem directly parallels the section of Virgil's Second Eclogue quoted earlier: much as Corydon offers the pleasures of love in the countryside to his Alexis, Marlowe's poem may be read as the invitation by one man to another to join him in exploring and enjoying their passion in a pastoral landscape. Though Marlowe isn't as explicit as Virgil is in the poem that is Marlowe's model, he's provided a love lyric that's entirely open to the interpretation that it celebrates love between men.[36] The fact that straight readers assume it must be about their own love only underscores the fact that, for those who are perceptive, Marlowe is placing male love on the same plane as love between men and women.

Barnfield wrote a number of homoerotic poems, including a series of sonnets that frequently have been compared and contrasted with those of Shakespeare; while Shakespeare's also address love between two men, they do so with much more intellectual and technical sophistication than Barnfield's. Still, as gay scholars recently have pointed out, the negative comparative criticism of Barnfield may have to do not only with his poetic ability, which of course isn't equal to Shakespeare's, but also with his exuberant, often playful affirmation of male love.[37] His most significant homoerotic poem also uses the theme of invitation, and is much more explicit than Marlowe's. Entitled "The Tears of an Affectionate Shepherd Sick for Love" (1594), it's presented as being spoken by a shepherd in love with a beautiful adolescent who's also being courted by a woman. Barnfield names the speaker Daphnis, after the beautiful shepherd of the Classical tradition, and the young man Ganymede, after the young male lover of Zeus in Greek mythology. The opening of the poem acknowledges but also challenges Christian condemnations of male love, and does so in a playful, sexually suggestive way:

> Scarce had the morning star hid from the light
> Heaven's crimson canopy with stars bespangled
> But I began to rue th' unhappy sight
> Of that fair boy that had my heart entangled;
> Cursing the time, the place, the sense, the sin;
> I came, I saw, I viewed, I slipped in.
>
> If it be sin to love a sweet faced boy,
> Whose amber locks trust up in golden trammels
> Dangle adown his lovely cheeks with joy,
> When pearl and flowers his fair hair enamels
> If it be sin to love a lovely lad,
> Oh then sin I, for whom my soul is sad . . .[38]

Ganymede doesn't return Daphnis's love with the same intensity, and therefore much of the poem takes the form of a passionate but unsuccessful invitation, modeled on that in Virgil's Second Eclogue:

> . . . If thou wilt come and dwell with me at home,
> My sheep-cote shall be strowed with new green rushes;
> We'll haunt the trembling prickets as they roam
> About the fields, along the hawthorn bushes.
> I have a piebald cur to hunt the hare:
> So we will live on dainty forest fare.
>
> Nay more than this, I have a garden plot,
> Wherein there wants nor herbs, nor roots, nor flowers
> (Flowers to smell, roots to eat, herbs for the pot),
> And dainty shelters where the welkin lowers:
> Sweet-smelling beds of lilies and of roses,
> Which rosemary banks and lavender encloses . . .
>
> . . . But if thou wilt not pity my complaint,
> My tears, nor vows, nor oaths, made to thy beauty,
> What shall I do? But languish, die, or faint,
> Since thou dost scorn my tears and my soul's duty;
> And tears contemned, vows and oaths must fail,
> For where tears cannot, nothing can prevail . . .[39]

Brokeback Mountain depicts a different sort of relationship, between two young men of the same age, and depicts them as conventionally masculine working-class American men, using none of the fanciful detail or courtly language employed by the two Elizabethan writers, but there's a fundamental similarity with their poems and with many other pastoral compositions based on Virgil's Second Eclogue. The theme of invitation is central to *Brokeback Mountain* as it is to so many works of the homoerotic pastoral tradition. During their reunion in 1967, Jack invites Ennis to make a life together in the country: "'Listen. I'm thinkin, tell you what, if you and me had a little ranch together, little cow and calf operation, your horses, it'd be some sweet life.'"[40] As in homoerotic pastoral poetry, the lover's invitation is rejected. Like Corydon and the other characters based on him, Jack is made to feel prolonged yearning, sadness, and nostalgia because the man he loves won't fully accept him. But unlike Virgil's Alexis and the other poetic characters modeled on him, who don't return the love that's offered them, Ennis does feel an intense sexual and emotional connection with Jack, but is afraid to accept Jack's invitation because of what he believes may happen if he's visible as a man-loving man and because of the shame he's been taught to feel about his love. In contrast to other homoerotic pastoral invitations, in *Brokeback Mountain* the homophobia enforced and instilled by society is the reason one man refuses the other's invitation. The film strongly develops the theme of invitation and rejection, showing Jack repeatedly raising the prospect of living together with Ennis, and Ennis repeatedly refusing. Only after Jack's death does Ennis begin to fully realize what he's lost in rejecting Jack. Both versions of *Brokeback Mountain* thus use the theme of invitation not only to affirm the value of male love, but also to demonstrate the brutality and destructiveness of homophobic hatred and violence.

The tragic mood that increasingly dominates *Brokeback Mountain* after Jack and Ennis must return to society at the end of their summer together, intensifying as Ennis rejects Jack's invitations and becoming complete with Ennis's overwhelming grief for Jack at the close of the narrative, connects it to the most emotionally and spiritually profound strand of the tradition of homoerotic pastoral writing, the elegy. From Hellenistic times to the present, writers concerned with friendship and love between men have used this form to express grief over the death of another man. Classical writers developed the elegy according to pastoral conventions, often presenting one shepherd's lament for another, and following the great revival of pastoral writing in the Renaissance, European poets drew on the tradition, employing conventional pastoral names, settings, and references in elegies honoring close friends who had died. Several of the greatest poets in English, including John Milton, Percy Bysshe Shelley, and Matthew Arnold, turned to the conventions of the pastoral elegy as a means of expressing grief over the death of close male friends. While his writing uses no explicit Classical conventions, one of Whitman's greatest poems is in the elegiac tradition, "When Lilacs Last in the

Dooryard Bloom'd" (1867), his lament for Abraham Lincoln and the dead of the Civil War. For gay writers confronting the catastrophic losses of the AIDS pandemic, the elegy also has provided an appropriate means of expressing grief, as in Paul Monette's beautiful and powerful collection mourning the death of his partner, Roger Horwitz, *Love Alone: Eighteen Elegies For Rog* (1988).[41]

The great elegies in English usually follow a structure that starts by expressing grief over the friend who has died, then remembering and honoring him, and finally moving toward some sort of reconciliation with the fact of his death. For writers who were able to accept religious conceptions of an afterlife, this last section usually expressed confidence that the spirit of the beloved man would live on. For modern writers less able to accept traditional religious hope, the conclusion of the elegy is more problematic, but may express some sense that the spiritual influence of the man who has been lost will continue. Most of the great English elegies undoubtedly weren't consciously intended to be homoerotic in our sense, but passages in them suggest an intensity of affection and grief with which many readers who are men who love men have identified strongly over the years. Because of the clear association of the conventions of the pastoral elegy with the homoeroticism of Greek and Roman culture, of which educated readers necessarily have been aware, the form tends to be suggestive not only of emotional but also of physical love. It's important to remember, too, that before the development of the negative medical-legal category of homosexuality in the late nineteenth century, the boundary between homosociality and homosexuality was less sharply drawn, and so there likely was more room for the expression of physical affection between male friends for earlier writers and readers.[42]

It's not necessary to discuss the major English elegies in any detail, but here are a few illustrations, indicating the intensity of emotion they present on the part of one man for another, and the ways in which they employ descriptions of pastoral landscape to express it. The first of the great pastoral elegies is John Milton's "Lycidas" (1638), which he wrote on the death of his friend Edward King, who was a student with Milton at Cambridge and also was a religious poet, and who drowned in a shipwreck in 1637 at the age of twenty-five. Milton presents them both as shepherds, giving King the conventional pastoral name of Lycidas. He first presents an idealized picture of their friendship, and then expresses his grief:

> . . . For we were nursed upon the selfsame hill,
> Fed the same flock, by fountain, shade, and rill.
> Together both, ere the high lawns appeared
> Under the opening eyelids of the morn,
> We drove afield, and both together heard
> What time the grayfly winds her sultry horn.

Battening our flocks with the fresh dews of night,
Oft till the star that rose at evening bright
Toward Heaven's descent had sloped his westering wheel.
Meanwhile the rural ditties were not mute,
Tempered to th' oaten flute,
Rough satyrs danced, and fauns with cloven heel
From the glad sound would not be absent long,
And old Damoetas loved to hear our song.

But O the heavy change, now thou art gone,
Now thou art gone, and never must return!
Thee, shepherd, thee the woods and desert caves,
With wild thyme and the gadding vine o'ergrown,
And all the echoes mourn.[43]

The poem moves toward acceptance of Milton's loss of his friend with the admonition: "Weep no more, woeful shepherds, weep no more, / For Lycidas your sorrow is not dead . . ."[44] and then the vision of him resurrected, "in the blest kingdoms meek of joy and love."[45]

One of Shelley's finest poems is "Adonais" (1821), his elegy on the death of his friend, the great lyric poet John Keats. The name Adonais, which Shelley gives to Keats in the poem, refers to the beautiful young nature god Adonis; the poem is modeled on Bion's "Lament for Adonis," which Shelley had translated into English. Shelley expresses his intense grief over the tragedy of Keats's death at twenty-four with the repeated exclamation, "O, weep for Adonais—he is dead!"[46] In the passage below, he presents the brilliant poetic ideas that Keats didn't live to express as being like his flocks, dying without the care of their dead shepherd:

O, weep for Adonais—The quick Dreams,
The passion-winged Ministers of thought,
Who were his flocks, whom near the living streams
Of his young spirit he fed, and whom he taught
The love which was its music, wander not,—
Wander no more, from kindling brain to brain,
But droop there, whence they sprung; and mourn their lot
Round the cold heart, where, after their sweet pain,
They ne'er will gather strength, or find a home again.[47]

Shelley doesn't have the confident Christian faith in resurrection that marks Milton's "Lycidas," but he does achieve a degree of reconciliation with the fact of Keats's death through a form of pantheism, saying that Adonais lives on because he "is made one with Nature . . . He is a portion of that loveliness / Which once he made more lovely . . ."[48]

The last of the major English elegies to rely directly on the conventions of Classical pastoral is Matthew Arnold's "Thyrsis" (1866), which he wrote about the death of his friend, the religious poet Arthur Hugh Clough. Arnold makes many references to the pastoral tradition and gives Clough the conventional shepherd's name of Thyrsis in the poem, but sets it in the landscape they both knew and loved, the hills from which one can see the "dreaming spires"[49] of Oxford. It depicts Arnold revisiting the area in wintertime, and remembering Clough as he sees once more the fields and trees they had admired on their walks together when they were students. As he walks through the winter landscape, Arnold anticipates how it will be in spring, and thinks of the cuckoo's song, saying

> . . . next year he will return,
> And we shall have him in the sweet spring days,
> With whitening hedges, and uncrumpling fern,
> And bluebells trembling by the forest ways,
> And scent of hay new-mown.
> But Thyrsis never more we swains shall see,
> See him come back, and cut a smoother reed,
> And blow a strain the world at last shall heed—
> For Time, not Corydon, hath conquered thee![50]

His walk eventually leads Arnold to the elm that was the favorite goal of his walks with Clough; he exclaims

> . . . O Thyrsis, still our tree is there!—
> Ah, vain! These English fields, this upland dim,
> These brambles pale with mist engarlanded,
> That lone, sky-pointing tree, are not for him . . .[51]

Arnold pictures his friend not in any Christian afterlife, but with Demeter, the ancient earth goddess:

> To a boon southern country he is fled,
> And now in happier air,
> Wandering with the great Mother's train divine
> (And purer or more subtle soul than thee,
> I trow, the mighty Mother doth not see) . . .[52]

Whitman uses none of Arnold's references to the shepherds, singing contests, and pagan deities of Classical pastoral in "When Lilacs Last in the Dooryard Bloom'd," but his elegy for Lincoln follows a pattern similar to the other great elegies, moving from intense grief, to a celebration of the man who has died, to reconciliation with the fact of his death. As with Shelley and Arnold, the understanding of the meaning of death that Whitman presents clearly isn't that of any formal religion; for him, death is to be welcomed as the "dark mother,"[53] the "strong deliveress"[54] who ends pain and suffering and makes new life possible. Whitman admired Lincoln greatly, and while he didn't know him as a personal friend, had a kind of acquaintance with him, since Lincoln took breaks from his exhausting work and went for carriage rides around Washington, and frequently would see and acknowledge Whitman, who was in the habit of taking long walks alone.[55] There's some evidence, too, that Lincoln may have read and admired *Leaves of Grass*.[56] As in the other elegies, Whitman turns to the beautiful living things in the natural landscape to express his feelings, though of course he employs plants and flowers that are typically American. The poem begins with an expression of grief as intense as that in any of the other great elegies:

O powerful western fallen star!
O shades of night—O moody, tearful night!
O great star disappear'd—O the black murk that hides the star!
O cruel hands that hold me powerless—O helpless soul of me!
O harsh surrounding cloud that will not free my soul.[57]

Then, amid the extraordinary national ceremony of Lincoln's funeral, Whitman presents himself as offering an appropriate token of his love, a sprig of lilac; the flower, like Lincoln, has great nobility, but just as the martyred president was a product of ordinary, working class America, it too is part of common, everyday life, blooming in the dooryards of thousands of American homes. And symbolizing Whitman's "manly love"[58] for him, the leaves are heart-shaped, and the blooms upright and phallic. Whitman then seeks appropriate ways to honor Lincoln, asking

O what shall I hang on the chamber walls?
And what shall the pictures be that I hang on the walls,
To adorn the burial-house of him I love?[59]

His response, of course, is that they should be pictures of the American landscape, the nation that Lincoln served and died for:

Pictures of growing spring and farms and homes,
With the Fourth-month eve at sundown, and the gray smoke lucid
and bright,
With floods of the yellow gold of the gorgeous, indolent, sinking
sun, burning, expanding the air,
With the fresh sweet herbage under foot . . .[60]

To honor the man he loves, Whitman chooses distinctively American pastoral images, what he calls, in "Song of Myself," "landscapes, projected masculine, full-sized and golden."[61]

Like Whitman's great poem for Lincoln, both versions of *Brokeback Mountain* are wholly American, presenting characters whose lives and language are pure products of American culture, and like Whitman they make no direct reference to European culture and its forms of expression. Yet *Brokeback Mountain* also can be seen as part of the tradition of the pastoral masculine elegy. While the early parts of both the story and the film establish a feeling of erotic liberation, of the shared, joyous expression of suppressed physical and emotional desire between men in a pastoral landscape, this then is countered by the fear that Ennis feels because of homophobic hatred, the long, painful struggle he and Jack face to maintain their love, the costs for them and their families, and finally the horror of Jack's murder. Both end with Ennis alone, grieving for Jack. Of course a man like Ennis knows and cares nothing about the literary traditions that just have been discussed, but like Whitman, he finds an eloquent way to express his grief and to honor his friend that recognizes the meaning of the American pastoral landscape in which they fell in love. In his trailer he hangs up the two bloody shirts, united together, one inside the other, though he must always regret that he made the mistake of resisting Jack's invitation to unite their lives together. Above the shirts he tacks up the postcard of Brokeback Mountain, a picture of their masculine landscape, to complete a simple shrine that expresses his grief for his friend and the value he places on their love for each other.

As a masculine elegy, *Brokeback Mountain* also is related to one of the most famous artifacts of American Western culture, the traditional cowboy song known either as "The Streets of Laredo" or "The Cowboy's Lament." Like a substantial portion of American folk music, the song derives from the rich Scots-Irish musical tradition, being based on an old Irish ballad, "The Unfortunate Rake." Most people are familiar with the sweet, sad tune and the words:

As I walked out in the streets of Laredo,
As I walked out in Laredo one day,
I spied a young cowboy all wrapped in white linen
Wrapped in white linen as cold as the clay.

"I see by your outfit that you are a cowboy"
These words he did say as I boldly stepped by,
"Come sit down beside me and hear my sad story,
I was shot in the breast and I know I must die . . .

It was once in the saddle I used to go dashing
Once in the saddle I used to go gay,
First down to the dram-house and then to the card-house
Got shot in the breast, I am dying today.
Oh beat the drum slowly and play the fife lowly,
Play the Dead March as you carry me along,
Take me to the green valley and lay the sod o'er me
For I'm a young cowboy and I know I done wrong . . ."[62]

In the song, the dying cowboy delivers his own elegy, expressing regret over the drinking and gambling that caused him to get shot, bidding goodbye to his family and friends, and warning others against following his example. The end of the song depicts the cowboy's death and its emotional impact on the man who's related his words in the song:

"Go bring me a cup, a cup of cold water
To cool my parched lips," the cowboy said;
Before I turned, the spirit had left him
And gone to its Giver—the cowboy was dead.

We beat the drum slowly and played the fife lowly,
And bitterly wept as we bore him along,
For we all loved our comrade, so brave, young and handsome,
We all loved our comrade although he'd done wrong.[63]

Those who've seen *Brokeback Mountain* may have noted that the filmmakers recognize the connection between the elegiac mood of the story and that of the song, and include a reference to it in the episode early in the movie in which Ennis returns to the camp on the mountain with supplies and is surprised by the bear. Before this accident, as Ennis rides along he hums a few bars of the song. This detail is suggestive in several ways: it shows how much pleasure Ennis takes in riding and in his work outdoors, and it indicates the mood of contentment he's begun to feel in being with Jack as their friendship develops. Whereas in the opening scenes in Signal Ennis is taciturn and closed, now he feels relaxed and open enough to enjoy an old cowboy song. Also, of course, although it can't be known by the character at the time, the song anticipates the grief Ennis later will feel at the loss of his comrade.

There's also a long tradition of poetry written in vernacular English by American writers who've worked as cowboys, which includes elegiac poems presenting the grief of one man for another. Probably the most famous is "The Lost Pardner," by Badger Clark. The son of a Methodist minister, Clark was born in 1883 and grew up in the Black Hills of South Dakota, partly in Deadwood. As a young man he worked in Cuba, became ill with "tropical fever," perhaps malaria, and worked on a ranch in Arizona for several years, recovering his health. He spent most of the rest of his life in South Dakota, becoming widely popular for his poems about cowboy life, particularly those collected in *Sun and Saddle Leather* (1915).[64] Clark's poetry reflects a period of life in the West when homosocial relationships between men were more accepted than they later came to be.[65] He remained a bachelor, and some of his poems celebrate the lives of cowboys who worked and lived together, "baching" with each other.[66] "The Lost Pardner" is remarkable for its description of a bond between two men that's clearly more important to them than any heterosexual relationship and for its emotional intensity and even the suggestion of an intimate physical relationship. Interestingly, the "pardner's" name is "Al," perhaps an echo of Corydon's Alexis.

> I ride alone and hate the boys I meet.
> Today, some way, their laughin hurts me so.
> I hate the steady sun that glares and glares!
> The bird songs make me sore.
> I seem the only thing on earth that cares
> Cause Al ain't here no more!
> And him so strong, and yet so quick he died,
> And after year on year
> When we had always trailed it side by side,
> He went—and left me here!
> We loved each other the way men do
> And never spoke about it, Al and me,
> But we both knowed, and knowin it so true
> Was more than any woman's kiss could be.
> What is there out beyond the last divide?
> Seems like that country must be cold and dim.
> He'd miss me, the same as I do him.
> It's no use thinking—all I'd think or say
> Could never make it clear.
> Out that dim trail that only leads one way
> He's gone—and left me here!
> The range is empty and the trails are blind,
> And I don't seem but half myself today.
> I wait to hear him ridin up behind
> And feel his knee rub mine the good old way.[67]

As will be discussed in the section below on the relationship between *Brokeback Mountain* and the tradition of the American Western, during the course of the twentieth century the kind of male intimacy described in Clark's elegy became less and less acceptable due to a growing awareness of the negative medical-legal category of homosexuality, and so the construction of masculinity in depictions of cowboy life came to exclude anything suggesting homoeroticism.

In concluding this discussion of the homoerotic pastoral tradition and *Brokeback Mountain,* it's important to point out that the elements of homoerotic pastoral to which the visual images of the movie version can be connected aren't restricted to writing, but include painting and photography as well. The most important and direct parallel in American art is with the work of Thomas Eakins, one of the greatest American painters and photographers, who studied in Europe in the 1860s and then made his career in Philadelphia until his death in 1916. The painting "Arcadia" (c.1883), which depicts three naked male adolescents in a lush, green summer landscape, deliberately evokes the conventions of pastoral poetry, and could be an illustration for a scene from one of the *Idylls* of Theocritus or from one of Virgil's *Eclogues*: as two of the young men recline on the grass, one playing Panpipes, the third stands before them, playing a reed flute. In his photographs, Eakins depicted himself and male friends, naked, in similar pastoral settings and poses, sometimes playing on pipes or flutes. One of his most famous large oil paintings, "The Swimming Hole" (1883–1885), approaches pastoral homoeroticism in a different way, avoiding any Classical references, and is like a scene from one of the *Calamus* poems of Whitman, who was a friend of Eakins and the subject of one of his finest portraits. In front of a sunny, warm summer landscape of trees and a distant green field, Eakins shows a placid river or pond with a rough stone pier, and six men, ranging in age from adolescence to maturity, all naked, swimming, diving, and lazing in the sun. The scene isn't imaginary, literary, or mythological, but is a group nude portrait of Eakins and some of his close male friends, including some of his art students. Even his dog, Harry, a big golden retriever, is pictured, swimming alongside Eakins himself.[68]

Modern gay painters and photographers have continued the homoerotic pastoral tradition, at least in terms of its general mood of delight in male beauty and companionship in garden-like settings that invite nakedness, as is the case in David Hockney's many paintings of men sunbathing and swimming and diving in pools in Southern California.[69] In some of his photography, Bruce Weber has followed the visual precedent set by Eakins in representing homoerotic pastoral scenes of naked men: the photographs of young men and dogs playing and swimming together collected in his most famous book, *Bear Pond* (1990), are directly reminiscent of Eakins's "The Swimming Hole." However, in contrast to Eakins, Weber's models tend to exemplify ideal standards of youthful male beauty that are strongly associated with men of Northern European background, suggesting a sense of racial and class privilege.[70] Despite their differences, all these various representations of men enjoying each other's company in natural settings that allow them to be naked are generally similar in mood to the scenes of erotic play between Ennis and Jack on the mountain, and bear a direct resemblance to the scene in the film in which the two men, reunited after four years apart, are able to go into the mountains together for several days, and on reaching their secluded destination, strip and, laughing and shouting, race each other to a cliff overlooking a river and leap in.

~

Brokeback Mountain is related in important ways not only to the homoerotic pastoral literary tradition that's so evident in poetry and visual art, but also to a distinctive general pattern of pastoral constructions in American culture which is familiar to most Americans and which ignores or actively repudiates associations with homoeroticism. To understand this connection, it's necessary first to discuss briefly the significance of idealized constructions of pastoral life in American history and literature, particularly the literary examples that are hostile to homoeroticism, and then to consider their relationship to the story and the film.

As many students of American culture have noted, the concept of a beautiful pastoral landscape at the edge of the wilderness has been of enormous importance throughout American history in defining the promise of American life. In the late eighteenth century, for those who were interested in liberal reform and the possibility of creating a freer economic, social, and political system, North America came to be seen as a place where a new and better kind of society, perhaps actually approximating the Arcadian state of happiness about which Europeans had dreamed for centuries, might be made a reality. The utopian fantasy of a comfortable agricultural life in a garden-like landscape, which had been articulated in pastoral poetry and art for the enjoyment of sophisticated elite audiences, began to be thought of as something that the enormous potential of the new continent might actually make attainable, and not just for a few but for a large portion of American society. American intellectual and political leaders such as Benjamin Franklin and Thomas Jefferson, and liberal Europeans such as St. John de Crevecoeur, imagined that the abundance of land in America could create a society in which most of those they saw as potential citizens—which their prejudices unfortunately limited to white men—could own land and become independent, self-reliant, prosperous farmers.[71] This ideal was used repeatedly to justify the violent expropriation of Native American land and the destruction of Native American civilizations, which were deemed inferior to the egalitarian agricultural society many white Americans believed they were building.[72] The ideal of an American pastoral republic, populated by virtuous farmers capable of self-government, persisted throughout the nineteenth century, even as corporate industry and technology increasingly transformed all aspects of American life, including agriculture.[73] Today, in an America that's become urbanized and industrialized, imagery of a simple agrarian life close to nature continues to appeal to many Americans, as seen in advertising, entertainment, and above all in the pastoral suburban landscapes and resort communities to which those who can afford to do so move in order to avoid the problems of urban society.[74]

Literary scholars have pointed out the prevalence of pastoral themes and pastoral imagery in American literature.[75] Some writers, especially during the late eighteenth and early nineteenth centuries, played important parts in articulating the liberal vision of an agricultural American republic, especially in patriotic poetry and in accounts of Western exploration and settlement and of the lives of frontier heroes such as Daniel Boone. Political oratory and popular writing frequently invoked references to the Arcadian ideal familiar to educated Americans from Classical literature, though of course ignoring the homoerotic elements of the Classical pastoral tradition, and presented America as a new Arcadia. In the heroic narratives of Western adventure that became a staple of popular literature (and eventually of movies and TV), the goal was to defend and expand this idealized agricultural society.[76] But as the transformation of American society by the forces of commerce, technology, and industrialization accelerated, other writers, including some of the most sophisticated critics of the society, began to contrast the dream of a pastoral life with the problems of the emerging urban world. A complex form of literary pastoral, in which an idyllic experience close to nature is juxtaposed to the increasingly aggressive commercialism and materialism of American society, with all of its costs for the environment and for human beings, developed in the work of many American writers. This pattern can be seen in the writings of some of the most important figures of nineteenth-century American literature, including Henry David Thoreau, Nathaniel Hawthorne, Herman Melville, and Mark Twain, as well as in the work of less well-known but significant writers of the period such as Sarah Orne Jewett, Hamlin Garland, and Frank Norris. In the first half of the twentieth century a number of important writers continued to develop this pattern, among them the novelists Willa Cather, William Faulkner, Sherwood Anderson, John Steinbeck, and Ernest Hemingway, and the historian Henry Adams. Some of these writers employ the contrast between life in pastoral or primitive nature and in the developing commercial society to make progressive critiques indicting Americans for increasingly embracing wealth and power and for exploiting other people and nature itself, as in Thoreau's *Walden* (1854), Twain's *The Adventures of Huckleberry Finn* (1885), Cather's *The Professor's House* (1925), Faulkner's *The Bear* (1942), and Steinbeck's *The Grapes of Wrath* (1939).[77]

For some American writers, though, their objections to the problems of urban, commercial, industrial society become entangled with constructions of gender in ways that are disturbing to anyone who values equality for women and for sexual minorities. Women hardly are responsible for the negative aspects of society as it's developed, and in fact have been treated in highly exploitative ways by it, but some male writers have responded to women as if they were an embodiment of forces that oblige male characters to conform to social demands. Women are equated with domesticity and so with the pressures on men to fulfill the requirements of the traditional male role, particularly in terms of supporting a family by working within the market economy. Involvement with women is perceived as entrapping men in the myriad of responsibilities of earning a living in a commercial, materialistic society. Literary works that construct women in this way frequently depict comradeship with other men as a liberating alternative to the oppressive obligations of domesticity, the responsibilities of making a living, and the larger problems of life in a complex, urban, industrial world. However, due to the intense homosociality of the escape that such works often present, and the general intensification of awareness of homosexuality and hostility toward it in the late nineteenth century and through much of the twentieth, they usually strongly disavow male homosexuality. The nostalgia for male freedom that these works present often takes the form of the fantasy of an escape "on the road" with other men; of course, Jack Kerouac's famous novel with this title exemplifies the pattern, as do many other works by writers of the Beat movement. It's also evident in the work of Ernest Hemingway.[78]

Hemingway's fiction often presents male characters who are soldiers, hunters, and outdoorsmen, epitomizing American concepts of masculinity, but as many readers have noted, it also frequently characterizes women in strongly negative ways, as making unbearable demands on men and so as driving them to escape their responsibilities. The escape, for Hemingway, sometimes takes the form of a retreat into nature, in some cases with a male companion whose undemanding friendship is in marked contrast to the behavior of the female characters. Certainly the most striking example of this pattern is in what may be Hemingway's most famous work, *The Sun Also Rises*, from 1926.[79] Set in Europe in the early 1920s, the novel centers on the frustrating relationship between an injured American veteran of the First World War, Jake Barnes, and Lady Brett Ashley, a beautiful, passionate, reckless Englishwoman. Like many of his best works, the novel expresses Hemingway's disgust with the catastrophe of the war. It constructs Jake as a victim of the pointless violence inflicted by warfare in modern society; though the exact nature of his wound never is described, he's been injured in a way that makes him impotent. Unable to consummate his relationship with Brett, he and she indulge in an endless, pointless round of socializing, drinking, and traveling with their other friends, typical of the disillusionment and skepticism of the "lost generation" who fought the war. For Jake, though he's presented as "loving" Brett, her sexual expectations are a source of pain, inflicting on him a continual awareness of what the war has done to him. Because of her, the pain from his wound is unending. At one point Jake escapes the frustration of a sexual involvement that never can be consummated, going off on a fishing trip with Bill Gorton, a friend from the States. As Hemingway presents it, this pastoral/primitive interlude by a mountain river in Spain is the only relief Jake can find. He and Bill enjoy each other's company, fishing and getting drunk and joking together, which is a comfortable contrast to the stress of Jake's involvement with Brett. But Hemingway is so vigilant against any implication that this homosocial escape may imply some degree of homoeroticism that he has Bill and Jake explicitly discuss and distance themselves from the idea of love between men. During a playfully sarcastic conversation as they set out on their trip, Bill expresses his affection for Jake, telling him that he's a hell of a good guy and that he's fonder of him than anybody on earth, but adding that he couldn't tell him that in New York, since it would mean Bill was a faggot. He then proceeds to burlesque the newly emerging psychological theories of homosexuality of the time, claiming that the Civil War happened because of a love triangle between Abraham Lincoln, General Grant, and Jefferson Davis, who, Bill says, were all faggots.[80] Hemingway's fear of association with male love is so strong that in an earlier episode, when Jake goes with friends to a dance hall in Paris, Brett is depicted arriving with an entourage of gay men who exemplify the effeminate stereotypes that Hemingway implies are typical of all men who love men. The careful grooming, excessive gestures, campy language, and flamboyant dancing of Brett's friends disgust and threaten Jake, whose impulse is to respond with violence to their mere presence. He says that somehow they always make him very angry, although he knows they're supposed to be amusing and that people should be tolerant, adding that he wants to take a swing at one of the men, to do anything to shatter what he describes as their attitude of superior, simpering composure.[81]

Considering *Brokeback Mountain* in relation to the homosocial yet homophobic perspective of Hemingway adds to the appreciation of what Proulx has achieved in her story. She reminds us, through the many parallels between the situation she describes and that in Hemingway's novel, of the intense suggestions of homoeroticism in his work, and in the kinds of male behavior his work reflects. *Brokeback Mountain* shows us two men who find their relationships with women unsatisfying, and who prefer to retreat together into a pastoral/primitive landscape on what ostensibly are "fishing trips," drinking together and enjoying each other's company—but also making love. Unlike the tormented characters in Hemingway, Ennis and Jack know that what they want is physical and emotional love with each other. Though both become involved in difficult relationships with their wives, women aren't the cause of their problems, homophobia is, and indeed their wives are victims of it as well. Proulx shows that straight men who hate and fear homosexuality are the source of the difficulties of the characters. Comparing the two works helps to demonstrate that, in spite of the disavowals of homosexuality in *The Sun Also Rises*, it, like many of Hemingway's other novels and stories, suggests intense attraction between men. For some readers today, Hemingway's discontented male characters, with their strong interest in hypermasculine pursuits, his demanding female characters, and his idealization of the escape provided by male friendships, all suggest a difficult struggle to repress homosexuality, an interpretation that only is reinforced by the macho postures the author continually adopted in his own life. While it's impossible to know, Hemingway seems to some to exhibit many signs of having been a frustrated closet case.[82] Of course, his fiction is just one example of a larger pattern of fantasy of escape from the problems of modern life, which, for some men, is constructed as involving an escape from women. What Proulx does in her story in a sense outs the intense, confused element of homoeroticism implicit in *The Sun Also Rises* and much of Hemingway's other work, and in the many fantasies of masculine comradeship in nature and on the road that continue to appeal to so many American men. Of course, this kind of fantasy is integral to the forms of fiction and film depicting Western adventure that I'll discuss in the next section of this chapter. One of the many dimensions of the brilliance of Proulx's story is that it forces readers to think about the similar narratives that so many American men enjoy, which depict male bonding away from women in natural settings, and obliges them to recognize that sexual attraction between men may be part of what makes these narratives appeal, though most men refuse to recognize it. What Proulx does thus reminds us again of the artificial boundary between the homosocial and the homoerotic that's imposed by the homophobia of American culture. By doing so, her story suggests how much healthier it might be for everyone in the culture to understand and overcome homophobic constructions of gender.

～

The relationship of *Brokeback Mountain* to the traditions of the American Western are more evident to most readers and viewers than the relationship to the European tradition of homoerotic pastoral art. Everyone in the United States knows some of the heroic narratives that Americans have told themselves about their nation's history and about the type of man that supposedly led American expansion across the continent. These stories, which make up the most important system of national fantasy for many Americans, have developed over more than two hundred years. Beginning in the eighteenth century with the wars between Native Americans and European colonists and then the rapid westward movement of settlers and the continuing conflict with native peoples after the American Revolution, white Americans formulated an imaginative explanation and justification of their actions. Building on the careers of actual frontiersmen, particularly Daniel Boone, they constructed an ideal image of the pioneer hero that articulated what they wanted to believe about themselves. This construction was widely expressed in the popular press, in oratory, in painting, sculpture, and popular lithographs, and in fiction, most importantly by James Fenimore Cooper, whose account of the life story of an ideal frontier hero in his five "Leatherstocking" novels defined many aspects of the heroic frontier narrative that so many white Americans desired. (Cooper calls his hero by many names: his given name is semi-comical, Natty Bumppo, but he's also called by the name that refers to his buckskin clothing, Leatherstocking, and by names that refer to his extraordinary prowess on the frontier: Hawkeye, the Pathfinder, the Deerslayer. In the chronological order of the events of his life the novels are *The Deerslayer* (1841), *The Last of the Mohicans* (1826), *The Pathfinder* (1840), *The Pioneers* (1823), and *The Prairie* (1827). In the period after the Civil War, the popular press, particularly dime novels, which were published in huge numbers and were very widely read, developed a related narrative form dealing with Western adventure, and began the idealization of the cowboy. Audiences could see dramatized representations of cowboy life and of battles with Native Americans in the performances of Buffalo Bill's Wild West Show, which anticipated the popularity of Westerns in motion pictures. The cowboy hero was defined further by Owen Wister in his highly popular novel, *The Virginian* (1901), which helped shape the evolution of heroic Western narratives in the movies as the medium emerged—the novel has provided the basis of five movie versions and a long-running TV series. Other popular Western adventure fiction, such as the novels of Zane Grey, also strongly influenced the development of Westerns in the visual media. Later Max Brand, Luke Short, and Louis L'Amour turned out more popular Western novels, many of which were filmed. In the twentieth century the cowboy became the most widely recognized American cultural ideal of manhood, the subject of movies, TV shows, popular fiction, country and western music, and advertising campaigns, particularly the one for Marlboro cigarettes.[83]

To understand the significance of *Brokeback Mountain* in connection to the tradition of the Western, it's important first to consider the ways in which the accounts of frontier adventure that have been so popular construct American history and American masculinity. From the time they began to be composed, narratives of Western adventure served to justify the conquest of Native Americans and the expropriation of their land. Unlike many writers of frontier adventure, Cooper sometimes shows a degree of ambivalence about the impact of expansion on native peoples and on the environment, but this is relatively rare, and most depictions of the conquest of the West until the mid-twentieth century present it in largely positive terms. Only in the period after the Second World War was there widespread consideration by popular writers and filmmakers of the historical process of expansion from the perspective of Native Americans. Traditional filmed and written Western narratives often juxtapose the way of life of white settlers to that of Native Americans, presenting the agricultural communities established by whites as a superior way of life, and frequently depicting white families, particularly women and children, as helpless victims of Indian violence. Stories of this kind often depict the struggle of white men, sometimes assisted by friendly Native American allies, to rescue women and children taken captive by hostile Indians. Accounts of the rescue of captives from Indians have been popular with white Americans since the late 1600s, when Puritan New Englanders who had been held by Native Americans along the New England frontier wrote about their experiences, and have continued to provide one of the basic plots for frontier narratives ever since. Most Americans are familiar with such representations from movies and perhaps also from the fiction on which many such films often are based. Two well-known examples are the most recent film version of Cooper's *The Last of the Mohicans* (1992), with Daniel Day Lewis as Hawkeye, Cooper's buckskin-clad frontier hero, and John Ford's famous film, *The Searchers* (1956), with John Wayne in what may be his most significant role, Ethan Edwards, the cowboy who devotes years to searching for and trying to rescue a white girl captured by Comanches.[84]

In stories involving captivity in particular, but in many other variations of frontier narrative as well, gender is of great importance. The general pattern is one in which Native Americans are depicted as aggressive, hostile males who threaten white settlers, attempting to kill men and to abduct women; Indians are constructed as potential rapists, and white men thus are justified in resisting them, since they're defending "their" women. While white men are active agents, penetrating the frontier and confronting enemies, white women are largely passive, and serve as signifiers of the civilized values the men defend. Because the goal of the white men who control the society that's expanding into the wilderness is to obtain, develop, and pass on property, women are of particular importance. In a sense, in a patriarchal society oriented toward property and profit, women are the most important form of property, since their reproductive role makes possible the continuity of patriarchal ownership from generation to generation. In contrast to white women, Native American women often aren't depicted at all, and the threat posed to Native American communities and civilizations by white expansion usually is ignored. Such narratives thus reverse the actual process of historical development, representing Indians as aggressors, and white Americans as defending their families and protecting women from rape. This pattern of narrative construction serves to justify white American expansion and the destruction of Indian peoples and their ways of life, presenting aggression as defense. Of course, this way of looking at the relationship of the United States to the rest of the world continues to affect the policies and rhetoric of American leaders, who consistently depict intervention abroad as defense. Some, particularly in the nations around the globe in which the United States has intervened militarily, may find it ironic that the nation with what's by far the world's largest, most powerful military force calls its department of war the "Department of Defense."[85]

Especially in frontier narratives from the period after the Civil War, which focus on the area of the High Plains, the Rockies, and the Southwest, and often feature the idealized cowboy as protagonist, white outlaws may figure as the enemies confronted by settlers. Native Americans also are presented as opponents of civilization in these forms of Western adventure narrative, and they and outlaws often are constructed similarly: both groups tend to be presented as largely or entirely male, without any commitment to families, homes, and productive economic property like that of the communities of white settlers, and outlaws also tend to be constructed as a sexual threat to the white women of the settler community. Whichever enemies those representing the westward expansion of white American society must face with the help of the cowboy hero, those enemies are fundamentally similar in their hostility to the values of the settlers, which are embodied in property, families, children, and especially female characters.[86]

As part of this ideological system of justification for imperial expansion, American masculinity has been defined in highly idealized terms. The pioneer hero, and especially the cowboy, has been constructed as a paradigm of American conceptions of masculine value. He's independent, self-reliant, brave, skilled at survival in the wilderness, and adept at the use of violence. He's smart, and has lots of practical knowledge, but he's not formally educated; his lack of cultural refinement clearly locates him as a populist hero with whom many men can identify. He's a man of action, not words. While women and weak men talk, he acts. In traditional gender ideology, a real man never makes himself vulnerable by opening up and sharing what he feels; to expose a need for others compromises independence and makes a man like a woman. The cowboy hero's function in many ways is a military one, deterring

aggression, avenging violence, and restoring order, but he's usually not presented as being part of an organized force, but as a free agent, though frequently acting in unison with a male companion who's subordinate but whose
assistance can be necessary to him. There's an element of rebellion against
male authority in the cowboy; most Americans disavow class differences and
class politics, but the cowboy and other popular action heroes betray a distrust and a dislike of authority that point toward a barely articulated feeling
of resentment toward those with property and power, though this almost
never achieves expression in class-conscious political action. Instead, this antagonism is directed outward, at those seen as enemies of the nation as a
whole, and thus actually serves to protect and maintain existing arrangements
of property and power.[87]

The cowboy hero isn't depicted as being perfect; his idealization allows
considerable latitude in his behavior in terms of violence, drinking, cursing,
and even sexual adventures with women who aren't identified with domesticity. While he often defends families and rescues women, he's usually been
presented as being single, as championing and avenging a domestic way of
life that he affirms but doesn't directly participate in. In some stories of Western adventure, he settles down with a woman at the end, but in many others
he leaves the community he's helped to save, continuing on his way and
maintaining his freedom. His lack of domestic ties leaves him free to act as
an independent agent of retribution against Indians, outlaws, or any other
threats to the white American community. But the emphasis on the cowboy
hero's freedom from domestic ties also indicates a deep ambivalence toward
the society he defends, and especially toward its most visible embodiment in
Westerns, women. Though women represent everything that must be protected, they also constrain men, and the cowboy's resistance to being tied
down by them anticipates the consistent element in American popular culture
of heterosexual male discontent with women and domesticity and of fantasies
of being on the road, with all the individual freedom that implies.[88]

In many versions of Western adventure, the cowboy hero is presented in
simplistic, highly idealized ways, as in the "B" pictures of the 1930s, but in
more sophisticated and complex fiction and movies he's often an ambiguous
figure. Frequently he's a man with a past as a gunfighter or even as an outlaw, and in some cases he's presented as being connected with or in some way
similar to the outlaw characters who oppose the community. In his very
strengths, especially his skills in the use of violence, he's potentially dangerous unless he subordinates his abilities to the needs of white society, and
many of the most interesting Western narratives center on the depiction of his
struggle to accept his responsibility to do so. The real drama often is concerned not with a struggle with obvious enemies of society, such as Indians

or outlaws, but with the hero's struggle to do right according to society's standards.[89]

Everything about the cowboy hero in narratives of Western adventure demonstrates his independence and self-reliance. He can judge and control other men, he's skilled in using weapons of all kinds, and his autonomy and freedom are illustrated by his ability as a horseman who's able to negotiate the dangers of the wild landscape. His relationship to people, weapons, animals, and nature itself is marked by knowledge and control. His knowledge of the land is especially significant, since it relates to his role as a defender of the expanding white American community. Not only does he know all the skills involved in hunting and tracking and every other aspect of wilderness survival, but he explores and understands the landscape, gaining the knowledge that allows him, and those who follow him and whom he defends, to take control of it. In some versions of Western adventure, he gains his knowledge from Native Americans, and in others from his own ordeals of survival in the wilderness. As some historians have noted, his intimate knowledge of the lay of the land, which allows him to penetrate it, to move freely in it, and to be able to control its inhabitants, parallels the relationship that American culture mandates between men and women. The cowboy penetrates and dominates the landscape the way a "real" man is supposed to penetrate and dominate a woman's body. While the cowboy often isn't presented as remaining part of the community, his intimate knowledge of the land facilitates continuing domination of it by white American society.[90]

The cowboy thus not only serves to rationalize the actual historical process of American expansion, but also as a model of American manhood, as an example of the sorts of behavior supposedly necessary to be an American man. In many ways his abilities are those that men are expected to have in order to survive in the American market economy, in which they must make it on their own and be willing to compete aggressively with other men to survive. In this model, perhaps a few other men who are close friends can be trusted, but in general men relate to men aggressively, as competitors who have to be shown their place. The cowboy's independence, self-reliance and self-control, and his aggressive, competitive attitude toward most other men all are the same fundamental qualities that have been prescribed to men for two hundred years by the advocates of self-advancement toward the American Dream. As mentioned in chapter 1, while this model of masculinity certainly can lead to success for some, it also keeps many poor men working hard on their own and tends to divide men from each other and to prevent collective action. The masculine ethic that prescribes stoicism and silence as the only ways to deal with personal struggle and suffering, stigmatizing emotion as feminine and therefore weak, functions to keep American men from sharing consciousness of the problems affecting their lives and work, and so serves to maintain things as they are in the society. The cultural changes of the 1960s and 1970s led to a shift that caused many to reject the idealization of the protagonists of Westerns and produced depictions of cowboys who were cynical antiheroes, but this new construction also emphasized, and even increased, the protagonist's independence and self-reliance. For many Americans today, the construction of masculinity typical of the earlier, heroic cowboy ideal continues to exert a strong appeal, and is exemplified by John Wayne, whose cult still persists nearly thirty years after his death.[91]

As contemporary historians of the American West have shown, popular Western narratives depart in many significant ways from what can be known about the actual history of the frontier. Most importantly, the perspective that presents white Americans as defending themselves against Indian aggression has functioned to erase the record of the effort to destroy Native American cultures and as a rationalization of a process of imperial conquest. Also, the life of the "cowboy," as he exists in literature and film, with his freedom to roam the frontier and to defend white settlers, is very different from the actual experience of the men who did the hard, poorly paid work of tending cattle in the West for those who controlled the cattle industry in the decades following the Civil War. Rather than being shaped by lone adventurers on horseback, the development of the West was shaped by those with capital to invest. The construction of the cowboy hero also is a distortion in terms of race: according to the image that's been so persistently popular in the culture of entertainment, he's white, and often is presented in juxtaposition to an enemy who are people of color, but in fact, according to the historians who've studied the social and economic history of cattle ranching, a substantial number of the men who worked with cattle in the West in the later nineteenth century were African American. Working and living conditions were difficult for actual cowboys, but the West offered an alternative to black men who wanted to escape economic, social, and political domination by racist whites in the segregationist South after the end of Reconstruction. Many other cattle workers were of Mexican background, part Indian, part Spanish.[92]

The idealization of the cowboy also is a distortion in terms of sexual attitudes and behavior. As has been discussed by historians who've begun to examine professions and communities in which men substantially outnumbered women, it's likely that among cowboys, as among other largely male working groups isolated from women, such as loggers, miners, and sailors, as well as the transient communities of hoboes, male-male sexual relationships were relatively common.[93] Historians of sexuality have shown that before the articulation of the medical-legal category of homosexuality toward the end of the nineteenth century and the resulting efforts by medical and governmental authorities to identify and suppress same-sex sexual relations, there weren't clearly defined boundaries between what today we would call homosocial and homosexual activity. Men who worked together, men who were friends, might also share sexual activity together. Though religious condemnations of sodomy, usually equated with anal intercourse, were widely known, these may not have been understood to apply to other forms of sexual interaction between men, particularly to mutual masturbation, frottage, or intracrural copulation. And even with explicit religious attacks on anal intercourse, there is substantial evidence that it still was widely accepted in many contexts, particularly among loggers and hoboes.[94] Some have suggested that those forms of work that necessarily were limited to men and were performed in all-male social contexts may have attracted men who resisted conventional domestic life and preferred to have close social and possibly physical relationships with other men.[95] There's scant direct evidence available about sexual relationships among men working in the cattle business in the period from the Civil War into the early twentieth century, though the records of observers, memoirs, and photographs indicate that cowboys lived on intimate terms together. They slept in close proximity to each other indoors and on the range, bathing together and often shaving and grooming each other, and often socialized together, including holding dances in which men danced with men, as was common in other all-male work environments. Some contemporary observers commented that some men who worked as cowboys seemed to avoid socializing with women, and to prefer the company of men, though they didn't infer that this signified same-sex desire.[96] One man who worked as a cowboy in Oklahoma in the early twentieth century, and who later became a sailor and after the Second World War was involved in gay communities in California, did provide explicit confirmation of same-sex relationships among cowboys. About friendships between cowboys that became sexual, he commented that "At first pairing they'd solace each other gingerly and, as bashfulness waned, manually. As trust in mutual good will matured, they'd graduate to the ecstatically comforting 69."[97] Intimate friendship between cowboys "was at first rooted in admiration, infatuation, a sensed need of an ally, loneliness and yearning, but it regularly ripened into love."[98] The popular cultural mythology of the cowboy not only ignores the substantial participation of men of color in the cattle business, but also erases the presence of men who loved other men. Indeed, in the construction of the cowboy in narratives of Western adventure in popular culture, his masculinity supposedly is antithetical to same-sex desire.

Whatever the actual degree of toleration or even acceptance of male-male sexual intimacy in the nineteenth century among men working in the West, as narratives of Western adventure came to be constructed in the twentieth century, given the growing awareness of the negative category of homosexuality, the idealized masculinity of the cowboy hero came to be defined in terms of the homophobia that was becoming increasingly intense in American culture. As American men became more aware of the medical and legal condemnation of forms of intimacy that formerly may have been accepted, models of masculinity developed that drew a clear boundary between acceptable homosocial behavior and anything that might suggest unacceptable homosexual behavior. To see evidence of this change, all you need to do is to look at nineteenth-century photographs of pairs or groups of male friends: before about 1900, men pose together leaning against one another, with arms over one another's shoulders or resting on one another's legs. Some photographs of male couples are particularly surprising, showing men with each other in intimate, affectionate poses whose connotations for those in the photographs are difficult to know for certain, but that immediately would be labeled "gay" by most people today.[99] Photographs of cattle workers taken in the last few decades of the nineteenth century are startling to modern viewers, showing men dancing together, bathing together, bedded down on the range next to each other, and seated and standing with their arms over each other's shoulders.[100] Such physical intimacy may or may not indicate the toleration of forms of sexual interaction that people today would call homosexual; we can't say for sure, but we can say that attitudes toward intimacy changed, and began to exclude gestures that could be seen as suggestive of sexual intimacy, given the emerging category of homosexuality. As he's been presented in popular literature and film since the early twentieth century, the cowboy hero shows little of this earlier easy intimacy with other men. Except for a trusted "pardner," who's never presented as being physically close to the protagonist in the ways just mentioned, his relations with other men often are competitive and confrontational; he challenges Indians or white outlaws, either forcing them to back down or fighting and defeating them. The images that come to mind are of cowboys in conflict with Indians on the range, or of gunfights in which a cowboy hero confronts another white man who's his enemy, draws quicker, and shoots him down.[101]

Before turning to *Brokeback Mountain,* the construction of the traditional Western hero's relationship with his sidekick needs examination. As mentioned, narratives of Western adventure in every medium frequently present the protagonist as having a close male friend who assists him. In Cooper's Leatherstocking novels, he's the Mohican warrior Chingachgook, and, as literary historians have noted, many other Western narratives follow a similar pattern, making the hero's companion a man of color. This pattern can be seen as a way in which white Americans differentiated between people of color who opposed them and those who would collaborate with them in the enterprise of expansion. Chingachgook, unlike the Hurons and others who resist the white settlers and take women captive, assists Hawkeye in subduing the frontier and rescuing captives, and clearly is in a position secondary to the white man. Of course, this pattern of racial subordination persisted well into the twentieth century, in constructions such as the relationship of the Lone Ranger and his Indian friend, Tonto. From the racist perspective of the dominant culture, racial difference confirmed the inferior status of the hero's companion.[102]

Even narratives in which the protagonist's sidekick is white usually make it clear that he's of subordinate status. Sometimes he's presented as an older man, or as a character whose weaknesses or foibles make him comic and so reduce his status in relation to the hero. He's seldom as strong, as competent, as handsome as the hero. With his limitations, he often serves as a foil to emphasize the completeness with which the cowboy hero exemplifies American conceptions of what a man ought to be. While many popular novels and movies present a Western hero who's assisted by another man, such relationships have come to be defined so as to clearly exclude any suggestions of romantic feeling or physical desire, given the increasing awareness of the negative category of homosexuality over the past century. The intense bonds between men depicted in so many narratives of Western adventure indicate the persistent appeal of male comradeship to many men, but also a growing tension with fears of physical attraction and contact between men, and a strong need to establish boundaries defining friendship as being separate from any behavior that possibly would result in labeling men as homosexual.[103]

In many Western novels and movies the cowboy hero's sidekick eventually dies, often getting killed as he fights enemies alongside the hero. The friend's death gives the added reason of vengeance to the cowboy hero's confrontations with his opponents, but it also sometimes allows the hero to be fully heterosexualized and integrated into the property-owning white community by replacing the relationship with the friend with one with a woman, though in many versions the hero doesn't settle down but departs from the community and so maintains his individual freedom. In *The Virginian*, for instance, the title character is obliged to hang his best friend, Steve, because Steve's become a cattle rustler; by the end of the novel, Steve's elimination allows the Virginian to marry the schoolmarm and to join the community whose property laws he's enforced.[104]

The Virginian is especially interesting since it was written at what seems to have been the time when the tension between homosociality and homosexuality was forcing American men, including writers who depicted them, to adopt more restricted attitudes toward types of intimacy that might suggest the possibility of homosexuality. Wister's perspective on intimacy between men is interestingly ambivalent. Despite the novel's overt endorsement of heterosexuality and marriage, readers often are struck by the continual implications of intimacy, including erotic attraction, between men. The narrator, an Easterner, consistently describes the Virginian in ways that stress how handsome and sexy he is. In the opening scene at the train station in Medicine Bow, before the character even is identified the narrator describes him climbing down from a fence "with the undulations of a tiger, smooth and easy, as if his muscles flowed beneath his skin,"[105] and then, seeing him at close hand, presents him as an exemplar of butch beauty:

> Lounging there at ease against the wall was a slim young giant, more beautiful than pictures. His broad, soft hat was pushed back; a loose-knotted, dull-scarlet handkerchief sagged from his throat; and one casual thumb was hooked in the cartridge-belt that slanted across his hips. He had plainly come many miles from somewhere across the vast horizon, as the dust upon him showed. His boots were white with it. His overalls were gray with it. The weather-beaten bloom upon his face shone through it duskily, as the ripe peaches look upon their trees in a dry season. But no dinginess of travel or shabbiness of attire could tarnish the splendor that radiated from his youth and strength.[106]

In the scene, the Virginian joshes an older man about getting married; watching and listening, the narrator startlingly reflects, "Had I been the bride, I should have taken the giant, dust and all."[107] The narrator's appreciation of the Virginian's sensuous, masculine beauty continues throughout the novel, and he repeats his playful fantasy of himself as a woman in relation to the handsome cowboy. While much of the novel is devoted to the Virginian's relationship with the woman he eventually marries, the novel also strongly emphasizes the importance and attraction of bonds between men; Steve is eliminated, but the admiring narrator succeeds him as the Virginian's sidekick. The novel suggests the continuing tension, for some American men, between the desire for close bonds with other men, and the fear of what they may signify.[108]

When considering *Brokeback Mountain* in relation to the American tradition of heroic Western narrative, it's important first of all to note the degree of shock, for some who read the story and especially for many who see the movie, of the idea that there even could *be* "gay cowboys." Both versions of *Brokeback Mountain* are startling to many people because they locate love between men directly in the system of iconography of the narrative tradition of the Western. The story and the film place a form of sexuality that supposedly is antithetical to American culture's construction of masculinity within a framework that's seen as epitomizing that construction of masculinity. Though Ennis and Jack aren't actually "cowboys," they're masculine white men dressed in worn Western clothes, riding horses through the mountains. They look and talk like what most Americans think of when they think of cowboys, and the landscape in which their story unfolds is one that's profoundly associated with stories of cowboy adventure, not only in scores of movies but in many novels. *The Virginian* is set in the mountains of Wyoming, in fact. Proulx's superb use of Western vernacular, both in her rendering of conversations and in the narrative voice she uses, immediately connects her story to the world of the Western for readers, as do her descriptions of the characters' clothing and horses and especially the wild landscape. The connection in the film is even stronger; many of its images could be directly from Westerns set in the Rockies, the Sierras, or the mountains of the Northwest, such as *Ride the High Country* (1962), *The Big Sky* (1952), *Bend of the River* (1952), or *The Naked Spur* (1953). The view of the Grand Tetons in the poster for *Brokeback Mountain,* of course, is the background for the action in one of the great Westerns in which a traveling gunfighter defends a helpless family of settlers from outlaws, *Shane* (1953). In their cinematography, Prieto and Lee recall types of scenes familiar to anyone who's seen Westerns: Ennis and Jack riding through the forest together, like a Western hero and his sidekick; the two men hunting on the wild slopes of the mountain; Ennis astride his horse, silhouetted against the sky. In the screenplay, in fact, in their notes describing a scene of one of the later trips the two men make together, McMurtry and Ossana specifically observe the parallels with the images of heroic male comradeship in the visual traditions of the American Western, saying that as Jack and Ennis ride through the mountains, they should look like Randolph Scott and Joel McCrea in *Ride the High Country*, only more life-worn.[109]

For modern viewers who've been taught to see the cowboy as an icon of a form of masculinity that's constructed as being in opposition to homosexuality, there's a constant feeling of surprise, since the two "cowboys" in *Brokeback Mountain* sleep together. Think of the scene just mentioned, of Ennis riding on the mountain, silhouetted against the sky; it occurs the day after Ennis first has sexual intercourse with Jack, when the film presents him as worrying about what's happening between them, and just a few hours before he decides to go into the tent with Jack again, for a night of lovemaking that's presented as being gentle, affectionate, and deeply necessary to both men. Or think of the first scene in the film between Jack and Ennis, outside the trailer: the way Ennis leans against the trailer, intensely aware of Jack but avoiding letting Jack see him looking at him, and the way Jack sizes up Ennis, observing him through the mirror; it almost could be an episode from a Western that builds up to a fight or a gun battle, but here it culminates in friendship and love.

The clothing the characters wear in the movie also contributes to the shock, at least for many straight viewers. What cowboys wear, in the traditional Western, is an integral part of their intense masculinity: the boots, jeans, belts, buckles, tailored Western shirts and jackets, bandanas, and cowboy hats, as well as the saddles, spurs, lariats, and horse tack involved in riding and roping, all are charged with a sense of masculine power. Of course Ennis and Jack don't wear sidearms, but in every other aspect of their dress they could take their places in just about any Western. The popularity of Western narratives has brought parallel popularity to Western wear; over the last century there have been periodic fads for Western clothing throughout the country, and of course in much of the West today the iconic attire of the cowboy is the basis for the actual clothing many people wear, not just for practical work outdoors, but as fashion generally in daily life. By dressing as cowboys, these American Westerners signify their participation in the Western as national fantasy, and especially in the traditional constructions of manliness associated with it. Cowboy clothes signify the kind of independent, self-reliant, competitive masculine power embodied by actors such as Gary Cooper, James Stewart, Joel McCrea, Randolph Scott, Clint Walker, Clint Eastwood, and of course John Wayne.[110] That two men dressed the way Ennis and Jack are dressed can fall in love and have sex may shock many straight viewers, but it isn't a surprise to many men who desire men, who are well aware of the sexiness of cowboy clothes. For years the cowboy has been a figure in gay pornography, and of course the masculinized fashions that gay men have developed draw heavily on working-class, outdoor attire, including clothing used by cowboys.[111]

One particular aspect of the clothing of the characters in the movie deserves comment in relation to the tradition of the Western: their hats. Western movies of the silent period and of the 1930s and 1940s established a clear pattern of symbolism in which the hero often wore a light-colored hat and his outlaw opponents black ones.[112] The fact that in most scenes Jack wears black or dark hats and Ennis white or tan ones can't have been inadvertent, especially given the care and awareness of movie traditions that the filmmakers show in other aspects of the film. At first, of course, the opposition of black and white seems to imply a judgment of the two characters, critical of Jack's relative openness about his sexuality and favoring Ennis's caution. As has been discussed, the movie presents Ennis as being more hesitant about his relationship with Jack during their summer on the mountain than does the story. This has played into the hostile and distorted readings of the film by those who want to condemn Jack as a "sexual predator," a black-hatted villain, and to see Ennis as his "victim." Such a reading either is plain stupid or is the result of willful distortion, since it's obvious in the film that Ennis is eager to maintain a relationship with Jack, though on terms that he can limit in order to maintain his public identity as a straight man; he clearly isn't Jack's "victim." Both Ennis and Jack are potential targets of other men who hate male love; it's their hatred that causes Ennis to resist Jack's invitations to live together, subjecting Jack to repeated rejection and disappointment, and which finally kills Jack just as Ennis has feared he himself might be killed. The fact that Jack wears a black hat is entirely ironic, since he's the victim of straight men who hate men who love men, especially man-loving men who are willing to allow their love to become visible, like Jack.

While attacks on the movie haven't said so directly, undoubtedly part of what makes some viewers, especially straight men, so uncomfortable about the film is that it makes explicit the sexual implications of the celebration of the male body in the Hollywood Western. Unlike most other film genres, the Western has focused visual attention on the bodies of strong, handsome men, presenting them in costumes and situations that reveal both the muscularity and the sensuousness of their physiques. In contrast to the protagonists of detective or spy films, who usually are shown in some variant of the ordinary, dull business suit that's the attire of many men in society, the Western hero is allowed a remarkable degree of display in his costume, which simultaneously is strikingly elegant and roughly masculine, and which directs the viewer's gaze toward the strength and beauty of the male body. His clothing includes materials, particularly leather and denim, that not only are practical for hard work outdoors, but also connote masculine strength, combining them with other elements, especially metalwork, such as buckles, spurs, and conchos, that serve practical purposes and are hard and durable but also often are very finely, even extravagantly, crafted. He's dressed for work and for fighting, but, unlike any other male figure in the culture, with perhaps the exception of a soldier in a dress uniform, is permitted to wear what amounts to a display of masculine jewelry. His costume also highlights the most erotically compelling aspects of the male form: tailored Western shirts emphasize the breadth of his shoulders, the strength of his arms, and often are worn open, with a bandana at the throat, showing his neck and chest. Tight-fitting jeans show the muscular flesh of his thighs and hips. Chaps, worn to protect the legs by men who work with cattle, not only are made of leather and often are fringed and highly decorated, but also direct visual attention to a man's crotch and butt.[113]

Riding, of course, only further dramatizes the masculine power and beauty of the cowboy hero. It shows him in a position of control and independence, mastering a powerful animal and able to go wherever he wants, and raises him up above others, indicating his status as an autonomous man who answers to no one. In European culture, a man on horseback has epitomized male authority since Classical and feudal times, and the cowboy astride his horse demonstrates the belief that in America this kind of status is available to every man. His position on his horse not only subordinates those below, but focuses their attention on his legs, hips, and torso, stressing his muscularity. His position is implicitly one of sexual dominance, and also emphasizes his crotch, the focus of his male sexuality.

In Hollywood Westerns the male body then is celebrated by being shown in dramatic physical action. The cowboy hero is displayed not only riding through the landscape, but exploring it on foot, tracking and hunting, and in standoffs with other men that lead to violent confrontations. Many of these are gunfights, but Westerns also often include fistfights between men that exhibit the power and beauty of their bodies in detail; these often are succeeded by episodes depicting the protagonist's recovery, which not only further demonstrate his resilient masculine power but allow further displays of his body when he washes or is tended by others in the process of recovering his strength. The hero's body, particularly in action, dressed in sexually charged clothing and sometimes partly undressed, is one of the central images of the Western film. As suggested above, the only other film genre that depicts male bodies so extensively is the war film. But displays of masculine strength and beauty, of course, are everywhere in American society, though they're rarely commented on. Not only movies but sports coverage, especially on TV, scrutinizes male bodies, often clad in uniforms such as those in football and baseball that, like the cowboy's costume, simultaneously accentuate male strength and sensuality. For many young men growing up and gradually coming to realize that they're attracted to other men, sports, war movies, and Westerns permit opportunities for clandestinely admiring men, though of course the majority of men, who identify as straight and form the largest audience for these displays, would immediately resist the suggestion that sexual attraction is any part of their interest in them. Because of the intense homophobia of American society, far more men than those who actually will acknowledge it are attracted to other men to some degree, and many of them, whether or not they're able to say so to themselves, are drawn to visual displays of male bodies.[114]

Brokeback Mountain addresses the erotic element in the Western movie genre directly, forcing straight viewers to be aware of the sexiness of the cowboy figure that forms an important dimension of his appeal but that they would prefer to deny. As they're presented in the movie, neither Ennis or Jack even begins to approach the degree of stylized Western masculine elegance often seen in the costume of movie cowboys, since they're poor, hardworking ranch hands, but in their clothing both demonstrate the basic effects of the style. Ledger and Gyllenhaal wear fitted Western shirts that show their chests, arms, and necks, jeans that show their thighs and hips, and both, in the course of life and work outdoors, are shown nearly naked. They don't have any of the fancy elements of Western attire, except for the prize belt buckle Jack proudly wears, but as it is, their practical Western wear and gear enhances their masculine attractiveness as it does for men in any cowboy movie, or for any men today who wear the style. But unlike the majority of straight men who claim to be unaware of other men's bodies, or of how Western clothes can enhance them, the two men in *Brokeback Mountain* are presented as looking at each other and being aware of each other's bodies. As they stand by the trailer in the first scene, as they work with the sheep, as they mount and ride and dismount, as they wash and cook and drink and sit by the fire, they move from clandestinely appreciating each other to being able to gaze directly, to look and take pleasure in looking. For the male viewer who desires men but who's necessarily had to do much of his looking with care, and who's well aware of the beauty of male bodies in Westerns and the sexiness of cowboy clothes, it's liberating at last to see two "cowboys" look at each other the way he's often looked at them; for the viewer who repudiates the fact that some men look at men, it's an affront, particularly because it outs the Western as a genre filled with homoerotic images and possibilities. Of course, *Brokeback Mountain* not only outs the Western movie genre, but all the areas of American commercial popular culture that celebrate the male body through Western iconography, including country music and of course rodeo, particularly the sport that so appeals to Jack Twist, professional bull riding. The spectacle of the body of the cowboy, in the most elaborate Western attire, is offered on a weekly basis on TV by Professional Bull Riders, Inc., or PBR.[115]

By locating love between men within the iconographic system of landscape, clothing, and activities that are fundamental to the Western, *Brokeback Mountain* obliges readers and audiences to begin to recognize how the American national fantasy of Western adventure and particularly the idealized cowboy hero have distorted history and endorsed a homophobic construction of masculinity. Both the story and the film remind us that men who desire other men are everywhere, that many of them are conventionally masculine in appearance and behavior, and that they were and are among the "cowboys" of the West. As many man-loving men are well aware, there's no inherent connection between a man's gender behavior, clothing, and interests and his sexual orientation. One of the most alarming aspects of *Brokeback Mountain* for many people is that the relationship between Ennis and Jack is a reminder of the artificiality of the boundary that the dominant culture now forces men to draw between friendship and more intense emotional and physical intimacy. As mentioned earlier, the fact that *Brokeback Mountain* makes men recognize that friendship exists on a continuum with sexual attraction helps to explain the hostility it elicits among many straight men, and the fact that it sets male friendship and love within the most important American myth of national development and ideal masculinity makes the anger and ridicule it provokes all the more strident.

The two main characters in *Brokeback Mountain* relate to the construction of masculinity embodied by the cowboy hero in ways that differ slightly but significantly. From the start of the story and the film, it's clear that Ennis almost exactly fits this model of what an American man ought to be. It's also clear, especially in the movie, that while Jack is conventionally masculine in his appearance, conduct, and interests, he isn't quite as close to the traditional ideal as Ennis is. Jack rides and hunts and tends animals and competes in rodeo, and can make it on his own, but he's willing to settle for a marriage that gives him some security. The most striking difference is that Jack is much more openly emotional than Ennis. Jack talks more, gestures more, laughs more, and, as both versions of the narrative develop, gets frustrated and angry more. Jack is more open and vulnerable, and doesn't have the laconic, stoic reserve that's so striking in Ennis. The filmmakers emphasize this difference in the scene, early in the friendship between the two men, when Ennis tells about his childhood and his family, and Jack smiles and tells him it's more than Ennis has said in two weeks, getting the reply that it's more than he's said in a year. As mentioned, the filmmakers add episodes that emphasize that Jack isn't as good a rider as he claims to be, and that he's not as good a marksman as Ennis. At first the relationship between the two men seems almost as if it will follow the pattern of the traditional Western, in which, if the tough, silent, self-reliant hero has a friend, the friend clearly is subordinate and expendable. This pattern even continues once the two men fall in love. Although the traditional Western avoids any suggestion of male physical intimacy, when Ennis and Jack begin their sexual relationship it seems to parallel and confirm the power relationship between the hero and his sidekick: Ennis takes the supposedly masculine role of inserting his penis, and Jack the supposedly feminine role of receiving it. Ennis is a top, and Jack's a bottom. Openness, of course, can refer not only to emotional expression, but also to sexual behavior; in both ways, Ennis fits what most people think of as a more masculine role, Jack a more feminine one.

As the story and the movie proceed, however, it becomes evident that Ennis's seemingly strong and independent type of masculinity is a response to intense fear, and that he's much less courageous than Jack. Jack's willing to commit himself to live with Ennis, but Ennis's fear of being attacked if others identify him as a "queer," as well as his shame at what he's been taught to believe it would mean about him, make him afraid to embrace a life with Jack. Jack knows how hostile other men can be, particularly given the hatred and violence his father directed at him as a child, but he's brave and willing to take the risk; Ennis's fear of what others will think and do makes him afraid to be himself. At first Ennis seems the epitome of American masculine independence, but ultimately he's not independent at all, and is intimidated and controlled by other men. His masculinity is based on fear and shame, and turns out to be a trap, causing him to resist his own ability to love, to try to direct it in a way that isn't right for him or anyone else, thus hurting Jack and Alma and himself. In order to fit what he's been told defines a man, he denies his own type of manhood. Ennis is tough and stoical, but these qualities cause him to try to endure what no one should have to endure, a rejection of basic sexual and emotional needs. Unlike Jack, he doesn't have the courage to understand and accept himself and to go ahead and try to build a life founded on his actual nature. As in many versions of the traditional Western, in *Brokeback Mountain* the hero's sidekick gets killed, but here he's not an expendable assistant to a hero who really doesn't need anyone else. Instead, Jack's murder devastates Ennis, showing him how much he loved and needed Jack and how much he has lost by trying to fit his culture's definition of being a man. Jack's death indicates the costs of being closed to contact with others and to one's own emotions and sexuality. Jack's openness, his willingness to express his feelings and his need for Ennis, stand as a corrective to Ennis's limitations. Both versions of *Brokeback Mountain* provide a critique of American masculinity that offers the disturbing but potentially liberating insight that it stems from a fear of other men that actually destroys individuality. Their criticism of the effects of established definitions of masculinity is especially relevant to the situations of men who feel attraction to other men, but it also has potentially constructive implications for those straight men who are able to think objectively about the limitations of the dominant American model of what it means to be a man.

Although at first the relationship of the two men to the land in *Brokeback Mountain* may seem superficially similar to that of the main characters in the traditional Western, it's quite the opposite. Like typical cowboy heroes, Jack and Ennis know the land and can survive on it and travel through it easily and successfully. They think nothing of spending months on the mountain, at the edge of wilderness, in dangerous terrain with violent weather far from any help if there's an emergency and with no means of communication with anyone else. Later, after they get back in contact with each other, they go on a series of trips into mountain wilderness areas all around Wyoming, with only their horses and guns and gear, and ride and hunt and camp for weeks at a time. But unlike the heroes of traditional Western adventure, their goal isn't to know and control the land in order to make it safe for the expansion of white society, but rather to escape that society, at least temporarily, as completely as possible. The wilderness is the only place where they can be free of the threat of homophobia that surrounds them everywhere in society. Wilderness, for them, is valuable not in terms of property that they, or other men whose interests they protect and serve, can make use of, but as a refuge from other men. Unlike the heroes of Western adventure, their goal isn't to penetrate the landscape and to assist the society that seeks to dominate it, but to avoid domination. Whereas in many of the more sophisticated Western narratives, the drama concerns whether or not the protagonist will use his abilities to serve the society, and the narrative is constructed to encourage the reader or audience to expect that finally he will, in *Brokeback Mountain* a sympathetic reader or viewer wants the two men—especially Ennis—to repudiate the society that repudiates their love.

The way that Ennis and Jack escape to nature relates *Brokeback Mountain* to the cultural tradition referred to earlier, which provides progressive criticism of society by juxtaposing its destructive impact on human beings with a retreat into a pastoral or primitive environment. Annie Proulx, like a number of other writers critical of American society and its values, presents the region of transition from agricultural land to wilderness as a refuge for those who've been disillusioned by society. As noted before, in the story there's none of the confused hostility toward women that distorts some works that follow this pattern, such as those of Hemingway, and in fact *Brokeback Mountain* helps to illuminate the limitations of such thinking. Proulx's story is more akin to *The Adventures of Huckleberry Finn*: much as Ennis and Jack find the Wyoming mountains to be a safe space where society's homophobic prejudices don't apply, the raft on the Mississippi offers Huck and Jim a safe space away from the racism that threatens Jim and would separate him from Huck. In both cases, though, even in the refuge of nature the characters must struggle with the beliefs they've internalized from their society, Ennis with his own homophobia and Huck with his own racism. While Twain forbears and doesn't give his novel a tragic ending, Huck, after a series of comic yet appalling experiences with his drunk, violent father, his manipulative "friend" Tom Sawyer, and a parade of conmen, crooks, and lynch mobs along the Mississippi, finally decides he wants no more of "sivilization"[116] and that he's going to "light out for the Territory."[117] In Twain's novel and in Proulx's story, in contrast to traditional heroic narratives of Western adventure, the goal isn't to explore the landscape and to assist in bringing it under the control of American society, but to get away from that society by escaping into primitive nature. As discontent with American society has grown and more white people have begun to admire and idealize the culture of Native Americans, some major Western adventure narratives also have followed this pattern. The most striking recent example is the extremely successful movie, *Dances with Wolves* (1990), in which Lt. John Dunbar, played by Kevin Costner, flees from the violence of the Civil War and the corruption and ignorance of other white men, and is assimilated into the culture of the Sioux. The film takes the tradition of the narrative of Indian captivity and stands it on its head: here whites pose the "savage threat" and Indians offer a superior way of life. Forster's *Maurice*, too, has elements of a primitivist escape, since Maurice and Alec go beyond the limits of agricultural England to make their livings together as woodcutters in the remnant of the Greenwood.[118]

It's important to distinguish narratives of escape into wilderness from those that present primitive nature as an opponent to be conquered, as in Jack London's stories and novels set in the Alaskan wild or on the high seas or in Edgar Rice Burroughs's endlessly popular Tarzan tales. In narratives like these, the goal is to battle against nature, to display superior strength and power, to prove that one is the fittest and can survive. The Social Darwinist construction of nature in such narratives serves not to criticize society and reject its values, but to demonstrate and justify the aggressive, individualistic construction of masculinity that's pervasive in America, celebrating the domination of other males and warning of the shame resulting from being dominated. In contrast to this sort of primitivism, in *Brokeback Mountain* Ennis and Jack don't want to show that they can impose their wills on the wilderness, but, like Huck Finn, to retreat into it in order to avoid letting other men impose their wills on them.[119]

In its critique of homophobic American constructions of masculinity and its presentation of an escape into nature, the movie version of *Brokeback Mountain* uses the magnificent Western landscape it presents through its beautiful cinematography quite differently from traditional Hollywood Westerns. When Alan Ladd arrives in the landscape of the Grand Tetons in *Shane* and commits himself to defend the farm families there, or when John Wayne rides through the towering buttes of Monument Valley to search for and rescue the white women held captive by Comanches in *The Searchers*, their actions ultimately serve to make the land safe for the expansion of American society. They assist society in inscribing its power on the landscape. For viewers who can accept such narratives uncritically, the magnificence of the land ultimately serves as a confirmation of the magnificence of the men and the society that conquer it. While many of the scenes depicting the Wyoming wilderness in *Brokeback Mountain* look similar, with their sweeping vistas of grand peaks, distant plains, and brilliant skies, the romantic images of the Western landscape presented by Ang Lee, Rodrigo Prieto, and the others who assisted them function differently, not endorsing society and its conquest of nature, but depicting nature as a refuge from society's ignorance and brutality and indicating the naturalness, for Ennis and Jack, of their desire.[120]

This difference from the significance of landscape in traditional Western movies points toward a larger cultural issue involving nature that may assist in explaining one of many causes of hostility toward the film. Since long before the development of motion pictures, the landscape of the West has been constructed in ways that closely associate it with traditions of American national ideology. Not only have Western landscapes been the settings of the innumerable narratives of conquest and expansion in the name of the defense of white settlement that many Americans have desired since the late eighteenth century, but in themselves such landscapes have become icons of national identity. Most Americans and many people around the world immediately recognize representations of the mountain cliffs of Yosemite, the geysers of Yellowstone, or peaks like Mount McKinley as national symbols of the United States. For most Americans, these landscapes are familiar from photographs in school textbooks or TV documentaries, and they appear recurrently in our culture, on posters, on calendars, on postage stamps, in commercial and political advertising. In the mid-nineteenth century, of course, such sites first became known to the public through painting, particularly the distinctive American approach to landscape art sometimes referred to as the Hudson River School or Luminism. Started by Thomas Cole and developed by his brilliant student, Frederic Church, the movement included numerous painters who concentrated on epic images of the American West, most notably Albert Bierstadt and Thomas Moran. Like other American landscape painters of the period, Bierstadt and Moran were influenced by the Romantic conception of the sublime in nature; the category of the sublime referred both to the powerful natural forces that one could witness in the wilderness, which were seen as a manifestation of divine power, and to the exalted emotions such natural spectacles evoked. Bierstadt in particular was a master of the sublime, often depicting mountain scenes of storms and sunsets, marked by intense light and dramatic shadow, and rendered with almost surreal attention to detail. The work of Bierstadt, Moran, and other painters of sublime Western scenes had a lasting influence on the American taste for landscape, influencing photography as well as cinematography, especially the way landscape is presented in Western films. From the nineteenth century on, such landscape images have been a source of great national pride for many Americans; Europeans may have ancient castles, cathedrals, and palaces, but the United States has magnificent natural landscapes equal to or surpassing any in the world. The scenes of Brokeback Mountain in the film work within this tradition, presenting magnificent mountain views similar to those many Americans equate with their nation's history and identity. Placing male love in a visual context so charged with national pride and even religious overtones likely is another reason for the indignation toward the film on the part of homophobic viewers.[121]

Just as the movie challenges the mythologized version of the American relationship to the landscape constructed in popular Westerns, so too does Annie Proulx's story. She doesn't approach the landscape in which the story is set from a perspective that idealizes and sentimentalizes ranching and farming. Unlike the nostalgic fantasies of the supposed simplicity and happiness of ranch and farm life in popular entertainment and advertising, her writing, grounded in her historical training, recognizes the fundamental fact that human lives often are shaped by the economic system in which people get their livings, and that in turn an economy often is shaped by the nature of the land in which it functions, particularly the limitations of the resources that human beings can use. With its short summers and harsh winters, Wyoming isn't conducive to the kind of agriculture Americans like to sentimentalize in popular fiction, movies, and advertising. Much of its economic development has involved extractive industries, particularly mining, petrochemicals, and logging, or the business of cattle ranching, which mean hard work and low wages for the people who do it, and substantial profits for absentee owners who often live far away and have little concern about the human or environmental impact of their businesses. Proulx is intensely aware of the beauty of Wyoming's landscape, both its agricultural and its wilderness areas, but she recognizes the harshness of life and work in both.[122]

One last point needs to be noted about the significance of the setting of *Brokeback Mountain* and its possible relationship to the anger the story and the film have generated. Certainly placing a depiction of romantic love between two men in the magnificent Western landscape that's integral to the nation's most significant construction of homophobic masculinity is an important source of hostility, but there's an additional factor, connected to the use of pastoral imagery. In employing as a setting a beautiful pastoral landscape at the edge of wilderness, both versions not only challenge deeply held American beliefs about national history and about what it means to be a man, but also aspects of religious mythology that are inseparable from the assumptions the majority of Americans make about the supposed superiority of heterosexuality. Images of pastoral landscapes are directly related to many aspects of Christian mythology, and to the fundamental creation myth of the Judeo-Christian tradition. As it's described in the Book of Genesis, and in literature and art based on the Genesis story, the Garden of Eden has been pictured in pastoral terms, and the Garden of Eden is directly associated by many with the ideal of heterosexual marriage as endorsed by many organized Christian churches. According to the traditional Anglican marriage service in the original version of *The Book of Common Prayer*, the sacrament of marriage is "an honourable estate, instituted of God in the time of Man's innocency."[123] The first marriage supposedly occurred in Eden before the Fall. Especially for fundamentalist Christians and others who interpret the Bible literally, some of their hostility toward *Brokeback Mountain* may come from the fact that it constructs desire between men as the sort of innocent, passionate, romantic love that supposedly is the property of heterosexuals only and that they honor with marriage, and places it within a landscape which, for all its wildness, is Edenic. According to the slogan used by some of the more bitter religious opponents of same-sex marriage, "God created Adam and Eve, not Adam and Steve." The movie in particular makes visible one of the worst nightmares of homophobes who call themselves Christians, showing two male lovers—not Adam and Steve but Jack and Ennis—passionately making love and innocently enjoying each other's naked bodies in the Garden.

The pastoral imagery of *Brokeback Mountain* offends those whose homophobia is based in their religion in other ways as well. The fact that Jack and Ennis are sheepherders associates them directly with a vast body of Christian belief and imagery concerning sheep and shepherds. In Christian tradition, Jesus often is figured as the Good Shepherd and His followers as His flock. The very word for minister in many Protestant denominations, "pastor," means shepherd, and of course Jesus Himself is the "Lamb of God." In the film, the men repeatedly are shown tending to their sheep in ways that suggest parallels with pastoral Christian imagery. As they go up the mountain with the sheep, we see Jack carefully carrying a weak lamb across his saddle, then Ennis riding with an even smaller one safely strapped into a sack, its little head poking out. Some images in the movie directly echo Christian iconography that's been used in painting, sculpture, and other forms of religious decoration for two thousand years. While ascending the mountain, at one point Jack carries a lamb over a stream, bearing it across his shoulders exactly the way Jesus often is pictured as the Good Shepherd. Once they reach the pastures, Jack is shown tending to an injured lamb, holding it on his lap as he gently pulls a thorn from its hoof.

The movie and the story have been denounced by religious homophobes because they dare to say that men who love men have just as much value as men who love women; both versions present the love between Jack and Ennis as a profound emotional connection that's as powerful as any marriage, and suggest that, given the natures of the two men, it would make far more sense, in a world that wasn't saturated with the hatred of same-sex love, for them to be married to each other. The film in particular surrounds them with images that subtly invoke Christian religious imagery and suggest the spiritual meaning and power of their love, which must be very provoking to those whose religions teach them to hate and attack same-sex love. Fortunately, some more enlightened religious denominations that affirm and welcome sexual minorities are countering this hatred, and some progressive ministers have praised *Brokeback Mountain* for showing the destructiveness of homophobia and the intensity of love that's possible between men.[124]

NOTES

1. "In Paths Untrodden," l. 18, Whitman, *Leaves of Grass* (Ninth edition/1892).

2. See the author's comments on the setting of the film in "About *Brokeback Mountain*: FAQs," annieproulx.com.

3. On sexual minorities and rural space, see Sumartojo, "Contesting Place;" Heibel, "Casa Nova"; Brown, *Closet Space*; Little, *Rural Geography*; Lindhorst, "Practical Implications"; Kramer, "Batchelor Farmers"; Van Hoven, *Spaces*; and Cloke, *Country Visions*.

4. Proulx, "Brokeback Mountain," 30.

5. Proulx, "Brokeback Mountain," 15.

6. Proulx, "Brokeback Mountain," 15.

7. Proulx, "Brokeback Mountain," 15.

8. "Interview with Annie Proulx," *The Missouri Review*, Vol. 22, No. 2, 1999.

9. Proulx, "Getting Movied," 134

10. Proulx, "Brokeback Mountain," 26.

11. "In Paths Untrodden," ll. 1, 8, Whitman, *Leaves of Grass* (Ninth edition/1892).

12. "In Paths Untrodden," ll. 3–5.

13. "In Paths Untrodden," l. 2.

14. "In Paths Untrodden," l. 10.

15. "In Paths Untrodden," l. 17.

16. "Recorders Ages Hence," l. 9, Whitman, *Leaves of Grass* (Ninth edition/1892).

17. There's a vast critical literature on the pastoral tradition in poetry which is beyond my knowledge to discuss, though, as someone who loves American and gay literature, I'm strongly interested in the history of a tradition that's had so much influence. For those who want to learn about the significance of the pastoral for men who love men, I think the best place to start is Summers, *Literary Heritage* (cited above). See particularly the entries on "Pastoral" by M. Morgan Holmes; "American Literature, Gay Male, 1900–1969," by Joseph Cady; "Elegy," by Stephen Guy-Bray; "English Literature: Renaissance," by Claude J. Summers; "Greek Literature, Ancient," by Louis Crompton; "Poetry, Gay Male," by Gregory Woods; "Roman Literature" by Louis Crompton; and those on Barnfield by George Klawitter; Forster, Marlowe, and Milton by Claude J. Summers; Shakespeare by Bruce R. Smith; Theocritus by Raymond-Jean Frontain; Virgil by Louis Crompton; and Whitman by Robert K. Martin. Also see Gregory Woods, *A History of Gay Literature*, cited above; Byrne R. S. Fone, "Arcadia and the Homosexual Imagination," in Stuart Kellogg, ed., *Literary Visions of Homosexuality* (Binghamton: Haworth, 1983); Gregory W. Bredbeck, *Sodomy and Interpretation: Marlowe to Milton* (Ithaca: Cornell University Press, 1991); David M. Halperin, *Before Pastoral: Theocritus and the Ancient Tradition of Bucolic Poetry* (New Haven: Yale University Press, 1983); Bruce R. Smith, (Chicago: University of Chicago Press, 1991); Claude J. Summers, ed., *Homosexuality in Renaissance and Enlightenment England* (Binghamton: Haworth, 1992); and David Shuttleton, "The Queer Politics of Gay Pastoral," in Richard Phillips, *et. al.*, eds., *De-Centring Sexualities: Politics and Representations beyond the Metropolis* (London: Routledge, 2000).

18. See Fone, "Arcadia"; in Summers, *Literary Heritage*, see entries on "Pastoral" by Holmes; "Greek Literature, Ancient," "Roman Literature," and Virgil by Crompton; and Theocritus by Frontain; as well as Woods, *History*.

19. In Summers, *Literary Heritage*, see entry on Theocritus by Frontain; and Woods, *History*.

20. In Summers, see entry by Frontain; also see *Theocritus: Idylls and Epigrams*, translated by Daryl Hine (New York: Atheneum, 1982); and Woods, *History*.

21. In Summers, *Literary Heritage*, see entries on "Pastoral" by Holmes; "Elegy" by Guy-Bray; "Greek Literature, Ancient," by Crompton. and Woods, *History*.

22. In Summers, *Literary Heritage*, see entry on Virgil by Crompton; As well as Woods, *History*.

23. In Summers, *Literary Heritage*, see entries on "Pastoral" by Holmes, Virgil by Crompton; and Woods, *History*.

24. "Second Eclogue," *The Eclogues of Virgil*, translation by J.W. MacKail, 1934.

25. "Second Eclogue."

26. See Summers, *Literary Heritage*, entry on "Pastoral" by Holmes; and Woods, *History*.

27. See entry by Holmes; Wood, *History*.

28. See Summers, *Literary Heritage*, entries on "Pastoral" by Holmes; "English Literature: Renaissance" and Marlowe by Summers; Barnfield by Klawitter; and Shakespeare by Smith; and Woods, *History*.

29. See Summers, *Literary Heritage*, entries on "Pastoral" by Holmes; Barnfield by Klawitter; and Marlowe by Summers; and Woods, *History*.

30. See Summers, *Literary Heritage*, entries on "Pastoral" by Holmes and "Elegy" by Guy-Bray.

31. See Summers, *Literary Heritage*, entry on Whitman by Martin; and Woods, *History*.

32. See Summers, *Literary Heritage*, entry on Forster by Summers; and Woods, *History*.

33. On the historical development of hostile religious and legal constructions of male love, see Greenberg, *Construction*, and Adam, *Rise*.

34. James Schamus, one of the producers of the film, discussed the planning that went into the poster and the advertising campaign in *Newsweek's* review. See Sean Smith, "Forbidden Territory: In Ang Lee's Devastating Film, *Brokeback Mountain*, Jake Gyllenhaal and Heath Ledger Buck Hollywood Convention," *Newsweek*, Nov. 5, 2005.

35. Christopher Marlowe, "The Passionate Shepherd to His Love," in M. H. Abrams, *et. al.*, eds., *The Norton Anthology of English Literature*, Fourth Edition, (New York: Norton, 1979).

36. See Summers, *Literary Heritage*, entries on Marlowe by Summers and Virgil by Crompton; and Woods, *History*.

37. See Summers, *Literary Heritage*, entry on Barnfield by Klawitter; and Woods, *History*.

38. Barnfield, "The Affectionate Shepherd," in Neil Powell, ed., *Gay Love Poetry* (New York: Carroll and Graf, 1997).

39. Barnfield, "Shepherd."

40. Proulx, "Brokeback Mountain," 28.

41. See Summers, *Literary Heritage*, entries on "Elegy" by Guy-Bray and "Pastoral" by Holmes; and Woods, *History*. Paul Monette, *Love Alone: Eighteen Elegies For Rog* (New York: St. Martin's, 1988).

42. See Summers, *Literary Heritage*, entry on "Elegy" by Guy-Bray; and Woods, *History*.

43. John Milton, "Lycidas," ll. 23–41, in Abrams, *Anthology*.

44. "Lycidas," ll. 165–166.

45. "Lycidas," l. 177.

46. Percy Bysshe Shelley, "Adonais" (throughout), in Abrams, *Anthology*.

47. "Adonais," ll. 73–81.

48. "Adonais," ll. 379–380.

49. Matthew Arnold, "Thyrsis," l. 19, in Abrams, *Anthology*.

50. "Thyrsis," ll. 72–80.

51. "Thyrsis," ll. 171–174.

52. "Thyrsis," ll. 175–179.

53. "When Lilacs Last in the Dooryard Bloom'd," l. 143, Whitman, *Leaves of Grass* (Ninth edition/1892).

54. "Lilacs," l. 147.

55. On Whitman and Lincoln, see Daniel Mark Epstein, *Lincoln and Whitman: Parallel Lives in Civil War Washington* (New York: Random House, 2005).

56. See Epstein, *Lincoln and Whitman*.

57. "When Lilacs Last in the Dooryard Bloom'd," ll. 7–11, Whitman, *Leaves of Grass* (Ninth edition/1892).

58. "For You O Democracy," l. 9, Whitman, *Leaves of Grass* (Ninth edition/1892).

59. "When Lilacs Last in the Dooryard Bloom'd," ll. 78–80, Whitman, *Leaves of Grass* (Ninth edition/1892).

60. "Lilacs," ll. 81–84.

61. "Song of Myself," ll. 647, Whitman, *Leaves of Grass* (Ninth edition/1892).

62. "The Streets of Laredo" or "The Cowboy's Lament," traditional American cowboy song.

63. "Laredo."

64. On Clark's life, see Jessie Y. Sundstrom, *Badger Clark, Cowboy Poet with Universal Appeal* (Custer: Badger Clark Memorial Society, 2004; Badger Clark Memorial Society: http://www.badgerclark.org, July 29, 2007).

65. On the greater acceptance of physical intimacy among men in the West before about 1900, see Packard, *Queer Cowboys*; Quinn, *Same-Sex Dynamics*; and Boag, *Same-Sex Affairs*.

66. Charles Badger Clark Jr., "Baching," *Sun and Saddle Leather* (Boston: R.G. Badger, 1915).

67. "The Lost Pardner," Clark, *Sun and Saddle Leather*.

68. On Thomas Eakins and homoeroticism, see the Gay, Lesbian, Bisexual, Transgender, Queer Encyclopedia: "Arts: American Art, Gay Male, Nineteenth Century," entry by Richard G. Mann (http://www.glbtq.com/arts/am_art_gay_19c,4.html, July

29, 2007); and "Arts: Thomas Eakins," entry by Carla Williams (http://www.glbtq
.com/arts/eakins_t.html, July 29, 2007); Emmanuel Cooper, *The Sexual Perspective:
Homosexuality and Art in the Last Hundred Years in the West* (New York: Routledge,
1994); and James M. Saslow, *Pictures and Passions: A History of Homosexuality in
the Visual Arts* (New York: Penguin, 1999).

69. On the art of David Hockney, see the Gay, Lesbian, Bisexual, Transgender,
Queer Encyclopedia: "Arts: David Hockney," entry by John McFarland
(http://www.glbtq.com/arts/hockney_d.html, July 29, 2007); Cooper, *Sexual Perspective*; and Saslow, *Pictures and Passions*.

70. On Bruce Weber's homoerotic photographs, see the Gay, Lesbian, Bisexual,
Transgender, Queer Encyclopedia: "Photography, Gay Male: Post-Stonewall," entry
by Ken Gonzales-Day (http://www.glbtq.com/arts/photography_gay_post_
stonewall.html, July 29, 2007); and "Bruce Weber," entry by Jason Goldman
(http://www.glbtq.com/arts/weber_b.html July 29, 2007).

71. The two most important studies of the pastoral idea of America and its influence are Henry Nash Smith, *Virgin Land: The American West as Symbol and Myth*
(Cambridge: Harvard University Press, 1950/1978) and Leo Marx, *The Machine in
the Garden: Technology and the Pastoral Ideal in America* (New York: Oxford, 1964).

72. On the development of justifications and rationalizations for the destruction of
Native American cultures, see Richard Slotkin's fine three-volume study: *Regeneration through Violence: The Mythology of the American Frontier, 1600–1860* (Middletown: Wesleyan University, 1973); *The Fatal Environment: The Myth of the Frontier
in the Age of Industrialization, 1800–1890* (New York: Atheneum, 1985); and *Gunfighter Nation: The Myth of the Frontier in Twentieth Century America* (New York:
Atheneum, 1992); also see Richard Drinnon, *Facing West: The Metaphysics of Indian-
Hating and Empire-Building* (Minneapolis: University of Minnesota Press, 1980);
and Robert F. Berkhofer, *The White Man's Indian: Images of the American Indian
rrom Columbus to the Present* (New York: Vintage, 1979).

73. On the persistence of the pastoral idea of America in the nineteenth and early
twentieth centuries, see Smith, *Virgin Land*.

74. On the prevalence of the pastoral impulse in American recreation, popular entertainment, suburban design, and advertising, see Marx, *Machine*; Kenneth T. Jackson, *Crabgrass Frontier: The Suburbanization of America* (New York: Oxford, 1985);
J. Schmitt, *Back to Nature: The Arcadian Myth in Urban America* (New York: Oxford, 1990); and Judith Williamson, *Decoding Advertisements: Ideology and the
Meaning of Advertising* (London: Marion Boyars, 1978).

75. On the pastoral in American literature, see Marx, *Machine*; Annette Kolodny,
*The Lay of the Land: Metaphor as Experience and History in American Life and Let-
ters* (Chapel Hill: University of North Carolina Press, 1984); and Lawrence Buell,
*The Environmental Imagination: Thoreau, Nature Writing, and the Formation of
American Culture* (Cambridge: Harvard University Press, 1996), and *Writing for an
Endangered World: Literature, Culture, and the Environment in the United States and
Beyond* (Cambridge: Harvard University Press, 2003). John Cooley provides a sum-
mary of critical discussion of the pastoral in American literature in his introduction to

his edited volume, *Earthly Words: Essays on Contemporary American Nature Writing and Environmental Writers* (Ann Arbor: University of Michigan Press, 1994).

76. On the development of the pastoral idea of America in the eighteenth and nineteenth centuries, see Smith, *Virgin Land*, and Marx, *Machine*. Will Wright relates the Western in particular to widespread American economic and social beliefs and practices in *The Wild West: The Mythical Cowboy and Social Theory* (Thousand Oaks: Sage, 2001).

77. On this aspect of pastoral writing in challenging the direction of American society, see Marx, *Machine*.

78. On the perennial fantasy of escape from women, domesticity, and responsibility, see Barbara Ehrenreich, *The Hearts of Men: American Dreams and the Flight from Commitment* (New York: Anchor, 1987).

79. Beginning in the late 1960s, there was widespread critical reevaluation of Hemingway, particularly of his representation of women, influenced by progressive feminist criticism of gender and power; more recently, some critics have challenged perspectives that locate Hemingway as a misogynist. The critical discussion of his complex and often contradictory attitudes toward gender and sexuality is interesting and valuable, but in my view his works express an impulse to withdraw from the responsibilities represented by women, a strong attraction to homosocial relationships, and a corresponding anxiety to distinguish the homosocial from the homosexual. His hostility toward men who love men isn't only evident in his writing, but in well-documented episodes in his life, notably in his relationships with F. Scott Fitzgerald and Jean Cocteau. See the Gay, Lesbian, Bisexual, Transgender, Queer Encyclopedia: "Literature: Ernest Hemingway," by Gregory Woods (http://www.glbtq.com/ literature/hemingway_e.html, July 29, 2007), also Richard Fantina, *Ernest Hemingway: Machismo and Masochism* (New York: Palgrave Macmillan, 2005).

80. Ernest Hemingway, *The Sun Also Rises* (New York: Scribner, 1926), 116.

81. Hemingway, *Sun*, 20.

82. To begin exploring the complex issue of Hemingway's attitudes toward sexuality and gender, see glbtq.com: Woods, "Ernest Hemingway" (http://www.glbtq .com/literature/hemingway_e.html, July 29, 2007) and Fantina, *Hemingway*.

83. For many years the Western was dismissed by intellectuals and literary, film, and cultural scholars, but as a result of Smith's discussion of the genre in *Virgin Land* (1950), serious discussion of it increased. The studies on which I've drawn are John Cawelti, *The Six-Gun Mystique* (Bowling Green: Popular Press, 1971); Will Wright, *Six Guns and Society: A Structural Study of the Western* (Berkeley: University of California Press, 1975), and Wright's *Wild West*; William W. Savage Jr., *The Cowboy Hero: His Image in American History and Culture* (Norman: University of Oklahoma Press, 1979); Jane Tompkins, *West of Everything: The Inner Life of Westerns* (New York: Oxford, 1992); Lee Clark Mitchell, *Westerns: Making the Man in Fiction and Film* (Chicago: University of Chicago Press, 1996); Richard Aquila, ed., *Wanted Dead or Alive: The American West in Popular Culture* (Urbana/Chicago: University of Illinois, 1996); Kent Ladd Steckmesser, *The Western Hero in History and Legend* (Norman: University of Oklahoma, 1997/1967); Chris Packard, *Queer Cowboys*; and

Slotkin, *Regeneration*; *Fatal Environment*; *Gunfighter Nation*. All of these studies are useful in understanding the historical development of the genre in literature and film. Berkhofer, *White Man's Indian*, provides important discussion of the representation of Native Americans in American popular culture. On the continuing appeal of the mythology of the Western for many who live in the American West, see Jane Kramer, *The Last Cowboy* (New York: Harper Collins, 1978).

84. Slotkin, *Regeneration*, *Fatal Environment*, and *Gunfighter Nation*, and Berkhofer, *White Man's Indian*, provide particularly insightful discussions of changing representations of Native Americans; analysis of narratives of captivity is central to Slotkin's great three-volume study.

85. Probably the most accessible brief overview of major aspects of the Western is Cawelti, *Mystique*. On race, gender, and property in Westerns, see Slotkin, *Regeneration*, *Fatal Environment*, and *Gunfighter Nation*; Tompkins, *West of Everything*; Mitchell, *Westerns*; and Wright, *Six Guns* and *Wild West*.

86. On outlaws and gender in Westerns, see Cawelti, *Mystique*.

87. On the Western hero in relation to individualism, community, and gender, see Cawelti, *Mystique*; Slotkin, *Regeneration*, *Fatal Environment*, and *Gunfighter Nation*; Tompkins, *West of Everything*; Mitchell, *Westerns*; and Wright, *Six Guns* and *Wild West*. I've discussed the indirectly expressed but significant element of class discontent in the construction of popular film action heroes in "Every Which Way but Lucid: The Critique of Authority in Clint Eastwood's Police Movies," *Journal of Popular Film and Television*, Vol. 10, No. 3, Fall 1982, reprinted as "Dirty Hero: The Critique of Authority in Clint Eastwood's Police Movies," in Christopher D. Geist and Jack Nachbar, eds., *The Popular Culture Reader, Third Edition* (Bowling Green: Popular Press, 1983). Though I don't discuss the cowboy hero specifically, I believe the argument I make is applicable, not only to the Westerns of Clint Eastwood but to others.

88. On the Western hero and women and domesticity, see Cawelti, *Mystique*; Wright, *Six Guns* and *Wild West*; Tompkins, *West of Everything*; and Mitchell, *Westerns*.

89. On the moral ambiguity of the Western hero and his ambivalent relationship to the community, see Cawelti, *Mystique*.

90. On the Western hero's relationship to people, animals, and the landscape, see Cawelti, *Mystique*; Wright, *Six Guns* and *Wild West*; Tompkins, *West of Everything*; and Mitchell, *Westerns*.

91. On the Western hero and the American masculine ideal of competitive individualism, see Wright, *Wild West*; Tompkins, *West of Everything*; and Mitchell, *Westerns*; on the changes in Westerns in the 1960s and 1970s, see Mitchell, *Westerns*.

92. For general discussion of the findings of social historians concerning probable social, economic, and demographic conditions in the cattle business in the later nineteenth and early twentieth centuries, in contrast with representations of the cowboy, see Packard, *Queer Cowboys*; Clyde A. Milner II, Carol A. O'Connor, Martha A. Sandweiss, eds, *The Oxford History of the American West* (New York: Oxford, 1996); and Richard White, *A New History of the American West: "It's Your Misfortune and None of My Own"* (Norman: University of Oklahoma Press, 1993). In part due to the lack of accurate records, there's considerable debate about what proportion of those

working with cattle in the West were African American, but some estimate 25 percent, and others as high as 40 percent. Though correct figures probably aren't obtainable, it's clear that there were many African American cowboys, and that until relatively recently popular fiction, film, and TV rendered their presence almost invisible. For detailed discussion of this specific topic, see Philip Durham and Everett L. Jones, *The Adventures of the Negro Cowboys* (New York: Dodd, Mead, 1966); Savage, *Cowboy Hero*; William Katz, *The Black West: A Documentary and Pictorial History of the African American Role in the Westward Expansion of the United States* (New York: Harlem Moon, 2005); and Blake Allmendinger, *Imagining the African-American West* (Lincoln: University of Nebraska Press, 2005).

93. On sex in all-male work groups, see Boag, *Same-Sex Affairs*; Higbie, *Indispensable Outcasts*; Quinn, *Same-Sex Dynamics*; Beneman, *Male-Male Intimacy*; Fellows, *Farm Boys*; and Packard, *Queer Cowboys*.

94. On sexual activities between men in all-male work groups, see Boag, *Same-Sex Affairs*; Higbie, *Indispensable Outcasts*; Quinn, *Same-Sex Dynamics*; Beneman, *Male-Male Intimacy*; Fellows, *Farm Boys*; and Packard, *Queer Cowboys*.

95. Beneman, *Male-Male Intimacy*; Boag, *Same-Sex Affairs*; and Packard, *Queer Cowboys*, raise the possibility that forms of all-male work may have attracted men who desired men. Scholarship on sailors and on pirates also suggests that there may have been a process of self-selection in which men who desired intimate relationships with other men chose to go to sea . For instance, see B. R. Burg, *Sodomy and the Pirate Tradition: English Sea Rovers of the Seventeenth Century Caribbean* (New York: New York University Press, 1995), and Burg, *An American Seafarer in the Age of Sail: The Erotic Diaries of Philip C. Van Buskirk, 1851–1870* (New Haven: Yale University Press, 1994).

96. Packard, *Queer Cowboys*, provides documentation of the intimacy of cattle workers in daily life, particularly through numerous photographs. Also interesting in terms of attitudes of cattle workers toward sex and gender, though without extensive discussion of same-sex intimacy, is Blake Allmendinger, *The Cowboy: Representation of Labor in an American Work Culture* (New York: Oxford, 1992).

97. Manuel Boyfrank, in Manuel Boyfrank Papers, International Gay and Lesbian Archives, West Hollywood, as quoted in Walter L. Williams, *The Spirit and the Flesh: Sexual Diversity in American Indian Culture* (Boston: Beacon, 1986).

98. As quoted in Williams, *Spirit*.

99. For photographic images of physical intimacy and affection between men in the nineteenth and early twentieth centuries, see David Deitcher, *Dear Friends: American Photographs of Men Together, 1840–1918* (New York: Abrams, 2001), and John Ibson, *Picturing Men: A Century of Male Relationships in Everyday American Photography* (Chicago: University of Chicago Press, 2006).

100. Numerous photographs and drawings presented by Packard (*Queer Cowboys*) indicate that types of affectionate physical contact which today might be labeled "gay" by many were widely accepted among cattle workers in the nineteenth and early twentieth centuries.

101. On individualistic, aggressive, competitive relations between men in Westerns, see Cawelti, *Mystique*; Wright, *Six Guns* and *Wild West*; Tompkins, *West of Everything*; and Mitchell, *Westerns*.

102. On race in the presentation of the Western hero's companion, see Packard, *Queer Cowboys*.

103. On constructions of the Western hero's sidekick, see Packard, *Queer Cowboys*.

104. On the elimination of Steve and the relative heterosexualization of the Virginian, see Packard, *Queer Cowboys*.

105. Owen Wister, *The Virginian: A Horseman of the Plains* (New York: Macmillan, 1901), 2.

106. Wister, *Virginian*, 4.

107. Wister, *Virginian*, 4.

108. See Packard, *Queer Cowboys*, for perceptive discussion of the implicit homoeroticism of *The Virginian*.

109. McMurtry and Ossana, "Screenplay," 70.

110. On the history and popularity of Western wear, see Tyler Beard and Jim Arndt, *One Hundred Years of Western Wear* (Layton: Gibbs Smith, 1993), and Holly George-Warren and Michele Freedman, *How the West Was Worn: A Complete History of Western Wear* (New York: Abrams, 2006).

111. On cowboy wear and gay men, see Cole, *Gay Apparel*.

112. On black hats/white hats and other aspects of costume in Westerns, see Cawelti, *Mystique*.

113. On the spectacle of the male body in Westerns, see the detailed and insightful discussion in Mitchell, *Westerns*.

114. See Mitchell, *Westerns*.

115. See the Professional Bull Riders, Inc., (PBR) website, http://www.pbrnow.com, July 29, 2007.

116. Mark Twain, *The Adventures of Huckleberry Finn*, ed. Sculley Bradley *et. al.*, (New York: Norton, 1977/1885), 229; Huck says he doesn't want Aunt Sally to try to "sivilize" him.

117. Mark Twain, *Huckleberry Finn*, 229.

118. Roderick Frazier Nash provides a useful introductory discussion on primitivism in American popular culture in *Wilderness and the American Mind* (New Haven: Yale University Press, 1967).

119. See Nash, *Wilderness*.

120. Cawelti, *Mystique*; Wright, *Six Guns*; Tompkins, *West of Everything*; and Mitchell, *Westerns*, all provide insightful discussions of the significance of the landscape in Westerns.

121. On Bierstadt and other painters of sublime Western scenery, see Matthew Baigell, *A Concise History of American Painting and Sculpture* (New York: Harper, 1996), and *Albert Bierstadt* (New York: Watson-Guptill, 1988); as well as the perceptive discussion in Mitchell, *Westerns*. On paintings of sublime landscapes and American nationalism, see Nash, *Wilderness*, and Barbara Novak, *Nature and Culture: American Landscape and Painting, 1825–1875* (New York: Oxford, 1981).

122. On agriculture and extractive industries in Wyoming, see Michael Malone and Richard W. Etulain, *The American West: A Twentieth Century History* (Lincoln: University of Nebraska Press, 1989).

123. "The Form of Solemnization of Matrimony," *The Book of Common Prayer,* 1662 Version.

124. On pastoral Christian imagery, see Gerhart B. Ladner, *God, Cosmos, and Humankind: The World of Early Christian Symbolism* (Berkeley: University of California Press, 1996); Robin M. Jensen, *Understanding Early Christian Art* (New York: Routledge, 2000); Jaroslav Pelikan, *The Illustrated Jesus through the Centuries* (New Haven: Yale University Press, 1997); and Gabriele Finaldi, *et. al., The Image of Christ* (London: National Gallery, 2000). On progressive Christians who support same-sex relationships, see Prologue, endnote number 34.

Chapter Four

"We Do That in the Wrong Place We'll Be Dead": Hatred and Fear

Even on Brokeback Mountain, which seems to offer a refuge where they're free to play and tease and wrestle and have sex, Jack and Ennis are seen and condemned by Aguirre; even in the most remote, idyllic place, love between men remains vulnerable to hatred. In both the story and the film, Aguirre's contemptuous observation of them comes at the moment when Ennis and Jack feel their greatest joy, chasing and grabbing each other half-naked and making love in the sunshine in one of the mountain meadows. Underscoring the sense of his intrusion and their vulnerability, Proulx inserts her description of Aguirre's surveillance into her most substantial description of Jack and Ennis's sexual play. As she says, sharing their passion night and day on the mountain makes them feel like they're flying, like they're invisible, but then adds that they don't know that one day Joe Aguirre watches them for ten minutes through his binoculars, until they button their jeans and Ennis goes back to the sheep.[1] On the mountain, once they've made love for the first time, Ennis and Jack can look at each other completely, not just furtively glancing so as to avoid being noticed. And they no longer have to hide their enjoyment of each other, but bring it out of the tent, into the sunshine. Being on Brokeback Mountain permits the expression of the homoerotic gaze whenever and wherever the men wish. But they still are susceptible to being seen by straight men, to the "bold stare"[2] of Aguirre and men like him who hold their kind of love in contempt, and who do whatever they can to eradicate it from any space, social or natural, where it becomes visible to them. Ennis and Jack at last are able to see each other, but there's no place where they're safe from being seen.

In both versions of the narrative, the episode in which Aguirre watches the men is a warning of the efforts of the dominant society to suppress and marginalize same-sex love. Aguirre may disregard the Forest Service rules, but his reaction to the passion he sees between Ennis and Jack shows he completely supports the homophobic cultural rules against love between men. Though he doesn't act directly against Ennis and Jack as some men—including their fathers—would do, and he doesn't wield a tire iron, Aguirre still tries to thwart them, bringing them down from the mountain early, perhaps without enough justification from the weather, treating them with contempt, and then insulting Jack when he returns the next spring, looking for work—and for Ennis. In the film, when Jack comes back to ask Aguirre if he's got any work on Brokeback again, at first Aguirre dismisses him, saying he's got no work for *him*, which could just mean that he's not satisfied with the work Jack did the previous summer with Ennis. But then, when Jack acts on his real concern, and despite Aguirre's hostile attitude dares to ask if Ennis has been around, Aguirre responds with hatred to this indication of Jack's desire, disgustedly condemning him and Ennis for "stemming the rose," and orders Jack out of his trailer. The threatening sign that Aguirre's posted on his office door, though a warning directed at trespassers in general, suggests the threat of violence that marks his reaction to encountering the intrusion of male love into what he and men like him perceive as heteronormative spaces that they control by right. (While Randy Quaid's performance may not quite be worth the ten million dollars he tried to pressure Focus Features into paying him, he's certainly convincing in presenting Aguirre as an all-too familiar kind of straight bully.[3])

Aguirre exemplifies one stage on the spectrum of homophobic hatred, which runs from the kind of suspicion and contempt illustrated in the film in the reactions to Jack on the part of the rodeo clown and the men at the farm equipment dealership in Childress, to the sort of simmering hostility expressed by Aguirre and by Jack's father-in-law, through to the physical violence directed against sexually different men by straight men like John Twist and Ennis's father and by the men who finally murder Jack. Aguirre's surveillance of Jack and Ennis reminds us that the mountain and any other wild areas the men may retreat to are surrounded on all sides by a social landscape in which members of the majority are vigilant, and will condemn and attack any men they perceive as sexually different. Even in the wilderness, there's the potential of the presence of straight men who will attempt to exclude and punish sexual difference. The natural world itself is subject to the effort to maintain the dominance of heteronormativity through a process of panoptic surveillance. Men who love men are trespassers everywhere. Hatred of them is a constant threat, silencing them, making them hide their feelings for each other, often forcing them into relationships with women that aren't right for them or for the women, causing men who love other men to fear not only the society around them but also their own feelings, distorting and damaging their lives and their relationships with the men they love.[4]

By the time when Ennis and Jack grow up, the late 1940s, the 1950s, and the early 1960s, the medical-legal constructions of homosexuality and the homosexual had become pervasive in the United States. During the Second World War, the medical model of same-sex desire as mental illness had been adopted by the armed forces, and though many sexual minority people served and same-sex relationships often were tolerated due to necessities of wartime, the official condemnation of homosexuality subjected it to increased negative visibility. After the war, Kinsey's findings on male sexual behavior caused a sensation, making the public much more aware of male homosexuality, and the McCarthyite Red Scare caused widespread, highly negative news coverage of the supposed "security risk" posed by male homosexuals and constructed homosexuality in terms of subversion. Men who were attracted to men were routinely denigrated in the press as "pansies," "fairies," "fruits," "perverts," "degenerates," and "deviates." In June of 1964, just a year after the story of *Brokeback Mountain* begins, *Life* magazine published a sensational photo essay on the "sad and sordid" "secret world" of homosexuality, stressing male prostitution and promiscuity, effeminate and sadomasochistic stereotypes, criminal activity, and the supposed parallel between homosexuality and Communist "subversion." The article showcased the hostile psychological theories of Dr. Irving Bieber. As mentioned before, during the 1950s there had been widely publicized panics in which sexually different men were rounded up as "sexual psychopaths," a label that constructed homosexuality as mental illness, often linking it to accusations of child molestation and child murder. Such negative constructions of homosexuality had become more widely known following the sensation caused by the Leopold and Loeb "thrill killing" in Chicago in 1924, in which two young men who were lovers murdered a young male relative and neighbor. In 1947, the scandal concerning the relationships the tennis champion "Big Bill" Tilden had had with teenaged male prostitutes added to negative constructions of male homosexuality. There is substantial evidence of increased religious condemnation of homosexuality among evangelical Protestants and Mormons by the 1950s. Historians of sexual minorities have noted that homosocial behavior that had been routine became much less accepted; for instance, by the 1930s and 1940s photographs of high school and college athletic teams show little or none of the affectionate intimacy of earlier pictures, in which young men posed with their arms over each other's shoulders, their hands on each other's legs, or holding hands. Substantial investigation of the incidence of violence against sexual minorities hasn't been done, but one major case in 1936 had received national news coverage and so was widely known. The popular Hollywood actor Bill Haines, who was known in the industry to be gay, and whose resistance to studio efforts to force him into marrying had put an early end to his acting career, was severely beaten at a beach near Los

Angeles by a mob calling itself the "White Legion" and accusing Haines of involvement in child molestation. Throughout the United States, for young men experiencing same-sex attraction the time period of Ennis and Jack's childhood and adolescence was one when it had become particularly difficult to come to terms with same-sex desire.[5]

Despite the rhetoric about "wide open spaces" where you don't feel "fenced in," Wyoming and much of the Rocky Mountain West forty years ago provided little space where it was safe to be visible to others as a man who loved men, and despite the growth of urban sexual minority communities and the gay rights movement, visibility still is dangerous, as shown by the kidnapping, beating, torture, and murder of Matthew Shepard in Laramie in 1998, a year after Annie Proulx first published *Brokeback Mountain*. The dangers that are possible for men who love men in the rural West are captured powerfully in the documentary play and movie, *The Laramie Project* (2002), based on interviews with Laramie residents after Matthew Shepard was murdered. In *The Laramie Project* a gay rancher who grew up in Wyoming explains that although many residents of the area, when asked about sexual minorities, claim to have a "live and let live" attitude, what this really means is "if I don't tell you I'm a fag, you won't beat the crap out of me."[6] Certainly many sexual minority people respond to this climate with endurance and resourcefulness, continuing to establish social networks and relationships, though many find it necessary to minimize their visibility. In part as a result of the threat of violence illustrated by the murder of Matthew Shepard or that of Brandon Teena in Nebraska in 1993, some sexual minority people and allies in the area are increasingly active and visible in the effort to confront homophobia. It's important to realize that the Shepard and Teena murders, which shocked people throughout the nation and beyond, are only two examples of the many crimes of violence that are directed against people because of sexual and gender difference. Such crimes occur in every part of the United States.[7]

In the rural West, hostility and the threat of violence cause some sexual minority people to leave, becoming part of an exodus to large cities where there may be more community and more safety. In Proulx's story, Jack recognizes this, although neither he nor Ennis wants to give up life in the country and to be forced into exile. During their reunion at the motel, four years after their summer on the mountain, Ennis asks him if what's happened to them happens to other people, and what they do, and Jack replies that it either doesn't happen in Wyoming or if it does, maybe they go to Denver, and then says in frustration that he "don't give a flyin fuck."[8] Although Denver could provide more community with other sexual minority people, and perhaps somewhat more safety, the gay community developing there, like those in major cities throughout the country, would have been particularly hospitable to middle class men, and while Proulx doesn't say so explicitly, it's plausible that a rural, working-class man like Jack wouldn't have felt accepted. Also, cities often don't necessarily provide a refuge; harassment and violence against sexual minorities happen in urban and rural areas every day, a fact that most straight people know and care nothing about, but that members of sexual minorities are all too well aware of. Almost a hundred and fifty years ago Whitman dreamed of the possibility of a safe space where men could love men freely and openly:

I dream'd in a dream I saw a city invincible to the attacks of the
    whole of the rest of the earth,
I dream'd that was the new City of Friends,
Nothing was greater there than the quality of robust love,
    it led the rest,
It was seen every hour in the actions of the men of that city,
And in all their looks and words.[9]

In rural America and in urban America, the majority still has yet to permit man-loving men and other sexual minorities to have the safe space to be themselves that Whitman dreamed of.

Both the story and the film repeatedly stress the danger of being visible as sexually different in a society that's poisoned with homophobia. A little later in the story's account of the reunion episode at the motel, when Jack raises the question of what they can do to be together, Ennis expresses his fear of being seen, telling Jack they can't be "'decent together if what happened back there—' he jerked his head in the direction of the apartment—'grabs on us like that. We do that in the wrong place we'll be dead. There's no reins on this one. It scares the piss out a me.'"[10] Even when he's alone with Jack, Ennis is unable to acknowledge the value of their relationship, implicitly constructing it as "indecent," and barely being able to refer to it in words at all, indicating it only with a gesture. In the screenwriters' version of Ennis's statement, as a result of the homophobia he's been taught he only can refer to the love he and Jack share as "this thing." In the story, Jack confirms Ennis's fear of exposure when he tells Ennis how he went back to Aguirre's office the next June and that Aguirre made a crack about how Jack and Ennis had found a way to pass the time up on the mountain, and that Jack then noticed Aguirre's "big-ass"[11] binoculars and so figured Aguirre had seen them having sex. Jack hides the full account of Aguirre's treatment of him, not telling Ennis about his disgusted remark that they "stemmed the rose,"[12] but what Jack does reveal to Ennis is more than enough to increase Ennis's already intense fear.

As Ennis realizes, the power of the erotic and emotional attraction between him and Jack puts them in constant danger when they're together. It's natural for them to hug and kiss each other, but this natural desire has to be suppressed when they meet if there's any chance at all that other people can see them. The most vivid example of this comes when they first greet each other four years after Brokeback Mountain; when Jack finally arrives and they embrace and kiss on the steps of the apartment over the laundromat, Alma looks out the door and sees them, which accelerates the process of estrangement between her and Ennis. In contrast to the story, in which the two men are completely lost in each other as they hug, the film underscores the sense of the danger of exposure, showing Ennis interrupting their passionate embrace to look around them and move a few steps with Jack to a corner where he thinks they're less visible. The filmmakers' sensitivity to the frequent necessity, for men who love men, of avoiding being seen even includes the way they arrange the brief transition shot of the exterior of the motel where Jack and Ennis stay: Jack's truck is parked at the end of the building, showing that the men have rented the room that's the farthest possible from the motel office.

Throughout the story and the film, Ennis's fear of being seen with Jack, of becoming visible to his society as a "queer" and possibly incurring the homophobic violence that he witnessed as a boy, repeatedly affects his actions, causing him to separate from Jack at the end of their summer together, leading him to go ahead with an unsatisfying marriage with Alma in spite of his feelings for Jack, preventing him from taking up Jack's invitation to ranch together, causing him to try to have a relationship with the waitress in Riverton, and continually making him anxious and afraid that others may recognize his sexual difference from them. The film reinforces this point about the danger of being visible as a man who loves men in an episode that only is suggested in the story; Proulx mentions that when Ennis lets Jack know that Alma has divorced him, Jack mistakenly thinks that that means Ennis finally has overcome his fear and is ready to live with him, and so drives up to Wyoming, only to have Ennis disappoint him again. The screenwriters expand brilliantly on this detail, providing an episode in which we see Jack, so happy he's singing along with "King of the Road" on the truck radio, driving to surprise Ennis in Riverton. When Jack gets to Ennis's line cabin outside of town, Ennis is startled and pleased but uncomfortable, with his two little girls waiting for him in his truck. Jack drives in, honking the horn, jumps out and eagerly embraces Ennis, who's always delighted by his friend's presence and hugs him back, but then stops Jack as he reaches to grasp the back of Ennis's head and bring him forward for a kiss, and awkwardly takes Jack over to meet the girls sitting in the truck. Ennis isn't able to directly reject Jack's hope that they can live together, and lamely puts him off by telling him it's a bad time for a visit because it's his turn to take care of the girls, but the real reason for his refusal, his fear of exposure as a sexually different man, is painfully evident in his discomfort, as he and Jack stand by the cabin and talk, when a truck slowly drives past. Straight viewers may misunderstand or dismiss the episode, but for any man who's been in love with another man who's afraid of being seen in public together in an intimate situation that might make others ask questions, the scene is painfully familiar. For those who want to minimize the reality of homophobia in America, it would be an interesting experiment for two men to embrace and kiss in a public place—rural or urban, West or East—where other people are coming and going and looking.

Both versions of the narrative show that Ennis's fears of the homophobic hostility of his society are justified. As part of its account of Jack's experiences as a rodeo bull rider in Texas, the movie adds the significant episode, referred to above, involving the rodeo clown, Jimbo, that perceptively indicates the dangers that can come with being perceived as sexually different. Trying to make a career for himself on the rodeo circuit, and lonely and nostalgic for what he had with Ennis, Jack tries to initiate a friendship with Jimbo, who's assisted him in the arena after being thrown by a bull. The stress and danger of rodeo work can provide a strongly homosocial environment, creating bonds between men; Jack tries to determine if his relationship with Jimbo could extend beyond that. As he drinks alone in a cowboy bar after the rodeo, Jack spots Jimbo as the young man's getting himself a beer, and steps up and tells the bartender he'll pay for it, saying Jimbo's the best damn rodeo clown he's ever worked with. Jimbo's response is superficially polite, but something in Jack's manner, perhaps the eagerness and warmth he shows, causes him to decline the offer. Jimbo treats Jack with a degree of suspicion, and draws a clear boundary between the contact they've had as a result of confronting bulls together in the arena and anything more, telling Jack that assisting him is just his job. Jimbo then goes over to a group of his friends by a pool table and apparently shares his suspicions with them. As the men talk together and glance over at Jack across the barroom, Jack realizes he'd better leave. Nothing further is shown, but given the hostility to sexually different men in American society, it could lead to Jack getting harassed by the group of men and then getting attacked. While neither the story or the film explain the specific circumstances that lead up to Jack's murder, it's possible to infer from what both do tell us that it also is the result of having become visible to others as a man who loves men. After years of frustration at being kept on a short leash by Ennis, Jack attempts to establish a full-time relationship with a ranch neighbor near Childress—in the film, probably the character Randall Malone—with the plan of bringing him up to his parents' ranch in Wyoming to run it together, as he'd originally hoped to do with Ennis. Apparently other men find out about Jack's sexuality, corner him in an isolated place, and beat him to death.

The homophobic hatred and violence that intimidate Ennis and eventually kill Jack function to marginalize same-sex love, reducing its visibility, denying men like Jack and Ennis friendships with other men like themselves or any positive information. Forty years ago, for a young man growing up in the West, or in just about any other part of the country, knowledge about sexual difference was severely restricted, and consisted mostly of condemnation and hostile stereotypes, at least until he was able to locate others similar to himself. As Proulx has said in her comments on the story, Ennis and Jack are a "couple of home-grown country kids, opinions and self-knowledge shaped by the world around them"[13] and are "clearly homophobic themselves, especially the Ennis character."[14] The story suggests that the only other men they're aware of who may love men are those who stand out because they're stigmatized as being less than masculine, and who they'd feel little in common with as a result. As Ennis says to Jack at the motel in the story, when they discuss what they can do, given their love for each other, and given the hatred others feel for men who love men, "'Jack, I don't want a be like them guys you see around sometimes.'"[15] Often sexually different men who want to pass for straight avoid any connections with men who are out, especially if those men fit the majority's homophobic stereotypes, since the relationship might out them as well. Of course, this intimidation only further divides and disempowers sexual minority men.

It's important for readers today to recognize how antithetical American cultural constructions of homosexuality were to those of masculinity at the time the narrative opens. Homosexual men were defined in terms of effeminacy and mental illness, both of which negated being a man. For Ennis, given what his cultural context has taught him, his sexuality and his gender identity are in conflict. To love Jack openly means being placed by society in a category denigrated as being without masculinity. As a man with no property or position, his masculinity is one of the few things Ennis does possess that gives him status, and though neither version of the narrative addresses this issue directly, it's plausible that this would be an important factor for a man like him in fearing to be identified as a "queer." Jack eventually gains some security as a result of his difficult connection to the Newsomes, but Ennis remains poor, in part because when he's younger he wants jobs that he can quit easily to take time to be with Jack, and then later on because of his commitment to meet his child support payments. Also, Ennis's last name raises at least the possibility that he may be part Hispanic, which could make him even more concerned, in a racist society, not to lose the little status he has as a straight man. For a man in Ennis's situation, there are a lot of reasons to be afraid of being visible as a man who loves another man.

For both Ennis and Jack, the central source of their experience of homophobia has been their fathers, who exemplify the hatred of sexually different men that permeates the society. Both narratives present the homophobic brutality of Ennis's father first, but both strongly indicate that the same sort of hatred also may be the primary cause of Jack's estrangement from his father.

During their reunion in 1967, Ennis tells Jack about the homophobic murder whose horrifying aftermath his father made him witness, a murder that his father himself may well have committed. In the story, this comes in the scene at the motel, in their conversation in bed after sex, and is the fundamental reason Ennis gives for rejecting Jack's invitation to reconfigure their lives so that they can live together, "'[shooting his] airplane out a the sky.'"[16] In the film it comes slightly later, during the trip into the mountains that they take for a few days in the same reunion episode. It's difficult to say which representation of what Ennis saw as a child is more horrifying and sickening. In the story, Ennis explains that there were two men, Earl and Rich, who ranched with each other around where he grew up, and that his father always made a remark when he saw them. Though they were tough older men, they were treated like a joke. When Ennis was about nine Earl was found dead in an irrigation ditch. He'd been beaten with a tire iron, spurred, and then dragged around "'by his dick until it pulled off, just bloody pulp.'"[17]

Even though the male couple Ennis describes were normative in terms of gender behavior, where he grew up near Sage in southwestern Wyoming the fact that they lived together nonetheless caused them to be subjected to contempt and ostracism, and their visibility and vulnerability, living in isolation in a rural area, exposed one of them to being kidnapped, tortured, castrated, and murdered. The elimination of Earl amounts to a homophobic lynching—not only was he brutally killed, but his corpse was displayed, to make an example of him and to teach a lesson to anyone—including little boys like Ennis—about what can await men who allow others to see that they're sexually different. What happened to Rich isn't even said. The scene in the film, a flashback as Ennis describes to Jack what happened, is even more horrible, if that's possible, since the audience sees the contrast between Earl's hideously mangled corpse and Ennis as an innocent, helpless, terrified child. Ennis goes on to tell Jack that his father made sure that he and his brother saw it, and that his father laughed about it, adding "'Hell, for all I know, he done the job.'"[18] As they grow up, straight people begin to experience sexual desire in a society that, for all its contradictory attitudes toward sex, endorses desire between men and women; homophobia, especially as it's expressed by family members, makes that experience very different for young people who feel same-sex attraction. The impact on Ennis of having grown up, and having begun, at some level of consciousness, to be aware of attraction for men in a family controlled by a father who may have been a homophobic murderer, comes across in what he says to Jack next, which indicates the depth and intensity of the fear that's been instilled in him. He comments that if his father were alive and could see them right then "' . . . you bet he'd go get his tire iron.'"[19] Even in the anonymous security of the motel, with his friend lying against him in bed and his father long dead, the threat of Ennis's father's vicious homophobic rage is intensely real to him, so real that he can imagine his father trying to beat him to death. Ennis's experience is one that most members of the majority can't even imagine, but that many sexual minority people know all too well. He grew up and began to understand that there were men who loved men, and perhaps even had some sense that he had such feelings, with a father who would have wanted him dead if he'd known Ennis was a "queer," and might have killed him himself.

The story reinforces the reader's sense of the depth of fear of homophobic violence that Ennis experiences throughout his life by making repeated references to his thoughts about the murder weapon that was used to kill Earl. He mentions it twice to Jack at the motel, first when he tells about seeing Earl's corpse and then when he imagines what his father would do if he saw Ennis and Jack in bed together at the motel; then he thinks of it when he calls Lureen and again when Jack's father talks to him, and of course the image of it still is in his mind on the last page of the story. In the movie, Ennis's suspicions about what actually happened to Jack are shown as he listens on the phone to Lureen's flat, rehearsed account of Jack's death: as she tells her tale about Jack being knocked unconscious by an exploding tire as he tried to fix a flat on a back road, Ennis pictures the scene of what probably happened, and imagines three men beating Jack to death. The scene is short and horrifyingly violent, but it's clear that the weapon is a tire iron. Still, this powerful scene doesn't name the weapon, and in fact it apparently is confusing to some viewers who haven't read the story and aren't certain how to interpret it. In the story, as Lureen gives the details of her version of what happened to Jack, Ennis suddenly realizes she's lying: "No, he thought, they got him with the tire iron."[20] Not *a*, but *the*—the tire iron that's been so real and so frightening to Ennis ever since he was a nine-year-old boy, the one that was used—possibly by his father—to beat in Earl's face. Then, as Lureen talks on, Ennis wonders if he's right, and vividly imagines Jack's accidental death as Lureen claims it happened. Although the mix of artificiality and sincere emotion over Jack's death that Ennis senses in what Lureen says to him makes him unsure, meeting John C. Twist confirms that it was the tire iron. At the end of the story, as Ennis struggles with his grief over Jack's death, he gets a little consolation from his vivid dreams of Jack, who's present to him as the lively, loving young man he was when they were together on Brokeback Mountain. But with the eerie weirdness dreams so often have, the tire iron appears too; the scene in the dreams is their camp on the mountain, with the open can of beans with the spoon sticking out, the way Jack liked to eat them, but the "spoon handle was the kind that could be used as a tire iron."[21] Within the logic of Ennis's dream world, it's simply a fact that there are kinds of spoons that can double as tire irons. Tire irons, and what they signify about the constant threat of violence against men who love men, are inescapable for Ennis.

As Annie Proulx has said in interviews and in what she's written about the process of creating "Brokeback Mountain," the way homophobic violence continues to damage the lives of sexual minority people was one of the main factors causing her to write the story. As she put it in one interview, "America is a violent, gun-handling country"[22] where "beatings and murder of those who are different abound."[23] In an essay about the story, she explained the experiences that caused her to think about what it would have been like for "any ill-informed, confused, not-sure-of-what-he-was-feeling youth growing up in homophobic rural Wyoming."[24] One evening when she was developing her ideas for the story, she "listened to the vicious rant of an elderly bar-café owner who was incensed that two 'homos' had come in the night before and ordered dinner. She said that if her bar regulars had been there (it was darts tournament night) things would have gone badly for them."[25] Proulx goes on to say that "Brokeback Mountain" is

> a story of destructive rural homophobia. Although there are many places in Wyoming where gay men did and do live together in harmony with the community, it should not be forgotten that a year after this story was published Matthew Shepard was tied to a buck fence outside the most enlightened town in the state, Laramie, home of the University of Wyoming.[26]

Confirming her perspective, geographers, sociologists, and social workers who've examined the ways social space and sexual orientation are constructed in rural areas observe that members of the majority who are hostile to sexual minorities often perceive homosexuality as something alien, transgressive, and threatening, an intrusion into heteronormative territory that must be suppressed and excluded. In the rural West, as indeed anywhere in America today, men who love men and members of other sexual minorities continue to be the potential targets of the homophobic violence that damages Ennis and finally destroys Jack.[27]

In both versions of the narrative, we only gradually learn about Jack's father. At the start of their friendship, Jack makes it clear to Ennis that he's eager to be anywhere else than Lightning Flat, and he confides in Ennis that though he loves rodeoing, and his father also was good at it, his father never taught Jack anything, and never once came to see him ride. The full dimensions and causes of Jack's estrangement from his father only become clear after Jack is dead, when Ennis goes to the Twists' ranch to try to persuade them to let him fulfill Jack's own wish about his burial, to have part of Jack's ashes to scatter on Brokeback Mountain. What he finds at the ranch explains why Jack was so impatient to get away and make a life of his own, and shows Ennis that Jack had to contend with a father whose hostility wasn't much different from his own father's. Both versions powerfully convey a sense of John C. Twist's general bitterness and of his contempt for his son in particular. In the film, the actor, Peter McRobbie, effectively captures the character's anger, and Heath Ledger skillfully presents the dignity with which Ennis endures it. The way McRobbie presents Twist, glaring with disdain at Jack's friend, sarcastically describing Jack's dream that he and Ennis could move to the ranch, build a cabin, and make the place into a cow and calf operation, then pausing to underline his disgust by spitting into his cup, shows that Twist knows exactly who Ennis is. As the text describes Twist, he sits silently at the table, his hands folded, and stares at Ennis with an "angry, knowing expression"[28]; Ennis recognizes in him a "not uncommon type with the hard need to be the stud duck in the pond."[29] To Ennis's straightforward statement of his sorrow about Jack's death, and his offer to take his ashes to Brokeback to fulfill Jack's wishes, the father responds contemptuously, telling him that he knows where Brokeback Mountain is, and dismissing Jack, saying that he thought he was "'too goddamn special'"[30] to be buried in their family plot. He then turns angrily on Ennis, telling him how Jack used to say that he was going to bring Ennis up to the ranch and get it into shape, and dismisses Jack's "half-baked"[31] idea that he and Ennis could build a log cabin and help run and improve the ranch. He says that then that past spring, Jack had said he was going to leave his wife and come up to Lightning Flat with "'some ranch neighbor a his'"[32] from Texas, and build a cabin and help with the ranch. He bitterly concludes, "'But like most a Jack's ideas it never come to pass.'"[33] With this, everything's clear to Ennis: Jack's father knows the significance of Brokeback Mountain; he knows Jack was attracted to men and that Jack and Ennis were lovers; and Jack was murdered, as Ennis suspected when he talked to Lureen on the phone; and now that Jack is dead, his father will do whatever he can to thwart Ennis and to cover up Jack's sexuality—literally, by burying his ashes in the family plot, rather than letting Ennis take them to Brokeback Mountain. Jack *was* "special," in that he was sexually different and in that he had unique importance in Ennis's life, but his father is determined to erase everything that made Jack different and unique. The contempt and satisfaction that John Twist expresses in the failure of his son's dream of having a life together with a friend must be especially sickening to Ennis, since it was his own fear of men like Twist that prevented him from taking up Jack's invitation, and that, indirectly, put Jack in the situation that led to his murder.

In her depiction of Twist, Proulx shows the remarkable insight into the situations of sexually different men that marks the story throughout; she recognizes that although the father's hatred of Jack's sexuality and of his relationship with Ennis is intense, it still will go unspoken. Many sexually different men grow up in families where, sometimes from an early age, they and everyone else have a sense that they're different, but where the hatred and shame and guilt that the family has been taught to associate with same-sex attraction work to silence any open discussion of it. Both versions of the narrative suggest that Jack's parents have perceived his difference, but while everyone has been aware of the issue, it's never been discussed; instead, the struggle has been waged, as it continues to be waged after his death, over smaller issues that stand for the larger one.[34] The father's refusal to allow Ennis to have Jack's ashes and to let them be scattered where they ought to be, on Brokeback Mountain where Ennis and Jack discovered they loved each other, is a way of repudiating not only Ennis but also Jack's sexuality, of erasing the man he was and of restoring the father's control over him at last, with Jack buried in the family plot. Even in death, hatred of his sexuality keeps Jack from getting what he'd hoped for; as he says to Ennis on their last trip, "'. . . Fuck-all has worked the way I wanted. Nothin ever come to my hand the right way.'"[35] When Ennis is kindly given a reprieve from any more time with John C. Twist by the gentle invitation of Jack's mother to go see her son's room, he looks out its window down the gravel road stretching south, realizing that when Jack was a boy, that was the only road he knew.[36] Ennis now has a sense of how trapped Jack felt, why he was so eager to get away, to be as good a bull rider as his father, to make a life for himself, and perhaps then to come back and, with Ennis's support, to run the ranch on his terms, not his father's.

In the scenes at the Twist ranch the director and the actors convey Proulx's account of the episode with great power, but there's one aspect of it that probably had to be omitted from the screenplay since it involves a memory that comes to Ennis at the moment Jack's mother allows him to get away from the father, and would have involved a complicated flashback interrupting the sequence of events in the scenes in the ranch house. The memory that comes back to Ennis powerfully confirms John Twist's brutality, his contempt for his son, and particularly the element of sexual aggression in his abuse of Jack. Proulx explains that Ennis recalls a story Jack told him about his father. When Jack was a little boy of three or four and was struggling to learn how to use the toilet on his own, he kept missing it when he peed, angering his father. Once his father went into an uncontrolled rage, whipping Jack with his belt and then urinating all over him and ordering him to clean it all up. That was when Jack noticed that he was circumcised and his father wasn't. As he tells Ennis, "'. . . I seen he had some extra material that I was missin. I seen they'd cut me different like you'd crop a ear or scorch a brand. No way to get it right with him after that."[37] Though there's no specific suggestion here that John Twist perceived his little son to be sexually different, his brutal abuse of Jack indicates that when Jack was as young as three or four, his father already felt irrationally hostile toward him for some reason, hostile enough that when his son had the difficulty that virtually every child has in learning to use the toilet, John Twist repeatedly reacted with anger, and once completely lost control, beating Jack unmercifully and then subjecting him to a form of phallic domination and humiliation that strongly suggests that Twist saw his son as somehow sexually deficient and inferior. The way in which Jack learned to think of the physical difference that he discovered between himself and his father in this terrible episode of abuse confirms that there was something in his father's behavior that made Jack feel that he perceived him as different. Of course, there's no connection between sexual orientation and being circumcised or uncircumcised, but for Jack, the way he thinks of the fact that he's been "cut," as being like what a rancher would do to mark an animal by cropping an ear or scorching it with a branding iron, shows that John C. Twist's behavior toward him made Jack feel that, in his father's eyes, he was branded as different. In Jack's story, there's no mention at all of his mother; apparently she was powerless to intervene. The complex suggestiveness of Jack's name already has been discussed, but one additional facet of it deserves comment in light of Jack's estrangement from his father: though we're never told, Jack's actual given name may be John, like his father; indeed, his legal name may well be "John C. Twist Jr." The fact that he always goes by Jack serves to reinforce the sense of his difference and distance from his brutal father.

The instance of abuse Ennis remembers Jack describing in the story raises some important points about understanding the relations between parents and sons who grow up to be sexually different. As people concerned about the problem of homophobia are aware, for much of the twentieth century the dominant theories in psychology, as a result of fundamental homophobic assumptions, constructed homosexuality as a mental illness, and claimed that male homosexuality was produced by abnormal family relationships, in which a distant, hostile father and an overprotective mother supposedly somehow "caused" their son's sexual orientation toward males.[38] By the early 1970s, such theories of the "etiology" of the "disease" of homosexuality had been largely discredited by the work of responsible psychologists such as Dr. Evelyn Hooker, who carefully studied and compared homosexual and heterosexual men, and found no differences in terms of mental health.[39] In 1973 the American Psychiatric Association dropped homosexuality from its list of categories of mental illness, though even today a small minority of homophobic psychologists continues to maintain that homosexuality is an "illness" that they can "cure," and often collaborates with homophobic religious groups that advocate "reparative therapy" to "change" sexual minorities and supposedly make them "become" straight.[40] For many sexually different men, of course, the dysfunctional family model that was claimed to "cause" homosexuality doesn't accurately describe their family relationships at all; for those for whom it does, the relationship between the son's sexuality and the parents' behaviors in fact may be exactly the opposite of what homophobic psychologists have believed.

Rather than *causing* the son's sexual orientation, a father's hostility and distance and a mother's protectiveness may be the *result* of the boy's sexuality. Despite the persistence of beliefs that sexual orientation somehow can be "changed," there still is very little understanding of what produces it in the first place, whether the factors are biological or environmental or both. While some people only become aware of a same-sex orientation in adolescence or later, many sexual minority people report a feeling of being somehow different, even if they don't act differently from other children, from an early age, confirming the perception that sexual orientation is established very early in life.[41] Thus it may well be that some parents also, at some level, recognize subtle differences in a child who eventually will have a same-sex orientation, and react to them, fathers often with hostility and mothers often with a desire to protect a child they rightly perceive as being particularly vulnerable, given the father's behavior. In a strongly patriarchal, sexist culture like ours, many fathers perceive their sons as extensions of themselves, as somehow reflecting on their own masculinity; a son who seems sexually different can be seen not as a confirmation of a father's masculinity, but as a denial of it.[42] Since it's only relatively recently that psychologists have begun really to listen to the experiences and perspectives of sexual minority people, the accuracy of this explanation of the reactions of some fathers and mothers to sons who are sexually different needs to be explored. Once again, Proulx's story shows the extraordinary perceptiveness with which she has sought to consider and represent the experiences of men who love men. In her accounts of the process of writing the story, she hasn't gone into detail about friendships with men that may have assisted her in developing the narrative, but the sensitivity to the experience of sexually different men that she shows suggests that she may have discussed such experience at length with friends or relatives. What she's written is testimony to the degree to which straight people who've rejected homophobic assumptions can be open to understanding the experiences of sexual minorities and can become true allies against homophobia. Annie Proulx deserves the greatest respect as an ally in challenging homophobia.

While Proulx's depiction of the Twists is brief, it's full of suggestion, not only about John Twist and Jack, but also about Jack's mother. Proulx indicates that in addition to having brutalized his son, John Twist has sought to dominate his wife; the story suggests the profound linkage between homophobia and sexism, the ways in which homophobic straight men equate and denigrate women and sexually different men.[43] As she's presented in the story, Jack's mother is quiet and deferential toward her husband, allowing him to do most of the talking, and not directly challenging his insulting dismissal of her dead son's dreams and of his friend. But she does dare to implicitly contradict her husband, ignoring the thinly veiled homophobia in his condemnation of Jack for thinking himself "too goddamn special to be buried in the family plot"[44] and telling Ennis how even after he moved to Texas Jack used to come home every year to help his father on the ranch. She then explains that Jack appreciated how she kept his room the way it was when he was a boy, and invites Ennis to go up and see it—and escape her husband.

The film's presentation of Jack's mother is very powerful. As in the story, she seems tired and unwell, moving carefully as though she's recovering from an operation. When she and her husband talk to Ennis in the strangely bare, white kitchen of the run-down little ranch house, she stands aside as John Twist sits at the table and rants about their son. Though virtually silent, the actress, Roberta Maxwell, makes clear the great distance the character she portrays feels from her brutal husband. It's easy to see that perhaps the only refuge for a woman caught in such a loveless marriage would be to retreat into the religious ecstasy and promise of transcendent union offered by Pentecostalism. But as she's portrayed, Mrs. Twist indicates none of the condemnation of male love typical of Pentecostal ministries; she clearly recognizes the special relationship Ennis had with Jack, and rather than assisting her husband in thwarting it, tries to help Ennis, not only by inviting him to go upstairs to Jack's room, making it possible for him to get away from the father and closer to things that can maintain his sense of connection with Jack, but also assisting him when he comes back down and wordlessly shows her the shirts, getting him a paper sack to take them in. Roberta Maxwell's gestures are eloquent: as Twist sits at the table, bitterly repeating that Jack's ashes are going to go in the family plot, she stands with her back to him, facing Ennis, and carefully places the shirts in the sack, then grasps her throat as if trying to control the pain she feels, and gently invites Ennis to come back and see them again. Although she was unable to defend Jack when he was a child, and still can't stand up to her husband when he attacks Jack after his murder, it's evident that she's done what little she can to show her love for her son. The father denies Ennis Jack's ashes, but the mother makes it possible for him to have the bloodstained shirts, the only vestige of his friend Ennis ever can have to remember him by. It's never said directly, but it's probable that, in preserving Jack's room as it was, she also has protected and guarded the shirts, not washing out the blood, but respecting their importance to her son and preserving them in the hiding place where Jack placed them—a closet within a closet.

~

The homophobia that extends throughout the American social landscape, that makes virtually every public space unsafe for any expression of same-sex love, that damages and sometimes destroys the lives of men like Ennis and Jack, as well as the other people involved with them, finally is beginning to be subjected to serious analysis. Part of the power of *Brokeback Mountain* lies in the effectiveness with which it depicts the intensity of the homophobia that sexual minorities must confront, as well as the depth to which some members of sexual minorities internalize homophobic feelings. A consideration of theories about the causes and effects of homophobia can serve to demonstrate further the insightfulness of both the story and the film.

One of the most perceptive recent examinations of the causes of homophobia and of the ways in which it operates has been made by Elisabeth Young-Bruehl in her comprehensive study, *The Anatomy of Prejudices* (1996). Her work is founded on a thoughtful reinterpretation of psychoanalytic theory in relation to social, cultural, and historical factors. Building on models of character types, Young-Bruehl distinguishes between three varieties of homophobic prejudice: obsessional homophobia, hysterical homophobia, and narcissistic homophobia, though as she explains, the three often overlap, and elements of all of them often may be combined in particular homophobic beliefs, behaviors, expressions, and policies.[45]

Obsessional homophobia constructs sexual minorities as an alien, organized, subversive, dangerous group, determined to damage and destroy the lives of "normal" people; the right wing political organizations and fundamentalist religious groups that represent themselves as waging a valiant effort to expose a sexual minority "agenda" that "threatens" to "destroy the family" exemplify obsessional homophobic attitudes. Probably the other major example of obsessional prejudice with which most people unfortunately must be familiar is anti-Semitism, which constructs Jewish people in similar terms, as forming a powerful, dangerous, subversive international conspiracy. The construction of sexual minorities as being engaged in a secretive conspiracy to subvert American life has a long history; it first clearly developed following the Second World War, when the majority began to recognize how extensive the "problem" of homosexuality was, and constructed sexual "deviants" as a "subversive" threat to "normality," using much the same language it employed in its constructions of the political "deviants" of the Communist Party. The rhetoric of contemporary homophobic political and religious groups that seek to prevent the legal protection of sexual minorities from harassment and discrimination, and are striving to amend the Constitution to deny same-sex couples the rights and benefits of marriage, directly derives from the homophobic rhetoric of McCarthyism. James Dobson's Focus on the Family continually attacks what it calls "the gay agenda" to "homosexualize" America, and Pat Robertson's Christian Broadcasting Network reports that the film industry and the media in general are "controlled" and "manipulated" by a "gay mafia" as part of a "well-planned propaganda campaign"; such "reports" then are reinforced by discussions of "gay influence" on the media by homophobic commentators such as John Gibson and Bill O'Reilly on Fox News or by those like Joe Scarborough on MSNBC who construct efforts to challenge homophobia as "subversion." The Republican Party has engineered a strategy for winning close elections by attracting the votes of homophobes, in particular by attacking proposals to allow sexual minorities to serve openly in the armed forces and efforts to achieve marriage equality for same-sex couples. These are only a few current examples; many of the homophobic attacks on *Brokeback Mountain* discussed in the Prologue to this book also can be understood as examples of obsessional homophobia, and there are many, many more.[46]

In hysterical homophobia, hostility to sexual minorities takes the form of projecting onto them anxieties and fears about particular sexual desires and sexual behaviors that many members of the majority find compelling but are unable to acknowledge in themselves. The stereotypic construction of gay men as hypersexual, and particularly the persistent fascination with male-male anal intercourse, are indications of this sort of hysterical projection of forbidden desires onto the homosexual Other. A related stereotype of lesbians is the recurrent fantasy of the enticing but dangerous lesbian seductress, a sort of nightmare version of heterosexual male conceptions of female attractiveness. Young-Bruehl points out that for those who perceive sexual minorities primarily in terms of hysterical homophobia, the goal is not to eliminate them; instead, the existence and visibility of sexual minorities serve an important function, allowing hysterical homophobes to point to them as an example of what they themselves supposedly are not, to define themselves in opposition to those whom they have constructed as representing forbidden desire. There's a clear parallel here with the long, ugly history of racist stereotypes, in which men and women of African background were perceived as embodying the sexual desires that the white majority believed were unacceptable in themselves, and were constructed in animalistic and infantile terms. For many whites, the threatening stereotype of the black rapist, the fascinating stereotype of the black seductress, and the comic stereotype of the childish minstrel have fulfilled the purpose of representing desires and behaviors that such whites cannot accept in themselves. Similarly, for some heterosexuals, the stereotypes they have constructed of gay men and lesbians allow them simultaneously to express and deny homoerotic desires, curiosity about anal intercourse, and fantasies about unbridled male and female sexuality. Also, the majority defines the homosexual Other in terms of what it sees as a highly unacceptable degree of deviance from prescribed gender behavior; constructions of sexually different men as effeminate and of sexually different women as masculine function to provide simultaneously disturbing and reassuring examples of everything that the majority seeks to convince itself it is not. In the hysterical homophobic impulse, the homosexual Other is necessary as a fantasy figure whose continued presence permits members of the majority to disavow those aspects of their own sexuality and gender behavior that they cannot accept, to express their compulsive curiosity about them, and to reassure themselves, by contrast, of their own "normality."[47]

These two forms of homophobia identified by Young-Bruehl are of great importance in understanding the majority's perceptions of sexual minorities: the obsessional construction of sexual minorities is especially relevant for understanding the ideologies of homophobic religious and political organizations, and the hysterical construction assists in understanding some of the persistent negative representations of sexual minorities in mass entertainment, particularly commercial film and TV. Her analysis of the third form, narcissistic homophobia, is especially useful in explaining the intensity of interpersonal homophobic hatred and violence in American society, including the hostile social landscape that surrounds Jack and Ennis in *Brokeback Mountain*. In Young-Bruehl's model, narcissistic prejudice describes the perspectives of those who are unable to tolerate the fact that there are others who they perceive as being fundamentally unlike themselves, and who respond to those they perceive as Other by defining boundaries that exclude them, or even by trying to destroy them. The most pervasive expression of this is in sexism, in which many men respond to the anatomical differences between themselves and women by defining women as entirely separate and different from themselves, as non-men, and create a complex system of controls and boundaries to exclude them from many male activities, institutions, and locations. For men with narcissistic sexist attitudes toward women, any women who dare to engage in historically "male" activities or to enter historically "male" institutions or spaces are perceived as a profound threat to their own identity as male. As a result of this anxiety about women, many men also construct men who love men as Other, as men-women who are alien and who must be excluded or even destroyed. The narcissistic model helps to account for the persistent stereotype of men who love men as effeminate, as not really being men at all but pseudo-women; it also may account for the fact that masculine men who are known to be sexually different also are targets of homophobia.

Indeed, they may be especially enraging to narcissistic homophobes, since they may be seen as having "infiltrated" and "betrayed" activities, institutions, and spaces controlled by straight men. Also, for narcissistic homophobes, women who aspire to equal and fair opportunities, and especially those women who love women, are constructed as threatening male prerogatives by "trying to be" men. Among men with a narcissistic homophobic perspective, it's imperative to maintain boundaries against all those who supposedly are unlike "real" men, which results in intense antagonism toward men and women who are sexually different, in addition to sexist prejudice against women in general. Narcissistic homophobia thus can explain the intense concern in our society with maintaining boundaries between the homosocial and the homosexual, as in the fear many men express about the possibility that sexually different men will "invade" spaces where they want to be able to bond with other heterosexual men, such as sports teams, locker rooms, fraternities, or the armed forces. It also can explain the fear and rage many straight men experience when sexually different men become visible to them anywhere in "their" society—they perceive such men as Other, as feminine non-men, and as a threat to their identity and dominant status as men. To prove that they are "real" men, many straight men thus feel compelled to subordinate, exclude, and eliminate men who are sexually different.[48]

The hatred that confronts Ennis and Jack can be understood primarily as a manifestation of narcissistic homophobia. The men who kill Earl—perhaps including Ennis's father—can't tolerate the presence of a male couple, even if they are masculine in behavior and appearance, or maybe especially *because* they are, and have tried to take an equal place for themselves within the ranching community in the countryside around Sage. For narcissistic homophobes, not only do such men have to be eliminated, either by driving them out or perhaps even by murdering them, but their physical identity as men has to be erased: to show that a man who lives with another man isn't "really" a man, Earl's genitals must be destroyed, and their destruction made visible. As mentioned above, by exhibiting Earl's tortured, castrated corpse, men like Ennis's father not only eliminate the "threat" Earl himself poses, but make his body a public spectacle, creating a terrifying warning that serves to intimidate any other man-loving men who may dare to become visible in the society, much less to try to enter it on equal terms. This display of violence not only functions to intimidate, silence, and exile adult men who are attracted to men, but also to teach a lesson to the next generation, not just to Ennis and K.E. but to every boy and young man in the community, that there is no place in the society for any man who feels desire for other men. Not everyone would see the tortured corpse, but everyone would hear about it; it functions as an instrument of homophobic terrorism, serving to maintain and reinforce the boundaries intended to exclude male-male desire from the society. The message to men who are sexually different is clear: keep your sexuality invisible and pass, or, better yet, get out; if you don't, you're risking getting killed.

For a narcissistic homophobe like Ennis's father, the possibility that one of his own sons might be sexually different would be absolutely intolerable. Neither version of the narrative directly indicates that Ennis's father expresses suspicion that Ennis might be a "queer," though the story describes an episode in Ennis's childhood that suggests that the father believed that Ennis needed to behave in a more traditionally masculine way. Ennis tells Jack that when his older brother, K.E., repeatedly beat him up when he was a boy, their father got tired of Ennis crying and told Ennis to beat up K.E., taking him by surprise, and doing it over and over until K.E. got the message. "'Nothin like hurtin somebody to make him hear good.'"[49] To Ennis's father, the only solution to conflict between men, even for the boys within his own family, is physical violence. He doesn't intervene and teach K.E. that what he's doing to his younger brother is wrong, but instead teaches Ennis to respond with even greater violence than K.E. directs against him. Particularly given the possibility that some fathers may sense that their sons are sexually different even when they're young children, it's possible that a man like Ennis's father would demand that he use violence to prove himself in a situation like this, and that the father also would go out of his way to be sure that he "taught his son a lesson" about what should happen to men like Earl. For a man like Ennis's father, it's even possible that anxiety about his own son's sexuality might play a role in causing him to make an example of a man like Earl by kidnapping, torturing, castrating, and murdering him. It's conceivable that such a father would lynch a gay or queer man as a way of teaching his son that any element of same sex desire must be suppressed, and thereby maintaining the boundary that excludes it from his own family.

Narcissistic homophobic rage also can be inferred to be the main factor in John C. Twist's abuse of Jack. As with Ennis's father, it's plausible that Jack's father suspected that Jack was sexually different when Jack was a child, precipitating the episode in which the father beat him and urinated on him, causing their growing estrangement, making the father ignore Jack's career as a bull rider, and leading Jack to want to make a life for himself away from Lightning Flat, and perhaps to find a friend who could come back with him to the family's ranch and challenge his father. In the film, the compulsion that homophobic straight men feel to maintain boundaries that exclude sexually different men also can explain the attitude of the rodeo clown and the other men at the bar toward Jack, and the derisive comments about Jack by the two men in the office at the farm equipment dealership as they watch Jack through the window as he demonstrates a tractor. Right in front of Lureen, one cracks,

"Say, didn't that piss-ant used to ride the bulls?" to which the other replies, "He used to *try . . .*" Though the insults are not overtly homophobic, at some level the men perceive Jack as being somehow different, and dismiss and exclude him as being less than a man. They don't label Jack as a "queer," but perhaps react to the playful, boyish, self-mocking humor he consistently shows—presented with skill and charm throughout the film by Gyllenhaal—which, to the kind of men who have to believe that they're "stud ducks," seems unmasculine. Toward the end of the narrative, of course, the narcissistic homophobic fury that Ennis witnessed as a boy of nine is directed at Jack: straight men who find sexually different men an intolerable affront to their identity eliminate him, just as Ennis's father may have eliminated Earl.

An understanding of narcissistic homophobia not only can assist in explaining the murderous rage of the men who threaten Jack and Ennis in the social landscape of *Brokeback Mountain,* but it also can assist in explaining hostile reactions to the film, including its rejection for Best Picture by the Motion Picture Academy. By locating the story of the love between two men and the ways in which a hostile society thwarts it within the heroic, masculine, iconic system of the American Western, the story and the film challenge the most deeply held fantasies of homophobic audiences and critics. The narratives introduce sexual difference, which the homophobic majority assumes to be urban, decadent, alien, effeminate, entirely Other, where it's not supposed to be, in the heart of the American imperial foundation myth, in the world of the strong, silent, tough, ideal American man—the cowboy. No wonder there have been such intense objections to the film from those who can't acknowledge that there can be any intersection between American masculinity and homosexuality, such as the Wyoming woman who was widely cited in the press as saying that she'd never encountered a gay cowboy and that *Brokeback Mountain* was "all hogwash."[50] No wonder that obtuse "critics" misread the film in ludicrous ways, such as attacking Jack as a "sexual predator." No wonder that purveyors of homophobic hatred in the media ridicule it as "Bareback Mounting" and attack it as "The Rape of the Marlboro Man." No wonder that it's repeatedly been ridiculed and parodied by various so-called "comedians" on TV, or by homophobic country singers such as Alan Jackson. No wonder that students have chanted "Brokeback! Mountain!" to insult other teams at athletic events, or that frat boys were reported to have tried to humiliate pledges by making them dress as "Brokeback cowboys."[51] No wonder that there have been efforts to ban it from theaters, school libraries, and indeed entire nations.[52] And no wonder that some of the older, white, straight men who dominate the Motion Picture Academy refused even to watch it, much less to consider giving it the Academy Award. The hatred that's been mobilized against the film is precisely the hatred that the film and the story depict with such insight. The repeated instances of the rejection and dismissal of *Brokeback Mountain* prove the very point of *Brokeback Mountain,* that to many straight men, love between men is so intolerable that they're compelled to do all they can to suppress it, silence it, render it invisible. But despite their efforts, they're impotent to destroy it; the beauty and power of the story and the film counteract their hatred and stupidity, affirming the possibility and value of love between men.

Because they've been surrounded from childhood by the hatred of male love that contaminates American society, sexually different men necessarily internalize homophobia, and their lives and relationships often are distorted by fear and shame. Their parents are likely to casually dismiss men who love men as "faggots" and "queers," and their fathers sometimes are motivated by narcissistic homophobia to direct not just ridicule and contempt, but anger and violence against sexually different men. From an early age, schoolmates rank one another in terms of hegemonic masculinity, denigrating, ridiculing, and insulting boys who are perceived as deficient, excluding, intimidating, and bullying them, and thereby also giving a powerful warning to any boy who can pass as masculine but who privately feels attraction to males. Teachers often do nothing to interfere with this sort of abuse, using the excuse that "boys will be boys," and some actively target and abuse boys who are perceived as less than masculine. Equating homosexuality with weakness is endemic in school athletics. Coaches hold up "sissies" and "fruits" and "faggots" as examples of what no real boy ought to be. In some supposedly Christian churches, which claim to teach a "Gospel of Love," what often is taught is the hatred of sexual minorities. A boy who's starting to feel attraction to other males may have to attend church services with his family at which he hears that "Thou shalt not lie with mankind, as with womankind: it is abomination"[53] in the sight of the Lord, and that "Sodomites" deserve the retribution of hellfire.[54] Some of these problems for sexual minorities have begun to change to a degree because of increasing resistance by sexual minorities and their allies, at least in some areas of the country, but homophobic abuse of every kind continues to be widespread. In the 1940s and 1950s, for a boy growing up near Sage, Wyoming, in the southwestern corner of the state near the epicenter of Mormonism in Utah, with a father who directed contempt, rage, and violence at sexually different men, or for a boy growing up in the area of Lightning Flat, toward the east end of the Montana border, with a father so full of hatred that he could beat and urinate on a little child, it's no surprise that homophobia would become deeply internalized. For Ennis and Jack, the threat posed by the hatred of men who love men is not only outside, but inside themselves.

Surrounded by so much hostility, and with no neutral, much less positive information about homosexuality, and no others to provide support or even to talk to, the only possibility for a young man who felt attraction to other young men and wanted to continue to remain accepted in his family and community would be to remain silent and to pass as straight. Unlike members of racial or ethnic or religious minorities, members of sexual minorities don't grow up in families of people like themselves whose love and support can counteract the prejudice and discrimination of the larger society. A child growing up in a black family or a child growing up in a Jewish family unfortunately will encounter vicious instances of prejudice at school and when out in public, but fortunately at home he or she is with people whose humanity refutes the horrible stereotypes of racism or anti-Semitism. A young person who's sexually different usually is the only one in the family who is so, and often grows up in fear that family members will discover and attack that sexual difference. Few straight people can imagine what it's like to grow up in fear of your own family because of the basic nature of your sexuality. Often today, and especially in the period when *Brokeback Mountain* is set, sexual minority young people have to come to an understanding of their sexuality alone. Quite frequently the biggest struggle for a young man is to begin to acknowledge a love of other men even to himself.[55]

Neither Proulx nor the filmmakers tell us much about the adolescence of Jack or Ennis, but it's not difficult to guess. For a young man gradually becoming aware of an attraction to other young men in a hostile society, often the only thing he can do is to wait and see if he also can be attracted to women, and perhaps still can be the kind of man everyone around him expects him to be. In American society, heterosexuality is compulsory—young people are assumed to be heterosexual and are directed into heterosexual relationships by everyone around them. In rural Wyoming in the 1950s and early 1960s, in school and at church it would have been taken for granted that Ennis and Jack, like every other young man, were straight, and they would have been pushed into school dances and church socials and dating. Young men who didn't seem to conform in terms of gender and sexuality would face intense pressure, including harassment, discrimination, and violence, and they'd risk forfeiting the privileges and status conferred by conforming to standards of hegemonic masculinity. Often young men in this situation can't even begin to acknowledge their real sexual feelings to themselves, and go through the motions with girls, hoping their feelings about men will just go away. While young straight people are supported in their feelings, though often within the confines of rules about only having sex after marriage, young sexually different men in a strongly homophobic environment frequently must deny their feelings, even to themselves, which not only alienates them from other young men with whom they could and should be able to explore sexual and emotional attraction, but also alienates them from themselves. Whereas young men who are straight may be able to enjoy their sexual fantasies and dreams about women, and even to share and celebrate them with friends, many young men who fantasize and dream about other men not only have no one to talk to and share their feelings with, but also learn to fear and repress their own sexual desires. This profoundly destructive experience is one that few members of the majority, particularly men, understand or even acknowledge. Today there are far more resources available about sexual minorities, and they're far more visible than they were forty years ago, but many sexually different young people still struggle in isolation and silence. The story and the movie don't depict the lives of Jack and Ennis as adolescents, but it's possible to assume that before they encounter each other for the first time at Aguirre's trailer, each of them has experienced and struggled with the sexual appreciation of other men that the subtle, powerful first scenes of the film suggest they feel. For young men in their situation, while every voice they've heard in the culture condemns male love, its power still can't be ignored.

Most members of the straight majority have little awareness of what it means for a sexually different person to pass for straight. The minority who are real allies actually are interested and try to understand, but most heterosexuals couldn't care less. Especially in a small community where everybody more or less knows everybody else and there's little chance of remaining anonymous or largely invisible as there is in a city, passing entails an awareness of constantly being under surveillance. As a man gets older and remains single, or has marriage problems or gets divorced, scrutiny becomes more intense; people may ask why he's not involved with women, or try, as part of the constant process of making heterosexuality compulsory, to "fix him up." But a sexually different man who passes isn't only under surveillance by others; to avoid the possibility that they'll suspect his difference, he must keep himself under even more intense surveillance, monitoring himself for any behavior or interest that might give away his secret, engaging in relationships with women that often are without much sexual or emotional meaning for him, and that unfairly raise and disappoint the expectations of the women. If a man who tries to pass does act on his sexual attraction to other men, he may be so fearful of any real involvement that he may settle for brief, even anonymous sexual encounters, rather than risking a more serious and sustained relationship with a man that might raise suspicion. If he gets involved both sexually and emotionally with another man, he may fear being seen with his partner, and may feel forced to limit their contact, which is frustrating and damaging to both of them, and can destroy the relationship. Few straight people can imagine how painful it is to love someone and to find that he feels compelled to hide your relationship or avoid you or lie about who you are out of fear of being subjected to homophobic labels. Sexually different men who try to pass may become entangled in relationships with women and tell them nothing about their actual sexuality, and may marry, trying to make the marriage work, fathering children, and all the time still feeling drawn to men, and frequently being involved with them. In slang in gay culture, a marriage in which the husband continues to have relationships with men on the side, but passes and so gets to have the status society accords to married men, frequently is dismissed as a "cover marriage" or a "front." The cost of passing for straight can be enormous, to the men who get involved with men who pass, to the women who get involved with them, to their children, and above all to the men themselves who struggle to be something that they aren't, and shouldn't have to try to be.[56]

~

The fear that's been instilled in Ennis by the homophobic hatred around him sets in motion the tragedy of *Brokeback Mountain,* leading him to reject Jack and to try to pass as straight, hurting not just Ennis but eventually everybody else in his life. At the end of his wonderful summer with Jack, after being able to experience intense sexual and emotional desire with another man, and, even more wonderfully, having that desire reciprocated, Ennis fails to act on what he's discovered about himself, withdrawing from the connection he and Jack have made, and conforming again to the pattern of heterosexual relationships into which his life already has been compelled. To appreciate the difficulty of Ennis's situation and the causes and effects of his withdrawal from Jack, it's important to look closely at how the story and the film represent Ennis's response to what happens between him and his friend on the mountain.

As has been discussed in chapter 2, Proulx presents Ennis's withdrawal from Jack as coming abruptly at the end of their summer together. Although neither man can put their relationship into words and both reject labeling themselves "queer," before they leave the mountain there's no sign of doubt or hesitation on Ennis's part, as there is in the film. In Proulx's version, the only indication that Ennis feels anxiety comes in August, when the hailstorm makes the sheep drift and get among a herd in another allotment. After five days of struggling to sort out their sheep from the Chileans' and finally getting the numbers right, Ennis knows the sheep are mixed; Proulx comments, "In a disquieting way everything seemed mixed."[57]

The disquiet Ennis starts to feel culminates shortly afterward when he and Jack get word from Aguirre to come down. As so often can happen when someone becomes involved in a sexual relationship in which they feel strong desire but that their society rejects, Ennis seems to have gone ahead with his lovemaking with Jack, avoiding thinking about its implications until he's forced to do so by the fact that their time together is drawing to a close. When exactly they would leave the mountain wasn't specified, but depended on the weather and on Aguirre. As they descend, Proulx says "Ennis felt he was in a slow-motion, but headlong, irreversible fall."[58] The word "fall" reverberates with implications. The pastoral idyll that Ennis and Jack have enjoyed on the mountain has been truly Edenic, allowing them to feel free of constant surveillance and judgment by straight men—like their fathers, and Aguirre, and scores of others they undoubtedly have had to deal with in their work, at school, at church, and everywhere else—and spontaneously to embrace their desire, and each other. While it's wild and cold, the mountain, like the Garden of Eden, permits the unashamed acceptance of sexuality, manifested in the way Jack and Ennis strip and play and make love in the sunshine in the alpine meadows. The paradise of the mountain allows male love to be expressed in a state of innocence, in contrast to society, where it's suppressed by the knowledge that it's perceived as sin. The "fall" can be thought of as one away from nature, back to society with its corrupt and corrupting notions of sin, and its compulsory pretense of heterosexuality. And yet also in the garden the men have come to a knowledge about themselves of which each may only have been partly aware, or may not have had at all, and which Ennis clearly doesn't want to have. The freedom Jack and Ennis enjoyed on the mountain had to be temporary, because of the changing weather and the demands of Aguirre and the society he represents. They're forced back into the confines of masculinity as men have defined it, and away from each other. For Ennis, society speaks most loudly in the growing doubt and anxiety he feels in his own mind. He and Jack aren't shut out of Eden by a divine command, but by other men; there's no angel with a flaming sword, but the growing fear that's been instilled in Ennis himself.

The film necessarily can't employ the reference to the Fall used in the language of the story's narrator, but it does convey a strong impression of the contrast between the innocent, playful, passionate friendship Jack and Ennis enjoy on the mountain after Ennis overcomes his initial hesitation and the tension that arises between the men as they return to society, and it directly depicts Ennis's overwhelming sense of no longer being in control of himself that Proulx describes as a feeling of irreversibly falling headlong. In the story, in her account of their conversation in Signal, just before they separate at the end of the summer, Proulx briefly and enigmatically mentions that Ennis has punched Jack, but only explains what's actually occurred at the end of the story, as part of her description of the bloody shirts. In contrast to this, the film presents the fight between Ennis and Jack in chronological narrative sequence, in a series of scenes that powerfully depict Ennis's frustration and Jack's yearning. Proulx never explains specifically how the fight begins, but the screenwriters provide an explanation that's entirely in keeping with her account of the two characters and their relationship. The scenes start when Ennis and Jack are packed up and ready to begin the trip down the mountain. Jack looks up from tightening his saddle and sees Ennis, sitting on a rise in the meadow; as Gyllenhaal and Ledger are shown in the scene, they suggest that Jack can tell that Ennis is upset. Ledger projects a mood that seems both worried and closed, much as in the film's depiction of Ennis the day after the two men first have sex. At first Jack tries to engage Ennis in play in order to cheer him up, and perhaps to get him to talk about what they'll do now. Jack takes his lariat, approaches Ennis, and playfully lassos him as he sits, saying, "Time to get goin, cowboy." Jack's gesture with the rope expresses what he feels but can't say directly: he wants to stay tied to Ennis. Then Ennis gets up and starts walking toward the horses, and Jack laughs and continues to play, as they have all summer, heeling Ennis with the lariat, pulling him down into the grass. Ennis yells, "This ain't no rodeo, cowboy," then grabs the rope hard and yanks Jack off his feet; Jack laughs and they wrestle and tumble together down the slope of the meadow.

As it's been many times earlier over the summer, their wrestling is an expression of the male erotic play that ties them together, but this time it has an edge, because Ennis is anxious and tense, and it expresses his fear of maintaining a tie with Jack and his resentment of Jack as the representative of desires Ennis doesn't want to have. As Ennis makes their wrestling more aggressive, Jack accidentally knees him in the nose, causing a nosebleed; they stop, and Jack, concerned, tries to staunch the blood with the sleeve of his shirt, but Ennis clocks him with a single punch. The film vividly captures the description Proulx gives of the punch, in her presentation of Ennis's memory of it as he stands in the closet in Jack's room at the Twist ranch, holding the blood-stained shirts: Ennis recalls that, as Jack was trying to stop the blood with his shirtsleeve, he had suddenly swung and laid out the "ministering angel . . . wings folded."[59] As can happen between two men, the playful, erotic wrestling turns serious, becoming a medium for expressing underlying tension and conflict that can't be put into words. Ennis finally has been faced by the arrival of the inevitable day when he must come down from the mountain and confront a decision about his feeling for Jack and the relationship he already has committed himself to with Alma. Whether he had partly realized he loved men before meeting Jack, and had suppressed those feelings in an effort to conform to the expectations of men like his father and brother, or whether he only became conscious of his attraction to men when he met Jack, isn't explained, but either way he now is confronted by a question that he can't deal with, and expresses his frustration at his situation in a moment of violence against Jack. Jack isn't responsible for the dilemma Ennis faces, since the conflict is within Ennis himself, due to what he feels and what he's been taught. Ennis reacts to Jack's horseplay the way his father told him to deal with K.E.'s violence, taking him by surprise and throwing a sucker punch. "'Nothin like hurtin somebody to make him hear good.'"[60]

The punch itself expresses many dimensions of Ennis's conflict. For those who read the story, it's a reminder of the violence of the men who shaped Ennis's childhood, and implies a contrast between the two men Ennis punches, his actual brother K.E. and Jack, who turns out to be closer and more important to Ennis than any brother could be, especially one who's been abusive like K.E. The punch also shows dramatically that Ennis has no words to express what he feels, much less to define himself. He has no model for understanding male love, and no way to articulate its meaning and value; when confronted with the frustrating question of whether he can choose it over the kind of love his society has told him he should feel, Ennis only can react with physical anger at the person who represents the impossible choice that he doesn't want to have to make. Also, in the scene in the film, Gyllenhaal's sensitive presentation of Jack suggests that Ennis's rage may partly be provoked by the solicitous concern that Jack feels for him. As Gyllenhaal presents the character, Jack is shocked and regretful that he's accidentally hurt Ennis, and reaches behind his friend's head, gently pulling him toward him so he can stop the bleeding, softly saying his name and urging him to come to him. According to American gender ideology, women express compassion, not men, and men certainly never express it for other men; Jack's gesture would be especially threatening to a man like Ennis, since it epitomizes the way in which their relationship challenges prescribed gender boundaries and "feminizes" both of them. For Ennis, the only way to cancel out the unbearable implications of such "feminine" treatment by another man would be a punch. At the end of both versions of the narrative, the shirts are all Ennis still has to tie him to his memory of Jack, and are enshrined by him along with the postcard of Brokeback Mountain in his trailer—but they also always must remind him of the day he punched Jack. They symbolize the love the two men shared, but also the violence Ennis directed at his friend because he was unable to fully embrace their love, and that set in motion the painful development of their separate, difficult lives, which culminated in Jack's murder.

The scene in Signal when Ennis and Jack separate at the end of the summer is one of the most painful in either the story or the film. At the crucial moment when each man will say what he plans to do next, now that their job together is over, Jack is filled with hopes he's afraid to speak. He's the more self-aware of the two, and perhaps could envision the possibility that they could make a mutual commitment, deciding to find work in the same place and maybe even arranging to live together. The movie suggests that he has reason to hope that at least Ennis might want to work on the mountain with him again the next year, since when they were sorting out the mixed herds of sheep after the hailstorm, Ennis was concerned to do it right in order to please Aguirre in case they wanted work from him again. But nothing's been discussed and no plans made, and Ennis has punched Jack in the face, so to resolve the situation Jack asks whether Ennis is going to "'do this'"[61] the next summer, which ostensibly is a question about whether Ennis will work on Brokeback again, but also is an invitation to resume their friendship as well. Ennis replies "'Maybe not,'"[62] confirming Jack's sense of his withdrawal, and reminds Jack that he and Alma are getting married in a few months. He says he might try to get work on a ranch, and then asks: "'You?'"[63] All Jack can do now is tell Ennis where he can find him if Ennis changes his mind. In the story, Jack's response to Ennis's question about what he'll do is slightly longer than what he says in the film, and emphasizes that he's still hoping that Ennis may not withdraw. As Proulx presents it, Jack tells Ennis that he'll work on Brokeback again "'If nothing better comes along,'"[64] and then adds that he may go up to his father's place and help him over the winter, and then head for Texas in the spring, if he doesn't get drafted. Jack makes it clear that though he'll be available, Ennis needs to realize he may not be so always. But to Jack's outline of where he'll be, Ennis only can say, "'Well, see you around, I guess,'"[65] effectively bringing everything that's passed between them to an end with the most casual farewell possible.

Although the men say little in the episode, and the language through which they express themselves is spare and flat, the filmmakers recognize its significance, and that the very terseness of the conversation indicates its depth of meaning. Gyllenhaal and Ledger convey what the scene means for the characters' relationship with extraordinary skill, suggesting the intense emotion that they feel but can't express to each other or even to themselves. At the start of the scene, Ennis is helping Jack start his old truck, a friendly gesture, but also one that speeds their separation. As they talk, Ledger perfectly indicates how closed down and nervous Ennis is, only squinting briefly at Gyllenhaal, and then uncomfortably looking away, down and to the side. Gyllenhaal, in contrast, presents Jack gazing expectantly at his friend; the contrast between the hope in his beautiful eyes and the ugly bruise on his left cheek, where Ennis punched him, sums up Jack's impossibly painful situation. In the dialogue as the movie presents it, Jack answers Ennis's question about his plans by saying that he might be back to the mountain if the army doesn't get him; when Gyllenhaal says he may be back, he gives a tentative, expectant, almost frightened smile that perfectly suggests the way Jack still is holding on to his hope that Ennis may want to maintain a connection. Ledger presents Ennis's response with similar skill, standing at a distance from Gyllenhaal, his expression hard, as he replies. His words, though, are subtly different from those in the story; instead of "'Well, see you around, I guess,'"[66] a statement that casually ends their involvement and only suggests that they might run into each other again by chance, he presents it as a question, saying, "Well, I guess I'll see you around, huh?" This obliges Jack to respond and implicitly agree to the end of their involvement, but, unlike Ennis's words in the story, also seems to raise the slight possibility that Ennis might be open to Jack getting in contact with him again. Gyllenhaal's voice sounds weak and slightly embarrassed as he gives Jack's final resigned acknowledgement of the failure of the dream of staying together with Ennis, the answer he knows Ennis expects to get: "Right." Ledger hesitates and continues to look for a moment at Gyllenhaal, suggesting that Ennis perhaps may not quite be able to accept what he's doing to them both. They don't touch; then Ledger turns and walks away. In contrast, the story describes them employing the ritualized gestures of affection that are acceptable between straight men to express their feelings for each other: they shake hands and hit each other on the shoulder, then drive away in opposite directions. There's none of this in the movie, which gives a much more powerful sense of Jack's despair and Ennis's refusal to accept what he feels. After looking closely at this extraordinary scene, and many others in the film that display equally superb acting, it's more and more difficult to accept that neither actor received an Academy Award.

The fact that the film presents Ennis as being even poorer than Jack, too poor to own even a junk truck, reinforces the sense of the awkwardness and pain of their parting. If two men work together and become friends, and one of them owns a vehicle, he'll assume that he can help out his friend by giving him a ride. Even if they were going out of town in opposite directions, the one with the truck would help his friend by taking him to the best place to hitch. This gesture not only would help make sure his friend got a ride, but would prolong their time with each other, expressing their friendship in the indirect way that American men are taught to prefer. But as Ennis walks off, Jack drives out of the lot, past him, and down the street in the same direction Ennis is going, reinforcing the sense that the falling out between them has ended any further effort at intimacy. As Jack drives past Ennis, all he can do is take a last look at his friend in the rearview mirror.

The screenwriters add a scene on the mountain that prepares for the scene in which Jack and Ennis separate, reinforcing the sense of Jack's guarded hopes of maintaining his connection with his friend. On their last day on the mountain, when Jack tells Ennis that Aguirre wants them to come down early, Ennis objects, angrily pointing out that the weather doesn't really justify it since the snow melted in an hour, and then complains bitterly about losing a possible month's more pay. Jack responds by offering Ennis a loan when they get to Signal, but to this effort to help his friend, and to maintain the connection between them, Ennis reacts indignantly, telling Jack he isn't in the poorhouse and doesn't need his money. Jack's offer, of course, isn't meant to be patronizing, and he's almost as poor as Ennis, so to take the offer the way Ennis seems to take it doesn't make much sense, but of course it makes a great deal of sense given that what's really happening is that Ennis, already upset by having to make a decision about his relationship with Jack, is giving a rebuff to Jack's effort to remain connected to him. In this scene as well, the acting is very strong, Ledger showing the frustration and anger that will explode in their fight shortly afterward, and Gyllenhaal looking hurt and confused by his friend's rejection of his help.

For many men who desire men, Jack's situation is an all too familiar one. Especially for young men who feel attraction to each other but aren't able to acknowledge it, determining where they stand with each other often is awkward and difficult. Two young men may delight in each other's company, and may begin a sexual relationship that they both desire, but still may find it impossible to discuss it and to decide what it means for them, since to do so would mean actually acknowledging what they feel and what it means about them. To go ahead and accept sexual difference and the labels it entails is a step that many young men struggle against taking, which can make it impossible for them to make their relationships work. Some young men, like Jack, are more able to accept what they want, though they may not be able to be out and to accept the negative outsider status of being known to be sexually different. At the end of their summer together, while Jack understands what he wants, he's afraid of what Ennis's reaction may be if he says it, so he hopes and waits, knowing he's likely to be rejected but still hopeful that Ennis can overcome his fear. When they part in Signal, their fight has made Jack nearly sure that Ennis will reject him, and so he's already secretly taken Ennis's bloodstained shirt to remember him by, as a token of his physical presence and the passion they shared. For men like Jack, there's no one to turn to, no community of others like himself that he knows and can ask for support and companionship when he's been rejected. As he was before he met Ennis, he's alone, an isolated man who desires other men in a homophobic society, and having the bloody shirt is the only way he can console himself and affirm the value of the love he and Ennis had. When Ennis brings their parting to an end, Jack already is grieving at the loss of his friend, though he does his best not to show it, and goes along with the superficial manner Ennis adopts. One of the many superb aspects of the film is the manner in which Gyllenhaal conveys a sense of how Jack just barely suppresses the pain he feels at being rejected and manages to say goodbye to Ennis in the way Ennis wants.

Once again, Whitman was the first in America to directly articulate the emotions a man can feel when a man he loves rejects him, especially in a society in which love between men is forced to remain unspoken. Whitman laments the loss of a friend's love in "Hours Continuing Long," a poem originally included in the *Calamus* section in the 1860 edition of *Leaves of Grass*, and then omitted by Whitman thereafter, probably because of the condemnation of the homoerotic content of many of his poems by homophobic reviewers. In the central part of the poem, Whitman describes his despair:

Hours discouraged, distracted—For he, the one I cannot content
    myself without—soon I saw him content himself without me;
Hours when I am forgotten (O weeks and months are passing, but I
    believe I am never to forget!)
Sullen and suffering hours—(I am ashamed—but it is useless—I
    am what I am;)
Hours of my torment—I wonder if other men ever have the like, out
    of the like feelings?
Is there even one other like me—distracted—his friend, his lover,
    lost to him?
Is he too as I am now? Does he still rise in the morning, dejected,
    thinking who is lost to him? And at night, awaking, think who is lost?
Does he too harbor his friendship silent and endless? Harbor his
    anguish and passion?
Does some stray reminder, or the casual mention of a name, bring
    the fit back upon him, taciturn and deprest?[67]

The silent pain expressed so well by Gyllenhaal in the scene in which the two men separate makes it easy to imagine the ongoing sadness and regret that lie ahead for Jack, the intense sense of loss and loneliness that Whitman knew and had the courage to say in his poem. Unlike members of the straight majority, whose love relationships are affirmed throughout the society, and who can count on friends and family members for support when love fails and they feel the pain of being left alone, society's homophobia frequently means that members of sexual minorities who struggle with relationships with those they love, especially when they're young, do so in a kind of isolation that straight people can't even begin to imagine. A young man grieving over rejection by a man he loves, as Jack does, and who like Jack is isolated by the effort to pass, can't turn to anyone for compassion and reassurance; he has no friends he can trust enough to disclose his sexuality or his relationship to, and there's no possibility of receiving understanding from his family. If Jack were to tell his parents about his grief over losing Ennis, his father could well attack him, and very likely would disown him. Being forced to pass deprives many men who desire men of the most basic forms of support that straight people take for granted.

One of the triumphs of Whitman's work, for himself and for man-loving men ever since, is that Whitman helped to initiate a process of sharing personal experience among men who loved men that was a step in beginning to build modern gay communities. The publication of "Hours Continuing Long" in 1860, along with the other poems in *Calamus*, helped to overcome precisely the isolation and despair that Whitman presents in the poem, to begin to create a sense of community and support among men who love men, at least among those who were able to read Whitman's work.[68] But for many men, like Jack, there continued to be—and still continues to be, in many places—no visible community of others who can sustain a man who loves other men as he struggles to accept himself and to find someone to love. Despite the intense despair Whitman expresses, he also retrieves a profoundly valuable kind of knowledge from his unrequited love—despite the shame he's been taught to feel, he's able to acknowledge to himself his identity as a man who loves men—to say, "I am what I am." In a similar way, while Jack suffers intensely when Ennis rejects him, at least he can acknowledge to himself what Ennis cannot, that the most important thing for him in his life will be to be with another man. He doesn't do it in words, but he does it by taking and keeping the shirt, which affirms for Jack the value of what he knows Ennis felt and what he still feels for Ennis.

Jack has no way of being aware of it, but his grief at Ennis's withdrawal is equaled by the pain Ennis inflicts on himself by rejecting Jack. Because Ennis feels obliged to conform and to try to be the kind of man his society has made clear is the only kind it will accept, he refuses the possibility Jack offers, and resumes his intention of marrying Alma, even though it's Jack he loves. Leaving his friend makes Ennis physically ill; according to the story, as he drives away, he has to pull over because he's overwhelmed with nausea, feeling like someone was "pulling his guts out hand over hand a yard at a time."[69] Though Ennis is sickened by what he's done, he's so repressed and alienated from his own feelings that he can't fully articulate to himself why he feels so bad. When he and Jack have their reunion four years later, he makes the intensity of his feeling for Jack clear, telling him how after they split up he had to pull over and try to puke, thinking he'd eaten something bad, and that it "'Took me about a year to figure out that I shouldn't a let you out a my sights. Too late then by a long, long while.'"[70] In the film, Jack drives off in his old truck, watching Ennis in the rearview mirror for what he thinks must be the last time, as Ennis walks away, his few belongings in a sack slung over his shoulder. Then as Ennis goes down the street, he suddenly staggers into an alley between two buildings, kneels down, and retches. In contrast to the story, the film presents Ennis as being more immediately aware of the reasons for what he feels: full of rage at his own emotions and because he felt he had no choice but to reject Jack, he curses and slams his fist into the side of the building he's leaning on, then sobs. In the screenplay, the screenwriters stress his degree of awareness of what he's done, saying, "Jack's leaving proves too much . . . pain, longing, loneliness overpower Ennis—emotions stronger than he's ever felt for another person consume him: he feels as bad and confused as he ever has in his life. Conflicted—he is angry at himself, for all that has happened, and for all that he is feeling."[71] As if to underline the point that there's virtually no place in society where a man who loves another man can be free of surveillance, at just that moment a cowboy walks past, and seeing Ennis crouched in the alley by the wall, looks and hesitates; Ennis shouts, "What the fuck you lookin at? Huh?" As an ironic reminder of the love that Ennis just has refused, the cowboy's jacket and hat look strikingly similar to Jack's, almost as if Jack had returned to offer his love to Ennis one more time. The two versions of the narrative handle this episode differently, but both depict Ennis in fundamentally the same way. His fear makes him back away from the prospect of building a life with a man he loves and who loves him, and traps him in his effort to conform to the life he thinks a man must have in order to be a man.

Although both Jack and Ennis come across as masculine men in the story and the film, Ennis is more traditionally masculine than Jack. Where Jack's boyish playfulness and greater ease in acting on his sexual desires show him to be the more open and emotional of the two, Ennis is more reserved and less demonstrative, and, though Jack certainly is athletic and strong, Ennis is physically the stronger of the two. Ennis is the kind of man who feels more comfortable outdoors than indoors, who doesn't know ketchup is a condiment. But, as mentioned in the previous chapter, while Jack's personality may seem softer and so in some ways more feminine, he's actually more courageous than his friend. Ennis typifies the ideal of masculinity in the Western cowboy tradition, being adept at handling as well as stoically enduring any physical challenge, but paradoxically he's not really as strong a man as Jack. Jack's willing to take the risk of being who he is and loving Ennis and even proposing to make a life with him, whereas Ennis is too afraid of the consequences to take up the possibility Jack implicitly offers him at the end of their summer together. Both know the brutality of men who take it upon themselves to enforce the compulsory heterosexuality of their society, but Jack's better able to resist the fear generated by endemic homophobia and to try to be himself. Perhaps the only way to successfully oppose those who hate love between men would be to be together. For Ennis, fear becomes the force that defines his life, causing him to back away from the prospect of a life with Jack, to go ahead with his plan to marry Alma, and to trap himself—and, though he and they can have no way of foreseeing it, Jack, and Alma, and even Lureen and the three children—in lives that are damaged because of his struggle to pass for straight. Even once Jack returns and invites Ennis to make a life together, Ennis repeatedly rejects his offers. Of course, it's impossible to locate responsibility or blame on Ennis, since like Jack he's struggling to understand himself and what his life can be amid just about the worst possible conditions, in a society that denies him any knowledge or assistance, but ironically his effort to avoid what men like his father do to men like Earl ruins everything for him and Jack, and hurts many others besides. By trying to save his life, he winds up destroying it, and Jack's as well. He's unable to embrace the gift of love that the two men have discovered together on Brokeback Mountain.

NOTES

1. Proulx, "Brokeback Mountain," 15.
2. Proulx, "Brokeback Mountain," 16.
3. "Actor Randy Quaid Sues Over Payment for 'Brokeback' Role," Associated Press, *San Francisco Chronicle*, March 24, 2006 (http://www.sfgate.com/cgi–bin/ article.cgi?file=/n/a/2006/03/24/entertainment/e093215S06.DTL, July 29, 2007).
4. On public space, including both the social space of communities and the open space of the countryside, as the domain of homophobia and heteronormativity, see Sumartojo, "Contesting Place"; Heibel, "Casa Nova"; Brown, *Closet Space*; Little, *Rural Geography*; Lindhorst, "Practical Implications"; Van Hoven, *Spaces*; Cloke, *Country Visions*; and Kramer, "Batchelor Farmers."
5. On U.S. military policy, the McCarthy purge, and the Sioux City and Boise panics, see Miller, *Out of the Past*; also see Gerassi, *Boise*, on Boise, and Miller, *Sex-Crime Panic*, on Sioux City. The famous *Life* magazine article is "Homosexuality in America: A Secret World Grows Open and Bolder," by Paul Welch, William Eppridge, and Ernest Havemann, June 24, 1964, Volume 56, Number 26. On the Leopold and Loeb case, see Hal Higdon, *Leopold and Loeb: The Crime of the Century* (Urbana/Chicago: University of Illinois, 1999). The case has reverberated through the years, inspiring Patrick Hamilton's play *Rope* (1929; entitled *Rope's End* in the United States); Alfred Hitchcock's movie, *Rope* (1948), based on the play; Meyer Levin's novel, *Compulsion* (1956); the movie *Compulsion* (1959), based on the novel; and Todd Haynes's movie *Swoon* (1992.) On the films and the case, see the entry in the Gay, Lesbian, Bisexual, Transgender, Queer Encyclopedia under "Arts" entitled "Screenwriters," by Craig Kaczorowski (http://www.glbtq.com/arts/screen writers.html, July 29, 2007). On Tilden, see Frank Deford, *Big Bill Tilden: The Triumph and the Tragedy* (New York: Simon and Schuster, 1976). On the growth of religious condemnations of homosexuality by the mid-twentieth century, see Quinn, *Same-Sex Dynamics*, and Howard, *Men Like That*. On changes in male poses in photographs, see Quinn, *Same-Sex Dynamics*. On Bill Haines, see William J. Mann, *Wise-*

cracker: The Life and Times of William Haines, Hollywood's First Openly Gay Star (New York: Penguin, 1998).

6. *The Laramie Project*, by Moises Kaufman and the Tectonic Theatre Project (New York: Vintage, 2001); HBO movie written and directed by Kaufman, 2002.

7. The abduction, torture, and murder of Matthew Shepard in Wyoming in 1998 and the trial of those responsible made homophobic hatred and violence, as well as resistance to them, more visible to many straight people. The two murderers repeatedly changed their stories, trying to evade responsibility for what they had done and to make it seem as if it weren't motivated by homophobia, and some officials and reporters facilitated this misrepresentation. Possibly the most vicious homophobes in the nation, the "Reverend" Fred Phelps and his followers, were present during the trial and insulted Matthew Shepard, his family, and all those who had been shocked by his murder. But many local sexual minority people and allies protested against homophobia; one of the most moving instances of this was the "Angel Action," in which people wearing white angel wings screened from view Phelps, his fellow bigots, and their signs reading "God Hates Fags" and "Matt in Hell." Local people opposed to homophobia gave powerful testimony in *The Laramie Project* and the murder led to the organization of the Matthew Shepard Foundation, based in Casper, which advocates legislation punishing hate crimes against those who differ in sexuality and gender expression.

Other similar cases in which people have been murdered because of their sexuality or gender behavior have occurred around the country. There are far too many to list, but some in the last decade include: Julianne Williams, 24, and Laura Winans, 26 (bound, gagged, throats slit, when hiking in Shenandoah National Park, Virginia, 1996); Billy Jack Gaither, 39 (beaten, burned; Sylacauga, Alabama, 1999); Gary Matson, 50, and Winfield Mowder, 40 (tortured, shot in their bed in their home; Happy Valley/Redding, California, 1999); Eddie Northington, 39 (beaten, decapitated; head left prominently in a park known as a gay cruising area; Richmond, Virginia, 1999); Steen Fenrich, 19 (beaten, dismembered by his stepfather; Dix Hills, New York, 2000); Danny Lee Overstreet, 43 (assassinated in a gay bar by a gunman who was enraged at gay men because his last name was "Gay"; Roanoke, Virginia, 2000); "J.R." Warren, 26 (beaten; Grant Town, West Virginia, 2000); Fred Martinez Jr., 16 (beaten; Cortez, Colorado, 2001); Sakia Gunn, 15 (stabbed to death because she acknowledged that she was a lesbian when confronted while walking home; Newark, New Jersey, 2003); Scotty Joe Weaver, 18 (beaten, strangled in his home; Bay Minette, Alabama, 2004); Ryan Skipper, 25 (beaten, stabbed; Winter Haven, Florida, 2007); Andrew Anthos, 72 (while riding home on a bus, confronted by a man who demanded if he was gay; beaten in front of his home; Detroit, Michigan, 2007); and Aaron C. Hall (beaten; Crothersville, Indiana, 2007).

The case of the rape and murder of Brandon Teena in Nebraska in 1993 was less extensively reported than the Matthew Shepard case when it occurred, but became widely known as the result of two important films, the documentary, *The Brandon Teena Story* (1998), and the drama, *Boys Don't Cry* (1999), which increased general awareness of the challenges faced by transgender people. After Brandon Teena was raped by men who had learned that he was anatomically female, he sought assistance from law enforcement authorities, who failed to intervene and prevent the rapists from murdering him. The sheriff in the case referred to Brandon contemptuously as "it." Transgender people often are the targets of particular hostility and violence. Attacks on them now are receiving more attention, as in the recent case of the murder of Gwen Araujo, 17 (beaten, strangled; Newark, California, 2002), but some murders of transgender people are given less coverage, perhaps partly because of racial prejudice, as in the case of Nizah Morris, 47 (beaten; Philadelphia, 2003).

Again, it can't be stressed enough that these are only some of the fatal attacks on lesbian, gay, bisexual, transgender, queer, and questioning people in this period. Also, there have been many brutal attacks that fortunately haven't resulted in death, though they have caused physical and psychological injury; of course, all such attacks function as a warning to sexual minorities, threatening and intimidating people throughout the society. And there are many more individuals, particularly vulnerable young people trying to understand their own sexuality and gender, who take their own lives because of the hostility around them.

Awareness of murders of sexual minority people has increased demands for legislation and enforcement against hate crimes directed at people because of sexual and gender difference, but in Nebraska, where Brandon Teena was murdered, the hate crimes law still does not mention crimes directed against those who differ in gender identity, and Wyoming has failed to pass any hate crimes legislation in almost a decade since the murder of Matthew Shepard. Despite continuing efforts, there is no federal law criminalizing acts of violence based on sexuality and gender expression, and George W. Bush has explicitly threatened to veto such legislation if Congress passes it. Information on hate crimes against sexual minorities is available from the Human Rights Campaign (http://www.hrc.com, July 29, 2007), the National Gay and Lesbian Task Force (http://www.thetaskforce.org, July 29, 2007), the Matthew Shepard Foundation (http://www.matthewshepard.org, July 29, 2007), the National Center For Transgender Equality (http://www.nctequality.org, July 29, 2007), and the Transgender Law Center (http://www.transgenderlawcenter.org, July 29, 2007).

8. Proulx, "Brokeback Mountain," 30.
9. "I Dream'd in a Dream," Whitman, *Leaves of Grass* (Ninth edition/1892.)
10. Proulx, "Brokeback Mountain," 27.
11. Proulx, "Brokeback Mountain," 27.
12. Proulx, "Brokeback Mountain," 27.
13. Proulx, "Getting Movied," 130.
14. Proulx, "GettingMovied," 130.
15. Proulx, "Brokeback Mountain," 29.
16. Proulx, "Brokeback Mountain," 30.
17. Proulx, "Brokeback Mountain," 29.
18. Proulx, "Brokeback Mountain," 29.
19. Proulx, "Brokeback Mountain," 29–30.
20. Proulx, "Brokeback Mountain," 45.
21. Proulx, "Brokeback Mountain," 54.
22. "Interview with Annie Proulx," *The Missouri Review.*
23. "Interview with Proulx."

24. Proulx, "Getting Movied," 130.
25. Proulx, "Getting Movied," 130.
26. Proulx, "Getting Movied," 130.
27. On the heteronormative, homophobic construction of public space, see Sumartojo, "Contesting Place"; Heibel, "Casa Nova"; Brown, *Closet Space*; Little, *Rural Geography*; Lindhorst, "Practical Implications"; Van Hoven, *Spaces*; Cloke, *Country Visions*; and Kramer, "Batchelor Farmers."
28. Proulx, "Brokeback Mountain," 48.
29. Proulx, "Brokeback Mountain," 48.
30. Proulx, "Brokeback Mountain," 48.
31. Proulx, "Brokeback Mountain," 49.
32. Proulx, "Brokeback Mountain," 49.
33. Proulx, "Brokeback Mountain," 49.
34. On the struggles within families that often surround the suspected homosexuality of a child, particularly boys, see, from various fields, Richard Isay, *Being Homosexual: Gay Men and Their Development* (New York: Farrar, Strauss, and Giroux, 2001); Kevin Jennings and Pat Shapiro, *Always My Child: A Parent's Guide to Understanding Your Gay, Lesbian, Bisexual, Transgender, or Questioning Son or Daughter* (New York: Simon and Schuster, 2003); Robert Bernstein, Betty DeGeneres, Robert MacNeil, *Straight Parents/Gay Children: Keeping Families Together* (New York: Thunder's Mouth, 2003); R. W. Connell, *The Men and the Boys* (Berkeley: University of California Press, 2000); Paul Monette, *Becoming a Man: Half a Life Story* (New York: Harper, 1992); and Alan Downs, *The Velvet Rage: Overcoming the Pain of Growing Up Gay in a Straight Man's World* (Cambridge: Da Capo, 2006).
35. Proulx, "Brokeback Mountain," 39.
36. Proulx, "Brokeback Mountain," 50.
37. Proulx, "Brokeback Mountain," 50.
38. See Miller, *Out of the Past*, for a sound introductory overview of hostile constructions of homosexuality in the field of psychology; Adam, *Rise*, also is useful.
39. For an introductory discussion of Hooker's achievements and their impact in changing understandings of homosexuality among psychologists and psychiatrists, see Miller, *Out of the Past*.
40. On the change in the position on homosexuality in the professions of psychology and psychiatry, see Miller, *Out of the Past*; Adam, *Rise*; and Bayer, *American Psychiatry*. The main organization of the small minority of psychiatrists and psychologists who still argue that sexual orientation can and should be "changed" is the National Association for Research and Therapy for Homosexuality (NARTH), which is associated with homophobic religious groups, including Focus on the Family. Their views are rejected by the American Psychological Association, the American Psychiatric Association, and the American Medical Association, among many others. One of the most visible figures in NARTH is Dr. John Nicolosi, author of several books on "changing" homosexual orientation, including, with his wife, *A Parent's Guide to Preventing Homosexuality* (2002). (Sexual minority people who've survived growing up with homophobic parents can imagine how much damage such a book can do, in legitimizing and facilitating parental efforts to "change"—or, more accurately,

suppress—a sexually different child's sexual orientation). Another prominent member of NARTH, Dr. Gerald Schoenewolf, brought considerable attention to the organization in 2005, publishing an essay on its website in which he referred to Africa as a "jungle" and argued that African people who had been abducted into slavery in America were "better off." On the ex-gay movement and the psychologists involved in it, see Wayne Besen, *Anything but Straight: Unmasking the Scandals and Lies behind the Ex-gay Myth* (Binghamton: Harrington Park, 2003), and Chris Bull, *Perfect Enemies: The Battle between the Religious Right and the Gay Movement* (Lanham: Madison, 2001). On Dr. Schoenewolf's views, see Southern Poverty Law Center: "Essay by Promoter of 'Ex-gay' Movement Sparks Racism Charges," Brentin Mock, Oct. 6, 2006 (http://www.splcenter.org/intel/news/item.jsp?aid=84, July 29, 2007).

    41. See Isay, *Being Homosexual*; Jennings, Shapiro, *Always My Child*; Bernstein et. al., *Straight Parents*; Monette, *Becoming a Man*; and Downs, *Velvet Rage*.

    42. See Isay, *Being Homosexual*; Jennings, Shapiro, *Always My Child*; Bernstein et. al., *Straight Parents*; Monette, *Becoming a Man*; and Downs, *Velvet Rage*.

    43. Suzanne Pharr, *Homophobia: A Weapon of Sexism* (Berkeley: Chardon, 1997) provides an insightful discussion of the many ways in which sexism and homophobia can be understood to be interconnected.

    44. Proulx, "Brokeback Mountain," 48.

    45. See Elisabeth Young-Bruehl, *The Anatomy of Prejudices* (Cambridge: Harvard University, 1996.)

    46. For introductory discussion of McCarthyism and homophobia, see Miller, *Out of the Past*, and Adam, *Rise*; Dobson, Robertson, and the Republican Party are discussed in Bull, *Perfect Enemies*; I've discussed Gibson, O'Reilly, and Scarborough in the Prologue.

    47. See Young-Bruehl, *Anatomy*.

    48. See Young-Bruehl, *Anatomy*; also see Pharr, *Weapon*.

    49. Proulx, "Brokeback Mountain," 28.

    50. *Casper Star-Tribune*, "Release of *Brokeback Mountain* Creates a Buzz," Deirdre Stoelzle Graves, Oct. 31, 2005 (http://www.casperstartribune.net/articles/2005/10.31/news/wyoming/06c2ae836ae836d988c5d872570aa00211854.txt, July, 27, 2007). In the article, Sandy Dixon, the woman who believed there weren't any gay cowboys, was refuted by Chuck Browning, a gay man from Wyoming who is a champion rodeo rider in the International Gay Rodeo Association. The article was referred to in the press around the nation. Interestingly, it should be noted that the mayor of Casper at the time, Guy Padgett, is an out gay man.

    51. At Gonzaga University, a Jesuit institution in Spokane, Washington, basketball fans harassed members of a visiting team by chanting "Brokeback! Mountain!" at them; see *The Advocate*: "Basketball Fans Asked to Stop Chanting *Brokeback Mountain* Insult," Feb. 14, 2006 (http://www.advocate.com/news_detail_ektid25416asp, July 29, 2007). At the University of Vermont, the Phi Gamma Delta ("Fiji") fraternity was suspended during the investigation of an alleged incident of hazing, reportedly involving dressing pledges in cowboy clothes and subjecting them to homophobic humiliation; see *The Chronicle of Higher Education*: "Fraternity Suspended for Alleged Homophobic Hazing," April 6, 2006 (http://www.chronicle.com/news/article/236/

fraternity–suspended–for–alleged–homophobic–hazing, July 27, 2007). Charges were brought and later dismissed, and the Vermont State Attorney General's Office said that though it believed the incident had occurred, there wasn't enough evidence to appeal the dismissal; see "Attorney General's Office Drops UVM Hazing Case," May 12, 2007 (http://www.wcax.com/global/story.asp?s=6507922, July 29, 2007). The description of Jack as a "sexual predator," the reference to the film as "Bareback Mounting," the idea that it constitutes "The Rape of the Marlboro Man," and the ridicule by TV "comedians" and by the singer Alan Jackson all are discussed in the Prologue.

52. The fact that Larry H. Miller, a wealthy Mormon who owns the Utah Jazz basketball team, cancelled showings of the film at his Salt Lake City theater when he realized what it was about was widely reported; see "Miller Speaks Up On *Brokeback*," Deborah Bulkeley, *The Deseret News*, Jan. 17, 2006 (http://www.deseretnews.com/dn/view/1,1249,635176966,00.html, July 29, 2007). In Austin, Texas, St. Andrews Episcopal School refused a three million dollar donation when the donor, one Cary McNair, made it contingent on the removal of *Brokeback Mountain* from a twelfth grade recommended reading list. McNair denounced the story as "pornographic material concerning deviant behavior"; see "Donor Pledge Returned to Sender; How Much Is Intellectual Freedom Worth? For One Texas School, It's Priceless," Shannon Maughan, *Publisher's Weekly*, Dec. 5, 2005 (http://www.publishersweekly.com/article/CA6288794.html, July 29, 2007). Among the nations seeking to ban the film were the Bahamas, Malaysia, and the United Arab Emirates; in general it was unavailable in Muslim nations. It was excluded from theaters in the People's Republic of China; interestingly, it was a big hit in Taiwan, the birthplace of Ang Lee.

53. *The Holy Bible*, King James Version: Leviticus, Chapter 18, Verse 22.

54. On the much-debated and apparently much-misinterpreted story of Sodom and Gomorrah in Genesis, Chapter 19, see David Helminiak, *What the Bible Really Says about Homosexuality* (Tajique: Alamo Square, 2000), and John J. McNeill, *The Church and the Homosexual* (Boston: Beacon, 1993).

55. On the difficulties of adolescence for sexual minorities, see Jennings, Shapiro, *Always My Child*; Bernstein, *et al., Straight Parents*; Isay, *Being Homosexual*; Monette, *Becoming a Man*; Downs, *Velvet Rage*; and Plummer, *One of the Boys*.

56. The problems involved in passing for straight are a central issue in much the work of many sexual minority writers, particularly of fiction, poetry, and autobiography. Texts that seem to me to be particularly relevant to *Brokeback Mountain* because of the periods they deal with and the kinds of men they depict are James Baldwin's brilliant novel, *Giovanni's Room* (New York: Delta, 2000/1956); Martin Duberman's autobiography *Cures: A Gay Man's Odyssey* (New York: Dutton, 1991); and Monette's *Becoming a Man*. On passing for straight and a comparison with racial, ethnic, and religious passing, see Brooke Kroeger, *Passing: When People Can't Be Who They Are* (New York: Perseus/Public Affairs, 2004). On representations of passing in literature, see Elaine K. Ginsberg, ed., *Passing and the Fictions of Identity* (Durham: Duke University, 1996), particularly the essay by Valerie Rohy, "Displaying Desire: Passing, Nostalgia, and *Giovanni's Room*." On the many problems involved in cover marriages, see Fritz Klein and Thomas Schwartz, *Bisexual and Gay Husbands: Their Stories, Their Words* (Binghamton: Harrington Park, 2002); Amity Pierce Buxton, *The*

Other Side of the Closet: The Coming-Out Crisis for Straight Spouses and Families
(New York: Wiley, 1994); and Jean S. Gochros, *When Husbands Come Out of the*
Closet (Binghamton: Haworth, 1989).

There are parallels and differences between passing by sexual minority people and
other sorts of passing, by light-skinned people of color or by Jewish people and members of other ethnic or religious minority groups. The long and important history of
women who have passed as men should be considered as well. Most sexual minority
people are less visible to the majority than most people of color are, and so it's often
easier for them to pass, though that doesn't necessarily mean their lives are easy,
given all the problems that can result from trying to pass for straight. Of course, there
are many people of color who are different from the majority in terms of sexuality and
gender, some of whom understandably may try to pass for straight in order to avoid
the oppression of at least one form of prejudice. For sexual minority white people,
passing for straight allows them to maintain the status and privilege of being identified with the dominant racial and sexual groups in society. In relation to *Brokeback*
Mountain, though neither version explicitly identifies Ennis del Mar as being partly
Hispanic, his last name suggests this, and it's plausible that for him his anxiety about
retaining his status as a straight man would be compounded by anxiety about his
racial/cultural identity, given anti-Hispanic prejudice.

57. Proulx, "Brokeback Mountain," 16.
58. Proulx, "Brokeback Mountain," 17.
59. Proulx, "Brokeback Mountain," 51.
60. Proulx, "Brokeback Mountain," 28.
61. Proulx, "Brokeback Mountain," 17.
62. Proulx, "Brokeback Mountain," 17.
63. Proulx, "Brokeback Mountain," 17.
64. Proulx, "Brokeback Mountain," 17.
65. Proulx, "Brokeback Mountain," 18.
66. Proulx, "Brokeback Mountain," 18.
67. "Hours Continuing Long," ll. 4–11, Whitman, *Leaves of Grass*, 1860 edition.
68. The importance of Whitman in inspiring shared consciousness, community,
and action among man-loving men has been widely recognized and discussed. For an
introduction, see Summers, *Literary Heritage*, entry on Whitman by Robert K. Martin; also the Gay, Lesbian, Bisexual, Transgender, Queer Encyclopedia: "Literature:
Walt Whitman", by Martin (http://www.glbtq.com/literature/whitman_w.html July
29, 2007); also see Martin, ed., *The Continuing Presence of Walt Whitman: The Life*
After the Life (Iowa City: University of Iowa, 1992.)
69. Proulx, "Brokeback Mountain," 18.
70. Proulx, "Brokeback Mountain," 26.
71. McMurtry and Ossana, "Screenplay," 28.

Chapter Five

Separate and Difficult Lives: Love

After leaving Jack at the end of their summer together Ennis continues with the plans he and Alma had made earlier and they get married late in 1963. Though the story is more explicit than the film, both make it evident that he still feels strong homosexual attraction, focused on his memories of Jack, but that like many other men with similar feelings he goes ahead and establishes what appears to be a "normal" heterosexual life, fulfilling the expectations of his family, friends, and community. He keeps his desire for male love and his memory of what he shared with Jack entirely secret, as part of his commitment to passing as a straight man. Outwardly he epitomizes the masculine ideal of much of American society: he's physically strong and able and economically independent, working at demanding outdoor jobs, laying asphalt, tending stock and doing ranch work, taking an extra job at a ranch on weekends so that he can keep his horses there, meeting his obligations to his family, and stoically enduring the challenges his life presents. Inside, however, are thoughts and feelings that he speaks to no one, which separate him from Alma and from everyone else. From the start of his marriage the knowledge that Ennis has of his own sexuality and the questions about himself that he struggles with alone and in silence necessarily cause a degree of distance from Alma that gradually grows, eventually leading to the failure of their marriage. There's no way she can know about what he feels, and, as with Ennis, the culture hasn't given her any information that would help her to understand. The way he wants to have sex with her is an expression of what he desires, but it's not possible for her to know its significance at this point. The only person he knows who could understand his needs is Jack, who Ennis has closed out of his life. Even if Ennis never were to see Jack again, the experience the two men have had together has confirmed for Ennis a sense of difference that always must separate him from his wife and family and community, and must put his outward life at odds with his own strongest feelings. For a man in Ennis's situation, who desires physical and emotional intimacy with a man but denies his desires, who marries a woman and starts a family, passing as heterosexual, there necessarily must be a sense of "twoness,"[1] of trying to be one sort of man to others, and even to himself, but still of feeling within himself that he's another sort of man. Being in this situation requires constantly holding back the deepest part of yourself from the people who love you, and who you've committed yourself to love. It's bad for everyone.

Jack doesn't deny his desire for love with a man in the way that Ennis does, but he doesn't know anyone else like himself other than Ennis, and can't forget the intensity of their connection. As mentioned before, late the next spring he returns to Signal, hoping that Ennis may have come by to ask Aguirre for a job on Brokeback Mountain again, attempting to reconnect with Jack; Aguirre dismisses Jack and then insults him when Jack asks if Ennis has been around. In the film, once Jack goes to Texas to try to make a living in rodeo, he's depicted trying and failing to start up a friendship with a man who attracts him, the rodeo clown, Jimbo. Although Jack can accept what he wants more than Ennis can, he also seems to share Ennis's concern to maintain his identity and status as a straight man, and this necessarily limits the possibility of Jack finding another man like himself. In the mid 1960s in cities in the West, as in most American cities, there were bars with a reputation for being places where sexually different men went, and there also were certain public places where men clandestinely cruised each other, but there's no indication in either version of the narrative that at this point in his life Jack's willing to try to meet men in these ways. Like Ennis, Jack isn't a city boy, and so, as he's presented in the film, he tries to meet men in the kinds of places he's familiar with, cowboy bars in rural towns, which isn't likely to work out, and easily can lead to trouble. At best it's only likely to result in meeting another man like Ennis, who may well be unable to commit himself to an ongoing relationship, and at worst, as the episode with Jimbo suggests, it can result in a rejection that could turn violent. The story, unlike the film, does indicate that on his travels on the rodeo circuit Jack may have been able to find someone to have a brief sexual relationship with, though there's no suggestion that it was anything more than that, and no indication of where or how it happened. When they talk at the motel, Ennis asks Jack if he does it with other guys, which Jack emphatically denies, but Proulx contradicts him, commenting that Jack "had been riding more than bulls, not rolling his own,"[2] although she tells us nothing more. The film does depict Jack going to a male prostitute in Mexico, but this is much later, after Ennis's divorce.

Whatever encounters Jack's had with other men between 1963 and 1967, the limited opportunities available to a man like him necessarily prevent him from finding anyone who captures his feelings the way Ennis did. Both the story and the film indicate that Jack falls into his relationship with Lureen for a mixture of reasons related to his poverty and to his situation as a single man who's strongly attracted to other men, but whose concern to pass as straight limits his contacts with men who desire men. When he tries to make it as a bull rider, Jack is very lonely and also very poor, only making a few thousand dollars a year, as he tells Ennis at the motel. The story doesn't describe how he becomes involved with Lureen, but the screenwriters imagine a very plausible account of what happens. They present Lureen Newsome as a kind of small-town Texas Princess who can get whatever she wants from her Daddy; when Jack returns her hat to her during the barrel race at the Childress County Fair Rodeo, she takes one look and knows he's something else she wants to have. Later in the evening at the cowboy bar, when they see each other again across the room and she looks at Jack in a way that shows she's interested, the bartender tells Jack about the big farm-machinery business Lureen's father owns, and that information, and Lureen's boldness in acting on her attraction, soon have them dancing together to Mary McBride's "No One's Gonna Love You Like Me," a song whose lyrics emphasize the loneliness and sadness Jack's feeling when he and Lureen meet. Lureen takes the lead, and next they're in the backseat of Daddy's red Thunderbird, Lureen getting on top of Jack and taking off her clothes, and they're married shortly afterward. On the DVD, this episode is given the appropriate title, "Roped In."[3] Like many men who want to be with other men but who aren't able to accept it and to go to places where men meet men, Jack's involvement with the straight people around him causes him to conform to society's expectations. He can find few men who are interested in him in the way that Ennis was, but there certainly are women, like Lureen, who are, and Jack's poor and lonely, and so he's pleased when a pretty, rich, determined girl like Lureen wants him. While we're never told, it also may be that Jack, like many other men who realize they desire men, gets involved with a woman hoping that he'll turn out to have a strong enough attraction to her to make a heterosexual life work for him. But as with Ennis, because Jack's sexual and emotional desires take him toward men rather than toward women, the marriage is potentially weak from the start, and Daddy, L. D. Newsome, only makes it worse. It's easy to imagine that Jack, once he's married to Lureen, must begin to compare living with her with the life he wanted to have with Ennis, and that he becomes more nostalgic for his friend. Also, marrying Lureen means replacing his painful relationship with his own father with the grating daily struggle to put up with a father-in-law who thinks he's yet another "stud duck." Understandably, after a couple of years of this, Jack takes the risk, despite the punch Ennis dealt him, to drop him a line and see if he wants to meet the next time Jack's on his way to make one of his dutiful visits to his parents in Lightning Flat.

The marriages of Ennis and Alma and of Jack and Lureen are sure to encounter trouble. Both men do feel physical attraction to their wives and have sex with them and father children, and both also feel affection for their wives, and real delight in their children. But the film and particularly the text indicate that both men find much more pleasure and satisfaction in sex with a man than with a woman, and that each man continues to remember and miss the other. They can be described as bisexual, but the use of this term doesn't represent their situation very well, since what each feels for the other is substantially stronger than what he feels for his wife. American culture's deep distrust of sexuality has prevented careful study and description of varieties of sexuality, but it's obvious to most people who try to think clearly about it that a binary model that categorizes most people as "heterosexual" and a small minority as "homosexual" is a simplistic reduction of the complexity of the sexual feeling and experience of many people. At least the use of the term bisexual begins to recognize that there may be people whose feelings can't be described adequately by either binary term, but this term has limitations too, seeming to suggest that a bisexual person is equally attracted to people of each sex, which of course often isn't the case. In the ongoing discussion of sexuality in American culture, it's increasingly being recognized that it's more accurate to describe the varieties of sexuality as a spectrum ranging from attraction only to people of the opposite sex, through a variety of gradations and combinations of attraction to people of both sexes, to attraction only to people of the same sex, much as Kinsey and his associates suggested nearly sixty years ago.[4] Some people consistently experience their sexuality as taking a particular place on this spectrum, while others may experience it as changing and shifting from one point to another over time. In such a model, Jack and Ennis would be nearer the end of the spectrum representing homosexuality; the strongest sexual desire each experiences is to have sex with a man, though each is able to have a sexual relationship with a woman. Both clearly have stronger emotional connections to each other than to their wives. Indeed, it's important to note that for both men, limitations and pressures resulting from homophobia are important factors in causing them not to remain together and to marry their wives. While neither ever labels himself, from their talks together about what they feel and do with each other in comparison with Ennis's relationship with Alma and Jack's with Lureen, it's clear that their sexual orientation is strongest toward men, though they can function as "heterosexuals" as part of the effort to pass for straight.

To call what Ennis and Jack do in marrying their wives a "decision" or a "choice" doesn't make much sense, given the pressures on each of them. In a world unlike our own, in which different types of sexual attraction along the spectrum weren't subjected to judgment and often to condemnation, and instead in which all were equally accepted and supported by society, Ennis and Jack would have the freedom to explore and understand their particular sexualities, and might well be together. But in a society filled with hatred and violence against same-sex love, and constant pressure to conform to the "norm" of heterosexuality, this is impossible, and both go ahead and marry women. For some who read or watch *Brokeback Mountain* this probably seems a fate that nowadays most men who love men can avoid, given the large urban gay communities, the activity of support organizations for sexual minorities, the many sources of information in the gay press, and the extensive communications network now provided by the Internet, which, even for those in isolated communities, can help men to make social and sexual connections with other men. To assume this, however, overlooks the continuing power of homophobia, which causes many men who desire men, especially in contexts whose culture and religion are strongly hostile to sexual minorities, to avoid accepting their desire. Many continue to be unable to identify as men who love men, and continue to try to pass for straight, often marrying women and starting families. The extent and persistence of the so-called "ex-gay" movement is evidence of the degree to which homophobia, especially in the ways it's fomented by some religious groups, still causes many men to try to reject same-sex attraction and to struggle to live as if they were straight. As those who've investigated the "ex-gay" movement report, it's made many conflicting and unreliable claims about its supposed "success" rate in "helping" men and women to "come out of homosexuality," and in fact the movement's main effect seems to be merely to repress same-sex desire and to reinforce "normative" gender behavior among those who get caught up in it. Those leading the movement, whether they can acknowledge it or not, simply exploit and profit from the homophobia that continues to be rampant in the United States. Also, ironically, "ex-gay" organizations appear to provide a context in which some people struggling with strongly internalized homophobic religious ideas may meet others of the same sex and establish intimate relationships. Certainly many people would say that sexual minority people have the right to define themselves as they want to, and to try to "become" straight if they really believe that that's possible or preferable, but it's ludicrous to present such actions as if they were independent, personal "decisions" or "choices," given the homophobic hostility and pressure toward social conformity that cause them to try to "become" straight.[5]

Trying to pass as a member of the sexual majority entails continual fear and secrecy, and demands continually withholding and often lying about what one actually feels and thinks. For a man who passes as straight and yet who has clandestine relationships with other men, it's necessary to fabricate an elaborate system of lies to hide and protect his secrets. While virtually all people find they have to lie from time to time, few people are estranged enough from others that they actually enjoy doing so; lying causes a profound sense of distance from others, with which most people can't be comfortable. Also, quite simply, it's a lot of work; to lie all the time about where you're going and what you're doing in order to hide a relationship means always having to keep track of the lies you've told, having to make sure they're consistent, and having to carefully sustain all the details of the false version of your life that you're trying to maintain. It also means trying to make sure that those with whom you're secretly involved are as committed to, and careful about, lying as you are, which usually is impossible. Most people who try to pass find themselves anxious and disgusted with having to lie constantly, and the stress from this can lead to depression and to a range of self-destructive efforts to cope, including becoming dependent on alcohol or drugs. The effort to pass also can lead to intense frustration, especially with the limitations of the heterosexual relationships in which a person who passes can become involved. Relations with parents, siblings, friends—and particularly spouses, for those sexual minority people who marry people of the opposite sex—often become oppressive because of the constant struggle to be what one isn't in order to satisfy their expectations. Continual frustration can lead to explosions of rage. Most straight people can't imagine the isolation and frustration experienced by sexually different people who try to pass, as they struggle with desire and shame and guilt, with few or perhaps any others like them to talk to, surrounded by straight people with their assumptions that everyone else who matters is straight, and their negative ideas about sexual minorities, expressed in the casual homophobic comments so common among straight people. For some, such a life can become so bad that the only way out is suicide. And today, of course, with the widespread problem of HIV, those who can't accept their sexuality, and who deny it to the people with whom they're involved, are at greater risk for being exposed and exposing others. As those who've endured it have attested, a life trying to pass often isn't much of a life at all.[6]

When a man who's struggled to pass finally does come out, or is forced out by pressure from others or by some unforeseen incident, the straight people he's surrounded himself with, who've assumed that he too is straight, may be indignant to learn that he's "lied" to them and "betrayed" them. Of course, in the case of a man who's married and established a family, for his wife and children to discover that he's attracted to men can be very difficult for them and can irreparably damage their relationships with him, leaving them bitter and angry, destroying the family that he's tried to build. The disappointment of family members is entirely understandable, but it often makes it impossible for them to recognize how the circumstances of living in a homophobic society can force a man into trying to pass, and make him betray and lie to himself first of all. Trying to pass for straight usually isn't a calculated decision, and constructing it in terms of "betrayal" and "lying" misses the fact that for most men who do it, it's an effort to avoid accepting an aspect of their own identities that they've been taught to fear and be ashamed of. Such men usually fall into the pattern of passing in adolescence, and do so as an understandable reaction to homophobia, as an effort to survive in a hostile society. Men who pass often hurt the others in their lives, but blaming them alone misses the actual cause of what's happened, that they've tried to pass because of their fear of the hatred of sexual difference that extends throughout American society, often including the families they've grown up in. The problems caused by passing for straight aren't due to homosexuality but to homophobia.

Particularly since the development of the movement for sexual minority rights over the past forty years, some members of sexual minorities who've become involved in heterosexual marriages have found that when their spouses become aware of the source of difficulty in the relationship, they're met with understanding and support. There are wives and husbands who, when they learn that the person they're married to identifies as sexually different, have enough awareness of the situation of sexual minorities in a homophobic society that they're able to assist them and to remain on close terms. Even if the marriage ends in divorce, which often is the only sound solution, it's possible for some people to respect the sexual orientation of their former spouses and to continue to be friends and to share responsibilities to children. People who are able to do this understand that the person they married didn't want to mislead or hurt them, but was unaware of, or unable to accept, a sexuality that society condemns and tells them should be a source of shame. Such spouses deserve praise and support for trying to understand the difficult situations that those they've married often have been forced into by homophobia.[7]

But in the turmoil of a failing marriage, even today, with more information available about the destructive effects of homophobia, this degree of understanding and empathy can be difficult to achieve. And in American society today, many voices, especially those of the homophobic leaders of religious organizations such as the Catholic Church, the Southern Baptist Convention, the Church of Jesus Christ of Latter-Day Saints, and a host of Pentecostal and fundamentalist organizations, including some of the most profitable and politically influential televangelist "ministries," and the many religious and political groups mentioned earlier that have attacked *Brokeback Mountain,* all continue their efforts to put responsibility on homosexuality, not on homophobia. These groups assume that heterosexuality alone is "natural" and "normal" and that everyone can and should conform to it, dismissing the testimony of sexual minorities that what they experience is natural and normal *for*

them, and denouncing physical and emotional desire between people of the
same sex as "sin," "intrinsic evil," or even "demonic possession."⁸ They assume that all men can and ought to feel sexual attraction to women, and that
when a man's sexual attraction to other men is a factor in the failure of his
marriage, the responsibility is entirely his own, for "giving in" to "sinful" impulses that supposedly have been divinely forbidden. It's impossible for them
to recognize that same-sex love is natural for some people, that what's unnatural is teaching people to hate and repress it, and that fear, shame, lies, and
the impossible effort to be what one isn't are no basis for a marriage. The issue is not, as religious homophobes see it, that some people "give in" to the
"sin" of homosexuality, that a man like Ennis "betrays" his wife and family
with a man like Jack, but instead that men like Ennis and Jack shouldn't be
pressured into marrying women in the first place, and indeed ought to be free
to love and marry each other.

The story and the film vividly render the growing problems for each man
and for those in his life caused by his attempts to maintain his relationships
with women. From the beginning of both marriages there are limitations and
tensions between Ennis and Alma and between Jack and Lureen that are inherent in the relationships, resulting from the fact that neither man's sexuality fits him for a heterosexual marriage, and that become evident before the
two men resume their relationship. These fundamental problems between the
men and their wives are presented in the text, and most aspects of them are
developed convincingly in the film, though some are given little emphasis
and others considerably more, which invites comparison and contrast of the
two versions of the narrative. Despite the omission of certain elements in the
film, in general the screenwriters perceptively expand on what Proulx has
said, and provide convincing accounts of the costs for everyone of the effort
to pass. The story describes the troubles between Ennis and Alma in detail,
and the film presents them accurately and movingly, and also adds powerful
representations of Jack's marriage with Lureen and his struggles with her father, the experience of the children in both families, particularly Alma Jr., and
the failed relationship between Ennis and Cassie, the waitress in Riverton.

ENNIS AND ALMA

To understand the depth of the problems between Ennis and Alma, it's useful
to look closely at what Ennis says to Jack about himself when they get together again in 1967, four years after their summer together. One of the most
substantial differences between the two versions of *Brokeback Mountain* involves this reunion episode; though some of the same issues are raised in both

versions, they're presented differently, and some are omitted entirely in the film. In the story, the scene at the motel is one of the most extended that Proulx gives of Jack and Ennis together, and provides much more explanation of Ennis's understanding of his own sexuality and of the problems posed by his marriage than is presented in the film. As the two men lie in bed after passionately making love, they discuss what's happened to them both over the previous four years. First each tells the other how satisfying it is to be with him again: as mentioned before, after praising Ennis's ability in intercourse, and crediting it to "'all that time a yours ahorseback,'"[9] Jack explains how his desire to make love with Ennis made him "'redline'"[10] it to meet up with him. Ennis's response shows that he's been thinking about Jack all the time, and that he's regretted the way he ended their friendship: "'I didn't know where in the *hell* you was. Four years. I about give up on you. I figured you was sore about that punch.'"[11] As Jack recounts his struggles as a rodeo rider and lists the serious injuries that have made him decide he's going to quit, Ennis playfully responds, expressing his appreciation of Jack's body, "'Sure as hell seem in one piece to me.'"[12] He then tells Jack that since separating from him and marrying Alma, he's been thinking and thinking about his sexuality, trying to understand how to explain it to himself: "'You know, I was sittin up here all that time trying to figure out if I was—? I know I ain't. I mean here we both got wives and kids, right? I like doin it with women, yeah, but Jesus H., ain't nothin like this. I never had no thoughts a doin it with another guy except I sure wrang it out a hunderd times thinkin about you.'"[13] Like a lot of men who grow up in isolation and ignorance because of homophobia, Ennis has had almost no information to work with in explaining his sexuality to himself, and assumes that sexuality must fit one of two supposedly opposite categories: you're either a normal man or you're a "queer." There's no acknowledgement of the spectrum of sexuality, that some men are attracted to both women and men, that for some the attractions are relatively equal, that for others they're stronger to one sex than to the other. Given how deeply Ennis has internalized the homophobia that's been directed at him, it's no surprise that the first thing he thinks about is that, given the binary model he has of sexuality, he can't be a "queer," and neither can Jack, since they both have wives and kids. Ennis also tries to support this reassuring assumption with the point that he never thought about doing it with another man. This reinforces a sense of the degree of internalized homophobia and sexual repression in Ennis's character: though he finds the greatest degree of satisfaction in what he and Jack do, his sexual desires are focused only on Jack, the one man with whom he's ever had sex, and aren't generalized to include other men. To confirm his sense that this must mean that he "ain't," Ennis questions Jack about whether he's had sex with other men; apparently Jack's eagerness to please

Ennis causes him to assure him he hasn't, although as mentioned before, Proulx contradicts Jack's assertion with her comment that he "had been riding more than bulls, not rolling his own."[14] Significantly, in their conversation as Proulx depicts it, Ennis's homophobia is so strong that he can't even bring himself to *say* the word "queer."

In the story, much of what Ennis tells Jack as they lie in bed together is at odds with his belief that he can't be a "queer," whether he acknowledges the significance of what he says or not: the pleasure he finds in having anal intercourse with a man and the fact that throughout his marriage with Alma Ennis has been masturbating as he thinks about Jack show how much stronger his attraction is to him than to women. Ennis also confirms the depth and intensity of his emotional attraction to Jack when he tells his friend about how rejecting Jack made him physically sick, and that it took almost a year of thinking about himself to realize why he needed Jack so much. Ennis tells Jack with regret that "'I shouldn't a let you out a my sights,'"[15] but that by the time he was able to understand what he felt, it was "'too late then by a long, long while.'"[16] Although Ennis's fear of being labeled queer and becoming the target of homophobic violence, along with the love and responsibility he feels for his daughters, makes him reject Jack's plan for ranching together, it's clear that what Ennis feels for Jack is substantially stronger than what he feels for Alma, and that if he could have felt less fear and shame and confusion, he would have stayed involved with Jack, and indeed might have realized that he shouldn't commit himself to getting married and starting a family.

The way that Ennis has preferred to have sex with Alma since marrying her confirms what he says about his sexuality to Jack in the scene at the motel, although Ennis keeps this fact about his sexuality to himself. In a scene describing Alma and Ennis at home shortly after the birth of their second daughter in 1966, Proulx presents Ennis slipping his hand up the sleeve of Alma's blouse, lowering her down on the bed while he caresses her ribs, breast, belly, and knee, then moving his fingers up into her genitals, stimulating and satisfying her, and then rolling her over and doing "quickly what she hated."[17] Although Ennis does have vaginal intercourse with Alma and they have two children, he also apparently often wants her to allow him to have anal intercourse with her, and seeks to make it acceptable to her by trying manually to give her the sort of stimulation she likes, to compensate for doing "what she hated."[18] Once again, as they do in the scenes in which Jack and Ennis have intercourse, the filmmakers have the integrity and courage to go ahead and show what's described in the text. In both versions of the narrative, it's evident that what Ennis prefers with Alma is to have the kind of sex that he valued so much with Jack. Even though they omit his comments to Jack at the motel about how he "'wrang it out a hunderd times'"[19] thinking about Jack, it's still clear in the film that Ennis isn't satisfied by the kind of sex that Alma wants, and is nostalgic for what he did with Jack. In the story, his comments about masturbating while thinking about Jack even raise the suggestion that when he has anal intercourse with Alma, it's Jack who is in his mind.

In a series of scenes that go beyond the story, the film suggests more about Ennis's motivations in going ahead with his plan to marry Alma. The scene of Ennis and Alma's wedding follows immediately after the scene in Signal the previous August, when Ennis is overcome by gut cramps and pounds his fist against the wall in the alley just after leaving Jack. Before the scene in the alley ends, as Ennis is kneeling and sobbing against the wall, we already hear the voice of the minister at the wedding intoning the Lord's Prayer: ". . . forgive us our trespasses as we forgive those who trespass against us," suggesting the guilt and shame that Ennis has been taught to feel and that play a role in his rejection of Jack and his determination to get married like a "normal" man. As the scene shifts to the wedding, the first image is that of Ennis, his face strained as he repeats "Lead us not into temptation, but deliver us from evil . . .," reinforcing a sense of the role of guilt in what he is doing. The wedding scene also is significant because it indicates the sense of obligation Ennis feels to conform to the expectations of his society, to make his brother and sister and their families proud of him, and especially to try to do right by Alma by fulfilling the commitment he made in getting engaged to her. In a subtle moment of dialogue at the close of the wedding ceremony, the screenwriters even suggest that the cheery minister may sense some hesitation on Ennis's part. Ennis looks dour and nervous, standing next to Alma, who's shyly beaming, and the minister, after telling Ennis that he may kiss the bride, jokes that if Ennis doesn't, *he* will. The general response is characteristic of the continual enforcement of heterosexuality in society: everybody laughs, as if to ask, what man *wouldn't* want to kiss a sweet-looking bride like Alma?

The film depicts the happiness that Alma and Ennis are able to enjoy, showing them during the first winter of their marriage laughing with each other as they toboggan in the snow, and at a drive-in movie theater later on, in the spring, where as they sit together in his truck she moves his hand to her stomach to show him that she's pregnant, but it also suggests that, as with many young couples, economic struggles and the demands of child raising lead to stress and tension. In a scene set in 1966, shortly after the birth of their second child—named Jenny in the film, Francine in the story—Ennis comes home from work to find that Alma has her hands full trying to do a wash at the sink and cook and care for the two little babies all at the same time. When he goes into the bedroom to check on the younger girl, who's in her crib, coughing because of her asthma, Alma calls to him to ask him to wipe the older girl's nose, and he yells back that if he had three hands he could.

In the next episode, which is the one that concludes by depicting Ennis and Alma having anal intercourse, the film also suggests a degree of tension between them in the conversation they have about where they live and how much they have to live on. Alma sits down behind Ennis on the bed and embraces him, and, after talking briefly about how the little girls are, asks if they can move to town, where there'd be other children for the girls to play with and they'd be nearer a doctor. He responds by expressing the pressure he feels to earn enough to support all four of them, saying rents are too high in town; she counters by proposing they move to a cheap apartment over the laundromat in Riverton that she could fix up, which he resists, saying she could fix up the place they're in if she wanted to. Throughout the conversation, as they counter each other's concerns about where to live, Alma and Ennis caress and kiss each other. For any couple, regardless of sex, disagreements that result from the demands of daily life often can be tempered and perhaps overcome by the mutual attraction both people feel. Alma responds excitedly to Ennis's caresses, but then as he leans over on top of her, he rolls her over on her stomach and positions himself behind her, as she weakly protests. Because of Ennis's sexuality, and particularly his nostalgia for Jack, sex between Ennis and Alma can't resolve their disagreements, and only will increase the tension developing between them. Whereas the film's lyrical score adds to the feeling of intimacy in the scenes between Jack and Ennis, music only is used in the first two scenes between him and Alma, when they play in the snow and go to the drive-in, and not after. In the bedroom scene just described, the only sound other than their conversation is the whistling of the Wyoming wind.

As he's depicted in both the story and the movie, Ennis is a man whose sexuality is more homosexual than heterosexual, but who refuses to label himself as "queer" or to participate in the queer sexual and social world as it existed for other men at the time. Ennis doesn't go to any of the public places, such as highway rest stops, parks, restrooms, or theaters that queer men in rural areas and small cities had defined as places for clandestine encounters. For some rural men who desired men, it was possible to find casual sex, and sometimes more serious and sustained relationships with other men, through such places and contacts, but Ennis doesn't act on his sexual feelings in this way, remaining in his marriage with Alma and only expressing his desire for men in his fantasies about Jack. When Jack returns, Ennis resumes his sexual relationship with him, but never becomes more actively involved in the queer world, in contrast to Jack. Ennis's reasons aren't stated directly in either version, but his concern to retain his status as a straight man and to avoid the dangers of being visible as sexually different apparently prevent him from identifying as queer, much less as gay.

The frustrations generated by Ennis's situation as a young married man with two children, and with an unspoken and unfulfilled yearning for sexual and emotional bonds with another man, explode in an extraordinary scene in the film depicting an episode imagined by the screenwriters. On the Fourth of July, 1966, the little del Mar family joins many others in Riverton at an evening picnic to watch the fireworks. As an amateur band plays "The Battle Hymn of the Republic," they spread out a blanket and begin unpacking their food, surrounded by other families and couples; then a pair of drunk bikers sits down behind them, leaning back and sharing a bottle as they speculate loudly about how much "pussy" there is "on the hoof" in the crowd around them. Alma gives Ennis a frightened look, and he turns to the two men and quietly asks them to keep it down because of his little girls. This reasonable request provokes the bigger of the two drunks to say "Fuck you!" to Ennis, and then to insult him further to the other biker, attacking Ennis's sexuality, suggesting that he's typical of the kind of married man who's lost interest in sex: "Asshole probably stopped puttin it to the wife after the kids come, you know how that is." As the fireworks begin to explode above the crowd, Ennis hands Jenny over to Alma, ignoring his wife's fearful murmured suggestion that they should move, and stands and confronts the two men. The smaller one stands and tells Ennis to listen to his "old lady's" advice, at which Ennis suddenly knocks him down and almost simultaneously kicks the bigger man, who's getting up too, in the face, knocking him backwards, and screaming that he'll knock out half their teeth. The camera takes the perspective of the bikers cowering on the ground, showing Ennis towering above, against the sky filled with the rockets' red glare and bombs bursting in air, as Alma and the two girls, almost as frightened as the bikers, stand timidly to one side, their tiny figures huddled together.

This scene, which, like the rest of the film, is superbly acted, directed, and shot, is full of complex and intriguing implications. Viewed on its own, separately from the rest of the film, it might seem to be a depiction of a simplistic, idealized, heroic American masculine archetype, the husband and father willing to risk his life against even the most intimidating threats in order to protect his wife and children. Similar episodes are a staple of action films and thrillers that appeal to audiences by depicting the vengeance taken by ordinary Americans against the threats they perceive to their safety in the world around them. There's a long list of films in which typical nuclear families are confronted by criminals, terrorists, monsters, even space aliens, and are defended by a father who's an ordinary guy forced by circumstance to become a hero, courageously meeting the challenge that threatens to destroy his loved ones. Some examples that come to mind are *Jaws* (1976), *Cape Fear* (1991), and *War of the Worlds* (2005).[20] Ennis's defense of Alma and the two little girls, with patriotic music playing and fireworks exploding, looked at separately might almost seem like a scene that could feature the likes of Sylvester Stallone or Jean-Claude Van Damme.

In the context of *Brokeback Mountain,* however, this episode expresses a remarkable range of challenging and contradictory suggestions. The viewer of the film knows that the man defending his family not only cares about and wants to protect them, but also that he's a man who loves men. As with the scenes on the mountain, which locate love between men in an iconic wilderness setting in which, according to the heroic narratives of the dominant culture depicting the conquest of the continent, male love supposedly doesn't, indeed, *cannot* occur, so too in the Fourth of July scene *Brokeback Mountain* places a man who loves men within another set of images fundamental to the national myth of manhood that supposedly are antithetical to male-male desire. In doing so, it challenges all of the assumptions and stereotypes concerning sexually different men—that they're urban, affluent, effete, single, and childless. In the scene Ennis is presented as an ordinary working-class American father who, when confronted by dangerous thugs, responds with fury, and a fury that's focused, relentless, and potentially deadly. The bikers he defeats represent everything that supposedly is alien to the American family, that it cannot possibly contain and still *be* a family: they're crude, dirty, foul-mouthed, violent, and, most significantly, they're single men on the make, targeting women for sexual use. Their obscene, anarchic, threatening sexuality is in total contrast to the values of commitment, love, and responsibility associated with the ideal of the family. The construction of the scene in terms of these apparently polar opposites creates an extraordinary tension indicating the intensity of Ennis's inner turmoil. To everyone else, he may seem to be the ideal husband and father, ready to lay down his life for his wife and children, but he himself is aware that his own sexuality is in contradiction to his outward, heterosexual role, and potentially is a force with much more disruptive potential for the family he's committed himself to build than the external threat posed by the two bikers. Though what he's felt for Jack is as deeply emotional as the traditional ideal of romantic love between a man and a woman, Ennis's society would condemn it as being even worse than the gross heterosexual lust of the bikers. By allowing himself to be compelled into marriage and passing by the expectations of family, friends, church, and society generally, and by his plans with Alma in particular, Ennis has entangled himself in a situation in which his own strongest desires may tear his family apart. His internal conflict is much more troubling to him than any external threat, which helps to explain the fury with which he confronts the bikers. The homophobic society whose national identity is being celebrated and affirmed during the scene has taught Ennis to understand his desire for men in the most negative terms, as a form of male sexuality inferior even to the brutal heterosexual desire of the bikers. It's plausible that, for him, they represent the disruptive sexual energy that he believes he has to suppress in himself, and that he projects onto them his fear and anger at the sexual desires he believes he must control. And perhaps, even more disturbingly, his rage is not only at the bikers and at what he secretly feels in himself, but also at the circumstances of his life, at his responsibilities as a husband and father, and at those for whom he's responsible. In their notes on the aftermath of Ennis's attack on the bikers, the screenwriters perceptively indicate that Alma and the little girls stare at Ennis in shock at the intensity of the fury they've witnessed in him;[21] at some level the wife and children of a man in Ennis's situation might sense that his anger was due in part to frustration with his commitment to them. Ennis can be seen not only as defending his family in the scene, but also, paradoxically, as exploding with frustration and rage *because* of them. For men who pass, the responsibilities of a heterosexual marriage may become a trap; despite their commitment to their families, they may find those families constricting and stifling to their most profound feelings.

Both versions of the narrative thus establish the tension between Ennis and Alma long before Jack's visit in 1967; Jack's return to Ennis's life doesn't suddenly disrupt the marriage and take Ennis away from Alma, but simply increases the distance already developing in the marriage because Ennis is passing for straight. Proulx recognizes this in a subtle detail in her description of Alma just after she's seen Ennis and Jack embrace on the steps of the apartment when Jack arrives for his visit. As Ennis awkwardly introduces Jack to her, Alma tries to limit the time the two men can have together; when he sees her taking a dollar out of her pocket, Ennis correctly guesses that she's about to ask him to buy her a pack of cigarettes in order to get him to come back sooner, a ploy that he counters by telling her that they've already got some. Proulx describes how Alma starts to ask him to get the cigarettes, speaking in her "misery voice."[22] The problems in the marriage are such that prior to ever knowing about Jack or about Ennis's love for him, Alma's "misery voice"[23] is a well-established aspect of her interactions with her husband, a manifestation of the conflicts in their marriage.

For a woman in Alma's situation, her marriage must be as frustrating and difficult as it is for her husband. Just as Ennis's understanding of sexuality is limited and distorted by the society's homophobia, so too Alma's must be. For a young, churchgoing, heterosexual woman growing up in Wyoming in the 1950s and 1960s, homosexuality, if she even were aware of it at all, would have seemed entirely alien, something strange and disturbing that was another manifestation of the unknown decadence of big cities far away. She might have encountered a few men who fit homophobic stereotypes, but they would seem quite unlike all of the "real" men in her life. According to prevailing stereotypes, a man like Ennis couldn't possibly be attracted to another man, since unlike "'them guys you see around sometimes,'"[24] Ennis is archetypically masculine. That her husband might be attracted to a man would be the last thing she'd think.

Alma, like Ennis, isn't out of her teens when they marry, and clearly she's sexually inexperienced and in love with him. The problems they encounter as young people with little money trying to care for two little children of course would be obstacles that Alma would have expected, and would be ready to deal with together with Ennis, and would expect mutual physical and emotional attraction to assist them in overcoming. What would be surprising, confusing, and disappointing would be their sexual incompatibility, especially his desire to do "what she hated."[25] Since, as is stressed in the story, Ennis has intense sexual fantasies concerning Jack, and repeatedly masturbates thinking about him, it's likely that Alma necessarily would become aware of a degree of distance from Ennis, particularly in their sexual relationship but also more generally that she would sense that there were important, intimate things that he kept from her. For any couple, the feeling that one's partner keeps certain things private or may have secrets that won't be shared always causes distance, limiting the possibility of a feeling of trust and security. Also, because women in American culture are taught to be concerned to please men and to try their best to adjust their lives to satisfy the needs and demands of men, it's likely that a woman in Alma's situation might worry that it was something about *her* that accounted for the sexual incompatibility and distance in her relationship with her husband. She might wonder whether she really was attractive enough for him, or if something was wrong with her for not wanting to do what made him happy. And just as Ennis has no one to turn to for support, and no sources of information and advice, Alma probably wouldn't either, since for a young wife to admit to others, even her closest relatives or friends, that she felt that something was going wrong in her marriage, especially something involving sex, and anal sex at that, would be a source of embarrassment and shame. Then to accidentally see her husband passionately embrace another man would be a total shock, a completely unimagined, unexpected explanation of all the problems in their marriage, and one that would be so confusing, so disturbing, so embarrassing that she might well be unable to speak about it with him or with anyone else, and would have to struggle with its implications in silence. Also, since Ennis has a temper and deals with frustrating situations with violence, at times Alma might well be physically afraid of him. Homophobia not only isolates and injures Ennis, but Alma as well.

When Jack comes back into Ennis's life, both the story and the film stress the powerful contrast between the passion that they feel for each other and the limitations of their relationships with their wives. After replying to Jack's message, Ennis takes the day off on June 24th when Jack's supposed to arrive and waits at home for him all afternoon, dressed in his best shirt—white with black stripes, reminiscent of prison uniforms and prison bars. In the film, although Alma isn't presented as particularly noticing it, Ennis is anxious, smoking and drinking beer and worrying—perhaps because of the way he parted from Jack four years earlier—that his friend may not show. In both versions, Jack's arrival immediately makes Ennis react with a sexual and emotional intensity that he's never shown toward Alma—although when he greets Jack he accidentally *does* show her what he feels for his friend, irrevocably changing his relationship with her, and ultimately leading to her decision to divorce him. Proulx's description of the scene, involving a characteristically virtuosic sentence, simultaneously presents the joy of the two men in being reunited and Alma's perspective on what happens between them. In late afternoon, when there's thunder in the distance, Jack pulls in driving his old pickup. When Ennis sees Jack get out, his worn hat tilted back, he's "scalded"[26] by a "hot jolt,"[27] and runs out on the landing and closes the door; Jack takes the stairs two at a time to meet him. When they embrace, Proulx says they

> hugged mightily, squeezing the breath out of each other, saying, son of a bitch, son of a bitch, then, and easily as the right key turns the lock tumblers, their mouths came together, and hard, Jack's big teeth bringing blood, his hat falling to the floor, stubble rasping, wet saliva welling, and the door opening and Alma looking out for a few seconds at Ennis's straining shoulders and shutting the door again and still they clinched, pressing chest and groin and thigh and leg together, treading on each other's toes until they pulled apart to breathe and Ennis, not big on endearments, said what he said to his horses and daughters, little darlin.[28]

The "hot jolt"[29] that "scalds"[30] Ennis describes the intense physical effect on him of seeing Jack again, his immediate emotional and sexual response which comes as a flash of erotic energy. Like most American men, he and Jack greet each other and express their bond as friends not with sentimental language, but roughly and playfully, through affectionate cursing, much as many male friends will jokingly insult and punch each other to show affection. But just as their friendship transcends the boundaries that are imposed on men by society's constant efforts to maintain separation between the homosocial and the homosexual, their physical contact goes far beyond the playful punches of straight male friends, and they "mightily"[31] hug and squeeze and then kiss. The metaphor of the right key easily opening the lock is a powerful expression of the completeness with which their kiss finally ends the frustrating sense of limitation each man has felt with his wife; for Ennis, kissing Alma, or for Jack, kissing Lureen just wasn't the right key to fit and make the lock tumblers turn, but for Ennis and Jack to kiss each other unlocks everything. The kiss opens the lock of sexual repression that's been imposed on each of them by trying to live as straight men. As so often is the case in her story, Proulx shows extraordinary insight into the experience of people who are attracted to members of their own sex: as has been attested by many sexual minority people who've struggled to live as straight people, trying to make love to people of the opposite sex often feels awkward and empty, whereas finally being able to embrace and kiss someone of their own sex to whom they're attracted feels utterly right and natural. Proulx's metaphor also suggests the way in which the reunion of the two men loosens their connections to their wives, and locks Ennis and Jack together again. She details their sensations as they become lost in each other, two stubbled faces scratching, kissing so hard and deep it brings blood, bodies pressing together all along their lengths as if they would try to get each part so close that they could merge into one. And that moment, as they forget everything in the joy of being with each other again, is what Alma sees, the shock that explains to her the reason for the distance she's felt from Ennis. With what Ennis says to Jack as they pull apart for a moment to breathe, Proulx reminds us that the distance between Ennis and Alma already has developed long before Jack returns to Ennis: to express what he feels about Jack, Ennis turns to the few sentimental words he uses for those he really loves, his horses and his little girls. He'll call one of his horses, or one of his girls, or Jack—but not Alma—"little darlin."[32]

As is true throughout the film, the acting and directing in this pivotal scene are convincing and powerful. With subtlety and effectiveness, Ledger shows the sudden transformation of Ennis's mood, from doubt that Jack will show up, and possibly guilt at the reason he may not come, to overwhelming pleasure at being with him again. The shot of Ennis as he comes out the door of the apartment, greeting Jack, who's down below, having just gotten out of his truck, adds a significant moment of dialogue not in the story or the screenplay. In keeping with the rough, playful insults the men use to express their love for each other, as Ennis stands on the porch and makes the gesture of opening his arms to welcome Jack, anticipating their hug, he shouts "Jack *Fuckin* Twist!" smiles, and punctuates what he's said, slamming his hands down on the railing. The all-purpose obscene expletive used for emphasis by American men when they talk together perfectly expresses the complexity of the characters Proulx created and the film depicts: it simultaneously typifies the harsh friendliness of ordinary, masculine American men, and also underlines that the friendship of these two ordinary, masculine American men includes fucking. Also, of course, it further elaborates the richly complex significance of Jack's name: each part of "Jack *Fuckin* Twist" alludes to an aspect of the intense sexual attraction that Ennis feels for Jack, and that Jack feels in return. The name directly manifests the sexual bond between them, which they're about to renew, when they go to the motel. It reminds us of the contrast between the strained sexual relationship between Ennis and Alma and the mutual fulfillment Jack and Ennis are able to enjoy together.

Gyllenhaal and Ledger embrace and kiss with power and conviction—so much so that they earned "Best Kiss" at the 2006 MTV Awards, and that, according to Gyllenhaal, it felt to him like Ledger had broken his nose.[33] The passion of the scene is emphasized by Santaolalla's score, which has been absent through nearly all of the scenes depicting the marriages of the two men, only beginning to return when Ennis receives Jack's postcard. As already has been mentioned, the film slightly changes the way the two men hug, emphasizing Ennis's fear of exposure. Whereas in the text they embrace and kiss when they meet on the stairs, in the film they embrace, but then, as they're about to kiss, Ennis thinks of the necessity of secrecy, and pulls Jack with him toward a corner of the landing by the wall where he thinks it's less likely they'll be visible, and then they kiss. Ennis's precautions would be effective to prevent them from being seen by anyone passing on the street, but not from being seen by Alma, who looks out at just that moment. For a man who tries to pass, surveillance is a threat not only in public but also within his own family and home. The reunion is ecstatic for Jack and Ennis, unlocking and releasing their sexuality and emotions and locking them together again as a couple, but for Alma what she sees unlocks the door to an understanding of Ennis she never could have imagined, and accelerates the process of unlocking their marriage.

Both the story and the film give powerful, moving descriptions of the impact of this episode on Alma, and the way it eventually leads to her decision to divorce Ennis. In the story, after her unexpected glimpse of "Ennis's straining shoulders"[34] as he and Jack kiss, she quickly shuts the door, then opens it again when the two men have pulled apart. As they turn to Alma, both Ennis and Jack are visibly affected by the passion they feel at being together again, Ennis's chest heaving to get his breath, Jack so excited he shakes and trembles like a horse tired from running, making the floorboard on the stairs vibrate. There's nothing Ennis is able to say except to try to maintain appearances, politely introducing Jack to Alma and Alma to Jack, then making an awkward gesture at explaining their excitement by saying that he and Jack haven't seen each other in four years. There's no interaction between Alma and Jack, and her subdued agreement with Ennis's attempt at explaining, and then again when he tells her that he and Jack are going out drinking and may not be back that night, should indicate to them that she has some understanding of what's happening. When the baby's cry leads Ennis to tell Jack about his two little girls and how much he loves them, the fact that he says nothing similar about her isn't lost on Alma, who Proulx says stands there silently, her mouth twitching, as if she's struggling with all the things she can't say. Jack volunteers the news that he's married to Lureen and has a little boy, but this evidence of his ostensible heterosexuality doesn't do anything to ease the situation. As the men get ready to leave, Jack's polite acknowledgement that he's pleased to have met Alma elicits no reply, only her desperate attempt to make Ennis come back sooner by trying to get him to buy cigarettes. What's happening between the three people is going to change all of their lives, but it's so painful and difficult to confront, especially because it requires acknowledging homosexuality, which their society only has given them ideas and words for repudiating, not for understanding, that none of them can say any of the things that have to be said, and so all of them retreat into a charade. All three of them realize what's happening, but none of them can deal with it.

The shock, despair, and anger that Alma silently goes through as a result of seeing Ennis with Jack are expressed with sensitivity by Michelle Williams in the film. In the scene while Ennis is waiting for Jack to arrive, when Alma suggests to him that they get a babysitter and all go out to dinner, Williams indicates the eagerness Alma feels to do a little bit of socializing, something she and Ennis rarely have time or money to do. Her cheerfulness in proposing that they all go out to dinner perhaps also shows that Alma is hopeful to try to resolve some of the tensions she and Ennis have felt with each other. Then when she opens the door and sees Ennis and Jack, her shock is evident not only in her facial expression, eyes wide, lips parted, but throughout her body, as she struggles to breathe and to get away from the door. As Williams closes the door and retreats into the apartment, she hunches her shoulders and seems almost to shrink, to close her body against what she's discovered. She goes to the table, gets her purse and puts it over her shoulder, and seems to be getting ready to leave the apartment to get away from what she's seen when Ennis and Jack come in. She remains far from the door, almost inaudibly saying hello when Ennis introduces Jack, as she looks across the room at him and at Ennis with a frightened expression on her soft features. As Ennis explains that they may not be back that evening, the look of fear changes to one of hurt and pain as she nods and agrees.

In both versions of *Brokeback Mountain* what Ennis says to Jack during their 1967 reunion indicates the frustration he's felt with his marriage. Though the film cuts out his comments about masturbating while picturing Jack, about his questioning of his sexual orientation, and about regretting he let Jack "'out a [his] sights,'"[35] it makes it clear that he's found marriage with Alma unsatisfying and frustrating. As he says to Jack in the scene in the film when they lie in bed together talking at the motel, he feels he's stuck with what he's got, that he only has time for making a living to meet his obligations to his family. He's prevented from accepting Jack's invitation to live together by the commitment he feels to his daughters, and most of all by his fear of what he'll lose and what can happen to him if he's perceived as a "queer," but a strong feeling of attraction to Alma isn't a factor.

The film adds an episode depicting Ennis's return to the apartment the morning after his night with Jack at the motel; in contrast to the story, in which he calls Alma to tell her that he and Jack are going to go on a fishing trip for a few days, here Ennis only tells Alma when he comes back to the apartment. As the episode opens, Alma sits at the kitchen table, apparently having been up all night unable to sleep because of what she now knows. When she hears Jack's truck, she wipes the tears off her face, but when he comes in Ennis doesn't embrace her, only greeting her to tell her he and Jack are going fishing, and then hurries from room to room to grab the things he needs to take. Alma's resentment shows as she argues with him about why Jack doesn't come in for coffee and whether Ennis's foreman will tolerate him taking time off, but she can't confront him about the real issue, the meaning of his relationship with Jack. As Williams presents Alma, she stands huddled in her thin robe, giving herself the reassuring hug that Ennis hasn't. Ledger presents Ennis as being so absorbed in getting ready to leave with Jack, and so anxious about what Alma may know, that he hardly even looks at her or listens to her. When she asks why Jack doesn't come in to have coffee, Ennis's reply is to say, distractedly, that Jack's from Texas, a *non sequitur* that would be funny if the circumstances weren't so painful. At one point, to keep packing, he has to go past her as she stands in a doorway, and Ledger almost seems to avoid her as he pushes past, though as he leaves, after picking up Alma Jr. and kissing her goodbye, he makes it a point to kiss Alma— on the cheek. As the two men get into Jack's truck to drive off, Williams presents Alma standing at the window, holding Alma Jr. against her face and starting to cry, and making a weak effort to wave goodbye. In the episode, Williams convincingly presents the astonishment, confusion, anger, and despair that Alma feels, and that will shape her marriage until she finally divorces Ennis.

The events of Jack's arrival illustrate the strain imposed on everyone when a sexually different person tries to pass, especially when that person has become entangled in a cover marriage. Alma had known there must be some reason for the distance between her and Ennis, but not what it was; the cause is so unexpected that it leaves her in shock, able only to go through the motions of her relationship with him. Nothing he says can change the fact, as Proulx says, that she's seen what she's seen. As very often is the case for Americans when confronted with the information that someone they know is sexually different, homosexuality is so burdened with negative meaning as to be impossible even to acknowledge, much less to discuss in any constructive way. It literally is "unspeakable." If the sexual incompatibility between Alma and Ennis was difficult for her to talk to anyone about before, what she knows now would be impossible. How could she go to a relative or a friend and say that she saw her husband kissing another man, and not get a response of complete incredulity that challenged her own credibility? Who would believe that a man like Ennis was in love with another man, especially in a society in which it's accepted that straight men can and should spend time in homosocial activities bonding with their buddies? Just as Ennis or Jack or any other sexual minority person in a homophobic society often has to struggle alone without support or guidance, homophobia often makes family members of sexual minority people struggle in isolation and silence too. Frequently the only thing people in such circumstances can do is to go on pretending that things really are as they seemed to be before, hoping that perhaps somehow they actually may *become* the way that they were supposed to be. They have almost no words to express how things really are, and to try to put things into words would be so difficult and painful it could tear their lives apart.

Because Alma must struggle in isolation and silence with what she knows about Ennis, she never is able to understand it or its significance. Both the story and the film make it clear that Alma feels betrayed by Ennis much as she would if she had learned that he was secretly involved with another woman he preferred to her, rather than with a man. It never is possible for him to help her see that, because of his sexuality, letting himself be pressured into getting married at all was the mistake, and that fear and shame prevented him from respecting and acting on the sexual attraction to Jack that he discovered well before he married Alma. How could Ennis articulate these things to Alma, when he barely can articulate them to himself? Reading the story or watching the film, it needs to be remembered that in the mid 1960s there was no real public dialogue about homosexuality, particularly away from urban centers, that the small, courageous homophile movement was scarcely noticed and was disparaged if it was, and that homosexuality was represented by most in the media, government, and religion in terms of perversion, criminality, and corruption. Ideas about respect for differences in sexual orientation, and especially about the need to support members of sexual minorities as they struggle against the pressures of homophobia, seeking to question and understand their sexuality and to make choices that are right for them, were unavailable to most people, and were inconceivable for a man in Ennis's situation. The word homophobia, and the concept that many of the problems faced by sexual minorities are due to society's prejudices, simply didn't exist.[36] Neither he nor Alma can be blamed for what happens to them, since it results from ignorance and fear on a scale few individuals could challenge. Today members of sexual minorities finally have made themselves more able to speak for themselves, and to generate constructive dialogue about sexuality and homophobia, providing ideas and information that can help many people to keep from becoming involved in cover marriages that only can hurt them and the people they marry. Still, homophobia continues to pose many obstacles to understanding and accepting same-sex attraction, and to force many people, especially those isolated and kept ignorant by their communities, into heterosexual relationships and marriages that aren't right for them or for their spouses.

Ennis's response to his situation with Alma and Jack isn't right, but it's completely understandable. He doesn't know what Alma's seen, though her coldness when he introduces her to Jack should make it clear to him that she must have suspicions, but there's no confrontation to challenge the fiction that he and Jack are just old buddies who go out for a night of drinking, or that the next day they just decide on the spur of the moment to go off on a fishing trip. It's unimaginable for him to voluntarily explain the situation to Alma, thereby destroying his identity as a straight man. The only bearable thing for Ennis to do is to maintain the fictions they've all tacitly accepted, which will allow him to continue hiding his sexuality within his cover marriage to Alma and to try to recapture what he had with Jack. He already has established a pattern of hiding his sexual desires, of masturbating while thinking of Jack; in the film he also has felt compelled to evade Alma's questions about Jack and to lie about who Jack is, telling Alma, when Jack's postcard comes, that they were "fishin buddies," keeping their summer together on Brokeback Mountain a secret. Now Ennis becomes caught up in a process of continual lying to Alma and his daughters. Hurting any of them is the last thing he wants; he still cares about Alma and loves the little girls, and feels responsible for all three of them, and he's also in love with Jack. But continuing to pass only can hurt them all, trapping Alma and the girls in a family based on the endless lies of a cover marriage and forcing Jack to stay with Lureen, constantly waiting for the few times Ennis and he can be together. The only real solution would be to talk openly about what's happening and to find an answer that would cause as little suffering as possible, but the fear and shame and ignorance that surround same-sex love prevent Ennis from being able to take this step, and so he, and everyone in his life, becomes trapped.

Following the episode of the reunion between Jack and Ennis, Proulx gives a short description, filled with painful detail, of the ensuing decline of the marriage between Ennis and Alma over the next seven years. The embrace Alma saw between Ennis and Jack, the fact that Ennis takes "fishing trips" a couple of times a year with Jack but never takes a vacation with her and the little girls, his dislike of socializing, his preference for low-paying ranch jobs that oblige her to work as a grocery clerk to cover their bills, and their sexual incompatibility gradually increase her resentment. Dreading having another child, she asks Ennis to use condoms, which causes him to tell her he'll stop having intercourse with her if she doesn't want his children; she mutters to herself that she'd have them if he'd support them, and thinks to herself that anyway, what he likes to do "don't make too many babies."[37] Finally she divorces Ennis and marries the grocer she works for. In her account, Proulx recognizes that the failure of a marriage often isn't expressed in dramatic conflict, but instead in occasional, bitter moments of contempt and rejection, in cold refusals of intimacy and casual jibes that inflict hurt that never goes away. Above all, it's shown in the growth of indifference between two people.

Proulx's choice of detail in having Ennis and Jack call their retreats into the mountains together "fishing" trips, as opposed to hunting trips or some other evasive term, is full of irony for the reader, since certainly Alma and perhaps Lureen can tell that there's something "fishy" about this explanation of the relationship of the two men, and also since in the vernacular the word "fish" is a crude, offensive synonym for female genitalia, the antithesis of the actual sexual interests of the two men. Sexually, what really appeals to Jack and Ennis sure isn't "fish."

The film depicts the difficult moments between Ennis and Alma that Proulx describes, and adds several others that enlarge the significance of the narrative. Immediately after it presents the first reunion between Jack and Ennis, the film provides an episode indicating the perspective of the two little girls, showing how the growing rift between Alma and Ennis affects them. It opens outside the little apartment over the laundromat, with Alma Jr. and Jenny going back and forth on a swing set, as Ennis and Alma argue in the apartment above. The girls stop playing and try to listen as the argument escalates, Ennis challenging Alma for getting ready to leave for work without serving the dinner she's prepared, Alma rushing out and down the stairs while she angrily tells him she's already promised to take the extra shift at the grocery store. The argument may seem to put Ennis entirely at fault, until you consider why Alma may be so eager to leave, and why Ennis may be so irrationally angry: Alma may want to get to work not only to get away from Ennis but also to be with the grocery store manager, named Monroe in the film, and Bill in the story. She has plenty of reason to be angry and frustrated with Ennis, and to seek love elsewhere, but unfortunately circumstances make it impossible for them to discuss Ennis's dilemma, how it affects her, and how they could deal with it. The scene stresses the cost for the two little girls: as Alma hurries off, Ennis following her and swearing, the girls watch silently, frightened and confused by their parents' anger. Embarrassed, and concerned to think of the effect of the argument on them, Ennis turns toward them and ventures to ask if they want a push on the swings, only prompting them to say no and to start swinging on their own again, as he angrily kicks a trash can and goes back inside. Anybody who's seen the sad effects of a divorce on little children can recognize how this scene captures the way the escalating fighting and bitterness between hostile parents who are unable to discuss their problems can cause children to close in on themselves and become more and more distant.

Shortly after this, the film continues its account of the relationship between Ennis and Alma with an episode in which Ennis is busy packing for one of his trips with Jack. Clearly the decline of the marriage has reached another stage, in which, without ever discussing what's gone wrong, Ennis and Alma now coolly tolerate each other. This prepares the audience for the final phases of the relationship, in which Ennis and Alma stop having sex and reject each other completely. As Ennis busily packs his gear for the trip, Alma sits by indifferently, reading the newspaper, then mentions that there's an opening at the power company that might mean good pay. As Proulx's account explains, Ennis doesn't want the kind of higher-paying job that he can't leave easily for his trips with Jack, and so the film shows him quickly evading her suggestion by faulting himself, saying he's so clumsy he'd probably get electrocuted. The episode subtly suggests another pressure that may play a role in pulling Ennis and Alma apart, when Alma Jr. eagerly asks her father if he'll be back in time for the church picnic. He cheerfully agrees to go as long as he doesn't have to sing; he loves making his daughters happy, but seems to show some resistance to involvement with church. It's not likely that he'd feel much attraction to religion, given that at church he'd surely hear denunciations of anyone having sex outside of marriage, and also, given the growth of explicit religious condemnation of homosexuality in the time period of the story, that he might well hear the love he feels for Jack excoriated as an "abomination." While we aren't told, the family's involvement with church probably comes from Alma, and in part may well be her way of exposing Ennis to a condemnation of his sexuality with which she agrees, though she isn't able to say it to him directly.

At the start of the episode, before Alma makes her suggestion about the job, a detail as Ennis hurriedly packs suggests the constant reminders about standards of masculine gender behavior that pressure sexually different men who pass. The radio's on, tuned to some talk show whose announcer is telling a joke that centers on the contrast between two men in a bar; we never hear the punch line, but the setup makes it clear that it's part of the continuous process whereby the culture reinforces its concepts of masculinity: "You fellas hear the one about the great big guy, big hairy monstrous guy, musta beena construction worker all his life, and he's sittin in a bar next to this little bitty guy . . ." For a man like Ennis, reminders of the distance between what the culture says he's supposed to be and what he actually feels are everywhere.

The interaction between Alma and Ennis at the close of the episode also stresses this distance, and the constant tension it causes between husband and wife. As Ennis is about to go out the door, Alma asks in a falsely chirpy tone if he's forgetting something, reminding him of the tackle box that he's left on the kitchen table. He goes to grab the prop that's necessary to his lie about his "fishing" trips with Jack, but she doesn't even look up from her newspaper, and he turns and walks out without a look or a word to her. With real insight, McMurtry and Ossana have elaborated on Proulx's narrative, showing the subtle but continual stress and pain, day in, day out, for a couple trapped in a cover marriage.

In a slightly later scene, the filmmakers develop the suggestion of the possible significance of homophobic religion in the breakdown of the del Mars's marriage. The family is shown in the little living room of their apartment during the evening, Alma knitting, Ennis on the other side of the room, stretched out on the sofa drinking a beer and watching a murder story on TV, as the little girls play on the floor. As Alma did when she and Ennis were waiting for Jack to arrive for his first visit, she expresses her desire for the kind of socializing that other married couples in Riverton enjoy, proposing that since it's Saturday night they could "smarten up" and go to the church social. Without even looking at her, indicating the depth of distance between them, Ennis questions and dismisses her desire to be with what he calls "that fire-and-brimstone crowd." Alma replies with bitter resignation that she thinks it would be "nice." For a heterosexual woman who wanted to have a "normal" marriage with a heterosexual man, it probably would be nice to get together of a Saturday night with other married folks who then would gather contentedly the next morning to listen to a preacher whose sermon might well include a condemnation of sexual infidelity. By the early 1970s, given the increased visibility of sexual minorities and the growing hostility of many religious denominations, it's not at all unlikely that the sermon might directly denounce same-sex love. For a wife who's embittered over her husband's failure to live up to her expectations, sexually, socially, economically, and in every other way, as Alma is, suggesting going to such a church social is an effective way to point out his failings and how they've defeated all of her expectations. Ennis's response to her suggestion goes right to the heart of the differences between them, and suggests the role of religion in them: while for her, the church is welcoming and represents the "normal" heterosexual life she feels he's cheated her out of, for him it's a hostile place where his deepest feelings are relentlessly condemned, though his commitment to passing forces him to suffer these attacks in silence, and he only goes there because she wants him to. The episode points up the impossibility for Ennis of explaining to Alma why what's happened has happened, or of her ever really knowing or understanding him, or feeling any forgiveness or compassion for him. The name "Alma" comes from Latin, meaning nurturing and kind, which of course Alma has a great capacity for being, as her relationships to the girls and to her second husband show, but sadly the ignorance and silence imposed by homophobia only make these meanings of her name ironic in relation to her attitudes toward Ennis. Both she and Ennis could give a great deal to the right partner, but their culture has trapped them in a relationship that's wrong for them and that damages both of them. The hostility between Ennis and Alma in this episode is confirmed by the one that follows immediately after it, apparently set on the same night, when they go to bed and begin to try to make love, only to argue bitterly about how much money Ennis makes and whether to use protection, which finally ends their sexual relationship for good, and makes the divorce inevitable.

The divorce doesn't free Ennis, but only traps him further. He now has to pay child support of two hundred and fifty dollars a month, which means he can't start and stop low-paying jobs the way he did before and has to plan ahead more carefully how many trips he can manage to take with Jack. He loves his daughters and feels responsible for them, and wants to meet his part of the divorce settlement to ensure that he can continue to have them spend time with him. The solution that Jack sees, of getting divorced from Lureen and coming back to Wyoming and starting a ranch with Ennis, is impossible for Ennis to agree to both because of his fear of being identified as sexually different and because of his commitment to his daughters. Running a ranch with Jack certainly might provide a steady source of income allowing Ennis to provide for the girls, and both he and Jack are good to children and would make good fathers, but given attitudes toward same-sex couples, especially in the 1970s and in the Rocky Mountain West, it's very unlikely that a court would grant Ennis the right to have his children visit him if he were living with Jack, and it might well deny him any contact with them at all. In any case, if he were living with Jack, a legal struggle over access to the girls, especially given Alma's hostility, certainly could have exactly the effect Ennis is most afraid of, making his relationship with Jack public knowledge, shaming him and inviting homophobic aggression. Like many same-sex couples, Ennis and Jack could do a good job of raising their children together if they were allowed to, but hostility to their relationship never even lets them get as far as discussing the possibility. This aspect of the trap Ennis finds himself in points to the struggle that many sexual minority parents continue to face today in trying to maintain access to their children.

The failure of the marriage only intensifies Ennis's anxieties about the possibility that others will question his sexuality. Both the story and the film show how this fear affects him in the episode at Thanksgiving with Alma, the grocer, and the two girls, shortly after the divorce. The movie follows the account in the story closely, elaborating plausibly on Proulx's description, depicting the house as a comfortable bungalow. Alma, clearly pregnant, politely serves a nice turkey dinner, the grocer is congenial, the girls are delighted to have everyone together, and Ennis shows it's all right by talking to them about horses, telling them jokes, and trying not to be a "sad daddy."[38] They're on the grocer's turf (in the film he sits at the head of the table, wielding his electric carving knife as a phallic token of his patriarchal position) but the girls clearly find Ennis far more glamorous, asking him for stories about his experiences as a bronc rider. He bashfully minimizes his ability, endearing himself even more to them. But everything disintegrates when Ennis helps Alma clear the plates and they talk in the kitchen. She presents herself as being concerned about him living alone, advising him that he ought to get married again, which of course just makes him feel trapped, as Proulx says, "too big for the room."[39] Their society's homophobia makes it impossible for her to have any understanding of his situation or his needs, and her advice is just a way of needling him, given her resentment of his relationship with Jack. The solution she proposes isn't a solution for Ennis at all, and she knows it. He counters her advice with, "'Once burned . . .,'"[40] a remark that places responsibility for the failure of their marriage on her, which isn't fair, though it's the only way he's able to express the frustration he feels at being told to repeat the mistake of getting married. The two of them have an opportunity to discuss what wasn't right between them, for Ennis to explain about himself and for Alma to begin to understand him, but of course neither of them's been provided with the concepts or the words to take it.

Ennis's remark about being "burned"[41] causes Alma, for the first time, to confront him directly about his sexuality, in the only way she can, which is to attack Jack. She demands if he still goes fishing with "'that Jack Twist'"[42] and then exposes the years of lies. She tells him how she always wondered why he never brought any trout home, and so, the night before one of his "'little trips'"[43] got out his creel case, which still had the price tag on it after five years, and tied a note on the end of the line, asking him to bring some trout home. She reminds him how he came back and said they'd caught and eaten a bunch of brown trout, but then tells him that when she got a chance to look in the case, the note still was there, showing the line never had touched water. In the movie, Williams presents Alma standing at the sink, staring straight ahead, not even looking at Ennis, and trembling with controlled anger. When Ennis dismisses the implications of what she's said, Alma finally releases the anger that's built up for so long, telling him not to lie to try to fool her, and then directly attacking Jack: "'Jack Twist? *Jack Nasty.* You and him—.'"[44] But, as Proulx says, Alma's overstepped the line for Ennis, and he grabs her arm, angrily telling her she knows nothing about it. This argument sums up their situation: Alma's got ample reason to feel bitter, having received little of the happiness and security that she'd hoped would come with marriage, and instead having made an incomprehensible and disturbing discovery about her husband and his friend, who she sees as a rival who's ruined her marriage. To her, the relationship between Ennis and Jack not only is an adulterous affair, but their sexuality is also something disgusting and shocking. But he's right, she knows nothing about why things happened the way they did. With Jack, well before he married Alma, Ennis had discovered what he really wanted, but was completely unable to accept what he'd found, and so rejected the person he loved and went ahead and married Alma, which he never should have done. Once Jack returned, it was impossible for Ennis to continue to deny what he felt, or to completely reject the man he loved a second time, and so he stumbled into the lying that she's known about for years. It was the only way he could try to keep what he had with Alma and still try to have something with Jack, and not lose the little status he has, given his poverty, of being a straight man—which may be the *only* status he has in his society, if one accepts the interpretation that he may be partly Hispanic. There's no way he can say any of this to Alma, much less tell her about the constant fear he's felt since childhood of being exposed and targeted for not being the "right" sort of man. And there's no way she ever could understand it, having no source of guidance about men like Ennis other than the uncompromising hatred preached everywhere in their society.

The terrible argument at Thanksgiving indicates one of the saddest and ugliest aspects of Ennis's situation: a man in the trap of passing, increasingly feeling frustration at the stress of maintaining the appearance of heterosexuality, may direct some of his anger at those closest to him. At the end of their summer together, Ennis punches Jack, and in the Thanksgiving episode he comes close to reacting to Alma by hitting her; he's ready to deal with difficult situations in the way his father taught him to deal with his brother, by using violence. Ennis keeps himself from doing this to Alma, but clearly she's in physical fear of him. Unlike the story, the movie explicitly shows that she's had some sense of the danger of his rage earlier, in the Fourth of July episode. When she argues with Ennis at Thanksgiving, Alma protects herself in the only way she can, saying she'll call her husband. But in doing so, she invokes the authority of a heterosexual male, implicitly threatening to tell him and everyone else about Ennis and Jack. Alma aligns herself with the forces of homophobia that have pushed Ennis into passing and into making the mistake of rejecting Jack and into marrying her. Ennis reacts to this threat with fury, threatening to make her husband—and her as well—"'eat the fuckin floor.'"[45] For an instant as he grips her arm and threatens her and her new husband, she glimpses the depth of fury he feels at the trap his life has been, though she can't understand its cause. To avoid making the terrible mistake of directing against her the rage that he feels at the forces that have distorted his life, the only thing Ennis can do is leave. In the film he storms through the living room, ignoring the startled grocer and the two alarmed little girls as he shoves on his hat and slams out. As for many sexually different men frustrated by the impossible demands of trying to pass for straight, Ennis's rage finally does explode, though fortunately not at Alma: Proulx says that after leaving the grocer's, Ennis goes to the Black and Blue Eagle Bar, gets drunk, has a brief fight, and leaves. The film changes this slightly, stressing the completely pointless and self-destructive effect of this sort of rage: Ennis picks a fight with the driver of a pickup truck outside the bar, and since the driver's bigger than Ennis, winds up getting the worst of it, getting knocked down and brutally beaten and kicked as he lies on the road.

The filmmakers build on the Thanksgiving episode with Ennis's family, going beyond the story and giving more of a sense of how Ennis's anxiety is intensified by the divorce, and so providing additional insight into his motivations regarding Jack and the waitress he meets in Riverton. As soon as the divorce comes through, Ennis's increased fear of being identified as sexually different is evident in the painful scene when Jack surprises him when he's with the two little girls outside the line cabin, and Ennis anxiously watches a neighbor drive by as he regretfully tells Jack they still can't be together. Being divorced by Alma, and then being confronted by her about his sexuality and his relationship with Jack, makes him even more afraid than before of the threat of exposure. The fact that Alma has completely turned against him, and that she may well have told the grocer why, as well as her association with the "fire-and-brimstone crowd" at the church, all mean that it's quite likely that gossip about the reasons for the divorce will start to spread. In small, rural communities, especially where conservative churches can play a leading role in determining opinion, there's little of the anonymity and privacy of large cities, and many of those who claim to be Christians self-righteously take it upon themselves to know other people's personal business and to police their behavior. This is especially true where sex is involved, and most of all concerning the "abomination" of homosexuality, as is evident in the "sex-crime panics" in communities such as Boise, Idaho, and Sioux City, Iowa, mentioned above, which targeted sexually different men as "sexual psychopaths."[46] Similarly, in Riverton, Wyoming, the news about why Alma del Mar divorced Ennis and married the grocer could be a sensation if it got around, especially because Ennis so completely defies the stereotypes about homosexuality that people assumed to be true. Although a concern with protecting her daughters from gossip might restrain a woman in Alma's situation, it's still quite possible that once her new husband knew what had happened the story would get out, and then there would be widespread indignation, making Ennis a pariah. Everyone would see the situation simply as one in which Ennis had victimized Alma to fulfill his own sick, sinful desires; few could conceive of his sexuality as deserving respect, or begin to understand the fear that drove him into the trap of marriage, and any who did would keep their mouths shut, out of fear of guilt by association. Anyone trying to defend a man who's sexually different would quickly be accused of being like him. It's no wonder, then, that after the divorce Ennis is glad to go back to living on the kind of "lonesome ranch" Alma disliked; as is the case for some sexually different men, both those who pass and those who don't, it's preferable to live in a place that's relatively private, providing some protection from exposure to the straight majority, and especially from surveillance by the busybodies who want to monitor everyone else's sex lives.

In the film, it's clear that once he's living alone again, Ennis's fear sometimes reaches the level of a sort of paranoia. During his next trip with Jack after the divorce, as Jack's telling about Lureen's growing obsession with her Daddy's business, Ennis suddenly asks, "You and Lureen, it's normal and all?" Jack assures Ennis that it is, causing Ennis to pursue the subject further with the question, "She don't ever suspect?" Jack shakes his head no, although there's some reason to doubt him, given his strong desire for sexual relationships with men, his trip to Mexico, and the growing distance between him and Lureen. Then, without telling Jack that Alma not only suspected but discovered his sexuality and confronted him about it, Ennis shares with Jack the constant anxiety that troubles him: "You ever get the feelin, I don't know, when you're in town, and someone looks at you, suspicious . . . like he *knows*. And then you get out on the pavement, and everyone's lookin at you, like they all know too?" Jack's response is to encourage Ennis to think about getting away, maybe to Texas, raising once more his invitation to live together. Though this would mean exposure, it also would provide Ennis with a kind of support he's never had. But given the heightened level of Ennis's fear, it's the last solution he has the courage to consider, and with angry and cruel words he dismisses Jack's idea as ridiculous and unworkable, given his own obligations to his girls and Jack's to Lureen and the Newsomes. Jack is the focus of Ennis's sexual and emotional desires, and is the only person he can turn to for any understanding of his anxieties, but paradoxically, because Jack's the man Ennis loves, he also represents the sexual identity that Ennis has been made to fear and hide. Jack epitomizes the very thing Ennis can't deal with, being a man who loves men, and so Ennis directs his frustration and anger over his insecure situation at Jack. One of the many costs of passing is that the very person you love most also can symbolize your greatest fears.

Ennis's confession to Jack of the intensity of his fear that his sexual difference will become known is followed immediately by the depiction of the way
he gets involved with Cassie, the waitress. The story only briefly mentions
this relationship, but the filmmakers develop it, convincingly relating it to Ennis's concern not to be identified as a "queer." One evening when Ennis is
drinking alone at the Wolf Ears Bar in Riverton, watching TV and oblivious
to the crowd and, at first, to her, Cassie picks him up. Whereas he's awkward
and shy with her, she has some of the kind of vivaciousness and determination Lureen shows with Jack, first trying to get Ennis to dance, which he's re-
luctant to try and unable to do, and then, when they sit and talk, boldly sticking her feet in his lap to get a foot rub. She tries to flirt, asking what he does,
but Ennis doesn't know how to flirt with women, and gives her the factual
conversation-killer of a reply that he spent the day castrating calves. Still,
Cassie persists; Linda Cardellini makes it clear that she's smitten, eager, and
hopeful. As she talks with Ennis, the song playing in the bar, Linda Ronstadt
singing "It's So Easy to Fall in Love," suggests the mistake she's making. In
a slightly later scene, the film indicates that Ennis and Cassie go out for a
time, though it's clear it doesn't amount to what she'd hoped, and in fact
there's no indication that they sleep together. With Cassie riding with him in
his truck, Ennis picks up Alma Jr. and the three go to the bar together of an
afternoon. Alma Jr. is a little hesitant and suspicious, and isn't encouraging
when Cassie let's her know she's seriously interested in Ennis, asking Alma
Jr., when they're alone, if she thinks he'll settle down again. With the insight
of a child who knows and loves her father, although she may not understand
his reasons, Alma Jr. disconcerts Cassie by telling her that maybe he's not the
marrying kind. Meanwhile Ennis stands across the room studying the juke-
box, listening to Tammy Wynette sing "D-I-V-O-R-C-E," which doesn't bode
well for Cassie's plans.

The last scene with Cassie comes after the relationship has ended; she
walks into a cheap bus station restaurant with another guy, but sees Ennis eating alone, and they talk briefly. As with Alma, it's impossible for Ennis to
share anything with Cassie about his actual feelings and needs and how
they've prevented their relationship from working. Cassie pretends to be
cheerful but obviously is hurt and angry, asking where he's been and if he got
the messages she left for him; clearly he's withdrawn from her, since being
with a woman simply isn't right for him. When he responds that he got the
message, glancing at her new boyfriend and making it sound like she's
dropped Ennis, rather than the other way around, she parries that Carl, the
man she's with, is nice, and, unlike Ennis, "even talks." She then expresses
her frustration with Ennis, exclaiming, near tears, that she doesn't get him.
Once again, like other men who try to pass, Ennis has put himself in a situa-

tion with a woman that only can hurt her, and can't satisfy him. Because the costs of being identified as sexually different are so high, some sexually different men try to make relationships with women work, hoping they'll feel enough of a physical and emotional connection to make it last, but often giving up because it just isn't what they need or want. As with Ennis and Cassie, this helps the man to maintain the appearance of being heterosexual, but it isn't the answer for him, and it's unfair to the woman. Ennis can't tell Cassie what she needs to know in order to "get" him, but he does say he's sorry, and faults himself, saying he probably was no fun anyway. But this only upsets her further, prompting her to disclose the degree of damage that can happen to a woman who gets involved with a sexually different man who passes as straight; she sobs that girls don't fall in love with fun, and then rushes off with Carl. Passing keeps Ennis's heterosexual credentials intact, but hurts Cassie much as it hurt Alma, pushes Jack away again and again, and leaves Ennis alone and miserable.

Ennis's dilemma exemplifies a link between homophobia and paranoia that's taken many years for responsible psychologists to understand. As has been mentioned, during much of the twentieth century the profession of psychology was dominated by hostile straight men who based their studies of homosexuality on seriously disturbed clients, and who, as a result of this sample and of their own unexamined homophobia, constructed homosexuality as a form of mental illness. In the view of such supposed experts, same-sex attraction resulted from abnormal family structure and frequently was associated with other serious mental illnesses, particularly schizophrenia and paranoia. Although this view was challenged and eventually discredited by the work of psychologists such as Dr. Evelyn Hooker, who studied more representative homosexual men and found them to be no more prone to mental illness than the heterosexual majority, the mental illness model of homosexuality still is aggressively propagated by a small minority of psychologists, in collusion with homophobic religious and political organizations. Over the past thirty years, as the study of the experiences of sexual minorities has opened up to respecting their own perspectives, it's become clear to many that in some people's lives there definitely *is* a connection between homosexuality and paranoia, while it's different from what hostile psychologists have claimed. Some sexually different people do experience intense fear and suspicion reaching the level of paranoia, but not because their sexuality is a mental disorder; as in Ennis's case, the conflict between what they need sexually and emotionally, and what they know society expects and will accept, causes constant anxiety that they may be rejected or attacked because of their sexuality. For those who try to pass and so remain isolated from supportive relationships with other sexual minority people, this fear and suspicion may become especially intense and destructive. But those who continue to attack homosexuality as a mental illness are too hostile and obtuse to recognize that the paranoia that sexually different people sometimes experience isn't a proof that their sexuality is a sickness, but in fact is a product of hostile attitudes toward sexual minorities throughout society, including those that are fostered by people like them who insist on constructing homosexuality as a mental disorder.[47]

JACK AND LUREEN

Proulx only briefly sketches Lureen and her father in the story through Jack's comments about them to Ennis, and presents Lureen herself in just one episode, the phone call Ennis makes to her when he learns Jack is dead. The depiction of the Newsomes and of Jack's relationships with them is the largest addition that the filmmakers provide, and, as with almost all their work, it respects and enhances the story. Jack becomes involved with Lureen for a variety of reasons, but intense sexual and emotional attraction aren't among them. Rodeoing in Texas, he's broke and lonely, unable to find a way to meet a man like Ennis; Lureen pursues him, and he's flattered and partly interested because she has money. Jack isn't motivated by the same degree of fear that causes Ennis to marry, but his experience with Lureen and her family also illustrates some of the problems encountered by sexually different men who pass for straight and wind up having to live more closely with straight people than they really want. Jack isn't effeminate in any way, but there's a gentleness and openness about him which contrast with the model of masculinity that dominated American culture at the time, and that still continues to be dominant in business, politics, and just about everywhere else, which defines a "real" man as unemotional and uncompromising. Fortunately, partly as a result of feminist critiques of traditional arrangements of gender and power, some straight men have become more open to expressing and sharing emotion, though most still have a long way to go. Some sexually different men find that qualities like those that set Jack apart are among the subtle elements suggesting possible sexual difference that are registered by their "gaydar," and some also know that such qualities often may attract straight women. Many women understandably find the emotional limitations of many straight men hard to take, and may find sexually different men more appealing because some of them are less closed emotionally than most straight men; it's plausible that this would be a factor in Lureen's pursuit of Jack. But the open expression of feeling by other men frequently makes many straight men uneasy and sometimes hostile, as is shown in their responses to Jack. This is evident in the story in Jack's father's treatment of him, and it's developed in the film in the attitudes of some of the straight men he encounters on the rodeo circuit and some who do business with the Newsomes' farm machinery operation, who react with various degrees of distrust and hostility. In the film, as Jack discovers after marrying Lureen, it affects every interaction he has with his father-in-law, making the relationship intolerable.

As he's presented in the film, L. D. Newsome is, as the screenwriters put it, plain and simple, a "prick."[48] He embodies a form of masculinity that everyone in the United States knows all too well, though he exemplifies a peculiarly Texan form of it. He's completely self-centered, interacting with the people around him entirely in terms of what they can or can't do for him. Their needs and feelings are invisible to him since his only concern is how they relate to his interests. And, because he's successful in his farm machinery business, those interests are substantial, so he's used to having a lot of people serve them, especially his family. The actor who plays him, Graham Beckel, effectively captures the regional qualities of the type: L.D. isn't interested in anyone else but L.D., and is as loud and brash as he can be in letting everybody know it. Appropriately, he's a big, beefy slab of a man who acts like he's used to steamrolling his way to whatever he wants. L.D. adores Lureen, who's his only child, but it's the kind of possessive love some fathers feel for a daughter who's Daddy's Girl. He obviously gives her whatever she wants, but he expects a lot in return, particularly that even as an adult and even after getting married she'll stay tied to him and always put him first. His relationship with his wife, Fayette (played by Mary Liboiron), parallels that with Lureen; she's well taken care of, but clearly her main job is taking care of him. Both women focus their attention on him, his business, his concerns; in an unsettling way, men like L.D. almost relate to their daughters as if they were additional wives, expecting daughter and wife to work together to serve him. Possessive fathers often have difficulty adjusting if their daughters marry, and in this particular case, since there's no son, it's especially problematic when another man comes into what almost functions as L.D.'s harem. Any man who married Lureen would find it an awkward situation, since marrying Daddy's Girl also means, in a way, marrying Daddy, but for Jack, given his own experience of abuse with his father, and his gentle, open personality, life with L.D. is an ordeal indeed.

After the first scenes showing Lureen and Jack at the rodeo, in the bar, and in the backseat of the T-bird, which stress how her glamour, money, and attention attract him and lead to their marriage, the film presents a scene right after the birth of their son Bobby, which shows just what Jack's gotten himself roped into. In their claustrophobic pink bedroom with its frilly curtains, knick-knacks, and matching pink Princess telephone, Lureen lies in bed happily

holding little Bobby. L.D. and Fayette crowd into the room, L.D. booming
that they've got a surprise for her. Fayette, done to a turn with her lacquered
beehive hairdo piled high, explains that they've got 120 cans of formula for
her, and then looks at her husband and asks where he put them. L.D.'s response makes Jack's place in the family hierarchy clear: "Oh hell, backseat a
the car where I left em. Rodeo can get em." No request, no politeness, not
even a direct statement to Jack, much less any recognition that Jack even has
a name—L.D. just tosses the car keys in "Rodeo's" direction and expects him
to do his bidding, and then sits himself down in Jack's place on the marital
bed to cuddle Lureen and Bobby, complimenting his daughter on her accomplishment: "Good job little girl! He's the spittin image of his grandpa." As if
this demonstration that L.D. evaluates everything in terms of its relationship
to himself weren't enough, he then turns to the baby's father, demanding that
he agree that the baby's the spitting image of his grandfather. L.D.'s ego is so
aggressive that it requires that Jack virtually deny his own paternal role, and
subordinate himself entirely, as a mere instrument of L.D.'s power in the
Newsome dynasty. In a sultan's harem, no other men except eunuchs were
tolerated, and if L.D. doesn't take it quite that far, he certainly won't tolerate
any hint of equality in terms of Jack's status. Like John C. Twist, L.D. has the
"hard need"[49] to be the "stud duck in the pond."[50] And interestingly, L.D.'s
gesture of tossing the car keys at Jack exactly parallels Aguirre's with the
watch in the episode in the Farm and Ranch Employment trailer at the start
of the film: as the screenwriters note, Aguirre sees that Ennis doesn't own a
watch, and will need one to meet the supply truck every week, and so he
tosses him a cheap watch "as if he's not worth the reach."[51] Lureen, of course,
knows and likes her place as Daddy's Girl, and gives Jack a sweet, helpless
look during Daddy's performance, as if to say, "What can we do? That's just
the way it is!" It's no surprise that the next episode in the film that relates to
Jack shows Ennis receiving Jack's first postcard, proposing their reunion. For
Jack, the experiment of life as a married man doesn't go well from the start.
He has a degree of economic security, but it's clearly dependent on keeping
his mouth shut around L.D. In the story, Jack continues to earn a living as a
rodeo rider for a time after getting married, though in the film it appears that
he starts working for L.D. quite soon after; in any case, eventually Jack becomes a salesman for L.D., and so he has to keep on L.D.'s good side. Lureen
has the kind of socially although not literally incestuous relationship with her
father that means that L.D., aided by Fayette, constantly mediates everything
the young couple does, assuming a proprietary attitude, since Lureen is
Daddy's Girl and Jack becomes Daddy's employee. Given that Jack's
strongest sexual feelings aren't for women to begin with, and then adding the
stifling atmosphere of his marriage, Jack's nostalgia for Ennis and for the

freedom, companionship, and love they shared on Brokeback Mountain makes him take the gamble of writing to Ennis to propose he stop by when he goes through Riverton, despite the bitter disappointment of the end of their relationship four years before. In the circumstances of Jack's life in Childress, it's easy to imagine his excitement when he receives Ennis's immediate reply: "you bet."[52]

Anne Hathaway gets Lureen just right, endowing her with the confidence and assertiveness of a girl who's always been given just what she wants, and who knows just how to ensure that she'll continue to get it, always being compliant to her Daddy's wishes. Her classically pretty face is striking, but as the film proceeds, in keeping with the customs defining feminine beauty in L.D.'s world, she adds more and more make-up, and her brown hair turns lighter, then gold, then platinum blonde, and keeps getting bigger and bigger. When we first see her, she's in a flashy, expensive red-white-and-black outfit for barrel-racing, but she's clearly an indoor girl rather than an outdoor girl at heart, and in the later scenes, which show her doing desk work for her father's business and socializing, she's immaculately and ostentatiously dressed, and covered with jewelry. She wears so many rings, and they're so big, that it's hard to imagine how she moves her fingers to do Daddy's accounts or cook the Thanksgiving turkey. Where Michelle Williams has a sweet, soft, girlish beauty that contrasts painfully with the bitterness and anger her character increasingly projects as the film progresses, Anne Hathaway's elegant features seem to become harder and more mask-like as Lureen compensates for aging by putting on more make-up. Hathaway uses her voice brilliantly, catching the accent of the Panhandle, sounding bright and lively at the start, but modulating it to indicate Lureen's growing alienation from Jack, so that it becomes harder and sharper in the scenes depicting their disagreements. By the end, in the awful phone conversation that indirectly tells Ennis that Jack has been beaten to death, the little Texas voice is, just as Proulx describes it, as "cold as snow."[53]

The additions provided by the filmmakers give Jack more than adequate reason for being ready not just to try to restart his relationship with Ennis, but, once they get together again, to go ahead and invite him to share his dream of ranching together. In both versions, Jack explains to Ennis that what makes the plan feasible is that L.D. dislikes him so much that he'd likely be willing to pay Jack off to get lost. This corresponds with the screenwriters' insights into L.D.'s character, particularly his concern to get a grandchild who's his "spittin image" in order to carry on his family, which means that from his perspective, Jack's become superfluous once he's fulfilled this purpose. Apparently what Jack felt for Lureen has diminished considerably by the time he sees Ennis again, partly because of the familial strings attached to the relationship.

Given that L.D. is the main man in Lureen's life, she'd probably acquiesce to the arrangement Jack proposes to Ennis. As Jack says in the story, though he cares about his son, he never was especially interested in having children himself, and so he'd be able to let Lureen and her family keep custody of Bobby if it came to that. The money from L.D. would make it possible for Jack and Ennis to move up to Jack's parents' ranch in Lightning Flat, put John C. Twist in his place, build a cabin of their own, and then whip the ranch into shape as a "little cow and calf operation."[54] While Jack doesn't say so in either version, given his warm personality it's likely he'd be glad to have Ennis's daughters visit with them if they lived together. It's not opposition from Lureen or her family that prevents the plan from working, but Ennis's own fear and shame, as well as his commitment to his little girls; even if Jack were to welcome them visiting, Ennis probably would be afraid that trying to arrange this would mean conflict with Alma and lead to exposure. Ennis rejects Jack's invitation, and after a few days together in the mountains, Jack has to retreat to Childress and put up with the Newsomes until the next time he can get away to Wyoming and be with Ennis.

In the film, right after the episode of the first reunion between Jack and Ennis, we see what sort of a life this means for Jack. As with Ennis and Alma, the sexual and emotional connection between Jack and Lureen isn't strong enough to override and compensate for the constant difficulties of daily life, especially in the suffocating little world that's run by L. D. Newsome. In the scene at the farm machinery business when the two sour old farmers look out the office window at Jack as he competently and entertainingly demonstrates a huge tractor, and dismiss him as a "piss-ant," Lureen sits working at the desk in front of them, looking pained by what they say, but says nothing to challenge them. After all, it'd be bad for Daddy's business, and the two men may be Daddy's friends—in any case, they're a lot like him. And it may be, given that she's a product of a culture that produces such men, and has been raised by one, that she shares their judgment. Where she once was attracted to Jack's boyish playfulness, now, surrounded by men like Daddy, she may be disappointed in Jack, and may wish she'd married a man who was more like L.D. The tension between her and Jack becomes overt in the next scene that shows them together, in which Lureen, as usual, is hard at work at a desk, this time in the plush office in their home, with a grim-looking amateur portrait of L.D. directly above, as if supervising both his daughter and her husband. Getting ready for a trip to Wyoming to "fish" with Ennis, Jack can't find his parka, and Lureen is too focused on her accounting to pay much attention. Though there's no indication that she's guessed that Jack loves Ennis, she clearly resents the time Jack takes to be with him, complaining that Jack always goes up to Wyoming, asking why Ennis can't come down to Texas, and reminding Jack that she and Daddy need him to demonstrate the new combines that are coming in. Jack keeps looking, mentioning the parka again, to which Lureen snaps that she doesn't have it and then criticizes him by criticizing their son, telling him he's worse than Bobby when it comes to losing things. This leads to more conflict, about the fact that Bobby is dyslexic and needs a tutor, and that Lureen hasn't helped Jack in persuading the school to get him one. Lureen seems to have become so involved in helping run Daddy's business that it comes before both her husband and her son. In contrast to Ennis and Alma in the parallel scene, Jack and Lureen kiss goodbye, but it's clear that, as Jack says to Ennis later, as far as Jack's marriage to Lureen goes, "we could do it over the phone."

Jack finally resolves the tension with his father-in-law in an episode at Thanksgiving set in the mid 1970s, created by the filmmakers as a parallel with the Thanksgiving dinner at the grocer's house at which Ennis argues with Alma. The dinner scene in the garish purple, white, and gold dining room at Jack and Lureen's house in Childress starts with L.D., as usual, making it clear to everyone that he expects to be in charge, even though he's a guest. Jack, seated at the head of the table, gets up to start carving the turkey that Lureen has prepared, when L.D. takes the carving knife away from him, telling him the "stud duck" does the carving, to which Jack graciously acquiesces. With their usual insight and respect for Proulx's text, the screenwriters have taken the telling barnyard phrase that Proulx has Ennis think of to describe the petty aggressiveness of John C. Twist, and have given it to L.D. as his own obnoxious title for himself. Their point's a good one: both men always think that they have to be the "stud duck," as indeed is the case for most of the other straight men in the film, including Aguirre and the farmers in the farm equipment office, and undoubtedly Ennis's father. The type of man who perceives every other man as a rival, who sees compromise as weakness, who has no sense of humor about himself, who can't take no for an answer, who always has to be right, is a type that America produces in great abundance, in business, in politics, in the West, in the East—and, at the moment, that America has in the White House. It's no wonder John Wayne still is a hero to men like this, thirty years after his death. Such men can't stand other men who don't care about being the "stud duck," seeing their lack of concern with competition and aggression as a sign of being "less than a man." Men who are gentle, or playful, or humorous, especially about themselves, as Jack is, are suspect, and men who love other men aren't men at all.

The screenwriters make the question of what it is to be a man into the spark that sets off Jack's confrontation with L.D. As the family begins to eat Lureen's Thanksgiving dinner, Bobby's attention is fixed on the football game on the big console TV in the living room; Lureen admonishes him, telling him to eat his dinner or she'll have to turn off the TV, and Jack seconds her, and then walks over and turns it off. L.D. overrides them both, lumbering across the fake tiger-skin rug to the TV, and telling his daughter/employee that if she wants her son to grow up to be a man, she ought to let him watch football. This last pronouncement on normative gender behavior clearly is aimed right at Jack, implicitly challenging him for having collaborated with a woman in denying the boy the salutary, masculinizing influence of football, and questioning Jack's own masculinity. Not only has L.D. appropriated the patriarchal position of host from Jack in Jack's own home, but now he's challenged Jack's place in relation to his son and his wife, and indeed has almost said right out that he isn't enough of a man. This finally does it for Jack, and he turns the TV off again, and then, as L.D. rises to turn it back on, stops him in his tracks, ordering the "old son of a bitch" to sit down and respect the fact that it's Jack's house and Jack's child, and that L.D.'s a guest, and threatening to knock his "ignorant ass into next week . . .!" Fayette and Bobby freeze, Lureen gives a faint smile, as if this is what she's wanted from Jack for a long time, and L.D. silently lurches back to his seat, stunned and confused, looking like a big balloon that's lost most of its hot air. Jack pauses for a minute, hand over brow, then rises and commences the supposedly archetypically masculine task of carving the turkey, since he's finally knocked L.D. off his perch. The stud duck may not be a dead duck yet, but now he's sure a lame duck. The acting in the scene is superb, and Gyllenhaal's gesture at the end, covering his eyes for a moment before taking over the carving, eloquently sums up Jack's situation: he's a different kind of man from all the L.D.'s, and yet if he has to, he can do what's necessary to compete with them, but why should he even have to? Jack puts L.D. in his place, and makes it clear that he can beat the old man at his own game, but ultimately it's not the game that Jack wants to play. He's been a bull rider, but it's also likely that one reason rodeo attracted him was the companionship it provided with other men. Just competing with men, fighting with men, trying to become stud duck, isn't what Jack wants; he'd rather make a life with another man as equals, as companions, as lovers, supporting each other, welcoming the other's strengths and compensating for his weaknesses and having the other welcome and compensate for his own. By reducing love between men to sex, homophobes completely miss the real point, for many men who love men, which isn't just the need for sex but the need for intimacy and equality with another man. This is the kind of friendship Jack briefly had with Ennis on Brokeback Mountain, and that he keeps hoping Ennis will be brave enough to try to have again. But being in L.D.'s world, even if he does beat L.D., isn't what Jack wants at all.

Though Lureen likes what she sees when Jack finally lets L.D. have what he deserves, she's fated to continue to be disappointed, since Jack isn't the kind of man her father is, doesn't want to be, and isn't interested in replacing him. When they met, she was attracted to Jack physically and found him charming, but he can't become something he's not. Many straight men and women may expect a man to behave like L.D., constantly trying to best other men, but that's just not what some men want. As with Alma and Ennis, Lureen never can understand what it is that Jack needs, and so never really knows or appreciates him for who he is. In contrast, for all their struggles with each other, Ennis and Jack know each other, and appreciate each other, and complement each other; Jack's playfulness opens Ennis up, and Jack needs Ennis's steadiness. If they could be together, they'd function much better as a couple than either man does with his wife. Trying to pass makes men like Jack and Ennis try to be what they aren't, depriving them of the kind of closeness to a man that they need, making them get involved with women and try to provide what they can't and shouldn't have to, and so disappointing and hurting everybody. Passing silences and isolates men like Jack and Ennis and forces them to try to create intimacy in opposite-sex relationships where it can't really happen, and leaves the women they marry confused, frustrated, and unhappy. Neither husband ever can tell his wife who he really is, and neither wife ever can really know her husband. Homophobia makes honest relationships between Jack and Lureen and between Ennis and Alma impossible.

~

The impact on both Alma and Lureen of being involved in a cover marriage is similar. Each gradually realizes that something's fundamentally wrong between her and her husband, but even though the issue becomes painfully clear to Alma, and remains obscure to Lureen for a longer time, in both cases the problems remain unspoken and unresolved, leading to chronic frustration and disappointment, while of different degrees. The two wives also are victims of homophobia. Neither husband is at fault; both are up against something so much bigger than they are that they have no idea how to deal with it, and neither wife has any guidance or support either. American culture teaches us that marriages should be founded on love, and that love between husband and wife can overcome many of the hardest challenges that life presents, but it's impossible for a wife ever to know and love a husband who can't be honest with her because he's trying to pass for straight. Fortunately for Alma, she realizes that the problems in her marriage don't really have to do with her, though unfortunately she never is able to understand Ennis's experience and perspective, or to accept and forgive, much less to offer him any support. She has the strength and determination to get out of the marriage, and sees that the grocer can offer her what Ennis can't. Lureen doesn't find a similar alternative, but she continues to put her energy into her Daddy's business, becoming a successful businesswoman and taking over the enterprise after L.D.'s death.

Each woman, fortunately, is able to cope with and overcome the limitations imposed on her life by a marriage that never should have happened in the first place.

For all the troubles they face, however, it needs to be recognized that both Alma and Lureen have a degree of social support that neither Ennis or Jack ever can have. Though certainly Alma may have faced some criticism for not staying with Ennis and "trying to make their marriage work for the sake of the children," perhaps particularly from the "fire-and-brimstone crowd" at her church, and in fact we're never told the rationale that she uses for the divorce, still a woman in her situation wouldn't be isolated and ostracized the way Ennis would be if the real reasons for the divorce became known. Alma goes from her marriage with Ennis directly into a relationship that's completely socially acceptable, a marriage with a respected, prosperous heterosexual man who gives her emotional support, financial security, a home, and more children. Ennis, in contrast, is left in constant fear that the divorce, and especially Alma's anger, will lead to the exposure of his sexual difference and the destruction of what little identity and status he has in the community. And how totally different Ennis's experience would have been from Alma's if, following the divorce, he had had the courage to take up Jack's offer and the two men had started living together, particularly in Riverton! Jack's dream probably wouldn't be as completely unworkable as fear causes Ennis to believe, especially if they moved away, but endemic homophobic hostility still would make it much harder to do, then or now, than the transition Alma makes to her marriage with the grocer. Similarly, while Lureen's marriage to Jack is a failure, and while it may even be that it becomes known that he leaves her for a relationship with the ranch neighbor, Randall Malone, and that this may be the cause of Jack's murder, still, she consistently has the support and money and prestige of her family. If there were a scandal in the community surrounding the end of her marriage and Jack's subsequent murder, all the blame would be put on him, and she'd receive sympathy from everyone as the innocent victim of a deceitful, wayward man who got what he deserved. Whatever obstacles they face, both women still have the protection of heterosexual identity, perhaps the most fundamental advantage accorded to the majority in a homophobic society, though it's almost completely invisible to any but the most thoughtful members of the straight majority. Straight people simply take for granted the status and privilege of being perceived as straight, and can't even begin to imagine the obstacles and threats that continually face sexual minority people who are out, particularly if they're visible to others by being in committed relationships with same-sex partners. Just in the process of doing the business of ordinary daily life, members of same-sex couples necessarily are obliged to reveal the fact of their domestic relationship with another person of the same sex, potentially exposing themselves and those they love to discrimination, harassment, and physical attack. In *Brokeback Mountain* neither Alma or Lureen has to face the isolation and fear that are the defining factors in the lives of their husbands, neither must continually hide who she is or the relationship she cares most about for fear of being socially exiled and becoming the target of violence.

JACK AND ENNIS

In the story and the film, the limitations Ennis and Jack face in their marriages are in total contrast to the power of the connection they feel when they have their reunion in 1967; being in each other's presence once more, the two men are overcome with a degree of physical and emotional excitement that's hard to control. Ledger and Gyllenhaal accurately convey Proulx's presentation of the awkward moment at the apartment door when Ennis introduces Jack to Alma, Ennis barely able to get his breath, and Jack nervously struggling to restrain what he feels. As the men stand next to each other talking about their children and trying to maintain the fiction of ordinary friendship, Proulx notes that when Jack's hand chances to graze against Ennis's, it's like "electrical current snapped"[55] between them. It's the kind of attraction that doesn't come often in life, but people who've felt it never forget it, and will recognize what's being depicted. To call it a feeling or a thought doesn't convey it at all—it's an intense attraction that involves the body, the mind, the heart, every part of a person's being. It's so strong that it's difficult to hide it or to keep it within the bounds of social convention; trying to do so is hard enough for straight people who feel it, but even harder for sexually different people, given that the society is ready to punish same-sex attraction if it becomes visible. It's a kind of passion that's almost unbearable if you feel it for another person and it isn't returned, but if two people feel it for each other and can express it and share it, it can become a bond stronger than anything else.

In the story, rather than presenting a series of episodes depicting the periodic reunions of the two men, as the filmmakers choose to do, Proulx briefly summarizes Jack and Ennis's experiences with each other over the years in a paragraph that then introduces an extended account of their last trip, in May 1983, which shows the pleasure they continue to take in each other's company. As she explains, for sixteen years, from 1967 to 1983, the men make several trips together a year into the mountain wildernesses that ring the western two-thirds of Wyoming. She lists the ranges of mountains, the Big Horns, Medicine Bows, Gallatins, Absarokas, Granites, Owl Creeks, the Bridger-Teton Range, the Freezeouts, Shirleys, Ferrises, Rattlesnakes, Salt Rivers,

Wind Rivers, Sierra Madres, Gros Ventres, Washakies, and Laramies. For a reader who doesn't know Wyoming, these names alone, some taken from the languages of the Native American inhabitants, some commemorating white men who promoted Westward expansion, and many noting natural features as well as the wild animals that live there, give a sense of the variety of the landscape, but to anyone who's been to Wyoming or who's lived there they evoke vivid memories of the immensity of the land and sky and the stark, dramatic beauty of the different mountains.

Proulx's depiction of their last trip, up to a group of unnamed little icy mountain lakes near the Hail Strew River drainage, indicates the balance of sexual attraction and emotional interdependence that's kept Ennis and Jack coming back together over the years. As she shows in describing the first day of the trip, they're easy and comfortable together, working well with each other in everything that's involved in packing into the mountains. Although it's a fine spring day full of the scents of conifers in the warm sun, the trail still is drifted with wet snow, so they leave it and ride through the woods, talking about the chance of a storm as they lead their horses. Ennis looks at the sky for storm clouds, but the sky's so clear and blue that Jack says he might "drown looking up."[56] They ride on during the afternoon, coming back to the trail, surprising a bear, and descend to the river, where they make camp and picket their horses without talking much, and then Jack opens a bottle of whiskey, takes a big drink and a long breath, and remarks "'That's one a the two things I need right now,'"[57] and caps it and tosses it to Ennis. As Proulx presents it, theirs is the kind of companionship in which two people enjoy being together and doing things together and know each other so well that few words are required. Packing up, riding together, finding their way, sharing their enjoyment of what they see, protecting each other, setting up camp, relaxing and drinking together, easily and comfortably lead to having sex and then to sleeping close to each other in the tent. There's no anxiety to entertain or please the other, simply shared happiness in each other's company. In a homophobic society, it's ironic that the only way two men who love each other can spend their days and nights together without causing any suspicion is in the quintessentially masculine activity of packing into the wilderness. In fact, this companionship actually reinforces the sense others have of the masculinity of men who do these things, while at the same time in the case of Ennis and Jack—and plenty of other men—it's also a way for them to be together to share their love for each other.

As Proulx describes it, this pattern of intimacy continues throughout the last trip, only interrupted, as it has been before, by the disappointment Jack feels because Ennis is afraid to make it permanent. Still, in contrast to their relationships with their wives, their intense connection works against the tension between them, drawing them back together again. On the evening of their third day in the mountains they have a talk by the fire while sharing a joint; Ennis mentions his relationship with the waitress in Riverton, leading Jack to tell what probably is a lie about having a relationship with a rancher's wife and then to express his frustration with the continuing separation that Ennis demands and to tell him how much he misses him when they're apart. While Ennis says nothing in reply, the conflict between them is resolved, at least for the moment, by physical affection and desire, as he puts his arm around Jack and pulls him close, and Jack slides his hand between Ennis's legs, and they lie together and talk and then make love on the ground by the fire. Their love for each other isn't able to overcome Ennis's fear or Jack's frustration, but over the years it's strong enough to keep them together. Even their argument at the end of the trip, though it's the worst Proulx describes between them and it leads Jack to try to have a relationship with another man, ends with Ennis and Jack trying hard to be reconciled with each other.

The film, unlike the story, is structured in alternating episodes, showing Ennis's life with Alma and Jack's life with Lureen, punctuated by the trips the men take together into the mountains. Whenever they meet, it's with a degree of excitement and pleasure in each other's company and a sense of the freedom to express their love that they find in nature that are in total contrast to the stressful routine of their relationships with their wives. The screenwriters' concern to emphasize this contrast probably accounts for a substantial difference between the depiction of the 1967 reunion in the story and its presentation in the movie; whereas Proulx only describes Ennis and Jack when they meet at the apartment and then as they lie in bed together at the motel, the filmmakers extend the episode, also showing the trip the men take together over the next few days and moving a portion of the dialogue that occurs at the motel in the story to a scene by their campfire in the mountains. This change allows the creation of a particularly powerful visual contrast between the depiction of their lives with Alma and Lureen and their experience with each other. With only a few exceptions at the start of Ennis's relationship with Alma and Jack's relationship with Lureen, the scenes showing their marriages are set entirely indoors. We see Ennis and Alma in the dingy kitchen and dimly lit bedroom of their line cabin, in the cramped apartment over the laundromat, and in the harsh glare of the fluorescent lights of the grocery store; Jack and Lureen are shown in the smoky bar where she "ropes him in" and in the over-decorated pink bedroom where she shows off the baby to L.D. The episode of the trip into the mountains liberates Jack and Ennis as well as the viewer from these small, ugly rooms and from the confining heterosexual relationships that take place in them, returning once again to the wide open spaces of the Wyoming wilderness.

After leaving Alma at the apartment Ennis and Jack drive into the mountains under a brilliant blue sky, park Jack's truck on a high point over a glittering river, strip their clothes, and run and jump into the water below. With its bright light, clear color, and sense of space, this episode directly recalls the scenes on Brokeback Mountain. Just as the scenes on Brokeback contrast with those that precede them in Signal, set in the dark, dirty interior of Aguirre's trailer and the smoky bar where Jack and Ennis first talk, the scenes in which the men swim naked contrast with those in which they're confined indoors with their wives. Their leap into the pure cold water is like a baptism back into the innocence and exuberance that they felt together four years earlier. The mood of liberation is emphasized by the gentle, lyrical music, which is associated with the companionship of Ennis and Jack throughout the film.

The scene that follows, as the men sit at evening by their campfire near a rushing river, directly recalls the Edenic quality of their summer together on Brokeback, the closeness of their experience there to paradise; as they sit together, Ennis looks up at the stars, and Jack playfully asks if he sees anything interesting up in Heaven. Ennis's reply indicates the delight he takes in being with Jack again: he smiles and says that he was sending up a "prayer a thanks" that Jack forgot his harmonica, recalling their fond teasing and music-making throughout the summer they shared. But as will happen over and over between them, this moment of shared joy raises the question, for Jack, of why it can't be permanent. Jack dares to say that it could always be like this, proposing that they start a little cow-and-calf operation together. Ennis immediately rejects the plan because both men already have their lives with their wives and children, which causes Jack to challenge Ennis, asking if what Ennis and Alma have really is a life. Ennis rightly defends Alma, since none of it's her fault, and the situation hurts her too, but Jack's correct, a cover marriage with years and years of the kinds of disappointments and frustrations he glimpsed when he saw Alma and Ennis at their apartment *isn't* a life, for either the man or the woman. He has no examples to guide him and no language to express his ideas, but Jack's comment suggests his awareness that trying to pass for straight will hurt everyone, including Alma and Lureen and the children. It would be better for them all to confront the problem, end the marriages, and free themselves and their wives. But, as Ennis says, the "bottom line" is his terror at the possibility of homophobic violence, and he recounts the horrific story of Earl's murder. Once more, as four years before, they're exiled from the garden, not simply by the external force of society's hatred, but by the power of that hatred in Ennis's own mind, checking the love that he feels. Ennis rejects Jack's invitation in the very place where they feel most free to love. By restructuring Jack and Ennis's reunion and depicting them not only in the motel but also by their campfire next to the river, the film emphasizes the fact that even in the wilderness they can't escape the fear and shame that Ennis feels.

As it is throughout the film, the acting in this episode is perceptive and powerful. At the start, during the playful joking about the harmonica, Ledger presents Ennis as lying back, relaxed and smiling. Gyllenhaal leans forward, looking directly at him as he presents Jack's invitation; Ledger's expression hardens as he refuses, and he sits up, putting on his hat, becoming more physically closed and turning his face away as he speaks. Yet at the same time he moves closer, sitting so near to Gyllenhaal that he's in easy reach as Gyllenhaal extends his hand and strokes his ear, suggesting Jack's effort to implore his friend not to reject his hope of living together. Ledger's use of his body in this scene perfectly indicates the ambivalence that Ennis feels, and that constantly tantalizes and frustrates Jack.

Despite the power of the episode of the first reunion as the filmmakers construct it, and the fact that Proulx's depiction of it, set only at the motel, lacks the dramatic contrast between the liberating open space of the mountain wilderness and Ennis's rejection of Jack's dream of living together, her account includes many significant elements that are lacking in the film's version of the episode. As the filmmakers present it, the dialogue between Ennis and Jack at the motel and in the mountains omits several of the most important things they say in the story, including their frank discussion of the pleasures of anal intercourse; Ennis's detailed account of his questioning of his sexuality and of the fact that, though married to Alma, he masturbates over and over thinking of Jack; his realization that rejecting Jack was what made him suddenly feel so physically sick after they parted; and his regret that he made the mistake of letting Jack out of his sights. By eliminating these parts of the conversation, the film reduces the audience's understanding of Ennis, making him seem more confused about his sexuality and less aware that he shouldn't have rejected the connection he and Jack made on Brokeback. The film also cuts out what Ennis tells Jack about the reasons for the punch, his explanation of how his experience with K.E. had taught him that there's "'nothin like hurtin somebody to make him hear good.'"[58] Also gone is the moment, when they're discussing what to do, when Jack says that some people go to cities like Denver, a solution that neither of them wants because it means exile from the country life that they love. Missing, too, is the moment when Jack's forced to beg Ennis to take a couple of days off with him in the mountains to "give [him] somethin a go on,"[59] which anticipates Jack's struggles with Ennis over the coming years. As it's presented in the film, the reunion episode is very strong, especially in terms of the moving acting and the contrast between the freedom suggested by the landscape and Ennis's inability to fully accept their love, but it does lack many of the powerful insights Proulx includes in it.

In the film, the first reunion is followed by a series of episodes that reinforce a sense of the liberation the men feel from the limitations of their cover marriages when they're able to be together in the mountains. In this structural pattern, the filmmakers intensify the connection of the narrative to the tradition of homoerotic pastoral, particularly as developed by advocates of male love such as Whitman, who present nature as offering the freedom that society denies, allowing men to express their love for each other. After several episodes that show the growing coldness between Alma and Ennis and the tension between Jack and Lureen, the film presents the first trip that Jack and Ennis take after their 1967 reunion, to the same campsite by the cliff next to the mountain river. Again, the wilderness with its lush trees, clear waters, and light-filled sky is in sharp contrast to the dreary kitchen where we've just seen Alma and the smoky office where we've just seen Lureen. The first scenes of the trip stress the rush of emotion the men feel at being able to be together, showing Jack waiting for Ennis at the camp he's already set up for them by the water; as he watches Ennis drive in, a smile fills Jack's face, and he excitedly shouts that Ennis is late, showing how eagerly he's anticipated being with his friend again. Ennis gets out of his truck and grins at Jack in return, and then, in a long shot, we see him walking into the campsite, telling Jack to look at what he's brought; though it's not fully audible, this is the scene in which the screenplay has him offer Jack the beans he's brought as a way of remembering their summer together on Brokeback. The episode continues with a depiction of the two of them riding along slowly together through sun and shadow in the woods by the riverside. As before, music is used throughout the episode, suggesting the happiness the men feel at being with each other again. Lyrical scenes of Jack and Ennis riding together are shown again at the start of the next depiction of one of their trips, set after the divorce, which culminates in their argument about whether Ennis might move to Texas. The riding scenes establish a contrast between the easy companionship that's possible between Jack and Ennis and the tension caused when Ennis's fears intrude. The film makes a similar contrast in its presentation of their final trip, which, as in the story, begins with a scene showing them sitting together at their campsite by a river at evening, sharing whiskey and a joint. The warm glow of the firelight creates a mood of intimacy directly echoing the firelit evening scene during the movie's depiction of their first camping trip together in 1967.

As the film presents the characters, although there's continued tension between Jack and Ennis over whether they can live together, every time they meet the joy they take in each other is affirmed. It's not just a matter of sexual attraction and sexual release as homophobic viewers and critics try to claim, but of pleasure in companionship, in being together as they ride through the mountains, do the daily tasks of setting up camp, cooking and cleaning up, eating, drinking, and sleeping together, always enjoying the sharing of each other's company. In keeping with the initiation of their love at Pentecost, the essence of their relationship is the profound communion that's possible between them. Even in the episode in the film when Jack surprises Ennis with the girls outside the cabin, having hoped the divorce meant that at last they could live together, despite the awkwardness of the situation the film stresses the intense happiness Ennis initially feels at seeing Jack, though he reluctantly rejects Jack's idea; as Jack jumps out of his truck, the screenwriters direct, "Ennis is surprised, puzzled as to why Jack is there, but is nonetheless—as always—thrilled to see him."[60] Throughout the movie's presentation of their trips together, it emphasizes the liberation that they feel in nature, where they're able to act in accordance with their own natures, contrasting this with the repression and frustration of the trap of life trying to pass by remaining within the confines of cover marriages.

The film's repeated use of riverside settings in the episodes in which the men are able to get together directly recalls its depiction of them on Brokeback; as was noted in the first chapter, during their summer on the mountain, both Ennis and Jack are shown in separate but parallel scenes, each of which depicts one of them as he washes in the clear water of the same stream, his thoughts on his absent friend. The river scenes that occur throughout the film indicate the vitality and purity of the passion that draws the men together, underlining the filmmakers' perception of it as a "force of nature." Yet because the flow of water suggests the continual passage of time, these scenes also indicate the temporary, transient aspect of the experience Jack and Ennis have together, the fact that there's "never enough time, never enough."[61]

Because of his intense love for Ennis, for many years Jack's able to put up with a life made up of extended separations, during which he does his best with Lureen and L.D., and waits and waits for the few weeks a year when he can be with Ennis and live the life that he had hoped that they always could have together. They get a week here, a week there, but not a life together. In twenty years, the amount of time that they can be with each other probably totals less than a year. Their periodic reunions in the mountains are idyllic, and are enough for Ennis and just barely enough for Jack, but even there, far from the problems of cover marriages, surveillance by straight people, and particularly the violent hostility of straight men, the force of homophobia always is present, and always makes Ennis curtail their time with each other.

Jack's situation of simultaneously being loved and rejected is a familiar one for many men who've loved another man who tries to pass; he wants to be with you, and loves you passionately when you're together, but also is ashamed of your relationship, fears being seen with you in public, lies about who you are to others, even avoids you or ignores you when it's possible that others may see. Few straight people have enough empathy for sexual minorities to be able to imagine or understand what this situation is like; perhaps the only analogy they can grasp is with a heterosexual relationship between a white person and a person of color, or between a Christian and a Jew, in which prejudice causes the person from the dominant group to fear and disavow intimacy with the person they love because of the fear of racial or religious prejudice. Straight people usually can just assume that society will affirm their relationship; members of sexual minorities who struggle to pass may find that the very person who loves them also is ashamed of them and denies them. Jack's experience shows how passing for straight not only can damage the lives of straight women who become involved in cover marriages with men who desire men, but also can hurt the other men with whom men who pass become involved as well.

Jack's love for Ennis is the strongest thing he feels in his life, but Ennis, by refusing over and over to fully accept it, eventually forces Jack to seek what he needs elsewhere. This happens gradually, and indicates no fundamental change in Jack's feelings for Ennis, but rather that his frustration and despair cause him to try to find some substitute for what Ennis is afraid to give him. By structuring the narrative as it does, as a series of alternating episodes depicting the marriages of the two men and their relationship with each other, the film is able to chart the gradual but cumulative effect of Ennis's repeated rejections on Jack. The episode when the divorce has come through and Jack hurries to be with Ennis, only to be turned away the moment he arrives, marks an important shift in their relationship. With convincing and moving subtlety, Ledger and Gyllenhaal indicate Ennis's discomfort and the sudden, sickening reversal of Jack's expectations as described by the screenwriters. As Ossana and McMurtry explain, Ennis

> realizes . . . what's happened: Jack thinks, mistakenly, that Ennis has come round, that this is their chance, finally, to be together. The smile leaves Ennis's face. Rubs his jaw . . . takes a deep breath. Uncomfortable . . . Jack looks at Ennis . . . and the smile leaves his face, too. Realizes now that he's made a terrible mistake: turns pale . . . his body sags under the weight of disappointment. Humiliated, then devastated.[62]

As mentioned earlier, Ennis is unable to explain his actual reasons to Jack, and gives the weak excuse that he has to care for his little girls that weekend, but, as the neighbor's truck drives past, Jack understands the real cause of the rejection, and gets back into his truck and drives off, sick at heart and wiping away tears. Ennis may be able to get by, just having sexual intimacy a couple of times a year, but Jack can't, and so, instead of driving back to Childress, he goes on south to Mexico, where he at least can have the sexual fulfillment he's been denied, and have it in anonymity. There's no indication of any conscious racism on Jack's part, but in confining his sexual activity to Mexico, he engages in a long-established pattern in which structures of racism and poverty enable men who are white, whatever their sexual orientation, to find inexpensive, anonymous sexual satisfaction. In the scene in which Jack picks up a hustler in Juarez the plaintive song in the background perfectly fits the frustration Jack feels with Ennis. It's the Cuban songwriter Osvaldo Farres's "Quizas, Quizas, Quizas," in which the singer laments that he's always asking when, where, how, and the one he loves always replies perhaps, perhaps, perhaps.[63] Though Jack is nowhere near as fearful as Ennis, and loves him so much that he's willing to risk the hostility that they might incur if they ranched together, at this point he's cautious not to have any involvement with other men that anyone in Childress might learn about. Eventually his frustration and especially his yearning for the kind of companionship that Ennis has refused him become so strong that he's willing to take a greater risk, with fatal consequences.

The next episode in the film in which Ennis and Jack meet culminates in Jack's last serious effort to try to get Ennis to consider living together, his suggestion that Ennis deal with his fears by getting out of Riverton and moving to Texas. After several idyllic riding scenes, we see Jack and Ennis at their campsite in the evening, washing their dishes after supper. At first their conversation has its usual intimate humor, as Jack describes his wife's obsession with business, the way she punches in numbers on her adding machine with the intensity of a rabbit with a coyote on its tail, which gets a laugh from Ennis. But mention of Lureen leads Ennis to express his insecurity about being able to pass as a heterosexual man, asking whether Jack's sex life with her is "normal and all," and describing his fears that other people he encounters "suspect." As Gyllenhaal presents them, Jack's responses to this interrogation suggest that Jack's holding back the truth from Ennis: his assurance that everything's normal and Lureen has no suspicions about his sexuality sound evasive and he looks edgy and uncomfortable as he gives them. Then, after years of waiting, hoping, and repeatedly being disappointed, Jack again broaches his hope that Ennis may finally decide to live with him, gingerly making his suggestion that Ennis might want to get out and move to Texas. This time Ennis's response doesn't directly address his fear of homophobic violence, but focuses on the problem of his concern for his daughters, and the fact that it's not likely he could maintain any contact with them if it became known he was involved with another man. But he doesn't aim his frustration at the prejudices and laws that would cut him off from his children, but at Jack: "Texas? Sure, and maybe you can convince Alma to let you and Lureen adopt the girls, and then we can just live together herdin sheep, and it'll rain money from L. D. Newsome, and whiskey'll flow in the streams . . ." Ennis is right, given the society they live in; moving to Texas and living with Jack probably would lead to Alma using the court system to cut Ennis off from the girls, as it probably would lead the Newsomes to cut Jack off from his son. But because Ennis accepts the society's belief that he and Jack wouldn't deserve to have contact with their children if they lived together, he's not able to recognize the injustice of separating sexual minority people from their children. Unlike Jack, he's not able to resist the idea that there's something wrong with his sexuality, or to assert the right of men who desire men to have the kinds of lives they want. Ennis isn't enraged by those who'd mistreat him because of his sexuality, but at Jack, who represents that sexuality. He speaks with brutal scorn, even ridiculing their time together on Brokeback Mountain.

Deeply hurt by what Ennis says, Jack retreats, expressing his frustration at the way Ennis accepts his life as it is. But Ennis can't let it go, and keeps on attacking Jack, referring to him contemptuously in the third person: "Jack Fuckin Twist, he's got it all figured out, ain't he?" From being the most affectionate form of masculine endearment, stressing his intense sexual attraction to Jack, Ennis's emphatic way of saying Jack's name now becomes a brutal repudiation. Homophobia isn't only an external force that constrains the men, but is an internal one as well, interfering with Ennis's ability to love and damaging his relationship with Jack. Where Jack's ready to take the first step toward demanding that his society grant him the space to live his life as a man who loves another man, Ennis isn't. While neither the story or the film is overtly political in any obvious way, the difference between Jack and Ennis reflects the difference between those sexual minority people who've been willing to risk identifying themselves to fight for their rights, and those who've been so intimidated by the majority that they stay silent.

No scene then is offered in this episode in which Ennis makes up with Jack, and their argument apparently leads to Jack's first serious consideration of finding a way to compensate for the emotional limitations Ennis imposes on their relationship. Jack's coped with the lack of sexual fulfillment by buying the services of a hustler in Juarez, but now he's open to the possibility of trying to establish a serious sexual and emotional commitment with another man. He doesn't actively pursue this possibility, but when the prospect arises, the film suggests that he's willing to try it. We next see Jack with Lureen in a dance hall, at a benefit dance for the county children's home. Seated at their table are another couple, Randall and LaShawn Malone, who the dialogue indicates the Twists gave a ride when the Malones' pickup broke down. Lureen's bored, Jack's restless, LaShawn naively chatters about herself, and Randall—an entirely conventional ranch foreman, big, bearded, in cowboy hat and Western dress jacket—seems subtly attentive to Jack. The tension between Lureen and Jack is evident in her sarcastic comments about the lack of interest husbands have in dancing with their wives, and the sense that neither man may be particularly interested in his wife becomes clearer when the two men are seated outside the dance hall, talking as they wait for Lureen and LaShawn. Jack suggests his indifference to Lureen by asking Randall why a woman will powder her nose when she gets home from a party, before she goes to bed. Randall doesn't point out that it might be because the woman wants to be attractive to her husband, and is interested in more than just going to sleep; instead he jokes about LaShawn's talkativeness. Then, after a pause, he tells Jack his employer has a fishing cabin and suggests that they go there some weekend and drink and fish. Jack doesn't make the proposition, but when it comes, he seems interested, though at that moment the wives return, and we don't hear his reply to Randall. The film doesn't say so specifically, but Randall likely is the ranch neighbor that John C. Twist mentions to Ennis after Jack's murder, who Jack had told his father, in spring of 1983, he hoped to bring up to Lightning Flat with him to fix up the Twists' ranch. The relationship that appears to develop between Jack and Randall isn't so much a rejection of Ennis, as it's an affirmation of how much Jack needs the companionship of another man. He'd hoped that his profound connection with Ennis could lead to them having a life together, but after Ennis ridicules Jack's suggestion that he move to Texas, Jack finally begins to shift to the hope that a relationship with Randall might be a substitute.

Following the scene with the Malones, on the last trip Ennis and Jack take together, in the spring of 1983, as they talk and smoke and drink by the river in the evening, Jack seems to try one final time to find out if Ennis really is satisfied with his life as it is, and if maybe at last he'd want to be with Jack after all. The film follows the story fairly closely, but expands a bit on Proulx's account of their conversation, perceptively having Jack ask why Ennis hasn't married again, perhaps fishing for some sign that Ennis has reached the end of trying to pass for straight. But Ennis's reply is to tell Jack that he's been seeing Cassie, and then to ask about Jack's relationship with Lureen. Ennis still is committed to trying to pass for straight, even to Jack, and he makes it sound as if he's actively pursued Cassie, when in fact it's the other way round. Jack then tells Ennis that he's got something going with the wife of a rancher in Childress, joking that he might get shot by either Lureen or the husband, and they both laugh. Though neither version ever directly challenges the truth of what Jack says here, it's likely a lie, and what Jack's actually referring to is his relationship with Randall. His loneliness probably has led him to follow up on Randall's interest in him, and their involvement runs a much greater risk than the fictitious heterosexual affair Jack jokes about to

Ennis. In a Panhandle town like Childress, if it got out that two married men were having an affair there easily could be violent consequences. Think about the pain of Jack's situation: he's with the man he loves, who keeps him at a distance and tries to pass for straight, and who's just told him about his relationship with a woman. Jack's all but given up on trying to get Ennis to be with him, and he's so lonely that he's taken the risk of having an affair with a married man who's his neighbor, but he can't say any of this to the man he loves and feels closest to. So he tries to make it into a joke, although what he's doing with Randall can get him killed. The desperation Jack feels is evident in the profoundly honest admission he makes to Ennis next. Unlike Proulx, the screenwriters word it without metaphor or humor, and so that it directly addresses Ennis's fatalistic belief that you've just got to stand things that you can't fix. Jack pauses, and then sadly looks out across the river and says: "Tell you what . . . the truth is . . . sometimes I miss you so much I can hardly stand it." As in the slightly different version of this episode in the story, in the film the evening ends with Ennis expressing in his actions the physical and emotional tie to Jack that his fear and shame keep making him deny: the next scene shows the men sleeping together in their tent by the river, Ennis curled up against Jack, his arm around him.

The last trip culminates in a brutal argument that shows how deep the differences are between the ways Jack and Ennis deal with their sexuality. It starts over the fundamental problem between them, the limited time Ennis can allow them to have together. The episode is closely similar in both versions, though in a few places the screenwriters make the dialogue more explicit, to cover ideas conveyed by the narrative voice in the story. Because he knows how disappointing Jack finds it is to wait and wait until they can be together, Ennis has put off telling him that his work and his financial obligations to his girls mean that they can't meet in August, and that Jack will have to wait until November. The story, incidentally, includes the detail that Ennis now is working as a hired hand at a cow-and-calf operation—ironically, the kind of ranch Jack had hoped they might own together someday.

Jack's disappointed by being forced to wait yet again, and because it means another trip in cold weather, and says sometime they ought to go someplace warm, like Mexico. Ennis resists, still trying to persuade Jack to make a Wyoming trip in November. In frustration, Ennis asks, "'You got a better idea?'"[64] and Jack bitterly replies, "'I did once,'"[65] reminding his friend that for two decades Ennis's fear has made him reject the suggestion of living together. Ennis then angrily confronts Jack, demanding if he's been to Mexico; in the film, he adds "Cause I hear what they got in Mexico for boys like you," making the accusation even more explicit. Not only does Ennis expect Jack to be able to accept their relationship with the limitations he's always required, but now for the first time he attacks Jack for needing any sexual contact beyond that. This confrontation, and especially the phrase, "boys like you," finally makes it fully explicit that Ennis not only is afraid of being attacked by others because of his sexuality, but that he still refuses to see himself as a "queer," that he needs to maintain the fiction of his own heterosexuality, and that he's contemptuous and afraid of Jack because Jack doesn't. Ennis isn't only afraid of homophobia in others; his concern to continue to pass is the result of his own homophobic hatred of men who accept same-sex desire, including the man he loves.

Jack's reaction is defiant, demanding why his going to Mexico is a problem. In the story, Proulx makes it clear that, sadly enough, Jack always has been aware Ennis feels this way, and that he's always dreaded that Ennis will challenge him about being able to accept his sexuality more than Ennis can. When Ennis demands to know about Mexico, Proulx comments that Jack had been braced for this sort of hostile question from him for years, but that now it came unexpected.[66] As she's shown throughout the story, before this Jack's awareness of Ennis's homophobia and of Ennis's expectation that Jack should be able to settle for the little that Ennis will give him always has made Jack keep back any information about his sexual involvements with other men.

As noted before, neither version of *Brokeback Mountain* is political in any explicit sense, but Jack's retort to Ennis is implicitly so; like millions of members of sexual minorities over the last several decades, he's reached a point where he refuses to lie about who he is and is willing to assert his right to have a life that acknowledges his sexual identity. The cultural changes of the 1970s have reached Jack and Ennis, as they gradually did most rural Americans: their hair is longer, they have sideburns, Jack has a mustache, they share a joint, and it may be that some of the ideas and language of the movement for gay rights also would have reached them, though even if they had, Jack's fear of Ennis's own homophobia certainly would prevent discussion of them. There's no suggestion at all that Jack has developed any articulate political awareness, but like many sexual minority people, his personal experience has caused him to be fed up with things as they are. Jack's taken the most basic individual step that's been fundamental to all efforts to challenge homophobia in the past forty years: he's no longer willing to settle for a way of living that puts keeping his sexuality invisible before having what he wants. In this way, he's like all those people who've come to identify, to themselves and others, as sexually different—gay, lesbian, bisexual, transgender, intersex, and queer, in the current, redefined meaning of the word. Jack refuses to continue to hide that he's a man who desires men, and has the courage to take the risk of trying to build a life that meets his sexual and emotional needs, to live with another man despite the reactions this may cause. He misses Ennis so much he can hardly stand it, and unlike Ennis, he's realized that maybe you don't *have* to stand it, that maybe you *can* fix it.

Jack's defiance directly threatens Ennis. It may be that part of what motivates Ennis's furious reaction to it is jealousy of the fact that Jack needs more than Ennis will give, that Jack's been involved with other men, but Ennis's rage is mainly directed at Jack's refusal to hide who he is the way Ennis feels he has to: "'I got a say this to you one time, Jack, and I ain't foolin. What I don't know . . . all them things I don't know could get you killed if I should come to know them.'"[67] Jack's refusal to continue to try to pass, his acceptance of his sexuality, and his sense that he has a right to sexual and emotional fulfillment, are so disturbing to Ennis that he orders Jack to keep his needs hidden and threatens to kill him if he doesn't. To convey the seriousness of the threat, in the movie when Ennis mentions the "things" he doesn't want to know and that he'd kill Jack because of, he punctuates what he's saying with a violent shove against Jack's chest, and spits just after threatening him, emphasizing his disgust and anger. The homophobic violence that endangers their love isn't only external, it's within Ennis as well. Ennis could do to Jack what his father did to Earl. His love for Jack is distorted and damaged by the force of narcissistic homophobia. For Ennis, loving another man has to be reduced to being a part of his life that can be kept separate and hidden, confined to certain times and certain places by boundaries that prevent it from intruding on the awareness of others—and of Ennis himself—and contradicting his identity and status as a supposedly normal heterosexual man. The wilderness isn't only a place where they can be safe to love each other; it's a place where Ennis can be safe from the implications Jack represents about himself. Jack, in contrast, by accepting his own sexuality and trying to respect his own physical and emotional needs, and above all by urging Ennis to involve his life fully with him, threatens Ennis's need to believe that he's "'not no queer.'"[68] Just as the narcissistic homophobes in the society around them, such as their fathers, Aguirre, the rodeo clown and his friends, and L.D. and his, can't tolerate any evidence of male homosexuality and constantly try to eradicate it, Ennis can't stand what Jack's acceptance of his sexuality means about him.

Jack refuses to back down, to deny his sexuality or his right to a complete sexual and emotional life with a man. He confronts Ennis, saying "'Try this one . . . and *I'll* say it just one time . . .,'"[69] telling him that they could have had a good life together but that Ennis refused to do it, so "' . . . what we got now is Brokeback Mountain. Everything built on that. It's all we got, boy, fuckin all, so I hope you know that if you don't never know the rest.'"[70] Jack furiously tells Ennis that he ought to count the few times he's let Jack get together with him over nearly twenty years, and *then* to challenge Jack about going to Mexico to get what he needs, *then* to threaten to kill him. In frustration, Jack shouts, "'I'm not you, I can't make it on a couple a high-altitude fucks once or twice a year. You're too much for me, Ennis, you son of a whoreson bitch. I wish I knew how to quit you.'"[71] In the story, Proulx says that, hearing this, Ennis stands as if he's been shot through the heart, his face grimacing, eyes tight shut, and fists clenched, and then drops to his knees, causing Jack to think he's having a heart attack. The film, however, has Ennis continue to accuse Jack before he collapses, angrily blaming him for his loneliness and poverty, which emphasizes that Ennis can't acknowledge that his own effort to resist his sexuality is the force that's distorted his life. Then as Ennis drops to the ground, Jack desperately hugs him, Ennis resists but then returns the embrace, and they make the effort to reconcile themselves. As Proulx says, they somehow "torque"[72] things back almost to where they'd been, like straightening a coat hanger to open up a locked car, then bending it back to its former shape. What they've argued about isn't news, and there's "[n]othing ended, nothing begun, nothing resolved."[73]

This episode highlights the contrast between Ennis and Jack discussed above in chapter 3 in relation to the ideal of masculinity in Western fiction and film. The American model of masculinity has important political consequences for everyone, including sexual minorities, since it not only teaches men that they must deny and hide their emotions and their need for other people, but also teaches them to respond to the suffering that results from this denial and hiding, both for others and for themselves, with stoicism and silence. The traditional ideal of male gender behavior disempowers men, forcing them to accept things as they are. For Ennis, it's impossible to fully embrace the love he feels for Jack or to acknowledge the pain caused by denying that love. The ideal of being a man prevents him from saying who he really is and what he really needs. Many see it as a form of masculinity that asserts independence and self-reliance, but in fact it's the result of fear of admitting the inner life of emotion or recognizing that one needs others, since this could lead to being judged and found less than a man by other men. Though Ennis's father's long dead, he and all the other men like him control Ennis's life. The heroic American ideal of the cowboy supposedly is based on the principle of being your own man, but Ennis's life shows that it really can be a way of living that keeps a man under the domination of other men.

Jack, however, is a different kind of man. He's committed to many of the same aspects of masculinity that Ennis is, but he's willing to accept what he feels for Ennis, to acknowledge that he needs another person and that that person is a man, and to say it and act on it. He hasn't closed down and denied his emotions, but can express them directly, in words, in gestures, in anger, in tears, in playfulness, in love. Unlike Ennis, he refuses to be trapped into a life of trying to pass because he's afraid of other men. He knows the hostility of

men like his father, and Ennis's father, and Aguirre, and L.D., but he isn't going to live his life for them. Jack's behavior isn't political in an organized,
collective, practical way, but he's gained the consciousness that's fundamental to all political action: he's begun to acknowledge who he is in relation to
the structure of power in his society, and to resist the ways in which that
power contradicts who he is. He refuses to accept things as they are. There's
a parallel here with Alma: like Jack, she refuses to accept the conditions of a
marriage that just won't work because of fundamental sexual and emotional
incompatibility, and she makes the decision to divorce Ennis and to start over
with a man who's really able to love her. The traditional gender ideal for a
woman is one that teaches her to deny her sexual desires, and when she marries to accept a sexual relationship on her husband's terms. Alma rejects this,
and instead of suffering in silence with Ennis, rebuilds her life. Unfortunately
Alma and Jack never would be able to discuss it, but there's an important similarity between them, in that both are brave enough to break with the constraints imposed on their lives by the traditional system of gender and power.

Ennis's anger at Jack comes in part from the fact that he expects Jack to
show the same stoicism he does in accepting their long separations and in enduring the sexual frustration and loneliness they produce. Because Ennis has
accepted domination by other men, he expects Jack to as well. In relation to
Jack, Ennis becomes the enforcer of the model of masculinity imposed by
men like their fathers and all the others who hate sexually different men. But
Jack isn't Ennis, and insists on his right to sexual and emotional fulfillment.
In the *Production Notes* for the film, Gyllenhaal makes an insightful comment about the differences between Jack and Ennis, based in turn on Ang
Lee's perceptions of the two characters. In response to a comment by Judy
Becker, the production designer for the film, about the look of Western towns
in the early 1960s, before the dramatic cultural changes of the next several
decades, Gyllenhaal says, "There's a metaphor of the whole West, how the
West was changing at the time from the Old West to the New West. Ang likes
to say that Jack represents the New West, and Ennis represents the Old West.
They're two people, two landscapes."[74] The shift in cultural attitudes noted
by Gyllenhaal and Lee is especially evident in attitudes toward masculinity.
Jack does represent a new approach to being a man that began in the 1960s
and that affected American culture generally, challenging the traditional construction of masculinity embodied in the cowboy hero admired and emulated
by so many American men. Partly in relation to the efforts of women to resist
the limitations imposed by the traditional construction of femininity, some
American men began to accept a less limited model of what it meant to be a
man, one that acknowledged emotion and personal connections. Though
American society continues to be one in which men enjoy far greater privi-

lege and power than women, since the period when the action of *Brokeback Mountain* begins there's been a degree of relaxation of the rigid restrictions imposed on male behavior, at least for some men in some cultural contexts. Contention over what it means to be a man is part of the much larger cultural struggle going on in this country. As Gyllenhaal and Lee recognize, Jack represents the new, more emotionally open, more vulnerable construction of masculinity, and Ennis the more inflexible, emotionally closed one that continues to oppose it. The characters of both Jack and Alma indicate the growing resistance, on the part of some men and many women, to accepting the stifling repression dictated by traditional definitions of gender.

Jack's suffering at being repeatedly rejected by Ennis because of Ennis's fear and concern to continue to pass directly parallels one of Whitman's most intriguing poems. It describes a relationship Whitman had with a man whose name isn't known, probably on Whitman's journey to New Orleans in 1848 when he was twenty-nine. The details are lost, but some scholars and critics believe that this was Whitman's first sexual relationship with another man, and that although it made him aware of the physical and emotional attraction to men that he later celebrated in his poetry, at the time he couldn't accept what he'd learned about himself, and fled the relationship, later coming to regret having done so. The poem focuses on the impact of Whitman's departure on the man, and on Whitman's memory of him and his regret over rejecting him. In Whitman's original manuscript, the poem reads:

> Once I pass'd through a populous celebrated city, imprinting on my brain
> for future use, its shows, architecture, customs, and traditions
> But now of all that city I remember only the man who wander'd with me,
> there, for love of me,
> Day by day, and night by night, we were together,
>
> All else has long been forgotten by me—I remember, I say, only one rude
> and ignorant man who, when I departed, long and long held me
> by the hand, with silent lip, sad and tremulous.—[75]

Not only did Whitman withdraw from the man, causing the man to feel the sort of despair that Jack feels over Ennis's withdrawals, but Whitman, like Ennis, also sometimes felt compelled to deny his sexuality because of fear of being identified as a man who loved men. The poem was published in 1860, in the edition of *Leaves of Grass* that presented the homoerotic *Calamus* poems for the first time, but Whitman seems to have thought it was too explicit, and altered it, changing it to refer to a woman, perhaps to make the poem acceptable to homophobic readers. The original handwritten version, which shows that the poem was written about another man, only was discovered in

1920, and even today many readers are unaware of the actual meaning of the poem, since many teachers, critics, and publishers either don't know or actively suppress the original version.[76]

Although the argument between Ennis and Jack doesn't change the deep feeling the men still have for each other, Ennis's anger apparently pushes Jack to decide to pursue things further with Randall. Both versions of the narrative offer similar details that suggest what probably happens, and show Ennis's pain as he gradually puts them together and realizes his own role in Jack's death. When the pattern of his relationship with Jack suddenly is interrupted by the return of his postcard to Jack seeking to confirm the November trip, stamped with the brutal official notification, "DECEASED," Ennis calls Lureen. Even when Jack is dead, the force of homophobia works to erase the love he and Ennis shared, and to hide the cause of Jack's death and to protect the men who are responsible for it. Even when Ennis is struggling with the shock of his friend's death and then the realization that he probably was murdered, Ennis maintains the fiction of just being an old buddy of Jack's, and says nothing that directly reveals his love for him. Whatever it is Lureen actually knows about Ennis's significance in Jack's life—and her own—she collaborates in this lie. Although Ennis is by far the most important person Jack knew, she agrees to relegate him to the vague category of being either the hunting buddy or the fishing buddy. As Lureen talks on, telling Ennis the version of Jack's death that's been fabricated to hide his sexuality and the fact that he was the victim of homophobic murderers, Ennis is forced to read between the lies. Her flat, emotionless account of Jack's death, delivered in a level, cold voice and sounding almost as if she's memorized it by rote, is what makes Ennis realize that it probably wasn't an accident, but that "they got him with the tire iron."[77]

The conversation between Ennis and Lureen is almost identical in both versions. In the film, it's particularly moving because so little is said and yet so much meaning is conveyed. As he is throughout, Ledger is entirely convincing, haltingly asking Ennis's questions, almost unable to speak but trying to keep the agony he feels from showing. Hathaway's presentation of Lureen is equally persuasive, suggesting how she's coped by retreating into a rigid, totally controlled pose, yet has cared about Jack and realizes who Ennis is and what's happened. When Ennis explains that Brokeback Mountain was where he and Jack herded sheep together in 1963, a look flickers in her eyes that suggests she understands why the place, and Ennis, were so important to her husband, but she then maintains the fiction that she's just telling the sad news of Jack's accidental death to another old friend of his. At the end of the phone call, her emphasis that Ennis should go see Jack's parents and ask to take his ashes to Brokeback Mountain indicates a degree of unspoken compassion for both Jack and Ennis. One small but significant difference in the story antici-pates the hostility that Ennis encounters from John C. Twist: in Proulx's ver-sion, Lureen mentions that she's never met Jack's parents, and that they didn't come to his funeral. The reasons for this aren't explained, but undoubtedly it's due to the hatred Jack's father feels for him.

Ennis's fear that Jack was murdered is confirmed when he visits Jack's par-ents and the father disgustedly tells him that Jack's plan to split up with Lureen and move to Lightning Flat with the ranch neighbor never came to pass. Apparently when Jack and Randall's relationship becomes known, Jack is targeted and murdered; the consequences for Randall aren't ever indicated. After Jack's gone, the shame and secrecy imposed by homophobia prevent anyone from ever acknowledging, much less respecting, the love between him and Ennis, and serve to hide the horrible crime that's been committed and to ensure that those who committed it will go unpunished. The homophobia of the majority causes some of them to direct terror and violence against sex-ual minorities and then renders that terror and violence invisible to the ma-jority as a whole, protecting the perpetrators and fostering the climate of vio-lence in which sexual minorities must live. For Ennis, as has happened to so many people who love someone else of the same sex when the person they've loved most is gone, the real nature of his relationship is denied, there's no recognition of his status in the life of the person he loved, and his right to mourn and to expect sympathy and support—or justice—is ignored. Like mil-lions of other men who've lost the men they love, Ennis is treated by others as having been "just a friend." The pain of this situation makes the kind ges-tures of Jack's mother all the more powerful; though she can't repudiate her husband's hateful words about their son, she shows Ennis that she realizes who he actually is, and respects him. The only recognition Ennis ever re-ceives of his grief over Jack's death, the greatest loss in his life, comes when she gently puts her hand on his shoulder and invites him to go up to Jack's room, allowing Ennis to find the two shirts.

The brief scene in the film showing Ennis's realization of what's happened to Jack, as he talks on the phone to Lureen, is horrific. In a green field by a railroad track, a setting that strangely echoes the landscape in front of Aguirre's trailer where Jack and Ennis first met, we see Jack, who's appar-ently been cornered by three men; as they march him in front of them, sud-denly one of them clubs him on the head from behind with a tire iron, he falls, and they beat him to death. As the sickening close-ups show, the particular targets of their furious violence are his crotch and his face. Even though he's stunned, he tries to fight them, but with three against one he can't, and as one of the assailants pulls Jack's legs open, another mercilessly kicks and stamps on his genitals. The third bashes his face in with the tire iron. To maintain the boundaries that many straight men need in order to be secure in their sense of their sexual identity, some of them will do everything possible to destroy any evidence of the existence of sexually different men among them. For them, Jack's individuality and his sexuality have to be eradicated.

Ennis is left alone, with the realization that repeatedly refusing Jack's love has caused Jack to try to find someone else who could give him what Ennis wouldn't, and that this has led to his murder. The last time they were together, Ennis threatened to kill Jack for trying to meet the sexual needs that Ennis refused to, because it threatened Ennis's sense of himself as a man; now other men who feared and hated Jack's sexuality have done what Ennis threatened, and have murdered Jack. The very thing that has terrified Ennis since childhood, that has made him afraid to accept Jack or to accept himself, now has happened to the man he loves, and because of him. By trying to escape homophobic violence, Ennis has caused Jack to be destroyed by it. Ennis's fear makes him put his concern to keep his identity as man who can pass for straight before his concern for the man he loves, and he loses him for good, and is left alone, with just his memories of Jack and endless regret for his death.

~

Over the last several decades, many sexual minority people have challenged the monopoly that straight people always have claimed on "family values," and have asserted their right to have families as well. Male couples and female couples have fought repeatedly for the right to keep and raise their children by earlier heterosexual relationships, to adopt children, and to have children by artificial insemination or with the assistance of surrogates. Now they are fighting for the right to have the commitments of partners of the same sex finally receive the array of advantages and benefits that straight couples simply take for granted. Some sexual minority people criticize this effort as an attempt to emulate and assimilate to the dominant heterosexual culture, with its models of monogamy. Certainly there are conservative gay and lesbian people who reject the positions of queer sex radicals that celebrate promiscuity and other forms of sexuality that aren't heteronormative, but not all advocates of equal treatment of same-sex couples do so. It's possible for same-sex couples who want to have the same benefits that married heterosexuals enjoy to respect and work together with those in the current queer movement as well. Not all of those who advocate marriage equality want to impose standards of heteronormativity on other sexual minority people.

The struggle to secure the full status of marriage for sexual minorities has provoked vicious and determined resistance from many in the majority, and may result in a constitutional amendment legally denying same-sex couples the rights that are accorded to straight couples, officially inscribing their second-class citizenship into the nation's most fundamental legal document. Despite the money and power of the political and religious groups striving to outlaw same-sex marriage, many sexual minority people are equally determined never to let this happen. In America today, increasing numbers of sexual minority people who have become involved in heterosexual marriages and who now realize that these relationships are in conflict with their basic sexual identities are coming out to their spouses and trying to restructure their lives to affirm their sexual and emotional need for partners of their own sex. Some spouses, much to their credit, are able to understand and accept this, and in many cases, through great effort, sexual minority people who are parents have succeeded in retaining their rights to their children. Couples of the same sex, especially those trying to keep and raise children, face hostility everywhere, but are determined to maintain their right to be considered as families too.

Reading or watching *Brokeback Mountain* and reflecting on these struggles and on the love between Ennis and Jack and the difficult situations they face with their wives and children, many people have been struck by the realization that in a less hostile society the two men and their children might have been able to become a family, and should have had the opportunity to if they wanted it. Given their sexuality, it's not right for either man to remain married to his wife, and neither wife is happy with her husband. Along with his love for Jack, the strongest connection with anyone that Ennis feels is his love for his little girls. Jack's concern with his son is substantially greater than Lureen's. If the two men were together, they would complement and support each other, and, as Jack realizes, probably could work together to achieve the economic success as ranchers that both have dreamed of since they were boys. Neither can fulfill the American Dream alone, but they might, if they were together. They both care about children, and could be fine fathers to the boy and the two girls if they were allowed to share in raising them. In the standard stereotype, gay men aren't interested in children, but in fact many men who love men have children and are good fathers; as Proulx says in her comments on the story, "the rural gay men I know like kids, and if they don't have their own, they usually have nephews and nieces who claim a big place in their hearts."[78] Thinking about the circumstances of their lives, as Proulx has imagined them and as the filmmakers present them, it's possible to glimpse the potential of a better marriage between the two men, and a better family, for them and for their children, than was feasible for them in the kind of marriage and family society forced them into. The thought of this possibility makes the pain and sadness of the ending of *Brokeback Mountain* greater.[79]

The question that *Brokeback Mountain* poses is fundamentally a political one, in the broad sense of the word, meaning the power or lack of power of various groups in a society. Is Jack's dream that two men can make a life with each other possible in America? Will the majority, with all its prejudice and hate, allow people of the same sex to live and love together, without facing the constant threat of discrimination, harassment, and violence? Like millions of sexual minority people today, Jack really doesn't ask for much, simply to be left alone and to be allowed to have the life that's right for him and for the person he loves. He never even gets as far as to raise the possibility that he and Ennis, if they lived together, might want to have access to their children and to play a role in raising them. Today, many same sex couples find that as they try to go about the business of daily life together, they face the prospect of insults and discrimination. Many who have children are denied access to them, and many are prevented from adopting children. Many couples in regions where local culture and religion are especially homophobic must fear for their safety. Sexual minority people hear their love denounced every day by politicians, pundits, and people who claim to be able to speak for God, or what they claim "God" is. In some areas, sexual minorities have achieved passage of laws to prohibit discrimination against them at work and in getting housing, but this sort of abuse still goes on throughout the country. There's no federal legislation to protect sexual minorities, and instead, if they even acknowledge their identity, they're excluded from the largest sector of the federal government, the armed forces, which sends everyone in America the message that the government views them as inferior. Both political parties oppose fully equal status and benefits for same-sex couples, and the present administration is in power in part because it caters to those who hate sexual minorities and want to see the Constitution permanently denigrate the value of their relationships. So Jack's simple dream, and the contempt and violence it provokes, really do have immediate political significance. Both versions of *Brokeback Mountain* depict the forces in America that prevent Jack's dream from being realized. The progress that's been made in challenging these forces only has been possible because millions of sexual minority people have had the courage to make the kinds of demands that Jack makes, despite the harassment and intimidation that this incurs. Like him, some who've asserted themselves have paid with their lives, and the prospect of homophobic violence is one that every out sexual minority person potentially faces. But no progress at all has been made by continuing to pass, as Ennis does. Despite the progress that's been achieved, homophobia continues to force sexual minority people to confront obstacles that most straight people can't begin to imagine, though of course straight people are responsible for them. Jack's dream is an expression of the suffering and the yearning that sexual minority people continue to feel, amid all the hostility of homophobia, for a world in which they merely can be free to be themselves and to love the people they love.

NOTES

1. In a particularly memorable passage in *The Souls of Black Folk* in which he describes the consciousness of racial difference that is forced upon African Americans by the racism of the white majority, W. E. B. DuBois says that "one ever feels his twoness" (W. E. B. DuBois., *The Souls of Black Folk*, ed. Donald B. Gibson, and Monica M. Elbert [New York: Penguin, 1996/1903], 5). Although racism and homophobia differ in many significant ways, one possible parallel that some have noted is in the sense of "twoness," of being part of American society but also of having another identity that many in the majority do not accept. Of course, one major difference is that many people of color cannot pass as members of the larger society, whereas many sexual minority people can. Still, the endemic homophobia of the dominant culture constantly reminds sexual minority people who pass of their difference and vulnerability. There are many people of color who are members of sexual minority groups as well, and who must negotiate a society shaped by racial prejudice along with prejudice concerning gender and sexuality. For thoughtful discussions of racism and homophobia, see McBride, *Abercrombie,* and Boykin, *One More River.*
2. Proulx, "Brokeback Mountain," 26.
3. *Brokeback Mountain.* Universal Studios DVD Number 26315, 2006.
4. See Kinsey, *op. cit.*, on the spectrum of types of sexual orientation, as well as discussions of bisexuality in Firestein, *Bisexuality*, and Burleson, *BiAmerica.*
5. See Besen, *Anything but Straight*, and Bull, *Perfect Enemies.*
6. On the costs of passing, see Baldwin, *Giovanni's Room*; Duberman, *Cures*; Monette, *Becoming a Man*; Kroeger, *Passing*; Ginsberg, *Fictions of Identity*; and Klein and Schwartz, *Husbands.*
7. On the struggles of spouses of those who pass for straight, see Klein and Schwartz, *Husbands*; Buxton, *The Other Side*; and Gochros, *When Husbands Come Out.*
8. Joseph Ratzinger is responsible for the phrase "intrinsic evil," which he coined in 1999 to condemn "homosexual acts," when he held the influential office of Prefect for the Congregation for the Doctrine of the Faith in the Roman Catholic Church, prior to attaining his present, even more powerful position. Homosexuality is described as "demonic possession" by many American Pentecostal Christians.
9. Proulx, "Brokeback Mountain," 24.
10. Proulx, "Brokeback Mountain," 24.
11. Proulx, "Brokeback Mountain," 24.
12. Proulx, "Brokeback Mountain," 26.
13. Proulx, "Brokeback Mountain," 26.
14. Proulx, "Brokeback Mountain," 26.

15. Proulx, "Brokeback Mountain," 26.

16. Proulx, "Brokeback Mountain," 26.

17. Proulx, "Brokeback Mountain," 19.

18. Proulx, "Brokeback Mountain," 19.

19. Proulx, "Brokeback Mountain," 26.

20. On the representation of fathers in commercial films, and the pattern depicting the ordinary father who heroically defends his family, see Sarah Harwood, *Family Fictions: Representations of the Family in 1980s Hollywood Cinema* (New York: St. Martin's, 1997), and Stella Bruzzi, *Bringing Up Daddy: Fatherhood and Masculinity in Post-War Hollywood* (Berkeley: University of California Press, 2006).

21. McMurtry and Ossana, Screenplay, 38.

22. Proulx, "Brokeback Mountain," 23.

23. Proulx, "Brokeback Mountain," 23.

24. Proulx, "Brokeback Mountain," 29.

25. Proulx, "Brokeback Mountain," 19.

26. Proulx, "Brokeback Mountain," 21.

27. Proulx, "Brokeback Mountain," 21.

28. Proulx, "Brokeback Mountain," 21.

29. Proulx, "Brokeback Mountain," 21.

30. Proulx, "Brokeback Mountain," 21.

31. Proulx, "Brokeback Mountain," 21.

32. Proulx, "Brokeback Mountain," 21.

33. MTV.com: "MTV Movie Awards Archive: 2006," June 8, 2006 (http://www.mtv.com/ontv/movieawards/archive/, July 29, 2007; Jake Gyllenhaal interview, *Elle* Magazine (U.S.), December 2004.

34. Proulx, "Brokeback Mountain," 21.

35. Proulx, "Brokeback Mountain," 26.

36. See Introduction, endnote number 48.

37. Proulx, "Brokeback Mountain," 31.

38. Proulx, "Brokeback Mountain," 32.

39. Proulx, "Brokeback Mountain," 32.

40. Proulx, "Brokeback Mountain," 32.

41. Proulx, "Brokeback Mountain," 32.

42. Proulx, "Brokeback Mountain," 32.

43. Proulx, "Brokeback Mountain," 33.

44. Proulx, "Brokeback Mountain," 33.

45. Proulx, "Brokeback Mountain," 34.

46. See Gerassi, *Boise*, and Miller, *Sex-Crime Panic*.

47. Beginning with Freud's interpretation of the case of Paul Schreber in 1911, many in the fields of psychiatry and psychology understood paranoid delusions as sometimes being the result of the projection onto others of unresolved incestuous or homosexual impulses. American Freudian theory tended to be far more hostile to homosexuality than Freud himself, constructing it as a serious mental disorder and linking it to severe mental problems such as paranoia. The important work of Dr. Evelyn Hooker and others in the 1950s and 1960s gradually led to recognition by many in

psychiatry and psychology that a same-sex orientation was not a mental disorder, though this perspective was strongly resisted by advocates of the sickness model, such as Drs. Irving Bieber and Charles Socarides. Even after homosexuality was declassified as a mental illness in the early 1970s, some, such as Socarides, one of the founders of NARTH, continued to construct homosexuality as mental illness, and as a cause of paranoia. Today, leading figures in NARTH explicitly reject the use of the word homophobia to refer to discrimination and hostility toward sexual minorities, instead narrowly defining homophobia as a phobic reaction to homosexual impulses that can result in projecting them onto others and developing paranoid delusions. The constructions of homosexuality and homophobia promoted by NARTH largely erase the problems of many sexual minority people—especially people like Ennis, who are isolated and without support—caused by living in a hostile society. Those who accept such constructions seem oblivious to the fact that a society that rejects same-sex desire can make some people who experience this desire fearful to the point of paranoia. And they seem incapable of recognizing the role that they themselves play in perpetuating social hostility to homosexuality—which, in the case of those in the fields of psychiatry and psychology, is sadly ironic, given the Hippocratic oath's command, "first, do no harm." See, for example, "Homophobia: A Scientific, Non-Political Definition" (Collected Papers of 2003 NARTH Conference; http://www.narth.com/docs/coll-breiner.html, July 29, 2007), in which a NARTH psychiatrist, Dr. Sander Breiner, specifically rejects the important and influential discussions of homophobia in Blumenfeld, *Homophobia: How We All Pay the Price.* Interestingly, in his statements on the NARTH website, Dr. Breiner repeatedly refers to homosexuality as a "perversion."

48. McMurtry and Ossana, "Screenplay," 65.
49. Proulx, "Brokeback Mountain," 48.
50. Proulx, "Brokeback Mountain," 48.
51. McMurtry and Ossana, "Screenplay," 4.
52. Proulx, "Brokeback Mountain," 20.
53. Proulx, "Brokeback Mountain," 47.
54. Proulx, "Brokeback Mountain," 28.
55. Proulx, "Brokeback Mountain," 22.
56. Proulx, "Brokeback Mountain," 36.
57. Proulx, "Brokeback Mountain," 37.
58. Proulx, "Brokeback Mountain," 28.
59. Proulx, "Brokeback Mountain," 30.
60. McMurtry and Ossana, "Screenplay," 62.
61. Proulx, "Brokeback Mountain," 39.
62. McMurtry and Ossana, "Screenplay," 63.
63. The music and lyrics for "Quizas, Quizas, Quizas" ("Perhaps, Perhaps, Perhaps") were composed in 1947 by Osvaldo Farres; it was made popular in the United States in a version in English by Nat King Cole.
64. Proulx, "Brokeback Mountain," 41.
65. Proulx, "Brokeback Mountain," 41.
66. Proulx, "Brokeback Mountain," 41.

67. Proulx, "Brokeback Mountain," 41.

68. Proulx, "Brokeback Mountain," 15.

69. Proulx, "Brokeback Mountain," 42.

70. Proulx, "Brokeback Mountain," 42.

71. Proulx, "Brokeback Mountain," 42.

72. Proulx, "Brokeback Mountain," 43.

73. Proulx, "Brokeback Mountain," 43.

74. *Production Notes*, 15.

75. "Once I Pass'd through a Populous City," Whitman, original manuscript version, in Gary Schmidgall, ed., *Walt Whitman, Selected Poems, 1855–1892, A New Edition* (New York: St. Martin's, 1999). (I have omitted the repetition of the words, "its shows," in the first line, which appears to be an alternative wording that Whitman was considering in contrast to the wording, "with its shows"). On the manuscript of the poem, also see Martin, *The Homosexual Tradition in American Poetry*.

76. The version of the poem published in 1860, which is that which has become widely known, reads:

> Once I pass'd through a populous city imprinting my brain for future use with its shows, architecture, customs, traditions,
> Yet now of all that city I remember only a woman I casually met there who detain'd me for love of me,
> Day by day and night by night we were together—all else has long been forgotten by me,
> I remember I say only that woman who passionately clung to me,
> Again we wander, we love, we separate again,
> Again she holds me by the hand, I must not go,
> I see her close beside me with silent lips sad and tremulous.

"Once I Pass'd Through a Populous City," Whitman, *Leaves of Grass* (Ninth edition/1892).

77. Proulx, "Brokeback Mountain," 45.

78. Proulx, "Getting Movied," 132.

79. On the movement for same-sex marriage, see George Chauncey, *Why Marriage? The History and Shaping of Today's Debate over Gay Equality* (New York: Basic Books, 2005).

Chapter Six

"What We Got Now Is Brokeback Mountain. Everything Built on That": Memory

The capacity of memory is fundamental to every aspect of our lives, and it's with good reason that we often worry about its decline or loss and strive to maintain it and improve it. It's deeply connected to the ways in which dominant cultural traditions shape the understanding of love. In our lives with those we love, memory can be a source of shared happiness and often of consolation, especially when those we love have left us. Nearly everyone treasures memories of people and places they've loved, of times with friends and lovers they never can forget, of favorite animals or of beautiful things they've seen or heard. One of the most mysterious and powerful aspects of the mind is the way, in the midst of some present action, a memory suddenly can come unbidden, so strong that it sweeps away the present and takes us back into the past. Nostalgia for someone we've cared for or for a place or time that's gone is one of the sweetest and yet saddest feelings. Sometimes the yearning that we feel for someone we've lost is so strong that it's not an overstatement to say that we feel haunted by memory, and we may almost feel that they're actually with us again. Memory can seem momentarily to undo the changes caused by time, but then as the vividness of our memory fades and we come back to the present, we're always reminded forcefully of the unrelenting passage of time, of the continual processes of change and loss and death. Memory can be the cause of grief and regret for things we've done that we'd do differently if we had the opportunity to do them over again, or for things we've failed to do that we now wish we'd done. Sometimes the memory of things done, or things undone, is almost unbearable, and we do almost anything we can to erase it and forget. Still, often even the pain and sadness of the memory of what we regret is preferable, as a connection with what we've lost, to forgetting it entirely. The beauty, sadness, and strength of memory are central to *Brokeback Mountain*.

Throughout their struggles with their cover marriages, Ennis and Jack continue to remember their summer together on the mountain. The power of this memory causes both of them to try to regain what they had there. Four years after their summer together Jack's intense memory of falling in love with Ennis at the same time of year, late spring, causes him to take the risk of proposing their reunion. While he also remembers the painful way that they parted, his message makes clear the intensity of his hope that he may be able to reach Ennis, which has led him to make the effort to find him: "'Friend this letter is a long time over due. Hope you get it. Heard you was in Riverton. Im coming thru on the 24th, thought Id stop and buy you a beer. Drop me a line if you can, say if you're there.'"[1] In his cautious invitation to Ennis just to let him take him out for a beer, and in asking Ennis for a reply "'if you can,'" Jack indicates that he doesn't necessarily expect that Ennis will want to renew their old intimacy, and that he won't be surprised if Ennis doesn't respond at all. Perhaps Jack would settle for just being able to see Ennis again, if he'd agree. Whatever will happen, Jack's memory of what they had is so strong that he's willing to try.

Ennis also has been remembering Jack. When he masturbates he pictures Jack and his nostalgia for Jack causes him to make Alma have sex with him the way Jack and he did. When Ennis gets Jack's message, he responds immediately, and then waits impatiently all day for him. In her description of Ennis as he waits, Proulx notes his vivid memory of eating with Jack during their summer together that causes him to tell Alma that Jack's not the restaurant type, the remembered image of their typical meal by the campfire, the "dirty spoons sticking out of the cans of cold beans balanced on the log."[2] When Jack arrives, after they embrace and kiss, as Jack and Ennis stand at the door talking to Alma, Ennis suddenly feels the nostalgia evoked by Jack's smell, the "intensely familiar odor of cigarettes, musky sweat and a faint sweetness like grass, and with it the rushing cold of the mountain."[3] As everyone knows from his or her own experience, certain smells arouse memories so powerfully that when we sense them, it's almost as if we're taken back physically through time and space to the moment when we experienced that smell before. Of all the five senses, for some reason, perhaps deeply related to our nature as animals, the sense of smell is most strongly connected to the power of memory. None of the other senses can bring back the past the way a certain scent can. Smelling Jack's body next to him for the first time in four years, it's as if Ennis is back on the cold, windy mountain again with him, in the separate world where they can be themselves. Any smell can be strongly charged with memory, but probably none so much as the particular scent of the body of a person you love.

During their first reunion, the fact that Ennis and Jack reconnect so strongly causes Jack to invite Ennis to live with him. Jack's dream, now that he's found Ennis again, is to take the steps that can make permanent what they had on Brokeback Mountain, to build a future on the memory of the past. In the film, as they sit by their campfire along the river, in a setting that recalls the mountain four years before, Jack broaches his plan by saying that it could always be just like this if they had a ranch together. Ennis shares the same memories, and is delighted to be with Jack again in the mountains as they were before, but the violence he remembers witnessing as a child competes with and supersedes the memory of being with Jack on Brokeback. As a result of Ennis's refusal, Jack is condemned to a life of constant waiting for the brief intervals when he can be with Ennis again, to constant remembering of what it's like to be with him as he struggles to cope with the limitations of his cover marriage to Lureen. Jack's love for Ennis is so strong that he's willing to settle for being with him only a few weeks a year. The memory of the mountain is a continual, painful contrast to trying to live like a straight man. For Jack, as for many people, perhaps the deepest kind of sadness comes from the recollection of past happiness in the midst of present suffering.

Of course, the power of the memory of their summer on Brokeback is strong for Ennis as well, and it keeps drawing him back to Jack. But it never is strong enough to overcome his memory of the terror he experienced as a child, not only in seeing Earl's tortured body, but in growing up in the house of the man who may well have murdered him. It can't overcome his persistent memory and fear of the tire iron that someone, perhaps his father, used to smash in Earl's face. It also can't overcome his fear of his own sexuality, and of Jack as a symbol of the love men can have for other men. Jack, of course, also carries terrible memories of the hatred straight men direct at those they see as different, like the one he tells to Ennis of being beaten and urinated on by his father, but unlike Ennis, he's able to overcome them. But the strength of the terrible memories Ennis carries with him prevents the two men from trying to return to what they shared. The past can't be recaptured. Even though Ennis and Jack travel all over Wyoming together during the course of nearly twenty years, making trips into just about every mountain wilderness in the state, as Proulx says, they never return to Brokeback.[4]

Not only do memories of the past haunt the lives of the two men, but they undoubtedly shadow the lives of Alma and Lureen. Both were strongly attracted to their husbands when they married them, and had hoped for traditional marriages and families, each expecting that the love between her and her husband could help to overcome whatever problems might arise because of finances, relatives, health, or age. Both women gradually realize that their hopes are going to be disappointed, though the reasons become clear much earlier for Alma, and probably only are fully revealed to Lureen by Jack's murder. The memory of the expectations they had when they got married must constantly come to mind in contrast with the ways their marriages actually worked out. And both women also always must remember what they've learned about their husbands, though they can't understand it and so can't forgive it. Obviously, for Alma, what she saw on the stairs of the apartment when Jack arrived is something she never can forget, as her anger at him and at Ennis in the episode at Thanksgiving shows. When Ennis calls Lureen after Jack's murder, her coldness and the lies she tells about Jack's death indicate the power of the awful memory that she'll spend the rest of her life trying to forget.

Memories of Jack also must constantly be with his parents. When Ennis visits them, the differences in the ways they remember their son are immediately obvious. For Jack's father, given his need to be the "stud duck," Jack's sexuality has been a source of anger and shame for a long time, though it's likely that it's never been discussed openly, and now that Jack's gone his father directs his contempt at Ennis, and at the memory of Jack, and perhaps also at Jack's mother. There's no direct evidence that the scandal surrounding Jack's death reached his parents, but it's quite likely it did, only adding to his father's disgust and his desire to obliterate any acknowledgement of who Jack really was. Although she's unable to challenge her husband's homophobic hatred of her child, Jack's mother shows her love for Jack in keeping his room as it was when he was a boy, and especially in preserving the shirts and in making it possible for Ennis to have them. Part of the immediate, unspoken bond between her and Ennis is that they both loved Jack and hold on to their memories of him. But the presence of Jack's father, and of course the fear and shame that surround love between men, make it impossible for Ennis and Mrs. Twist to share what they feel about Jack. One of the few things that even can begin to make the loss of someone we love bearable is sharing our memories of that person with someone else who felt the same way, but homophobia denies this consolation to Ennis and to Jack's mother. They both must suffer their loss alone in silence. Both of them will cling to their memories of Jack, but neither ever will have anyone they can tell about him. The grief a parent feels at losing a child is overwhelming, and it must be even more difficult for Jack's mother to bear since she must live every day in the presence of a husband who hated their son, who may well have wished him dead and clearly is satisfied now that he is. While she wants to remember her child, she's married to a man who only wants to forget him.

Over the years of their friendship, when Jack and Ennis are together, Jack always dreads the impending separation, which will leave him for months and months with nothing but his memories of their times with each other, and this leads to his repeated efforts to change Ennis's mind. Jack keeps raising the possibility of trying to recapture their past, and Ennis keeps rejecting it, until he finally drives Jack away. On their last trip, after jokingly telling Ennis about his supposed affair with the rancher's wife, Jack's comment in the film, "Tell you what . . . the truth is . . . sometimes I miss you so much I can hardly stand it," expresses his despair at being forced to live a life that mostly consists just of memories. As he says to Ennis when they argue, instead of actually having built an ongoing life with each other as Jack had hoped they would, the only extended time they've ever had together was that one summer long before: "[w]hat we got now is Brokeback Mountain. Everything built on that. It's all we got, boy, fuckin all . . ."[5] Instead of working and living together and sharing their lives, what life they have with each other only is made up of fragments, when they get together and briefly revive the memory of what they once had. All they really have is a memory.

The most powerful contrast between what is and what was, suggesting what might have been, comes in both versions of *Brokeback Mountain* at the end of the argument between Ennis and Jack on their last trip. After Jack reacts to Ennis's threat to kill him by telling Ennis that all they've been getting by on is their memory of their summer together, and Ennis collapses, they then try to reconcile and to "torque"[6] things back to where they'd been. In the film, as soon as Ennis falls, Jack runs over to him, embracing him, and after a moment of angry resistance, Ennis hugs him back. In both versions, the scene then changes to Jack's memory of another embrace, on an evening on the mountain twenty years before. Proulx's description is perfect in its eloquence, but unfortunately can't be quoted here in full; the scene in the film realizes her poignant description beautifully. Proulx explains that what Jack "remembered and craved"[7] without being able to "help or understand"[8] it was an evening during their summer together when he'd been standing by the fire and Ennis had come up behind him and embraced him, saying nothing, "satisfying some shared and sexless hunger."[9] They had stood together in the firelight for a long while, the sound of Ennis's pocket watch and the settling coals of the fire making them aware of the passage of time. Jack remembered that Ennis breathed quietly as he held him and hummed and rocked a little, the "vibrations of the humming like faint electricity."[10] This, and the beating of Ennis's heart, had lulled Jack into "sleep that was not sleep but something else drowsy and tranced . . ."[11] Ennis eventually had had to end their embrace, using a phrase his mother had used when he was a boy, saying, "'Time to hit the hay, cowboy. I got a go. Come on, you're sleepin on your feet like a horse,'"[12] and had given Jack a shake and a push, then mounted his horse to ride back to the sheep, telling Jack as he left that he'd see him the next day. Proulx concludes the description of what Jack remembers by saying

> Later, that dozy embrace solidified in his memory as the single moment of artless, charmed happiness in their separate and difficult lives. Nothing marred it,

even the knowledge that Ennis would not then embrace him face to face because he did not want to see nor feel that it was Jack he held. And maybe, he thought, they'd never got much farther than that. Let be, let be.[13]

Unlike their desperate embrace when they argue, this embrace is an easy, gentle, spontaneous expression of Ennis's need for Jack's companionship, and of Jack's need to be close to Ennis. Their embrace emphasizes the point that so many straight people refuse to get, that what they want to call "homosexuality" is far from being only a matter of sex, but is deeply concerned with emotion and the need for intimacy with another human being. For whatever reasons, not all people crave, or are satisfied by, closeness to a person of the other sex; some need closeness to a person of their own sex, and they need it just as much as members of the majority need it with the opposite sex. For both Ennis and Jack, the need to be with another man who also needs to be with a man meets a fundamental requirement of their being. As Proulx depicts it, and as Ledger and Gyllenhaal present it, it isn't only about sex, but also about a desire just as profound and important, which, when it's coupled with sex, can create the most intense romantic love. What Jack remembers shows that, for all his fear and anger, Ennis needs to be with a man just as much as Jack does. It's Ennis who hugs Jack, and who holds him, humming and easing him into a peaceful trance, in which the passing of time almost seems suspended, so that there's no anxiety about any impending separation. In contrast to their other experiences with each other, momentarily there's no sense of time or change or loss. It's a moment out of time, though remembering it becomes central to Jack's sense of loss.

Being with Jack gives Ennis a feeling of great contentment, which he expresses in this episode through music, much as the film also shows him doing earlier when he rides along and hums "The Streets of Laredo." When Ennis finally ends Jack's trance because he has to go to take care of the sheep, he draws on the memory of his mother, speaking to Jack with the kind of tenderness she showed Ennis when he was a child. As Proulx indicates here, while American culture has arbitrarily limited to women the capacity to express this sort of gentle, solicitous love, men are capable of it as well, and it can be a crucial part of the bond between two men. The tenderness of love doesn't necessarily have to be associated with gender. Men are capable of giving it, and one of the many costs, for everyone, of American culture's denigration of emotion as feminine, and thus as supposedly contradicting masculinity, is that it robs many men of this potential. It's one of the most important lessons many straight men could learn from some men who love men, if they were able to.

In showing the kind of strong, sustaining love that Ennis can give, this episode also reinforces the sense, not only on Jack's part but for the reader or viewer as well, of what the men lose because it's impossible for Ennis to accept Jack's invitation to make a life together. The love that Ennis shows here is the kind of love that can build a relationship, that can see two people through all the challenges that can come to a couple, through struggles with work and with money and with sickness. It's the kind of love that can build a family, that Ennis and Jack could have shared not only with each other, but, if others allowed it to be possible, perhaps also with Ennis's daughters and with Jack's son. The episode shows just why Jack's nostalgia for Brokeback Mountain is so painful, over the twenty years of separate and difficult life he and Ennis have, since Jack knows what Ennis is capable of, what he could have given Jack, if he could have let himself, and what it would have allowed Jack to give back to him.

Yet as Proulx notes, and as she says Jack realizes, even then Ennis wouldn't embrace Jack face to face. Even at the moment of sweetest intimacy, Ennis's fear and shame make it impossible for him to accept that the intimacy he wants is with another man. In this, the episode illustrates Ennis's profound resistance to his own needs, which condemns both him and Jack to lives of loneliness and frustration, punctuated by the brief but always curtailed happiness of their trips together, and which ultimately leads to Jack's murder.

The shock of Jack's murder destroys the minimal happiness in the pattern of Ennis's life, leaving him only with his memories of Jack, which he's unable to share with anyone. Once Jack is gone, Ennis feels constant nostalgia for him, along with the tormenting regret of the knowledge that Jack wouldn't be dead if he hadn't pushed him away. His fear and shame, his concern to keep his manhood intact, at least as his society tells him he should define his manhood, cause him to lose the most important person he'll ever have. For Ennis, the full realization of what he's had with Jack only comes once it's lost forever. In this regard Proulx's story bears comparison with one of the greatest works of fiction about men who love men, and about the costs for such a man of being concerned with adhering to what society says a man must be. Like Ennis, David, the narrator of James Baldwin's *Giovanni's Room* (1956), is so afraid of what loving a man may mean about himself, at least to the straight men who control the world around him, that he loses the most important relationship in his life. David is unable to accept his own feelings or the love he and Giovanni share, and rejects Giovanni, leading to his death, much as Ennis drives Jack away and causes him to make the decisions that provoke his murder. As Baldwin shows, David's tragedy is that he's unable "to say 'Yes' to life."[14] This is Ennis's tragedy as well. For Ennis, as for David, his concern with retaining what he's been taught must constitute his identity as a man only condemns him to loss, grief, guilt, and loneliness.

Along with the realization that rejecting Jack set in motion the events that led to his murder, one of the most painful things for Ennis must be to hear what Lureen and Jack's father have to say about Jack, and especially about Jack's memories of Brokeback Mountain. In response to Ennis's question about where Jack's buried, Lureen tells him, in a level, cold voice, that they put a stone up and explains that Jack had said that when he died he wanted to be cremated and to have his ashes scattered on Brokeback Mountain. Since she didn't know where that was and thought it might be near where he grew up, she tells Ennis that half of his ashes were buried in Childress and the rest sent to his parents. What Lureen says tells so much about Jack's despair: though he only was thirty-nine he talked about what should be done if he were to die, almost as if he knew it was about to happen. His yearning for Ennis and for what they shared and could have had together is evident in his wish about being buried on the mountain, but so too is the painful distance between him and Lureen. He never could tell her where or what Brokeback Mountain was; to tell her would have ended their marriage. And now that he's dead, and perhaps because of the way he died, she's got no interest in finding out. The estrangement between them is overwhelming in her next, dismissive comment, that knowing Jack she thought Brokeback Mountain probably was "'some pretend place where the bluebirds sing and there's a whiskey spring.'"[15] To this, Ennis, barely able to speak, offers the fact that they'd herded sheep together there in 1963, which could explain to her his meaning in Jack's life, if she wanted to know it, but then she just dismisses the significance of what he's told her, and Jack's significance as well, saying that when he said it was his place, she thought he just meant a place to get drunk on whiskey, since he drank a lot. The struggle and pain of being in a cover marriage, along with the impact of Jack's murder, have made it impossible for her to know or understand him. Why the mountain was Jack's favorite place, why he drank so much, why he was in such despair, and how Ennis could help her to answer these questions all are things Lureen has no wish to know.

In the contemptuous way Lureen dismisses Jack's memory of Brokeback Mountain, Proulx makes a connection with popular culture that's rich in significance. The lines Lureen refers to, "where the bluebirds sing and there's a whiskey spring,"[16] are from the "salty" original version of the old hobo song, "Big Rock Candy Mountain." The song was made popular in a sanitized form by Burl Ives in the 1950s, having first become widely known in the 1920s in a similarly cleaned-up version sung by Harry "Haywire Mac" McClintock, a hobo singer; its original version probably dates from the 1890s.[17] The song describes a hobo's idea of paradise, a mountain full of earthly delights where "they hung the jerk that invented work."[18] In the form that most people now know, made palatable to families with little children, the Big Rock Candy Mountain offers the pleasures of peppermint trees and lemonade springs, although in the original version they were cigarette trees and whiskey springs and there were streams of alcohol and a lake of gin. When it first began to be sung it depicted the Big Rock Candy Mountain as a dream of pleasure that an experienced hobo uses to invite a young man to come along with him on the road, to be his companion and sexual partner. In the original version, the song is presented as being sung by a "jocker" to the fellow he wants to persuade to be his "punk."[19] So, though of course Lureen could have no way of knowing it, the very way in which she dismisses Jack's memory of Brokeback Mountain encodes an allusion to the reason why it meant so much to him, because it was the site of his discovery of love with another man.

After his call to Lureen, Ennis goes to Lightning Flat, where Jack's father treats his son's memories of Brokeback Mountain not with the kind of incomprehension Lureen shows, but with overt hate. In contrast to Lureen, he tells Ennis he *knows* where Brokeback Mountain is, making it clear he knows what it meant to Jack and to his friend. Even when Jack's dead, his father's hatred won't allow the fulfillment of Jack's nostalgic wish to have his body returned to the place where he fell in love with Ennis, to make the connection with Ennis in death that Ennis refused Jack in life. For Ennis, the pain of hearing the indifference and scorn that Lureen and Jack's father feel for Jack's memories of the mountain must be excruciating, since he couldn't embrace those memories in the way that Jack could. In the film, in the argument with Ennis when Jack dares to suggest moving to Texas, Ennis dismisses the idea by ridiculing the memory of their summer together, even using some of the same words Lureen later does to dismiss Brokeback Mountain: "Sure . . . then we could just live together herdin sheep and it'll rain money from L. D. Newsome, and whiskey'll flow in the streams . . ." Ennis treated the idea of a life built on the love he and Jack shared on Brokeback Mountain as if it were as absurd as the hobo's vision of utopia in "Big Rock Candy Mountain." Once someone we love is gone, the memory of hard words we've said is especially painful, since there's no way what we've said ever can be taken back.

The nostalgia that's a central part of the experience of both Jack and Ennis in *Brokeback Mountain* connects the story and the film to popular traditions of Western narrative, especially movies, in a way that reinforces a sense of the current of homoerotic energy that's essential to the genre. As students of the Western genre have pointed out, despite the fact that the form has a long history and can be placed in many times and locales, the most usual setting is the High Plains, the Rockies, or the Southwest during the thirty or so years after the Civil War.[20] The classic Western is set in the past, and often explicitly evokes nostalgia for a time and place when men supposedly had greater freedom and opportunity than the present, when a man still could be a man. It simultaneously celebrates and grieves for a kind of heroic, independent American masculinity that many believe is increasingly difficult to achieve in today's world. Often, especially in later Westerns, the cowboy hero is presented as a tragic figure, who finds there's no place for him in the settled, developed West he helps to make possible. The movies often are a kind of lament over what's supposedly a lost masculine ideal. Though *Brokeback Mountain* isn't set in this distant period, and concludes in the recent past, it too is filled with nostalgia concerning men, not for some imaginary time and place when men could fulfill a fantasy of masculinity, but for the actual possibility of comradeship and love between two ordinary men. In its connection with the mood of nostalgia that's so important in the Western, the story of Ennis and Jack again suggests that what causes so many American men to be drawn to the Western and its cowboy heroes may be an unacknowledged yearning for closeness to other men.

At some time in our lives, most of us probably have felt the impulse to keep some object as a tangible reminder of someone we've loved. This impulse can be so strong that it makes some people hoard things that remind them of past love and happiness, or to go to the opposite extreme, to try not to give in to the desire to hang on to such reminders. Objects in and of themselves have no meaning beyond what we give them, but the simplest, most ordinary things can become charged with great significance to a person who associates them with someone they love. Such reminders can be among our most valuable possessions, but they also can be a continual source of pain, always making us think of how much we've lost. They become physical, tangible embodiments of the longing and pain of memory.

At the close of *Brokeback Mountain* Ennis owns almost nothing, and doesn't care; as he says in the movie to his daughter when she visits him at his trailer, "well . . . you got nothin, you don't need nothin." But he does have a possession of enormous value, at least for him: the two bloodstained shirts. They gain their meaning for him not simply as reminders of his summer with Jack, but because Jack himself gave them meaning, and saved them and treasured them for twenty years. Just as Jack always kept the feather from the eagle that he shot his first summer on Brokeback, still wearing it in his hat on his last trip with Ennis, he kept the two shirts.[21] Ennis's discovery of the shirts shows him again, once Jack is gone forever, how much Jack always loved him. The shirts show him that at the end of their summer, after their fight, grieving over Ennis's rejection and the likelihood that he never would see Ennis again, Jack stole Ennis's shirt, took it back with him to Lightning Flat, and united it with his own shirt as a reminder of the love he and Ennis had shared, and that he had hoped Ennis might want to continue. Jack carefully placed Ennis's shirt inside his own, expressing his sense of closeness to Ennis, showing that he wanted to think of Ennis close to him, inside him, as they were when they made love. Of course, the shirts, covered with Ennis's dried blood, also had to make Jack think of their fight and Ennis's angry rejection of him, but the blood also is an indication of their connection, of the union between them, a kind of blood brotherhood deeper than the connection of any two actual brothers.

Proulx's extraordinary depiction of the moment when Ennis discovers the shirts, hidden by Jack in a closet within a closet where they probably had been protected by his mother, shows the enormous impact on Ennis of what he finds. At first he only notices Jack's old jeans and boots, but then in a jog in the wall he finds hanging on a nail what he recognizes as "Jack's old shirt from Brokeback days."[22] It has his own dried blood on it, reminding him of their fight and how he surprised Jack with a sucker punch, the same way his father taught him to attack his brother, K.E. Just as Ennis's homophobic, brutally violent father taught him to deal with his brother, Ennis dealt with Jack, rejecting his love at the end of their summer, and then over and over again for years, leading to the final, fatal spilling of Jack's blood. Then, as he holds Jack's bloody shirt, Ennis realizes that it's not alone. The shirt seems to be heavy, until he sees that another shirt's been carefully worked inside Jack's. It's his own worn old plaid shirt that he thought he'd lost, "stolen by Jack and hidden here inside Jack's own shirt, the pair like two skins, one inside the other, two in one."[23] Now, seeing how the shirts testify Jack's love for him, Ennis is overcome, embracing the shirts much as Jack must have done on every trip to Lightning Flat, as Jack would think of Ennis and how much he longed to be with him and hold him. In the scene in the film, Ledger presents Ennis with the understated intensity that marks his superb performance throughout the film, holding the shirts, rocking slightly as he does so, recalling the scene depicting Jack's memory of their embrace on Brokeback, although now Ennis finally is able to embrace from the front, not from behind. When Ennis is ready to embrace Jack and to gaze into his face, to finally see and feel that it's Jack he holds, Jack is lost forever. As Proulx says in her description, as he hugs the shirts to himself, Ennis tries to recapture Jack's presence through the scent that moved him so powerfully before, pressing his face into the fabric and breathing deeply, "hoping for the faintest smoke and mountain sage and salty sweet stink of Jack but there was no real scent, only the memory of it, the imagined power of Brokeback Mountain of which nothing was left but what he held in his hands."[24] Ennis now knows the full cost of the fear and shame that made him refuse Jack. Jack is gone. All Ennis has is the memory of him, and the embodiment of that memory in the shirts. We hold on to things that evoke the memory of a person we love, but those things also are a source of pain and grief, since they continually remind us that the living person that we loved is lost to us forever. For Ennis, the shirts, as a kind of talisman of his love for Jack, and Jack's for him, must be especially painful, since the blood that marks them also always must remind him of his violent rejection of Jack, and of the violence of his death.

Although in Proulx's version of the narrative she mentions the shirts in the second sentence of the story, in her description of Ennis as he gets up before dawn one morning in his trailer after Jack's death, their significance to Ennis only becomes clear at the end, in her account of Ennis's discovery of them and then in her description of the simple shrine he makes for Jack. After he brings the shirts back from Lightning Flat to Signal, where Proulx says he now lives, he goes to the gift shop and looks for a picture postcard of Brokeback Mountain. They're out of them and the storeowner offers to order him a hundred, but he says that one's enough, and when it comes he carefully tacks it up in his trailer and hangs the two shirts below. As in "When Lilacs Last in the Dooryard Bloom'd," when Whitman asks, " . . . what shall the pictures be that I hang on the walls, / To adorn the burial-house of him I love?,"[25] Ennis chooses to honor Jack with a masculine landscape. Apparently Ennis doesn't have a photograph of Jack, but now he does have one of the place where they fell in love. As Proulx indicates, sometimes one photograph *is* enough, as a way of remembering something that changed your life forever and that you never forget. We live surrounded by photographic images, and are able to make hundreds, thousands, of them cheaply and easily. Commercial photographic images incite, embody, and commodify desires that never can be fulfilled. But for many people certain personal photographs, because they record a moment or a person or a place that's dear to us, become inestimably valuable. In holding an image, photographs can be consoling, but they also can be haunting and tormenting, since near as the image is, it's still only an image. It reminds us of the relative or friend or lover we've lost, but also that we never can be with them again. Photography embodies both the value and the pain of memory.[26] For Ennis, the postcard recalls his summer with Jack, and their trips together, and must also remind him that they're entirely gone. All he has is Brokeback Mountain.

As it does in so many other scenes, the film's depiction of what Ennis does with the postcard and the shirts adds to the richness of Proulx's already richly detailed narrative. During the course of the movie Jack and Ennis correspond only with postcards; while Jack's have pictures of Western landscapes, Ennis's, characteristically, are the ones you can buy at the post office that are blank. This makes it all the more striking that at the end he buys a card with a picture of the mountain, almost as if the card were a message of affirmation he's communicating to Jack. At the close of the film, when Ennis is alone in his trailer putting away the sweater that Alma Jr. forgot, he looks again at the two shirts and the postcard, which are on the inside of the closet door. Just like Ennis's love for Jack, still hidden in the closet. He carefully straightens the card and touches the shirts, and we notice that now the shirts are reversed, Ennis's on the outside, Jack's carefully placed inside of it, sleeves worked down into sleeves. This detail was a particularly thoughtful and sensitive gesture on the part of Ledger, and suggests the impact on Ennis of losing Jack.[27] He finally knows what he's had and lost, and now finally is able to indicate his regret and his wish that he'd given Jack the love and support and protection that Jack asked for, and was eager to give in return. Ennis's shirt now encloses and protects Jack's.

The last words Ennis speaks in both versions of *Brokeback Mountain* also indicate his realization of how much he's lost by not saying yes to what his life has offered him. In both the story and the film, as he stands in front of the shrine he's made, crying, Ennis says, as if his friend were standing in front of him once again, "Jack, I swear—"[28] without saying more. As Proulx points out, Jack never had asked Ennis to swear anything, and wasn't "the swearing kind,"[29] reminding us of Jack's gentleness and of the way he repeatedly invited Ennis to make their relationship permanent, but never made it a demand or tried to force Ennis into doing so. What Ennis swears to Jack we never know, but we can guess what it might be. Surely he would tell Jack that he loves him, and that he didn't want what happened to Jack to happen. Also, too, Ennis might well say that he didn't know that his own fear and shame would help cause it to happen, and that he wishes he could have things to do over again differently. He might wish he could assure Jack that if he could do things over, he would choose to live with him, and would love him and protect him. But while Ennis feels these things, he doesn't say them—Jack is no longer there to say them to.

The final scenes in the movie and the story are somewhat different, reflecting an important difference in structure between the two versions. Before comparing each version of the ending, it's necessary to consider the difference in structure. As mentioned, Proulx's narrative begins with Ennis getting up in the morning in his trailer some months after he's learned about Jack's death. He's been working as a hand for a rancher who's just gone out of business, and he has to leave early with his horses and try to find another job. He thinks briefly that he might have to stay with his married daughter, but there's no other mention of family or friends. Then, after Proulx recounts the whole history of the relationship between the two men, she concludes the story by returning to Ennis in the trailer after Jack's death. The film lacks this framing structure, and opens with Ennis's arrival in Signal in 1963, on the morning he and Jack meet. Also, in the final episode in the film, before the last scene, in which Ennis looks at the shirts, Alma Jr. visits him at the trailer, with the news that she's soon going to get married, which leads to a significant moment in their relationship.

The ending of the film is beautiful and poignant, suggesting that Ennis's continuing love for Jack, and his realization of how wrong it was to reject his friend, causes him to be more open with Alma Jr. As the last episode opens, Ennis apparently just has moved, and is putting the stick-on address numbers on the mailbox in front of his trailer when his daughter drives up to visit him. In earlier scenes, the film has emphasized the love that Alma Jr. feels for him, and has indicated that she'd like to be closer to him in a scene in which she asks if she could live with him rather than with Alma and the grocer. In that scene Ennis gently declines her request, saying his work takes him away too much, but the implication is that he also wants to protect his privacy. But in the final episode with Alma Jr. the film indicates that he becomes able to be closer to her, which mitigates the sense of his isolation and loneliness.

The car Alma Jr. drives up in is a flashy Camaro, and she explains that it belongs to her boyfriend, Kurt. The distance between Ennis and his daughter is evident in Ennis's comment that he thought she was seeing Troy, and in her reply that that was two years before. Perhaps Troy made more of an impression on Ennis than on his daughter, since Ennis persists, asking if Troy's still playing baseball, before she's finally able to begin telling him about Kurt, an oil worker whom she's been seeing for a year. Clearly, though Ennis cares about Alma Jr., he's seen her very little and doesn't know much about her life. When they sit and talk in the trailer, she explains that she's going to marry Kurt, telling her father that the wedding will be on June 5 at the Methodist Church, that Jenny will sing and Monroe will cater the reception. Ennis's concerned response startles and touches her: he asks if Kurt loves her. She assures him he does, and then tentatively invites Ennis to come. His first reaction is characteristic of the distance he's kept from everyone for most of his life, and which he's probably wanted from his ex-wife in particular, and which doubtless has been made stronger by his grief over losing Jack, which he can share with no one. As he did with Jack, he uses his obligations to his work to put Alma Jr. off, but then stops himself, pauses, and pours them both a drink for a toast, smiling at her and dismissing any concern about his employers, saying he reckons they can find a new cowboy. Though Alma Jr. never will know it, losing Jack makes Ennis see the damage that's done by continuing to reject others who love him, and so he refuses to hurt her the way he kept hurting Jack. Kate Mara, who plays Alma Jr., presents the impact of his decision with sensitivity, shyly beaming at what he's said. But as the screenwriters note, the smile he gives her in return "can't hide his regret and longing, for the one thing that he can't have. That he will never have."[30] Ennis may allow Alma Jr. to be a little closer to him, but he'll never tell her what she wants to know, what it is that always makes him so sad. Even with her, now the person in his life who loves him the most, he remains unable to say that once, long before, in late spring, the same time of year that she'll be married, he also fell in love. Her wedding to Kurt will be given support and encouragement by everyone, including Ennis, unlike the love he and Jack had, which was thwarted at every turn, most of all by Ennis's own resistance. For the audience, if not for Ennis, there's painful irony in a comment he makes to Alma Jr. when she first tells him she's seeing Kurt rather than Troy: he tells her that since she's nineteen, she can do whatever she wants. Ennis and Jack were the same age when they met, but an array of forces, both in society and in themselves, made it impossible for them to do what they wanted. Ennis now may be more open with his daughter because of what he's learned from his loss and grief, but even with her he has to remain silent about the memory of his love. After she leaves, as he stands by the closet looking at the two shirts and the picture of Brokeback Mountain, he speaks his last words in the film, "Jack, I swear . . ." affirming to his memory of Jack the love that he can tell to no one else. The last shot of the film emphasizes his isolation: we see the bare, windy plain through the window of Ennis's trailer, a complete contrast with the picture of Brokeback Mountain in the postcard.

Not only is the ending of the story different because Alma Jr. doesn't appear, but more importantly, in it Proulx enters Ennis's thoughts and feelings in a way that's central to the art of fiction and perhaps more difficult in film. To understand what she does, it's necessary first to look closely at the scene that opens the story, also set in Ennis's trailer after Jack's death. Unlike the filmmakers, Proulx gives Ennis no human connections to lessen his loneliness. "Ennis," in Gaelic or Celtic, means island, and he's entirely alone, like an island in the sea.[31] As he gets up and prepares to move out and begin the process of finding a new job and a new place to live, he only briefly thinks of his daughter, and just as someone who might provide a place to stay until he moves on. But, in a way that doesn't happen in the film, Jack is very much present in this opening scene, through the intensely real sexual dream that Ennis just has awakened from as the story begins. After describing the hard circumstances of Ennis's life, the fact that he faces a day with no job and no home and is uncertain even where he'll sleep that night, Proulx remarks that nevertheless he feels pleasure because he dreamed about Jack. She contrasts Ennis's situation, worrying about the day ahead as he warms up stale coffee by the sink in the trailer, with the happiness that the dream brings to his consciousness. He "lets a panel of the dream slide forward. If he does not force his attention on it, it might stoke the day, rewarm that old, cold time on the mountain when they owned the world and nothing seemed wrong."[32] For Ennis, the realities he has to face are softened by the memory of his dream of Jack, though, as Proulx notes, he can't force his attention on it. As we all know, the memory of a dream can't be made to come into our consciousness, and trying to subject it to conscious thought can simply push it away, until perhaps it comes again of its own accord. Also, for Ennis, it may be that too much thought, especially about what happened to Jack, may make it impossible to recapture the happy memory of the dream. But the memory of the dream is what may be able to help him get through the day.

Then in the final part of the story, Proulx returns again to Ennis's thoughts in the months after Jack's death, and explains more about the significance of his dreams about Jack. By beginning and ending the story with what Ennis thinks and feels after Jack is gone, Proulx locates the narrative of their experience together as Ennis's memory, reinforcing the mood of nostalgia and regret. She starts the final part by describing how Ennis arranges the shirts and the postcard in the trailer, adding that about then Jack began to appear in Ennis's dreams, as Jack was when Ennis first met him, with his curly hair and bucktoothed smile,

> talking about getting up off his pockets and into the control zone, but the can of beans with the spoon handle jutting out and balanced on the log was there as well, in a cartoon shape and lurid colors that gave the dreams a flavor of comic obscenity. The spoon handle was the kind that could be used as a tire iron. And he would wake sometimes in grief, sometimes with the old sense of joy and release; the pillow sometimes wet, sometimes the sheets.[33]

Because Ennis has acknowledged and accepted his love for Jack as he couldn't fully when Jack was alive, now Jack lives not only in his memory, but comes to him in dreams, almost as if he really were alive, young, and happy to be with Ennis, as he was when Ennis first fell in love with him — and before he rejected him. Although Ennis is entirely alone, in a way Jack still is with him, and helps him. Through all the difficulties of his life, Ennis's attitude has been a fatalistic, stoical one: "'if you can't fix it you got a stand it,'"[34] and now the love he and Jack had provides a source of strength that helps Ennis stand it. Even on a morning when Ennis faces the hard prospect of having no job and no home, the dream of Jack can "stoke the day."[35] Yet always in Ennis's passionate dreams of Jack there also is the memory of what happened to Jack, expressed in the surreal dream image of the can of beans with the spoon, threatening to become a tire iron, a startlingly distorted version of the memory of his meals with Jack on Brokeback Mountain that Ennis thought of as he waited for Jack on the afternoon of their first reunion. Even in his imagination's recreation of the sexual intimacy and ribald humor he shared with Jack, Ennis's awareness of the constant threat of violence, and perhaps of his own connection to it, intrudes. He always will have his love for Jack, and the memory of Jack's for him, but he never will be free of the knowledge that his rejection played a part in Jack's murder, and that he's partly responsible for the fact that, real as Jack seems in his dreams, when he awakens, Ennis is alone. Sometimes he'll have the comforting pleasure of his wet dreams about Jack, other times tears of grief that Jack is gone.

For a man like Ennis, the future probably holds a lot that he'll need the strength to stand. Instead of saying yes to Jack and to himself, he said no, and now when he realizes it was a mistake, it's too late, and he's alone, and likely will be for the rest of his life. In her comments about the origin of "Brokeback Mountain," Proulx, with her remarkable sensitivity about the lives of man-loving men in the rural West, has suggested what growing older may mean for a man like Ennis. She's explained that her thoughts for the story began to take shape when

> One night in a bar upstate I . . . noticed an older ranch hand, maybe in his late sixties, obviously short on the world's luxury goods. Although spruced up for Friday night his clothes were a little ragged, boots stained and worn. I had seen him around, working cows, helping with sheep, taking orders from a ranch manager. He was thin and lean, muscular in a stringy kind of way. He leaned against the back wall and his eyes were fastened not on the dozens of handsome and flashing women in the room but on the young cowboys playing pool. Maybe he was following the game, maybe he knew the players, maybe one was his son or nephew, but there was something in his expression, a kind of bitter longing, that made me wonder if he was country gay.[36]

As Proulx observes here, the "destructive rural homophobia"[37] that she makes her subject in the story doesn't take its toll only in the lives that are snuffed out, like Jack's or Matthew Shepard's, by straight men who can't stand the fact that there are man-loving men among them, or in the thousands of sexual minority people who are forced to give up their small communities, ranches, and farms and the landscape they love and go into exile in cities like Denver; it also costs the lives of men like the ranch hand she observed who was part of the inspiration for Ennis, who are condemned to a half-life of isolation and loneliness by the hatred that prevents them from loving other men. She recognizes one of the many truths of the ACT UP slogan, "Silence Equals Death," the fact that a life of silence in hiding really does amount to a kind of living death. As she points out in the same essay on "Brokeback Mountain," "Wyoming has the highest suicide rate in the country, and . . . the preponderance of those people who kill themselves are elderly single men."[38] Isolation, poverty, sickness all must contribute to this, and certainly many such suicides aren't men who desire men, but many certainly are. As historians have shown, there are man-loving men in rural areas who successfully establish relationships, though many testify to the repressive, limiting conditions they've experienced. At least the fear and shame that have kept Ennis trying to pass for straight didn't prevent him from having what he had with Jack, though for some sexual minority people, rural and urban, their own internalized homophobia keeps them from ever fulfilling their needs for sexual and emotional intimacy at all. And at least Ennis has his dreams, his imperishable memory of Jack, which may be enough to help him get by.

The last sentence of the story again reminds us of the profound spiritual importance of love, regardless of who it is that loves or is loved. After describing the vividness of Ennis's dreams of Jack, Proulx says, "There was some open space between what he knew and what he tried to believe, but nothing could be done about it, and if you can't fix it you've got to stand it."[39] For Ennis, as for many people, there's a distance between the hard facts of life and what he hopes may be true. Every morning when he awakens, it's to the knowledge that Jack is dead, but when he sleeps and Jack comes to him in his dreams, it's with such a sense of reality that it reinforces the belief that in some way Jack's spirit continues, that he's not entirely gone. Love can be so strong that it makes us hope that the connection we have with the spirit of the person we love can persist, posing questions about what happens after death that, in life at least, are unanswerable. Jack still is with Ennis, with the kind of daily intimacy that they weren't able to have when he was alive because of Ennis's fear and shame. Perhaps, Ennis tries to believe, they aren't separated forever. But there's no way to know, and all he can do is endure, with the support of his memory of Jack.

NOTES

1. Proulx, "Brokeback Mountain," 20.
2. Proulx, "Brokeback Mountain," 20–21.
3. Proulx, "Brokeback Mountain," 22.
4. Proulx, "Brokeback Mountain," 35.
5. Proulx, "Brokeback Mountain," 42.
6. Proulx, "Brokeback Mountain," 43.
7. Proulx, "Brokeback Mountain," 43.
8. Proulx, "Brokeback Mountain," 43.
9. Proulx, "Brokeback Mountain," 43.
10. Proulx, "Brokeback Mountain," 43–44.
11. Proulx, "Brokeback Mountain," 44.
12. Proulx, "Brokeback Mountain," 44.
13. Proulx, "Brokeback Mountain," 44.
14. James Baldwin, *Giovanni's Room*, 5.
15. Proulx, "Brokeback Mountain," 46.
16. Proulx, "Brokeback Mountain," 46.

17. On the development and versions of the song, "Big Rock Candy Mountain," see Higbie, *Indispensable Outcasts*, and Hal Rammel, *Nowhere in America: The Big Rock Candy Mountain and Other Comic Utopias* (Urbana/Chicago: University of Illinois, 1990). The song has a long history, probably being derived from a seventeenth-century English broadside ballad, "An Invitation to Lubberland." In English folklore, Lubberland, like Cockaigne, was an imaginary land of utopian plenty and pleasure.

18. From National Institute of Environmental Health Services/National Institutes of Health/Department of Health and Human Services Kids' Pages (niehs.nih.gov/kids/lyrics/bigrock/htm):"Big Rock Candy Mountain" lyrics.

19. On "Big Rock Candy Mountain," see Higbie, *Indispensable Outcasts*, and Rammel, *Nowhere*. In their discussions of hoboes, both Higbie and Boag (*Same-Sex Affairs*) provide thorough and nonjudgmental discussion of the sexual relationships between jockers and punks. Higbie briefly discusses "Big Rock Candy Mountain" and its representation of the jocker-punk relationship, though Boag does not. Although Rammel provides extensive discussion of the origins of the song and quotes a version of it that refers to jockers and punks, unfortunately he doesn't discuss the meaning of the two terms and avoids discussing the sexual aspect of the jocker-punk relationship, and so perpetuates the suppression of the song's significance in relation to men who desired men. Scholarship continues to be harmed by the impulse to erase evidence of same-sex desire. Though it's much more subtle than direct homophobic discrimination, this kind of erasure is a significant component of the spectrum of homophobia, and works to deny men who love men, and everyone else, knowledge of same-sex desire and relationships in history and culture.

20. See Cawelti, *Mystique*, on the limitations of the time period in which classic Westerns often are set.

21. Proulx, "Brokeback Mountain," 36.

22. Proulx, "Brokeback Mountain," 51.

23. Proulx, "Brokeback Mountain," 52.

24. Proulx, "Brokeback Mountain," 52.

25. "When Lilacs Last in the Dooryard Bloom'd," ll. 79–80, Whitman, *Leaves of Grass* (Ninth edition/1892).

26. On photography, desire, loss, and memory, see Roland Barthes (translator, Richard Howard), *Camera Lucida: Reflections on Photography* (New York: Farrar, Strauss, and Giroux, 1981), and Susan Sontag, *On Photography* (New York: Farrar, Strauss, and Giroux, 1973).

27. Diana Ossana discussed Heath Ledger's rearrangement of the two shirts in her interview with Anne Stockwell in *The Advocate*, February 28, 2006.

28. Proulx, "Brokeback Mountain," 54.

29. Proulx, "Brokeback Mountain," 54.

30. McMurtry and Ossana, "Screenplay," 96.

31. "Ennis" or "innis" means "island" in Gaelic or Celtic; "del Mar" means "of the sea" in Spanish.

32. Proulx, "Brokeback Mountain," 4.

33. Proulx, "Brokeback Mountain," 54–55.

34. Proulx, "Brokeback Mountain," 30.
35. Proulx, "Brokeback Mountain," 4.
36. Proulx, "Getting Movied," 129–30.
37. Proulx, "Getting Movied," 130.
38. Proulx, "Getting Movied," 131.
39. Proulx, "Brokeback Mountain," 55.

Chapter Seven

The Pair Like Two Skins,
One inside the Other,
Two in One: Myths of Love

Both versions of *Brokeback Mountain* challenge the majority's assumptions and prejudices, but possibly their most remarkable achievement is to locate love between men within the almost sacred space American culture reserves for myths of romantic love. Everyone in this country is familiar with the ideal of romantic love, since it's expressed in virtually all areas of cultural activity, from the most sophisticated creative works to the most commercial and popular. Some may be skeptical about it, others may analyze it critically, but it still shapes expectations of relationships for many people. Members of sexual minorities, growing up in American culture and sharing its beliefs, of course also often share this understanding of love, but the dominant culture has constructed romance only in terms of heterosexuality, explicitly excluding intimate relationships between people of the same sex. As most members of the majority construct same-sex desire, it consists merely of sexuality, often of the crudest forms; they usually ignore and often explicitly deny the emotional dimensions of relationships between couples of the same sex. Although many sexual minority writers, artists, and filmmakers have presented love between people of the same sex in romantic terms, their work usually only reaches audiences that primarily include members of sexual minorities. With the story and the movie of *Brokeback Mountain*, a heterosexual writer and heterosexual filmmakers have created narratives that represent love between men in the ways that many in the majority have assumed only are appropriate for themselves. In two highly crafted and sophisticated works of art, the creators of both versions of *Brokeback Mountain* assert the right of love between men to be placed on the same exalted plane as heterosexual love, within the genre of romantic tragedy. The movie, in particular, because it's been widely advertised, distributed, and discussed, forces members of the majority to recognize that sexual minorities and some members of the majority see love between people of the same sex as being entirely equal to heterosexual love.

As cultural historians have explained, the great emphasis that American culture and other cultures that are derived from European traditions place on romantic love isn't shared by numerous cultures around the world, and in fact only began to develop in Western Europe during the Middle Ages, in the aristocratic tradition of courtly love.[1] Since that time a complex array of conceptions has been created that construct romantic love in the terms that are accepted today in cultural systems that have been shaped by Europe, such as that in the United States, and that can be referred to as Western, in the broad sense that they're part of the cultural inheritance of Europe rather than Asia and Africa. According to these conceptions, romantic love is distinct from and superior to sexual desire because, in addition to strong sexual attraction, it also involves a profound emotional connection between people that gives meaning to their sexual involvement. It's not only a physical connection, but also a deeply emotional one, not mere lust, but love. Of course, romantic love sometimes is unrequited, but ideally it's mutual, and, when this is the case, it's thought of as providing the basis for a lifelong commitment. Western culture has defined marriage in terms of romantic love, instead of defining it as a pragmatic arrangement between families or individuals, as is the case in some parts of the world. The prevalence of the ideal of romantic love probably is related to the growth of individual autonomy, particularly for men, as a result of the development of capitalism in Western Europe and its colonies. Romantic love stresses individual choice in marriage, and creates an idealized conception of marriage that probably has served to encourage women to accept the unequal role within it that men have demanded they take. Women in particular are indoctrinated with belief in romantic love, but, though the culture makes different emotional and sexual scripts available to men, the expectations of romantic love often shape their lives as well.

Many other beliefs about romantic love are familiar: it often is thought of as something that takes us by surprise, with dramatic suddenness, and as being almost irresistible, impossible to control. Our language reflects this: we speak of "falling in love," of "love at first sight," of "endless love." Love often is constructed in terms of fate or destiny. We're taught to expect that there exists another special person who's right for each of us, "another half" without whom our lives can't be complete. Romantic love is deeply related to our experiences of time and change: we learn to anticipate it with hope, to yearn for it, to regret its failure, and to memorialize its loss. When it comes, we wish it could last forever, and feel nostalgia for it when it's gone. Perfect experiences of love often are constructed as moments when time seems suspended, as a kind of ecstasy outside of the daily experience of change and loss. Such constructions of love can be thought of as expressing, in personal terms, a utopian impulse, a yearning for a life that's better and happier than what people have. This transcendent aspect of constructions of romantic love associates it strongly with the desires for security and permanence and the fears of loss and death expressed for many people by religion.

Though some cultures lack the romantic construction of love or view the emotions and behaviors that many Americans associate with it quite differently, and often negatively, to many people in American culture it's simply assumed to be innate and natural, and isn't recognized as a cultural construction at all. Today, as a result of the development of critical analysis of the cultural construction of gender, some do recognize that the ideal of romantic love is culturally defined, and seek to challenge its predominance in perceptions of sexuality and gender. Still, the vast majority of people in American society accept it as an accurate description of the kind of love that's possible between two people, and indeed even some of those who are well aware of the analytical critiques of it, having grown up being influenced by the dominant cultural values of American society, still are influenced by it like everyone else. That it can be thought of as a cultural construction doesn't change the fact that romantic love is one of the most important ideals that shapes the lives of people in American culture today.

The contrast between the idealized representation of romantic love and the way the majority usually constructs same-sex love is stunning. If love between men or love between women is depicted at all by the majority, it's usually been in ways as remote as possible from the lofty, moving representations so frequent in constructions of love between members of the majority. Depictions of people of the same sex who are attracted to each other largely erase their emotional connection, reducing their relationships to mere physical lust, preventing any recognition that their relationships even qualify as love, which remains a category reserved for heterosexuals only. As mentioned before, men who love men often are constructed as dangerous sexual predators or as effeminate, contemptible victims, representations that cater to the fears of heterosexual men, and women who love women often are represented as exotic seductresses for the titillation of a heterosexual male audience. Male-male sex is constructed as being particularly unnatural and disgusting, and is the obsessive focus of many in the majority in relation to sexual minority men. Desire between people of the same sex isn't presented as it is to them, but as it appears to members of the majority, whereas narratives about love as the majority experiences it are presented from within the perspective of the heterosexual lovers involved. In the constructions of same-sex desire that are usual among the majority, there's none of the sense that love can be an overwhelming feeling of complete commitment to another human being, or of the compassion and sensitivity that male and female lovers are presented as feeling toward each other, or of the sense that being in love completes the self, that the person one loves is one's other half. If emotion is depicted between lovers of the same sex, it's often as the ugly, disturbing feelings most people would wish to disavow in themselves, jealousy, dependency, obsession, and rage. Above all, same-sex desire is presented as transient and promiscuous, not as true and lasting commitment.

Although styles of artistic expression change greatly over time, and some exaggerated idealizations of romantic love that moved people in the past no longer can be taken with the seriousness that they once were, readers and audiences in America today continue to be strongly attracted to depictions of the power of love, and of course often to seek to realize it in their own relationships. For centuries, artists in every area of cultural activity have honored heterosexual love in works intended to show the depth of love between man and woman, many of which are of great power and beauty. The depiction of romantic love is central to most of the major traditional art forms, particularly poetry, drama, the novel, song, opera, ballet, and painting. In high culture, idealized representations of love probably were most strongly embraced by serious artists who were part of the Romantic Movement, particularly during the first half of the nineteenth century. The shift toward realism in art in the later nineteenth century and then the Modernist Movement in the twentieth generally tended to cause many serious creative artists to depart from the idealization of love, or, if they depicted it, often to present it ironically, as being overwhelmed by the power of economic and social conditions, or even as a destructive illusion. Nonetheless, despite such changes in sophisticated taste, many writers, composers, painters, and sculptors, both those involved in innovative artistic movements and those seeking to appeal to a broad popular market, have continued to accept and honor many aspects of Western cultural traditions about love. In popular fiction and journalism, and in the new commercial media of artistic expression that emerged in the twentieth century, particularly movies, TV, and popular music, idealized representations of romantic love have been a central subject. Images of heterosexual passion and romance also are used to sell nearly every commodity on the market, and literally are everywhere in the advertising that saturates American society and shapes almost every mode of communication. Both sophisticated and popular audiences continue to want stories of the power of love, keeping some of the great examples from the past perennially popular, and eliciting the creation of new artistic expressions of the culture's beliefs about the possibilities of romantic love, some of which are highly conventional and cater to broad popular tastes, and some of which are sophisticated and innovative works of art.

As a result, there is an immense body of works in many areas of artistic expression that celebrate and idealize romantic love.

The long and rich tradition of the exaltation of love between men and women is known to almost everyone in at least some of its forms, and its varieties are almost endless. While the creative art produced by Western culture honors the love between men and women using various methods, perhaps the most fundamental, particularly in art that employs linear narrative, involves presenting romantic love in contrast to forces that oppose it. Everyone affected by Western culture is familiar with at least one of the variants of the great myth of tragic love.

The basic form of the myth, as it's been used especially by poets, playwrights, novelists, composers, choreographers, and filmmakers, is easily described: a man and a woman meet, are deeply drawn to each other, and fall passionately in love, each giving the other everything possible, yet some terrible force opposes them, and sometimes even may cause one or both of them temporarily to resist their love, though often they then embrace it again more strongly, even if it's too late. If the opposing force destroys one of the lovers, the grief of the one who remains serves to affirm the value of their love. This opposing force may be so great that in some versions it may destroy both of their lives, but the power of their love is represented as being even greater. In some depictions of love, particularly those that aren't concerned with the conventions of realistic representation, love may be presented as being so powerful that it even can transcend death. The force that thwarts love fails, and in its failure only demonstrates the greatness of love. Although of course physical attraction is part of the power of the love that unites the two lovers, it's presented not as aggressive and lustful, but as a pure, beautiful, mutual desire, inseparable from the gentle, affectionate, solicitous emotions that the lovers share and that ennoble them. Such tragic myths thus emphasize the spiritual nature of love, raising the sexual and emotional attraction between people of the opposite sex almost to the level of a religious experience. As it's presented in some narratives, tragic, romantic love becomes a kind of secular counterpart to the values of charity and self-sacrifice emphasized in some forms of Christianity. In representations of desire between people of the same sex, in contrast, rather than presenting their love as something noble and pure, and juxtaposing it to a destructive force, as in the great myths of tragic love between heterosexuals, the attraction between people of the same sex is *itself* represented as a destructive force.

Of the great tragic love stories that the majority tells about itself, probably the example from traditional high culture that's most familiar to many Americans is Shakespeare's *Romeo and Juliet* (1594). Here the opposing force that confronts the two lovers is presented as a social conflict: the innocence, purity, and beauty of the feelings of the young lovers for each other are countered by the brutal, pointless feud between the Montagues and the Capulets. Though the hatred between their families destroys the lives of the star-crossed lovers, it can't destroy their love, which Shakespeare presents as a transcendent, almost religious force that transfigures everyone at the end of the play, teaching a profound lesson of forgiveness and reconciliation. The contrast between love and social forces that oppose it is evident in many other versions of the myth of tragic love, such as some of the major works of fiction produced by the Romantic Movement, for instance the great novels of the Bronte sisters, Emily Bronte's *Wuthering Heights* (1847) and Charlotte Bronte's *Jane Eyre* (1847), which helped to define some of the conventions of what became the popular gothic romance. Such novels often present a female protagonist, and emphasize the ways in which differences in class and status, and the constraints of patriarchal culture, may interfere with her relationship with the man she loves. Because of the nature of its organization and structure, the myth of tragic love has lent itself to the depiction of a wide range of social problems that can affect individual relationships, and it's been used by sophisticated and popular artists to criticize inequalities of class, race, religion, and ethnicity. The force that opposes the lovers, and which can be criticized by contrasting it to their love, may be any sort of prejudice that divides people and leads to conflict.

With the development of realistic styles of artistic expression concerned with social criticism in the mid to late nineteenth century, some artists who rejected what they saw as the excesses of the Romantic Movement still made use of the basic structure of the myth of tragic love. One example familiar to many American readers is Edith Wharton's brilliant novel *The House of Mirth* (1905), in which Wharton shows the ways in which the snobbery and materialism of the turn-of-the-century New York upper class interfere with the emotions of the two main characters, Lily Bart and Lawrence Selden, ultimately preventing their love and destroying Lily. Of course, many other artists concerned with the realistic depiction of society completely rejected the hope expressed in the conception of romantic love. This is the case in a major work contemporary with Wharton's, Theodore Dreiser's *Sister Carrie* (1900), which was suppressed on publication because its characters are motivated solely by self-interest and the desire for material advancement, rather than the lofty and generous emotions idealized in romantic love. Carrie's choice of relationships with men on the basis of their material wealth rather than on any emotional connection with them, and her eventual success, was especially shocking to American readers. But even skeptical works such as this, by rejecting the possibility of romantic love, remind us of the power of the ideal.

The artistic Modernism that became prevalent in the twentieth century also often challenged the power of romantic love. A familiar example, already mentioned, is Hemingway's *The Sun Also Rises*, in which the wounded war veteran Jake Barnes and Lady Brett Ashley are deeply attracted and care about each other, but are unable to consummate their love because of Jake's sexual injury. The frustration of romantic love serves as a means to address the catastrophe of the First World War. F. Scott Fitzgerald's *The Great Gatsby* (1925) is a particularly imaginative reworking of the myth that raises profound questions about American culture. Here, although Gatsby and Daisy share an intense mutual attraction, their love is distorted by the values of the different social classes they come from. Gatsby idealizes Daisy as a symbol of the social world he's so ambitious to enter, and perhaps even as the ultimate possession that would confirm his inclusion in that world. Her allegiance to her own class ultimately causes her to reject their love. What truly makes Gatsby great, in the eyes of the narrator, Nick Carraway, is his willingness, finally, to sacrifice his success and even his life for Daisy, although she's unworthy of him. The nobility of his love ultimately is in contrast to the crude selfishness and materialism that cause Daisy to retreat, and that have driven Gatsby to get rich through crime. For Fitzgerald, a tragic story of resistance to love becomes a means of making a brilliant critique of the corrupting impact of the American Dream.

The great European traditions of performing art, of course, make extensive use of the myth of tragic love. Sometimes these art forms present it as being challenged by hostile social or cultural systems, as in Verdi''s *La Traviata* (1853) and *Aida* (1871) and Puccini's *La Boheme* (1896), but since opera and ballet lend themselves to highly imaginative styles of expression, they also are well suited to creating imaginary worlds presenting the tragic myth of romantic love in magical, fantastic ways, stressing the spiritual aspects of love. These art forms are unfamiliar to many Americans, but some know one important example, the ballet *Swan Lake* (1877), which perfectly represents the mythology through which Western culture privileges heterosexual love. In what's probably its best-known version, Prince Siegfried encounters the enchanted Swan Queen, Odette, over whom a cruel sorcerer has cast a spell that only can be broken if a mortal man loves her. Siegfried and Odette fall in love, and he pledges himself to her, but the sorcerer then manipulates him into violating his pledge, which will curse Odette to death. As Odette is about to die, Siegfried returns to her and she forgives him, though she can't escape the curse. She's forced to cast herself into the lake to drown, but his love for her is so great that he joins her, and the power of sacrifice and love destroys the sorcerer and frees the other swans from his spell. As Tchaikovsky's magnificent score closes, there is a somber but triumphant apotheosis, in which the two lovers are united in the afterlife. Like many other operas and ballets that affirm the value of love between men and women, *Swan Lake* presents love triumphing over all opposition, as a mystical, transcendent force that can conquer even death itself.

The persistent appeal of the myth of tragic love is evident in every aspect of American commercial popular culture. The ultimate example of the myth, at least in the English-speaking world, *Romeo and Juliet*, has been filmed repeatedly, and one of the most wonderful American musicals, *West Side Story* (1957), is based on it. In the musical, the two lovers, Tony and Maria, are separated not by family rivalry but by the ethnic hatred between Polish and Puerto Rican Americans. Although in contrast to the play the musical ends with the death of only one of the lovers, the message their love provides of the need to forgive differences that divide people is much the same as that in Shakespeare. Recent popular culture provides a version of the myth that everyone undoubtedly must be aware of, since it was so widely advertised, and so hugely successful, even if they haven't actually seen the movie: *Titanic* (1997). As in *Gatsby*, here the lovers are divided by differences of social class, though of course the effects of this division aren't developed with the complexity of Fitzgerald's novel. But, along with all its spectacular special effects, the film does provide an interesting reinterpretation of the myth of romantic love, incorporating the contemporary aspirations of women to autonomy and equality, though still presenting a male as the source of guidance for the main female character. At the start, Rose (Kate Winslett) is trapped by the class and gender conventions of the transatlantic elite, much like an Edith Wharton character, but her passionate affair with Jack (Leonardo DiCaprio) and his heroism and self-sacrificing love free her from the tyranny of her mother and of her fiancé, showing her the possibility of a life lived for herself on her own terms.

There are many differences between the various examples just cited; some use highly refined European artistic traditions of expression to create extraordinary imaginary worlds, others work within a framework of realistic representation, but generally they illustrate the continuing cultural pattern of the celebration of heterosexual romantic love. Such works of art reinforce the belief that the discovery of love between man and woman can be an experience of remarkable beauty, that their love can be innocent and pure, that it can resist and even transcend brutal opposition and hostility, and that rather than merely involving the uniting of two bodies, it can mean the uniting of two souls. Both versions of *Brokeback Mountain* differ substantially in stylistic terms from some of the forms of verbal, visual, and musical expression that have been mentioned, but they're related in that they too address the subject of romantic love. Both are the creations of heterosexual artists, but both claim a place for love between men in a territory of cultural expression that the majority has reserved entirely for itself.

Following the fundamental pattern of stories of romantic love, the story and the film of *Brokeback Mountain* present the love between Ennis and Jack as far more than sexual attraction. Indeed, it begins as friendship, and involves trust, mutual effort in work, and playful companionship long before it becomes a sexual relationship. For both men, a strong emotional connection is formed well before it leads to having sexual intercourse. When they do act on their sexual attraction toward each other, it's in ways that are satisfying to both of them. Whatever the reactions of some heterosexual male readers and viewers may be, within the context of the story and the movie, the passionate sexual interaction between the characters is presented as it is to them, natural, joyful, necessary, and fulfilling, and as a source of reinforcement of their emotional bond. Their sexual and emotional involvement grows and develops, leading to a profound connection that's lifelong, despite society's hostility and Ennis's fears and internalized homophobia. Their sexual passion continues, and is equaled by their need for each other's companionship. In this regard, both versions of the narrative place the relationship between Jack and Ennis directly in the category of romantic love, refuting the homophobic belief that passionate relationships between men must only be sexual and transitory, and can't have the emotional depth and richness of relationships between men and women. The filmmakers emphasized their awareness of the centrality of romantic love in *Brokeback Mountain* in the advertising campaign that they used for the movie, with the slogan "Love is a force of nature" and a poster whose design was deliberately modeled on that for *Titanic*. Just as the poster for *Titanic* is arranged vertically, showing the film's heterosexual lovers in close-up at the top, with the title and other information below, so the poster for *Brokeback Mountain* has Ledger and Gyllenhaal as Ennis and Jack next to each other at the top, the Wyoming landscape behind them, and the printed text underneath. According to reports on the movie's advertising campaign, the design was developed only after extensive examination of the posters for a large number of successful romantic films.[2]

In Western culture's construction of romantic love, it can become the basis of a continuing monogamous commitment. As critics of the ideology of romantic love rightly have pointed out, this ideal can be impossible to realize in actual relationships, but the dominant culture still teaches that men and women should aspire to love one another for life. Romantic love is presented as the foundation of marriage. Whether or not such a belief is realistic for most people, it does occur in some cases; as the emotional and sexual bond between Ennis and Jack is presented in both the story and the movie, it's so strong that if it weren't constantly impeded by homophobia, it could unite them for life. Their love could be the basis for the sort of monogamous relationship that the dominant culture solemnizes and honors as marriage. As Proulx and the filmmakers present the relationship of the two men, it reinforces the argument many sexual minority people and their allies now are making that same sex couples are just as capable of commitment as their heterosexual counterparts, and that therefore there's no rational reason for denying them the benefits and status of marriage. In both versions, all of the obstacles to a continuing relationship between Jack and Ennis, including Ennis's sense of fear and shame, ultimately are imposed from without, by society. It's important to note that substantial numbers of people who are sexually different have made it clear that they don't identify as gay or lesbian but as queer or in other ways, and that many have strong and well-reasoned criticisms of constructions of relationships that emphasize commitment and monogamy; those who reject what they perceive as heteronormative models of same-sex relationships also may reject the story and the film. But sexual minority people who value committed, monogamous relationships and support efforts to achieve marriage equality for same-sex couples are likely to be strongly affected by *Brokeback Mountain*.

Like many of the most moving depictions of romantic love, Proulx's story and Lee's film present the intense love between Ennis and Jack in opposition to a force that's its antithesis, and that, by contrast, shows the depth of their love. The bond between them, which at once is an egalitarian form of comradeship and the strongest form of sexual passion, is juxtaposed to the hatred and violence of men like Aguirre, their fathers, L.D., and the men who murder Jack. Proulx and the filmmakers repeatedly contrast the happiness that Jack and Ennis find in being with each other to the competitive, aggressive, brutal actions of the other men in their world. Although the mountain provides a place apart that allows love between men to flourish, a masculine landscape for masculine love, men who hate love between men dominate every other space. Homophobia is so pervasive that it affects the natural desire Ennis feels for Jack, driving him to reject his friend, and forces both men into the mistake of marrying women. Their separation causes both continually to feel nostalgia for the union they once had, and that Jack feels they could have maintained. Jack's memory of being embraced by Ennis on the mountain exemplifies the construction of romantic love as a utopian experience transcending time and defying change. As in some classic versions of the myth of tragic love, the force that opposes their love causes one of the lovers to betray the other, but ultimately this only serves to dramatize the importance of their love, when Ennis realizes what he's lost in rejecting Jack. As a result of Jack's murder, Ennis comes to understand how much he and Jack loved each other, the mistake he made in refusing to live with him, and the connection of his own fear and shame to Jack's death. The tragic loss of love confirms its meaning and value, for Ennis and for the reader or viewer as well.

Whatever perspective one takes on the traditional cultural construction of romantic love, cultural historians have shown that it developed as an alternative to the custom of arranged marriages, in which two families negotiated the marriage of a son and a daughter in order to create an alliance and to promote family interests. The cult of romantic love is, in part, a form of protest against this practice, and an assertion of the right of individual men and women to have the freedom to choose their own sexual and emotional partners. To many people today, the idea of an arranged marriage is repugnant, since it ignores the desires of individuals. In their construction, the two versions of *Brokeback Mountain* present homophobic hatred and prejudice as the social power opposing individual desire, and forcing Ennis and then Jack into marriages that society deems appropriate, but that violate the individual desires and natures of the two men, and of course also place their wives in situations that are wrong for them. In a sense, for each man and his wife homophobia results in a forced marriage that ignores individual feeling and freedom. Despite current reactionary efforts to erode legal conceptions of the right of privacy, many Americans believe strongly that adults have the right to control their personal lives and to choose their relationships for themselves. Thus *Brokeback Mountain* touches a deeply held belief concerning the freedom to love that's inherent in the conception of romantic love, and mobilizes it in asserting the right of people of the same sex to love one another if it's right for them. While many homophobic straight readers and viewers will continue determinedly to ignore or attack the story and the film, for some straight people, especially those who value the ideal of romantic love, *Brokeback Mountain* can move them to recognize that two men can experience romantic love as well, and that lovers of the same sex deserve the same freedom to love that lovers of the opposite sex assume as their right. This may account for the fact that many straight women have responded very positively to the movie.

By contrasting romantic love with hostility to it, myths of tragic love demonstrate the strength of feeling and commitment between two people, no matter how many oppose them, or how powerful those who oppose them are. Love is presented as being far more than physical attraction; it's presented as a spiritual force that can resist all opposition, that can transform others, and that can last beyond death. Though Romeo and Juliet die, their love changes their families forever, and brings about their reconciliation. Though Siegfried and Odette die, their love destroys the malignant power of the sorcerer, frees the other swans, and transcends death. Though Tony is murdered in the rumble between the Sharks and the Jets, Maria confronts them with what they've done and brings their feud to an end. Though Jack dies in the freezing water after the *Titanic* sinks, he leaves Rose with a lesson about the power of love and individual freedom and courage that transforms her entire life. Narratives of tragic, romantic love, despite the great differences between them in terms of style and presentation, emphasize the profound spiritual power of love. *Brokeback Mountain* differs stylistically from all these examples, but it too presents love as a transforming force that can't be destroyed.

Unlike many versions of the myth of tragic romantic love, the context of *Brokeback Mountain* is entirely ordinary. There's none of the elegance and glamour and fantasy so often employed in versions of the myth extolling heterosexual love. Except for the magnificence of the mountains in which Ennis and Jack are free to love each other, the settings either are run down and shabby, as in the places Ennis lives and the Twists' ranch, or cheap and garish, in the case of Lureen's home and the other settings associated with the Newsomes in Texas. The physical ugliness of the social environment reinforces a sense of the ugliness of its values, especially the contempt and hatred of men who love men. The main characters are uneducated working-class American men, who only are remarkable because their sexual difference sets them apart from the majority. Their speech is ungrammatical, sometimes crude, but full of the rich vernacular of everyday life. Both versions of the narrative present the lives of Jack and Ennis in a relatively straightforward, realistic manner, although in both cases with great subtlety. Aside from the frame depicting Ennis after Jack's death, Proulx's narrative recounts the experiences of the men in linear fashion, though it's rich in its use of vernacular language and in its presentation of significant detail. The film also presents their lives in linear sequence, in fact dropping the frame employed by Proulx, and simply telling the events of their story in chronological order. Prieto's cinematography is superb, suggesting the dull, constraining quality of the spaces in which the men live with their wives, in contrast to the light, color, and open space of the mountain and the other wildernesses where the men can be together, but it always seems a realistic presentation of actual places with which many Americans are familiar.

Against the realistically depicted ordinariness of the social world Jack and Ennis inhabit, with its physical and moral ugliness, the story and the movie present the depth and intensity of their love, linking it to the natural beauty of the mountains. Each version of the narrative places the reader or viewer within the perspective of the two men, showing their gradual, wonderful discovery of the love between them, demonstrating what it means to them. Their love is presented as they experience it, and it's contrasted to the contempt, hatred, and violence of the other men around them. As in other versions of the myth of tragic love, this contrast shows the greatness of love, and the stupidity and cruelty of the forces that oppose it. Other stories of tragic love have challenged a variety of forms of social prejudice and conflict, but *Brokeback Mountain* is the first directed toward a mass audience to directly challenge homophobia. In it, Annie Proulx and the filmmakers have taken the structure of the sort of story the majority uses so often to glorify its own love, and have used it brilliantly to challenge the majority's prejudice against love between men. As in other versions of the myth, the forces that oppose the love between Ennis and Jack ultimately are incapable of destroying what the lovers feel. The other men who affect their lives attack their love as something dirty, worthless, and hateful, but to Jack, and finally to Ennis in spite of his resistance, it's beautiful and natural, far more so than the heterosexual love that they've been taught that they should feel. Nostalgia for it draws them back together repeatedly, and keeps Jack hoping that Ennis eventually will accept his invitations to live together. After Ennis's rejections lead to Jack's murder, he finally does fully understand the significance of their love. Jack is dead, but their love is not, and it sustains Ennis. Even though he's alone, he still has the memory of Jack's love, manifested in the shirts. In the film, this helps him to open up to his daughter, and in the story, Jack's love is even more powerful. It's present not only in Ennis's memories and regrets, but in his dreams, in which Jack comes to him as a lover and gives him the support he needs to be able to stand what he can't fix. Although the movie and the story operate in terms of the conventions of realism, in settings similar to those of the ordinary daily lives of millions of Americans, like other versions of the myth of tragic love, such as those that use the most exalted verbal, visual, and musical means to tell their stories, they present love as a force that can resist death. There's none of the magical fantasy of poetry or opera or ballet, but even as in the grandest examples of the myth, love is transcendent, and can't be entirely defeated by the forces that oppose it. At the close of both the film and the story, Jack isn't completely gone, and Ennis still speaks to him as a living presence, when he stands looking at the two shirts and the postcard of Brokeback Mountain and says, "Jack, I swear . . ."

Perhaps one reason the story and the film have evoked such a strong response from so many men who love men is that they see that the love between Jack and Ennis is indestructible in an additional sense, because it lives on again and again in the lives of other men who love men, for whom the story and the film affirm the value of their deepest feelings. Despite the hostility to love between men that's everywhere in America, there always will be men who feel what Ennis and Jack have felt. In every generation, some young men will enjoy each other's company, and laugh and wrestle and play together, and fall in love with each other, discovering what they discovered on Brokeback Mountain. Certainly the meanings given to the desire of men for men differ from generation to generation, and from community to community, as proponents of the social constructionist perspective point out, but however it's constructed in a given social context, desire between men continually reappears. As he did so often, Whitman realized this, telling his readers in one of his greatest poems, "Crossing Brooklyn Ferry," that "[i]t avails not, time nor place—distance avails not . . .[j]ust as you feel . . . so I felt . . ."[3] and then speaking directly about the experience of being a man who loves men, which he knows there always will be others who share:

> [I . . . w]as call'd by my nighest name by clear loud voices of young men
>   as they saw me approaching or passing,
> Felt their arms on my neck as I stood, or the negligent leaning of their
>   flesh against me as I sat,
> Saw many I loved in the street or ferry-boat or public assembly, yet never
>   told them a word . . .[4]

As he has for generations, Whitman assures readers who are men who love men that they aren't alone, that despite the differences of time and place and distance there always have been and always will be men who love men. In that sense, male love never can be destroyed, no matter how much it's hated by men like those imagined by Proulx who murder Jack, or those who actually murdered Matthew Shepard. *Brokeback Mountain* not only speaks to men who love men, but also to other members of sexual minorities, and to straight people who are able to be allies of sexual minorities, validating their sense of the value of their love as well. For those who are secure enough in their own sexuality not to feel threatened by the ways in which men make love together, it's possible to recognize and respect the love between Jack and Ennis and other men as being like their own love, and to affirm the right of man-loving men to what they feel. This probably is one of the reasons that Ang Lee and so many others have responded to Ennis and Jack as real people, since they recognize the love between them as being real.

~

The story and the movie are intensely American in many ways. Both are set in a part of the landscape that everyone recognizes as being associated with the dominant culture's heroic constructions of the country's past, both center on characters who are emblems of the dominant culture's construction of masculinity, and both employ language that's rich in a type of slang that many ordinary American men use. While the problem of homophobia that both address unfortunately is global, it takes a particularly vicious form in America, given that the majority here has constructed love between men as being antithetical to their constructions of masculinity, and that hatred of same-sex love now is being exploited as a means of gaining political, economic, and social power. In presenting the love between Ennis and Jack, the story and the film draw on a rich variety of cultural traditions, some far older than the United States, some integral to its history. Both versions invoke the myth of tragic, romantic love, and demand a place within this tradition for love between men. Both allude to the ancient tradition of pastoral poetry, with its idealization of masculine love in a natural setting that reinforces the sense of the naturalness of that love, though they use none of its lofty language or formal conventions. At the close of the film, the filmmakers recognize that what Annie Proulx has created in many ways is a modern, realistically presented pastoral elegy set in the American West, in which one man, who fell in love with another when they were sheepherders, remembers his friend and grieves over his loss. To convey this elegiac mood, they choose to end the film with the poignant vernacular lament of one man for another, Willie Nelson's sweet, gentle rendition of the song, "He Was A Friend of Mine." The song fits the movie perfectly, expressing the sadness of a man who cries whenever he thinks of the friend he's lost, a man who never harmed anyone, and who died on the road, without ever having found what he wanted.[5]

NOTES

1. The first important study of the Western literary and cultural tradition of romantic love was Denis de Rougemont, *Love in the Western World* (New York: Pantheon, 1956), which was followed by his second book on the subject, *Love Declared: Essays on the Myths of Love* (New York: Pantheon, 1963). Other studies which are useful in understanding changing constructions of romantic love and marriage include Eli Zaretsky, *Capitalism, the Family, and Personal Life* (New York: Harper and Row, 1976); Anthony Giddens, *The Transformation of Intimacy: Sexuality, Love, and Eroticism in Modern Society* (Stanford: Stanford University Press, 1992); Stephanie Coontz, *Marriage: A History: How Love Conquered Marriage* (New York: Penguin, 2005); William R. Jankowiak, ed., *Romantic Passion* (New York: Columbia University Press, 1995); David R. Shumway, *Modern Love: Romance, Intimacy, and the Marriage Crisis* (New York: New York University Press, 2003); and Eva Illouz, *Consuming the Romantic Utopia: Love and the Cultural Contradictions of Capitalism* (Berkeley: University of California Press, 1997). Seidman, *Beyond the Closet*, relates issues of love and marriage to sexual minorities.

2. According to the producer, James Schamus, the poster for *Brokeback Mountain* wasn't modeled on posters for Westerns; instead, he studied the designs of the posters for more than fifty successful romantic films, and based the poster closely on that for *Titanic*. The two are strikingly similar in general composition: at the top, both show the heads of their two main characters, so close as to be touching but looking away from each other; the outline of Ledger's denim-clad shoulder in the *Brokeback Mountain* poster echoes that of the ship's bow in the poster for *Titanic*. See Sean Smith, "For-

bidden Territory: In Ang Lee's Devastating Film, *Brokeback Mountain*, Jake Gyllenaal and Heath Ledger Buck Hollywood Convention," *Newsweek*, Nov. 21, 2005.

3. "Crossing Brooklyn Ferry," ll. 20, 22, Whitman, *Leaves of Grass* (Ninth edition/1892).

4. "Crossing Brooklyn Ferry," ll. 79–81.

5. "He Was a Friend of Mine" is a traditional American song, versions of which have been sung by various performers, including Willie Nelson, Bob Dylan, Dave Van Ronk, the Byrds, Mercury Rev, the Grateful Dead, and the Chad Mitchell Trio. Dylan made an arrangement of the song in 1962, which is the version sung by Willie Nelson at the end of *Brokeback Mountain*.

Bibliography

BOOKS AND ARTICLES

Abrams, M. H., *et al.*, eds. *The Norton Anthology of English Literature*, Fourth Edition. New York: Norton, 1979.

Adam, Barry. *The Rise of a Gay and Lesbian Movement*. New York: Twayne, 1995.

Allmendinger, Blake. *The Cowboy: Representation of Labor in an American Work Culture*. New York: Oxford, 1992.

———. *Imagining the African American West*. Lincoln: University of Nebraska Press, 2005.

Altman, Dennis. *The Homosexualization of America*. Boston: Beacon, 1982.

Anderson, Eric. *In the Game: Gay Athletes and the Cult of Masculinity*. Albany: S.U.N.Y., 2005.

Aquila, Richard, ed. *Wanted Dead or Alive: The American West in Popular Culture*. Urbana/Chicago: University of Illinois Press, 1996.

Baigell, Matthew. *Albert Bierstadt*. New York: Watson-Guptill, 1988.

———. *A Concise History of American Painting and Sculpture*. New York: Harper, 1996.

Baldwin, James. *Giovanni's Room*. New York: Delta, 2000/1956.

Barrett, Jon. *Hero of Flight 93: Mark Bingham*. New York: Alyson, 2002.

Barthes, Roland. *Camera Lucida: Reflections on Photography*. (Trans., Richard Howard.) New York: Farrar, Strauss, and Giroux, 1981.

———. *A Lover's Discourse: Fragments*. (Trans., Richard Howard.) New York: Farrar, Strauss, and Giroux, 1978.

Bartlett, Neil. *Who Was That Man? A Present for Mr. Oscar Wilde*. London: Serpent's Tail, 1988.

Bayer, Ronald. *Homosexuality and American Psychiatry*. Princeton: Princeton University Press, 1987.

Bean, Billy, and Bull, Chris. *Going the Other Way: Lessons from a Life in and out of Major-League Baseball*. New York: Marlowe, 2003.

Beard, Tyler, and Arndt, Jim. *One Hundred Years of Western Wear*. Layton: Gibbs Smith, 1993.

Bellah, Robert N., Madsen, Richard, Sullivan, William M., Swidler, Ann, and Tipton, Steven M. *Habits of the Heart: Individualism and Commitment in American Life*. Berkeley: University of California Press, 1985.

Beneman, William. *Male-Male Intimacy in Early America: Beyond Romantic Friendships*. Binghamton: Harrington Park, 2006.

Benshoff, Harry M., and Griffin, Sean. *Queer Images: A History of Gay and Lesbian Film in America*. Lanham: Rowman and Littlefield, 2005.

Berger, John. *Ways of Seeing*. London: BBC/Penguin, 1972.

Berkhofer, Robert F. *The White Man's Indian: Images of the American Indian from Columbus to the Present*. New York: Vintage, 1979.

Bernstein, Robert, DeGeneres, Betty, and MacNeil, Robert. *Straight Parents/Gay Children: Keeping Families Together*. New York: Thunder's Mouth, 2003.

Bersani, Leo. "Is the Rectum a Grave?" Crimp, Douglas, ed.. *AIDS: Cultural Analysis, Cultural Activism*. Cambridge: M.I.T. Press, 1989.

Besen, Wayne. *Anything But Straight: Unmasking the Scandals and Lies Behind the Ex-Gay Myth*. Binghamton: Harrington Park, 2003.

Biery, Roger E. *Understanding Homosexuality: The Pride and the Prejudice*. Austin: Edward-William, 1990.

Blumenfeld, Warren J., ed. *Homophobia: How We All Pay the Price*. Boston: Beacon, 1992.

Boag, Peter. *Same-Sex Affairs: Constructing and Controlling Homosexuality in the Pacific Northwest*. Berkeley: University of California Press, 2003.

Boykin, Keith. *One More River to Cross: Black and Gay in America*. New York: Anchor, 1996.

Bredbeck, Gregory W. *Sodomy and Interpretation: Marlowe to Milton*. Ithaca: Cornell University Press, 1991.

Bronski, Michael. *The Pleasure Principle: Sex, Backlash, and the Struggle for Gay Freedom*. New York: St. Martin's 1998.

Brown, Michael. *Closet Space: Geographies of Metaphor from the Body to the Globe*. New York: Routledge, 2000.

Brown, Ricardo J., and Reichard, William, Ed. The Evening Crowd at Kirmser's: A Gay Life in the 1940s. Minneapolis: University of Minnesota, 2001.

Bruzzi, Stella. *Bringing Up Daddy: Fatherhood and Masculinity in Post-War Hollywood*. Berkeley: University of California Press, 2006.

Buell, Lawrence. *The Environmental Imagination: Thoreau, Nature Writing, and the Formation of American Culture*. Cambridge, Harvard University Press, 1996.

———. *Writing for an Endangered World: Literature, Culture, and the Environment in the United States and Beyond*. Cambridge: Harvard University Press, 2003.

Bull, Chris. *Perfect Enemies: The Battle Between the Religious Right and the Gay Movement*. Lanham: Madison, 2001.

Burleson, William E. *BiAmerica: Myths, Truths, and Struggles of an Invisible Community*. Binghamton: Haworth, 2005.

Butler, Judith. *Gender Trouble: Feminism and the Subversion of Identity*. New York: Routledge, 1990.

Buxton, Amity Pierce. *The Other Side of the Closet: The Coming-Out Crisis for Straight Spouses and Families.* New York: Wiley, 1994.

Cahill, Sean, and Burack, Cynthia. "Internal Enemy: Gays as the Domestic Al-Qaeda; A Report from the Family Research Council's Values Voters Summit, Sept. 22-24, 2006." National Gay and Lesbian Task Force.

Cawelti, John. *The Six-Gun Mystique.* Bowling Green: Popular Press, 1971.

Chauncey, George, Jr. *Gay New York: Gender, Urban Culture, and the Making of the Gay Male World, 1890-1940.* New York: Basic Books, 1994.

——. *Why Marriage? The History and Shaping of Today's Debate over Gay Equality.* New York: Basic Books, 2005.

Clark, Charles Badger, Jr. *Sun and Saddle-Leather.* Boston: Richard G. Badger, 1915.

Clemens, Samuel Langhorne (Mark Twain). *The Adventures of Huckleberry Finn*, ed. Sculley Bradley, *et. al.* New York: Norton, 1977/1885.

Cloke, Paul. *Country Visions: Knowing the Rural World.* Upper Saddle River: Prentice Hall, 2003.

Cohen, Ed. *Talk On the Wilde Side: Towards a Genealogy of Discourse on Male Sexualities.* New York: Routledge, 1993.

Cole, Shaun. *Don We Now Our Gay Apparel: Gay Men's Dress in the Twentieth Century.* Oxford: Berg, 2000.

Connell, Robert W. *Gender and Power: Society, the Person, and Sexual Politics.* Stanford: Stanford University Press, 1987.

——. *Masculinities.* Berkeley: University of California Press, 1995.

——. *The Men and the Boys.* Berkeley: University of California Press, 2000.

Cooley, John. *Earthly Words: Essays on Contemporary American Nature Writing and Environmental Writers.* Ann Arbor: University of Michigan Press, 1994.

Coontz, Stephanie. *Marriage: A History: How Love Conquered Marriage.* New York: Penguin, 2005.

Cooper, Emmanuel. *The Sexual Perspective: Homosexuality and Art in the Last Hundred Years in the West.* New York: Routledge, 1994.

D'Emilio, John. *Sexual Politics, Sexual Communities: The Making of a Homosexual Minority in the United States, 1940-1970.* Chicago: University of Chicago Press, 1983.

——, Turner, William B., Vaid, Urvashi. *Creating Change: Sexuality, Public Policy, and Civil Rights.* New York, St. Martin's, 2000.

Deford, Frank. *Big Bill Tilden: The Triumph and the Tragedy.* New York: Simon and Schuster, 1976.

Deitcher, David. *Dear Friends: American Photographs of Men Together, 1840-1918.* New York: Abrams, 2001.

Denny, Dallas, ed. *Current Concepts in Transgender Identity.* New York: Garland, 1998.

DePastino, Todd. Citizen Hobo: How a century of Homelessness shaped America. Chicago: University of Chicago, 2003.

Dotson, Edisol. *Behold the Man: The Hype and Selling of Male Beauty in Media and Culture.* Binghamton: Haworth, 1999.

Downs, Alan. *The Velvet Rage: Overcoming the Pain of Growing Up Gay in a Straight Man's World.* Cambridge: Da Capo, 2006.

Drinnon, Richard. *Facing West: The Metaphysics of Indian-Hating and Empire-Building*. Minneapolis: University of Minnesota, 1980.

Duberman, Martin. *Cures: A Gay Man's Odyssey*. New York: Dutton, 1991.

——. "'Writhing Bedfellows' in Antebellum North Carolina: Historical Interpretation and the Politics of Evidence." Duberman, Martin, Vicinus, Martha, Chauncey, George, Jr., eds. *Hidden from History: Reclaiming the Gay and Lesbian Past*. New York: Penguin, 1989.

DuBois, W. E. B. *The Souls of Black Folk*. Gibson, Donald B., and Elbert, Monica M., eds. New York: Penguin, 1996/1903.

Durham, Philip, and Jones, Everett L. *The Adventures of the Negro Cowboys*. New York: Dodd, Mead, 1966.

Dynes, Wayne, ed. *The Encyclopedia of Homosexuality*. New York: Garland, 1990.

Ehrenreich, Barbara. *The Hearts of Men: American Dreams and the Flight from Commitment*. New York: Anchor, 1987.

Epstein, Daniel Mark. *Lincoln and Whitman: Parallel Lives in Civil War Washington*. New York: Random House, 2005.

Fantina, Richard. *Ernest Hemingway: Machismo and Masochism*. New York: Palgrave Macmillan, 2005.

Fausto-Sterling, Anne. *Sexing the Body: Gender Politics and the Construction of Sexuality*. New York: Basic Books, 2000.

Fellows, Will. *Farm Boys: Lives of Gay Men from the Rural Midwest*. Madison: University of Wisconsin Press, 1996.

Fiedler, Leslie. "Come Back to the Raft Ag'in, Huck Honey." *Partisan Review*, June 1948.

——. *Love and Death in the American Novel*. New York: Stein and Day, 1960.

Finaldi, Gabriele, *et al. The Image of Christ*. London: National Gallery, 2000.

Firestein, ed. *Bisexuality: The Psychology and Politics of an Invisible Minority*. Thousand Oaks: Sage, 1996.

Foldy, Michael. *The Trials of Oscar Wilde: Deviance, Morality, and Late-Victorian Society*. New Haven, Yale University Press, 1997.

Fone, Byrne R.S. "Arcadia and the Homosexual Imagination." Kellogg, Stuart, ed. *Literary Visions of Homosexuality*. Binghamton: Haworth, 1983.

——. *Homophobia: A History*. New York: Picador, 2000.

——. *Masculine Landscapes: Walt Whitman and the Homoerotic Text*. Carbondale: Southern Illinois University Press, 1992.

George-Warren, Holly, and Freedman, Michele. *How the West Was Worn: A Complete History of Western Wear*. New York: Abrams, 2006.

Gerassi, Jon. *The Boys of Boise: Furor, Vice, and Folly in an American City*. Seattle: University of Washington Press, 2001/1966.

Giddens, Anthony. *The Transformation of Intimacy; Sexuality, Love, and Eroticism in Modern Society*. Stanford: Stanford University, 1992.

Gochros, Jean S. *When Husbands Come Out of the Closet*. Binghamton: Haworth, 1989.

Greenberg, David F. *The Construction of Homosexuality*. Chicago: University of Chicago Press, 1988.

Gross, Larry. *Up from Invisibility: Lesbians, Gay Men, and the Media in America.* New York: Columbia University Press, 2002.

Halberstam, Judith. *Female Masculinity.* Durham: Duke University Press, 1998.

Halperin, David M. *Before Pastoral: Theocritus and the Ancient Tradition of Bucolic Poetry.* New Haven: Yale University Press, 1983.

Harwood, Sarah. *Family Fictions: Representations of the Family in 1980s Hollywood Cinema.* New York: St. Martin's, 1997.

Heibel, Todd. "Blame It on the Casa Nova? 'Good Scenery and Sodomy' in Rural Southwestern Pennsylvania." Colin Flint, ed. *Spaces of Hate: Geographies of Discrimination and Intolerance in the U.S.A.* New York: Routledge, 2003.

Helminiak, David, *What the Bible Really Says about Homosexuality.* Tajique: Alamo Square, 2000.

Hemingway, Ernest. *The Sun Also Rises.* New York: Scribner's, 1926.

Herek, Gregory M., and Berrill, Kevin T., eds. *Hate Crimes: Confronting Violence against Lesbians and Gay Men.* Thousand Oaks: Sage, 1992.

———, ed. *Stigma and Sexual Orientation: Understanding Prejudice Against Lesbians, Gay Men, and Bisexuals.* Thousand Oaks: Sage, 1997.

Herman, Didi. *The Antigay Agenda: Orthodox Vision and the Christian Right.* Chicago: University of Chicago Press, 1997.

Herring, Scott, ed. "*Brokeback Mountain* Dossier." *GLQ: A Journal of Lesbian and Gay Studies,* Vol. 13, No. 1.

Higbie, Frank Tobias. *Indispensable Outcasts: Hobo Workers and Community in the American Midwest, 1880-1930.* Urbana/Chicago: University of Illinois Press, 2003.

Higdon, Hal. *Leopold and Loeb: The Crime of the Century.* Urbana/Chicago: University of Illinois Press, 1999.

Howard, John. *Men Like That: A Southern Queer History.* Chicago: University of Chicago Press, 1996.

Human Rights Watch. *Hatred in the Hallways: Violence and Discrimination against Lesbian, Gay, Bisexual, and Transgender Students in United States Schools.* New York: Human Rights Watch, 2001.

Ibson, John. *Picturing Men: A Century of Male Relationships in Everyday American Photography.* Chicago: University of Chicago Press, 2006.

Illouz, Eva. *Consuming the Romantic Utopia: Love and the Cultural Contradictions of Capitalism.* Berkeley: University of California Press, 1997.

Isay, Richard. *Being Homosexual: Gay Men and Their Development.* New York: Farrar, Strauss, and Giroux, 2001.

Jackson, Kenneth T. *Crabgrass Frontier: The Suburbanization of America.* New York: Oxford, 1985.

Jagose, Annemarie. *Queer Theory: An Introduction.* New York: New York University Press, 1996.

Janowiak, William R., ed. *Romantic Passion.* New York: Columbia University Press, 1995.

Jennings, Kevin, and Shapiro, Pat. *Always My Child: A Parent's Guide to Understanding Your Gay, Lesbian, Bisexual, Transgender, or Questioning Son or Daughter.* New York: Simon and Schuster, 2003.

Jensen, Robin M. *Understanding Early Christian Art*. New York: Routledge, 2000.

Johnson, Dirk. *Biting the Dust: The Wild Ride and Dark Romance of the Rodeo Cowboy and the American West*. New York: Simon and Schuster, 1994.

Katz, Jonathan Ned. *The Invention of Heterosexuality*. Chicago: University of Chicago Press, 1995.

———. *Love Stories: Sex between Men before Heterosexuality*. Chicago: University of Chicago, 2001.

Katz, William. *The Black West: A Documentary and Pictorial History of the African American Role in the Westward Expansion of the United States*. New York: Harlem Moon, 2005.

Kaufman, Moises, and the Tectonic Theatre Project. *The Laramie Project*. New York: Vintage, 2001.

Kimmel, Michael S. *Manhood in America: A Cultural History*. New York: Free Press, 1996.

———. "Masculinity as Homophobia: Fear, Shame, and Silence in the Construction of Gender Identity." Brod, Harry, and Kaufman, Michael, eds., *Theorizing Masculinities*. Thousand Oaks: Sage, 1994.

———, and Aronson, Amy. *Men and Masculinities: A Social, Cultural, and Historical Encyclopedia*. Santa Barbara: ABC-Clio, 2004.

Kinsey, Alfred, *et al*. *Sexual Behavior in the Human Male*. Philadelphia: Saunders, 1948.

Klein, Fritz, and Schwartz, Thomas. *Bisexual and Gay Husbands: Their Stories, Their Words*. Binghamton: Harrington Park, 2002.

Kleinberg, Seymour. *Alienated Affections*. New York: St. Martin's, 1980.

Kolodny, Annette. *The Lay of the Land: Metaphor as Experience and History in American Life and Letters*. Chapel Hill: University of North Carolina Press, 1984.

Kopay, David, and Young, Perry Deane. *The David Kopay Story*. New York: Arbor House, 1977.

Kramer, Jane. *The Last Cowboy*. New York: Harper Collins, 1978.

Kramer, Jerry Lee. "Batchelor Farmers and Spinsters: Gay and Lesbian Identities and Communities in North Dakota." Bell, David, and Valentine, Gill, eds. *Mapping Desire: Geographies of Sexualities*. New York: Routledge, 1995.

Kroeger, Brooke. *Passing: When People Can't Be Who They Are*. New York: Perseus/Public Affairs, 2004.

Ladner, Gerhart B. *God, Cosmos, and Humankind: The World of Early Christian Symbolism*. Berkeley: University of California, 1996.

Lees, Alfred W., and Nelson, Ronald. *Longtime Companions: Autobiographies of Gay Male Fidelity*. Binghamton: Haworth, 1999.

Levine, Martin. *Gay Macho: The Life and Death of the Homosexual Clone*. New York: New York University Press, 1998.

Lindhorst, Taryn. "Lesbians and Gay Men in the Country: Practice Implications for Rural Social Workers." Smith, James Donald, and Mancoske, Ronald J., eds., *Rural Gays and Lesbians: Building on the Strengths of Communities*. Binghamton: Haworth, 1997.

Little, Jo. *Gender and Rural Geography: Identity, Sexuality, and Power in the Countryside*. New York: Prentice Hall, 2001.

McBride, Dwight A. *Why I Hate Abercrombie and Fitch: Essays on Race and Sexuality*. New York: New York University Press, 2005.

McGowan, Jeffrey (Major, U.S. Army, Ret.). *Major Conflict: One Gay Man's Life in the Don't-Ask-Don't-Tell Military*. New York: Broadway Books, 2005.

McMurtry, Larry, and Ossana, Diana. "Brokeback Mountain: A Screenplay." Proulx, Annie, McMurtry, Larry, and Ossana, Diana. *Brokeback Mountain: Story to Screenplay*. New York: Simon and Schuster, 2005.

McNeill, John J. *The Church and the Homosexual*. Boston: Beacon, 1993.

Mackey, Richard A., O'Brien, Bernard, and Mackey, Eileen F. *Gay and Lesbian Couples: Voices from Lasting Relationships*. Binghamton: Haworth, 1997.

Malone, Michael, and Etulain, Richard W. *The American West: A Twentieth Century History*. Lincoln: University of Nebraska Press, 1989.

Mann, William J. *Wisecracker: The Life and Times of William Haines, Hollywood's First Openly Gay Star*. New York: Penguin, 1998.

Marcus, Eric. *Is It a Choice? Answers to the Most Frequently Asked Questions about Gay and Lesbian People*. New York: Harper, 2005.

——. *Making Gay History: The Half-Century Fight for Lesbian and Gay Equal Rights*. New York: Harper, 2002.

Martin, Robert K., ed. *The Continuing Presence of Walt Whitman: The Life after the Life*. Iowa City: University of Iowa Press, 1992.

——. *The Homosexual Tradition in American Poetry*. Austin: University of Texas Press, 1979.

Marx, Leo. *The Machine in the Garden: Technology and the Pastoral Ideal in America*. New York: Oxford, 1964.

Melton, J. Gordon. *The Churches Speak on Homosexuality: Official Statements from Religious Bodies and Ecumenical Organizations*. New York: Gale, 1991.

Messner, Michael. *Politics of Masculinities: Men in Movements*. Thousand Oaks: Sage, 1997.

Meyerowitz, Joanne. *How Sex Changed: A History of Transexuality in the United States*. Cambridge: Harvard University Press, 2004.

Miller, Neil. *Out of the Past: Gay and Lesbian History from 1869 to the Present*. New York: Alyson, 2006.

——. *Sex-Crime Panic: A Journey to the Paranoid Heart of the 1950s*. Los Angeles: Alyson, 2002.

Milner, Clyde A., II, O'Connor, Carol A., and Sandweiss, Martha A., eds. *The Oxford History of the American West*. New York: Oxford, 1996.

Mitchell, Lee Clark. *Westerns: Making the Man in Fiction and Film*. Chicago: University of Chicago Press, 1996.

Monette, Paul. *Becoming a Man: Half a Life Story*. New York: Harper, 1992.

——. *Love Alone: Eighteen Elegies For Rog*. New York: St. Martin's, 1988.

Mulvey, Laura. "Visual Pleasure and Narrative Cinema" (1975). John Caughie *et al.*, eds. *The Sexual Subject: A Screen Reader in Sexuality*. London: Routledge, 1992.

Nardi, Peter, ed. *Gay Masculinities*. Thousand Oaks: Sage, 2000.

——. *Gay Men's Friendships: Invincible Communities*. Chicago: University of Chicago Press, 1999.

——. *Men's Friendships.* Thousand Oaks: Sage, 2004.

Nash, Roderick Frazier. *Wilderness and the American Mind.* New Haven: Yale University Press, 1967.

Novak, Barbara. *Nature and Culture: American Landscape and Painting, 1825-1875.* New York: Oxford, 1981.

Osborne, Karen Lee, and Spurlin, William J., eds. *Reclaiming the Heartland: Lesbian and Gay Voices from the Midwest.* Minneapolis: University of Minnesota Press, 1996.

Packard, Chris. *Queer Cowboys and Other Erotic Male Friendships in Nineteenth-Century American Literature.* New York: Palgrave Macmillan, 2005.

Pannapacker, William. *Revised Lives: Whitman, Religion, and the Constructions of Identity in Nineteenth-Century Anglo-American Culture.* New York: Routledge, 2003.

Patterson, Eric Haines. "Every Which Way but Lucid: The Critique of Authority in Clint Eastwood's Police Movies." *Journal of Popular Film and Television,* Vol. 10, No. 3, Fall 1982. Reprinted as "Dirty Hero: The Critique of Authority in Clint Eastwood's Police Movies." Geist, Christopher D., and Nachbar, Jack, eds. *The Popular Culture Reader, Third Edition.* Bowling Green: Popular Press, 1983.

Pelikan, Jaroslav. *The Illustrated Jesus through the Centuries.* New Haven: Yale University Press, 1997.

Pharr, Suzanne. *Homophobia: A Weapon of Sexism.* Berkeley: Chardon, 1997.

Plummer, David. *One of the Boys: Masculinity, Homophobia, and Modern Manhood.* Binghamton: Harrington Park, 1999.

Polmar, Norman. *The Death of the U.S.S. Thresher: The Story behind History's Deadliest Submarine Disaster.* Stonington: Lyons Press, 2004/1964.

Pronger, Brian. *The Arena of Masculinity: Sports, Homosexuality, and the Meaning of Sex.* New York: St. Martin's, 1990.

Proulx, Annie. *Brokeback Mountain.* New York: Scribner's, 2005. (Also published in *Close Range: Wyoming Stories,* New York: Scribner's, 1999).

——. "Getting Movied." Proulx, Annie, McMurtry, Larry, Ossana, Diana. *Brokeback Mountain: Story to Screenplay.* New York: Scribner, 2005.

"Interview with Annie Proulx." *Missouri Review,* Vol. 22, No. 2, 1999.

Quinn, D. Michael. *Same-Sex Dynamics among Nineteenth-Century Americans: A Mormon Example.* Urbana/Chicago: University of Illinois Press, 1996.

Rammel, Hal. *Nowhere in America: The Big Rock Candy Mountain and Other Comic Utopias.* Urbana/Chicago: University of Illinois Press, 1990.

Ricketts, Wendell, ed. *Everything I Have Is Blue: Short Fiction by Working-Class Men about More-Or-Less Gay Life.* San Francisco: Suspect Thoughts, 2005.

Roediger, David R. *The Wages of Whiteness: Race and the Making of the American Working Class.* New York: Verso, 1991.

Rohy, Valerie. "Displaying Desire: Passing, Nostalgia, and *Giovanni's Room.*" Ginsberg, Elaine K., ed. *Passing and the Fictions of Identity.* Durham: Duke University Press, 1996.

Rood, Karen L. *Understanding Annie Proulx.* Columbia: University of South Carolina Press, 2001.

Rooney, Ellen, ed. *The Cambridge Companion to Feminist Literary Theory.* Cambridge: Cambridge University Press, 2006.

Rotundo, E. Anthony. *American Manhood: Transformations in Masculinity from the Revolution to the Modern Era.* New York: Basic Books, 1993.

de Rougemont, Denis. *Love Declared: Essays on the Myths of Love.* New York: Pantheon, 1963.

———. *Love in the Western World.* New York: Pantheon, 1956.

Russo, Vito. *The Celluloid Closet.* New York: Harper and Row, 1987.

Saslow, James M. *Pictures and Passions: A History of Homosexuality in the Visual Arts.* New York: Routledge, 1994.

Savage, William W., Jr. *The Cowboy Hero: His Image in American History and Culture.* Norman: University of Oklahoma Press, 1979.

Schmidgall, Gary. *Walt Whitman: A Gay Life.* New York: Plume, 1998.

———, ed. *Walt Whitman: Selected Poems, 1855-1892, A New Edition.* New York: St. Martin's, 1999.

Schmitt, J. *Back To Nature: The Arcadian Myth in Urban America.* New York: Oxford, 1990.

Sears, James T., and Williams, Walter L., eds. *Overcoming Heterosexism and Homophobia: Strategies That Work.* New York: Columbia University Press, 1997.

Seidman, Stephen. *Beyond the Closet: The Transformation of Gay and Lesbian Life.* New York: Routledge, 2003.

Shumway, David R. *Modern Love: Romance, Intimacy, and the Marriage Crisis.* New York: New York University Press, 2003.

Shuttleton, David. "The Queer Politics of Gay Pastoral." Phillips, Richard, *et al.*, eds. *DeCentring Sexualities: Politics and Representations beyond the Metropolis.* London: Routledge, 2000.

Sinfield, Alan. *The Wilde Century: Effeminacy, Oscar Wilde, and the Queer Moment.* New York: Columbia University Press, 1994.

Sloan, Lacey M., and Gustavsson, Nora. *Violence and Social Injustice against Lesbian, Gay, and Bisexual People.* Binghamton: Harrington Park, 2000.

Slotkin, Richard. *The Fatal Environment: The Myth of the Frontier in the Age of Industrialization, 1800-1890.* New York: Atheneum, 1985.

———. *Gunfighter Nation: The Myth of the Frontier in Twentieth-Century America.* New York: Atheneum, 1992.

———. *Regeneration through Violence: The Mythology of the American Frontier, 1600-1860.* Middletown: Wesleyan University Press, 1973.

Smith, Henry Nash. *Virgin Land: The American West as Symbol and Myth.* Cambridge: Harvard University Press, 1978/1950.

Sontag, Susan. *On Photography.* New York: Farrar, Strauss, and Giroux, 1973.

Steckmesser, Kent Ladd. *The Western Hero in History and Legend.* Norman: University of Oklahoma Press, 1997/1967.

Stockwell, Anne, "*Brokeback*'s Big Secrets" (Interview with Larry McMurtry and Diana Ossana), *The Advocate*, Feb. 28, 2006.

Stratton, W. K. *Chasing the Rodeo: On Wild Rides and Big Dreams, Broken Hearts and Broken Bones, and One Man's Search for the West.* New York: Harvest, 2005.

Stryker, Susan, and Whittle, Stephen, eds. *The Transgender Studies Reader*. New York: Routledge, 2006.

Sumartojo, Rini. "Contesting Place: Antigay and -Lesbian Hate Crime in Columbus, Ohio." Colin Flint, ed. *Spaces of Hate: Geographies of Discrimination and Intolerance in the U.S.A.* New York: Routledge, 2003.

Summers, Claude J., ed. Encyclopedia of Gay, Lesbian, Bisexual, Transgendered, and Queer Culture (glbtq.com).

———, ed. *The Gay and Lesbian Literary Heritage: A Reader's Companion to the Writers and Their Works, from Antiquity to the Present*. Revised Edition. New York: Routledge, 2002.

———, ed. *Homosexuality in Renaissance and Enlightenment England*. Binghamton: Haworth, 1992.

Sundstrom, Jessie Y. *Badger Clark, Cowboy Poet with Universal Appeal*. Custer: Badger Clark Memorial Society, 2004.

Tate, Laurence. "How They Do It in West Texas." *Harvard Gay and Lesbian Review*, Vol. 13, No. 4, July/August, 2006.

Terry, Jennifer. *An American Obsession: Science, Medicine, and Homosexuality in Modern Society*. Chicago: University of Chicago Press, 1999.

Tompkins, Jane. *West of Everything: The Inner Life of Westerns*. New York: Oxford, 1992.

Tuaolo, Esera, and Rosengren, John. *Alone in the Trenches: My Life as a Gay Man in the NFL*. Napierville: Sourcebooks, 2006.

Ultimate Brokeback Forum. *Beyond Brokeback: The Impact of a Film*. Livermore: WingSpan, 2007.

Van Hoven, Bettina, ed. *Spaces of Masculinities*. New York: Routledge, 2004.

Walters, Suzanna Danuta. *All the Rage: The Story of Gay Visibility in America*. Chicago: University of Chicago Press, 2001.

———. *Material Girls: Making Sense of Feminist Cultural Theory*. Berkeley: University of California Press, 1995.

Warner, Michael, ed. *Fear of a Queer Planet*. Minneapolis: University of Minnesota Press, 1993.

———. *The Trouble with Normal*. New York: Free Press, 1999.

Weinberg, George. *Society and the Healthy Homosexual*. New York: St. Martin's, 1972.

Welch, Paul, Eppridge, William, and Havemann, Ernest. "Homosexuality in America: A Secret World Grows Open and Bolder." *Life* magazine, Vol. 56, No. 26, June 24, 1964.

White, Richard. *A New History of the American West: "It's Your Misfortune and None of My Own."* Norman: University of Oklahoma Press, 1993.

Whitman, Walt. *Leaves of Grass*, Ninth edition. New York: Norton, 1973/1892.

Williams, Walter L. *The Spirit and the Flesh: Sexual Diversity in American Indian Culture*. Boston: Beacon, 1986.

Williamson, Judith. *Decoding Advertisements: Ideology and the Meaning of Advertising*. London: Marion Boyars, 1978.

Windmeyer, Shane, ed. *Brotherhood: Gay Life in College Fraternities*. New York: Alyson, 2005.

———, and Freeman, Pamela, eds. *Out on Fraternity Row: Personal Accounts of Being Gay in a College Fraternity*. Los Angeles: Alyson, 1998.

Wister, Owen. *The Virginian: A Horseman of the Plains*. New York: Macmillan, 1901.

Wooden, Wayne S., and Ehringer, Gavin. *Rodeo in America: Wranglers, Roughstock, and Paydirt*. Lawrence: University of Kansas Press, 1999.

Woods, Gregory. *A History of Gay Literature: The Male Tradition*. New Haven: Yale University Press, 1998.

Wright, Will. *Six-Guns and Society: A Structural Study of the Western*. Berkeley: University of California Press, 1975.

———. *The Wild West: The Mythical Cowboy and Social Theory*. Thousand Oaks: Sage, 2001.

Young-Bruehl, Elisabeth. *The Anatomy of Prejudices*. Cambridge: Harvard University Press, 1996.

Zaretsky, Eli. *Capitalism, the Family, and Personal Life*, rev. ed. New York: Harper and Row, 1976.

Zeeland, Steven. *The Masculine Marine: Homoeroticism in the U.S. Marine Corps*. Binghamton: Haworth, 1996.

INTERNET AND OTHER SOURCES

"A Local Author's Work Inspires *Brokeback Mountain* Production," University of Wisconsin, Madison: Campus News, Jan. 10, 2006; http://www.news.wisc.edu/11998

"Actor Randy Quaid Sues over Payment for *Brokeback* Role," Associated Press, *San Francisco Chronicle*, March 24, 2006; http://www.sfgate.com/cgi-bin/article.cgi?file=/a/a2006/03/24/entertainment/e093215S06.DTL

"Alan Jackson Sets the Mood," *Houston Chronicle*, March 16, 2006; http://www.chron.com/disp/story.mpl/chronicle/3726986.html

"Attorney General's Office Drops UVM Hazing Case," WCAX-TV News, May 12, 2007; http://www.wcax.com/global/story.asp?s=6507922

Badger Clark Memorial Society; http://www.badgerclark.org

Baehr, Ted, Movie Guide; http://www.MovieGuide.org

"Basketball Fans Asked to Stop Chanting *Brokeback Mountain* Insult," *The Advocate*, Feb. 14, 2006; http://www.advocate.com/news_detail_ektid25416asp

"Big Rock Candy Mountain," National Institute of Environmental Health Services/National Institutes of Health/Department of Health and Human Services Kids' Pages; http://www.niehs.nih.gov/kids/lyrics/bigrock/htm

Boehlert, Eric, "Cowboy Controversy," Rolling Stone, Feb. 10, 2006; http://www.rollingstone.com/news/story/9257407/cowboy_controversy

Breiner, Sander, "Homophobia: A Scientific, Non-Political Definition," Collected Papers of 2003 NARTH Conference; http://www.narth.com/docs/coll-breiner.html

"*Brokeback* Crossing Sexual Preference Divide," Internet Movie Database, Dec. 29, 2005; http://www.imdb.com/news/sb/2005-12-29

Brokeback Mountain entry; Internet Movie Database; http://www.imdb.com/title/tt0388795

Brokeback Mountain Focus Features/Universal Studios DVD 26315

"*Brokeback Mountain* Full Review," United States Conference of Catholic Bishops, Office for Film and Broadcasting, Dec. 30, 2005; http://www.usccb.org/movies/b/brokebackmountain.shtml

Brokeback Mountain Original Motion Picture Soundtrack, Verve/Forecast B0005604-02

"*Brokeback Mountain* Resource Guide," GLAAD; http://www.glaad.org/eye/brokeback_mountain.php

Bulkeley, Deborah, "Miller Speaks Up on *Brokeback*," *The Deseret News*, Jan. 17, 2006; http://www.deseretnews.com/dn/view/1,1249,635176966,00.html

Cahill, Sean, and Burack, Cynthia, National Gay and Lesbian Task Force Policy Institute, "Internal Enemy: Gays as the Domestic Al-Qaeda; A Report from the Family Research Council's Values Voter Summit, Sept. 22-24, 2006; http://www.thetaskforce.org/reports_and_research/internal_enemy

"The Castration of the Strawberry Roan," http://www.snif.numachi.com/pages/tiCASTROAN;ttSTRWROAN.html

"Conservatives Quick to Opine on *Brokeback*, Slow to Actually See Film," Media Matters, Jan. 20, 2006; http://www.mediamatters.org/items/200601200005

"Curtis Berates *Brokeback Mountain*," Feb. 5, 2006; http://www.contactmusic.com/new/xmlfeed.ns/mndwebpages/curtis%20berates%20brokeback%20mountain_05_02_2006

"Ernest Borgnine" biographical entry, Internet Movie Database; http://www.imdb.com/name/nm0000308

Finke, Nikki, "What Did I Tell You?" *Los Angeles Weekly*, March 5, 2006; http://www.deadlinehollywooddaily.com/what-did-I-tell-you

"Fraternity Suspended for Alleged Homophobic Hazing," *The Chronicle of Higher Education,* April 6, 2006; http://www.chronicle.com/news/article/236/fraternity-suspended-for-alleged-homophobic-hazing

Frichtl, Ben, "*Narnia* Gets Lion's Share of Box Office While Critics Hail 'Gay Cowboy' Flick," Concerned Women for America, Culture and Family Issues, Dec. 13, 2005; http://www.cwfa.org/articles/9689/CFI/misc/index.htm

Gay and Lesbian Athletic Foundation; http://www.glaf.org

Gay Games; http://www.GayGames.com

Gay Sports; http://www.GaySports.com

"Gene Shalit Offers Defamatory *Brokeback* Review on NBC's *Today*," GLAAD Action Alert, Jan. 5, 2006; http://www.glaad.org/action/alerts_detail.php?id=3849

Goldman, Jason, "Arts: Bruce Weber," Gay, Lesbian, Bisexual, Transgender, Queer Encyclopedia entry; http://www.glbtq.com/arts/weber_b.html

Gonzales-Day, Ken, "Photography, Gay Male: Post-Stonewall," Gay, Lesbian, Bisexual, Transgender, Queer Encyclopedia entry; http://www.glbtq.com/arts/photography_gay_post_stonewall.html

Graves, Deirdre Stoelzle, "Release of *Brokeback Mountain* Creates a Buzz," *Casper Star-Tribune*, Oct. 31, 2005; http://www.casperstartribune.net/articles/205/10.31/news/wyoming/06c2ae836ae836d988c5d872570aa00211854.txt

"Homosexual-Themed Films Assault Christmas Moviegoers," Traditional Values Coalition, Dec. 14, 2005; http://www.traditionalvalues.org/modules.php?sid=2535

Human Rights Campaign; http://www.hrc.com

International Gay Rodeo Association; http://www.igra.com

"Jake Gyllenhaal Interview," *Elle* magazine (U.S.), December 2004.

Kaczorowski, Craig, "Arts: Screenwriters," Gay, Lesbian, Bisexual, Transgender, Queer Encyclopedia entry; http://www.glbtq.com/arts/screenwriters.html

Kupelian, David, "The Rape of the Marlboro Man," *World Net Daily*, Dec. 27, 2005; http://www.WorldNetDaily.com/news/article.asp?ARTICLE_ID=48076

Lundegaard, Erik, "Love Makes *Brokeback* Oscar Favorite: Tale of Star-Crossed Lovers Attracts Audience, Academy Votes," Feb. 1, 2006; http://www.msnbc.msn .com/id/11102003

———. "Oscar Misfire: *Crash* and Burn: The Academy Takes Yet Another Step toward Irrelevance with Its Latest Pick," MSNBC, March 6, 2006; http://www.msnbc.msn.com/id/11700333

———. "Playing It Safe, Academy Awards Style," MSNBC, Jan. 26, 2005; http://www.msnbc.msn.com/id/6725814

McDonough, Kevin, "Tune in Tonight: Do Movies of the Past Decade Make the Cut?" United Features Syndicate, June 20, 2007; http://www.2.ljworld.com/news/ living/columns/tunein/?page=2

McFarland, John, "Arts: David Hockney," Gay, Lesbian, Bisexual, Transgender, Queer Encyclopedia entry; http://www.glbtq.com/arts/hockney_d.html

Mann, Richard G., "Arts: American Art, Gay Male, Nineteenth Century," Gay, Lesbian, Bisexual, Transgender, Queer Encyclopedia entry; http://www.glbtq.com/ arts/am_art_gay_19c,4.html

Martin, Robert K., "Literature: Walt Whitman," Gay, Lesbian, Bisexual, Transgender, Queer Encyclopedia entry; http://www.glbtq.com/literature/whitman_w.html

Matthew Shepard Foundation; http://www.matthewshepard.org

Maughan, Shannon, "Donor Pledge Returned to Sender; How Much Is Intellectual Freedom Worth? For One Texas School, It's Priceless," *Publisher's Weekly*, Dec. 5, 2005; http://www.publishersweekly.com/article/CA6288794.html

Mock, Brentin, "Essay by Promoter of 'Ex-Gay' Movement Sparks Racism Charges," Southern Poverty Law Center, Oct. 6, 2006; http://www.splcenter.org/intel/ news/item.jsp?aid=84

"MSNBC Airs Juvenile Homophobia on 'Imus in the Morning,'" GLAAD Action Alert, Jan. 20, 2006; http://www.glaad.org/action/alerts_detail.php?id=3854

MTV Movie Awards Archive: 2006; http://www.mtv.com/movieawards/archive

Murray, Rebecca, "Jake Gyllenhaal Talks about *Brokeback Mountain*: Jake Gyllenhaal on *Brokeback Mountain* and His Love Scenes with Heath Ledger," Your Guide to Hollywood Movies, About.com, *New York Times*, no date; http://www .moviesabout.com/od/brokebackmountain/a/brokeback112905.htm

National Center for Transgender Equality; http://www.nctequality.org

National Gay and Lesbian Task Force; http://www.thetaskforce.org

OutSports; http://www.OutSports.com

"Pat Robertson's Contradictory Theology," Media Matters, May 2, 2005; http://www .mediamatters.org/items/200505020002

"'Profam' Critic: *Brokeback*," Good As You, http://www.goodasyou.org/good_as_you/ 2005/12/profam_critic_b.html

Professional Bull Riders, Inc.; http://www.pbrnow.com

Proulx, Annie, "Note on Interviews;" http://www.annieproulx.com

"Scarborough Country" transcript, MSNBC, Jan. 17, 2006; http://www.msnbc.msn .com/id/10907413

17th Annual GLAAD Media Awards, New York, March 27, 2006; http://www.glaad .org/events/mediaawards/index.php

Slezak, Michael, "Are You Enjoying 'Jokeback Mountain'?" *Entertainment Weekly*: Movie News, Feb. 3, 2006; http://www.popwatch.ewcom/popwatch/2006/02/ are_you_enjoyin.html

Smith, Sean, "Forbidden Territory: In Ang Lee's Devastating Film, *Brokeback Mountain*, Jake Gyllenhaal and Heath Ledger Buck Hollywood Convention," *Newsweek*, Nov. 21, 2005.

"Snack Fairy: Cowboys," Commercial Closet, no date; http://www.commercialcloset .org/cgi-bin/iowa/portrayals.html?record=2660

Spines, Christine, "Western Union: Heath Ledger and Jake Gyllenhaal Put Their Careers on the Line—the Young Actors Play Cowboys in Love in *Brokeback Mountain*," *Entertainment Weekly*: Movie News, Dec. 2, 2005; http://www.ew.com/ew/ article/0,,1136232,00.html

Strand, Paul, "Homosexual Agenda Pushed in Movies Like *Brokeback Mountain*," Christian Broadcasting Network, Jan. 13, 2006; http://www.cbn.com/cbnnews/ 060113d.asp

"*Today* Show Reviewer Regrets *Brokeback* Comment," GLAAD Action Alert, Jan. 10, 2006; http://www.glaad.org/action/alerts_detail.php?id=3849

"Tony Curtis" biographical entry; Internet Movie Database; http://www.imdb.com/ name/nm0000348

Transgender Law Center; http://www.transgenderlawcenter.org

Turan, Kenneth, "Breaking No Ground: Why *Crash* Won, Why *Brokeback* Lost and How the Academy Chose to Play It Safe," *Los Angeles Times*, March 5, 2006; http://theenvelope.latimes.com/awards/oscars/env-turan5mar05,0,5359042.story

"U.S.C.C.B. Reclassifies Gay Western *Brokeback Mountain* After Complaints," Catholic News Agency, Dec. 16, 2005; http://www.catholicnewsagency.com/new .php?n=5643

Walls, Jeanette, "Interview with Heath Ledger and Matt Damon," MSNBC: Entertainment: Gossip, Aug. 25, 2005; http://www.towleroad.com/2005/08/heath_on_ brokeb.html

Whitty, Jeff, "Open Letter to Jay Leno," April 24, 2006; http://www.queerty.com/ queer/entertainment/an-open-letter-to-jay-leno-20060424.php

Williams, Carla, "Arts: Thomas Eakins," Gay, Lesbian, Bisexual, Transgender, Queer Encyclopedia entry; http://www.glbtq.com/arts/eakins_t.html

"Willie Nelson's Gay Cowboy," 365gay.com, Feb. 14, 2006; http://www.365gay .com/newscon06/02/021406nelson.htm

Woods, Gregory, "Literature: Ernest Hemingway," Gay, Lesbian, Bisexual, Transgender, Queer Encyclopedia entry; http://www.glbtq.com/literature/hemingway_ e.htmlw

Index

About the Author

Eric Patterson lives in central New York State with his partner of nineteen years, T.R. Forbes, who's a soil scientist and writer. They share interests in progressive politics; history; science; the environment; watching and identifying birds and animals; watching rugby (and rugby players); music; art; and literature and film, particularly fiction and movies about the lives of men who love men. They support organizations that help sexual minority people and people with HIV and organizations that help animals and the environment. They both enjoy the outdoors and living in the country, and use organic methods to cultivate about an acre of land around their house, with the assistance of their dog friend, Mina, a lively, devoted, mixed-breed (yellow Lab-ish) spayed female whose main interest is patrolling her yard for all species of rodents. With Mina they've explored the fields, woods, and creeks in the countryside near their home. They know a number of gay men in the area where they live, and value their friendship highly. T.R. presently is completing a novel based on his experiences in South America in the 1970's. At Hobart and William Smith Colleges in Geneva, New York, Eric teaches courses on American culture, American literature, and the history and culture of sexual/gender minority people, and advocates policies and practices that challenge heterosexist privilege and support full inclusion and equality for those who differ from the majority in sexuality and gender, and for people of all identities.